WALKABLE WESTCHESTER

SECOND EDITION

Jane and Walt Daniels

2014

NEW YORK-NEW JERSEY TR. CONFERENCE

Library of Congress Cataloging-in-Publication Data

Daniels, Jane.
Walkable Westchester / Jane Daniels, Walt Daniels.
p. cm. Includes bibliographical references and index.
ISBN 978-1-880775-86-8 (alk. paper),
ISBN 978-1-880775-88-2 (eBook)
1. Walking--New York (State)--Westchester County--Guidebooks. 2. Westchester
County (N.Y.)--Description and travel. I. Daniels, Walt. II. Title.
GV199.42.N652W4733 2014
917.47727 04--dc22
2014004128

Published by
New York-New Jersey Trail Conference
156 Ramapo Valley Road
Mahwah, NJ 07439-1199

Cartography: Allison Werberg
Book and cover design: Nora Porter

Front cover: Water-filled quarry in Sylvan Glen Park Preserve

Welcome to the second edition of *Walkable Westchester*, a comprehensive guide to the extraordinary walking opportunities in Westchester County.

We are blessed with a diversity of habitat, shoreline, woodlands, urban strolls and more in the 450 square miles in this county with its marvelous borders along both the Hudson River and the Long Island Sound. I am always amazed when I discover a new spot to meander, having been involved in the preservation of open space and building of parks for decades. *Walkable Westchester* helped me find a few more of the off-the-beaten-track gems that make the county so special.

This book is an encyclopedia of accessible open space in the county and more, listing scores of places and hundreds of miles of trails. It breaks the suggested walks down into the categories that help you find just what you are looking for, whether that's a short level walk along a flowered path or a hardy all-day trek. Looking for the coolest place on a hot, steamy day or where to take those snow-shoes after a winter storm? Check here first. Want to know what is ADA accessible or what areas are pet-friendly? Right here is your source. Rather go on a mountain bike or on horseback? Yes, those trails are listed here as well.

What I like especially is that this book includes lots of fascinating history and a feast of information for the naturalist in all of us. With useful maps for almost every park and trail, there should be little fear of getting lost. You can use this book as a veritable map to simple pleasures in the county.

So, cherish it, it's a resource, like our green spaces themselves. Thank you Jane and Walt Daniels for taking your passion and knowledge of the trails and laying them out for us to follow in your footsteps.

Linda G. Cooper
Regional Director, Taconic Region
New York State Office of Parks,
Recreation and Historic Preservation

DEDICATION

To all those who have worked to preserve open space
and
the many who shape the paths through it.

TABLE OF CONTENTS

FROM THE AUTHORS

Majestic trees against an azure sky, a brook rushing through a granite wash, birds chattering across an open field—these images might seem like fantasy in a suburban county so close to New York City. But for a hiker or just a stroller out seeking the embrace of nature, that haven is but a short distance away from anywhere in Westchester.

As avid hikers we found that information about hiking in Westchester was limited and scattered. We hoped to create a guide that would remedy that. After eight years of researching, hiking, and mapping almost 600 miles of trails at 186 locations, *Walkable Westchester* came into being.

Ever since publication of that first edition, we have been hearing from hikers about the thrill of discovering new places to hike using this guide. We hope this updated edition, with new areas added to the increasing list of accessible open space, will be helpful. The refinements and additions with plentiful background information on the parks and trails should appeal to the casual stroller, the adventurous hiker, history buff, or the curious naturalist in us all.

We hope that you will continue to enjoy the many walking opportunities in Westchester and can share the joy we have had in exploring them. Research into "green exercise," has shown that walking in nature can have a more wholesome effect on your health than walking elsewhere, even if for short periods.

For a healthy walk of any challenge, from a stroll along a level path to a scramble up a rocky mountainside, Westchester can be the perfect place. And in exploring it, perhaps you can find some peace, quiet, or just yourself.

Jane and Walt Daniels
Mohegan Lake, New York

ACKNOWLEDGMENTS

The second edition of *Walkable Westchester*, like the first, would not have been possible without the help of many dedicated people. Their work and ours were made much easier because of the base established with the first edition: the volunteers who checked trails, provided information, advice, and general assistance.

Aside from the cartographer, Allison Werberg, and the book designer, Nora Porter, all those involved in this project were volunteers.

Jim Simpson's advice and help with research and editing was invaluable. We cannot thank him enough for making a lengthy process enjoyable. Dianne Press copy-edited the text and Suse Bell did the indexing. Part of the editing and research was done at the Ossining Library, a splendid place with helpful reference staff.

Field checkers were an invisible, but essential part in producing this book. Three extraordinary field checkers, Carol Jensen, Erik Jensen, and Eileen West visited half of the parks donating 270 hours to revise the book. The following volunteers spent at least 15 hours working on the project.

Ken Blitz
Daniel Chazin
Merilee Croft
Peter Diamond
Mary Dodds
Zachary Gold
Carolyn Hoffman
John Jurasek
Mark H. Linehan

Catharine Raffaele
Will Raffaele
Anne Rahikainen
Kate Ray
Lynn Salmon
Fred Stern
Jacques Van Engel
Robert Willemann

Photo credits: All photos were made by the authors except for the following: Herb Chong [front cover, back cover, and back cover flap, pages 31, 413], Christine DeBoer [4], Paul Meck [xiv, 103], Anwer Querishi [1], Jim Simpson [37, 117, 139, 292, 333, 356, 376].

HIKER'S ETIQUETTE

A few guidelines for the polite and courteous hiker.
- Obey posted regulations including when the park is open and what is permitted.
- Keep to the right on wide or paved paths.
- Greet people you meet and let others know you are passing them. After all, everyone is enjoying the outdoors.
- Bikers yield to hikers and horses; hikers yield to horses.
- When meeting a horse:
  - Move to the downhill side of the trail.
  - Ask the rider if you are okay to stay where you are.
  - Stand quietly until the horse passes to avoid motions that might startle.
- Hike quietly. There is such a thing as noise pollution.
- When meeting a group of hikers, move to the side of the trail to let them pass.
- Leave only footprints; take only pictures.
- Pack it in, pack it out; even better, pick up any litter you find.
- Keep your dog on a six-foot leash.
  - Dogs running loose threaten wildlife.
  - Other dogs might not be friendly.
  - Some people are intimidated by dogs they don't know.

Understanding Trail Blazes
Each trail is identified by a distinctive color blaze nailed to or painted on a tree. The grouping of the blazes tells you what direction the trail goes.

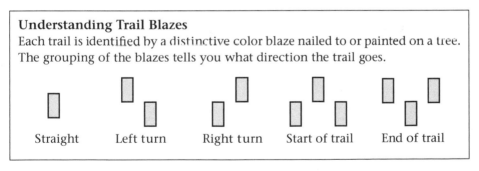

| Straight | Left turn | Right turn | Start of trail | End of trail |

Use of the information in *Walkable Westchester* is at the sole discretion and risk of the hiker. The New York-New Jersey Trail Conference and its authors make every effort to keep their publications up-to-date, however, trail conditions do change.

If you notice discrepancies or inaccuracies in this book, let us know. E-mail your comments to info@nynjtc.org; please include name of the park, the trail, the relevant page number(s), and the date of your observations.

When I Went Walking

In the spring, when I went walking
I took a co-worker who had never been on a hike
    to an old quarry with rusty cable.
We saw pink lady slippers and smelled the skunk cabbage.
She wants to go hiking again.

In the summer, when I went walking
I showed three ten-year-old boys a pond
    with frogs singing and slime around the edges.
We picked blueberries and ate them all.
They want to go hiking again.

In the fall, when I went walking
I pointed out to my friend the hawks flying by
    as we sat overlooking the Hudson River.
We enjoyed the colorful foliage along the trail.
We want to go hiking again.

In the winter, when I went walking
I heard the crisp snow crunch under my husband's boots
    and felt the cold air.
He shared hot chocolate from a thermos with me.
We will go hiking again.

When you went walking
Did you feel rain on your face, hear the birds sing, or find a spider?
You shared them with someone, I hope.
Will you go hiking again?

—Jane Daniels

Fishing at Sparkle Lake.

SECTION I

TINY TREASURES

- ◆ Have one mile or less of trails
- ◆ Offer a small scale introduction to nature
- ◆ Are in the neighborhood or close by

Bye Preserve

Pound Ridge • 0.6 mile, 23 acres

Sometimes you just need a place that is not too far away, just a walk or a short drive, for a small infusion of fresh air and open space. In Pound Ridge, such a place is Bye Preserve. As you enter the preserve on a narrow strip of land between houses, you will see a trail with white blazes (hiker lingo for painted trail markers) that heads downhill. The trail crosses a stream on stepping stones, follows a rocky gorge, and passes large boulders. At 0.4 mile the trail makes a sharp right turn. To the left, a trail leads into private property. The white trail reaches a junction which begins a loop. At the far end of the loop, there is a short connection to an unmarked woods road paralleling a stone wall and a property boundary. The walk down to, and then around the loop and back to the parking area is 1.0 mile. In 2004, The Nature Conservancy transferred the property to Pound Ridge Land Trust with supporting conservation easements held by the Westchester Land Trust.

DRIVING: From I-684, take Exit 4 (Route 172) and head east on Route 172. Drive through Bedford Village to where Route 172 ends at Route 137. Turn right onto Route 137 and go 2.3 miles. The preserve is across from the Pound Ridge Golf Club and just before the New York-Connecticut state line [41.175614N 73.564878W].

PUBLIC TRANSPORTATION: None available

For contact information, see Appendix, Pound Ridge Land Conservancy.

Carolin's Grove

Pound Ridge • 1.1 miles, 5 acres

A sense of serenity greets you as you drive into the parking lot at the entrance to Carolin's Grove. A large grove of Norway spruce planted in the 1930s gives a cathedral-like appearance to the site and invites visitors to pause, observe, and reflect. Robert Lawther donated the property to The Nature Conservancy in 1969 in memory of his wife, Carolin. In 2004, The Nature Conservancy transferred the property to Pound Ridge Land Conservancy with supporting conservation easements held by the Westchester Land Trust.

The simple trail system here resulted from the cooperative efforts of the town, a school, and a local nonprofit organization. The blue trail wraps around the town's ball and soccer fields and continues through the Pound Ridge Elementary School playground, providing the school with two outdoor learning areas.

From the parking lot on the side opposite a kiosk, the blue trail heads clockwise to parallel Route 137. It bears right and passes a white trail #1 at 0.1 mile. Reaching the edge of the woods, the blue trail skirts a ball field and heads down a paved service road. It turns right, passes a playground, crosses an open field and reenters the woods where the blazes resume. After passing white trail #2 at 0.4 mile, the

CULTIVATING OPEN SPACE

Westchester County has a long history in preserving the open space and the amount protected areas continues to grow. It was wealth of a different sort that is partly responsible: the affluent built country estates on large tracts and created bridle trail systems. Many of these tracts were later acquired or donated as open space and some of the trails remain.

There have always been those who valued open space. The Hudson Park on Long Island Sound dates from 1886. Residents in Larchmont came together to create Manor Park in 1892. But it wasn't until the 1920s that the county itself began acquiring land for parks and recreation and for parkways for private vehicles. Among those instrumental in this process were William L. Ward, who created an overall plan for county-owned recreational land and Agnes Meyer, who was instrumental in implementing that vision.

The hard times of the Depression in the1930's halted investment in new parkland, but instead existing parks were improved by the Civilian Conservation Corps. Post-war development saw a rise in bequests and the establishment of nonprofits. With the 1970s and 80s came an increasing environmental awareness and a rising concern over unchecked development. By the 1990s, concerned residents were banding together to stop intrusive developments and preserve over crucial open space with some purchases leveraged through group efforts.

Since 2000, the 27 new parks have been protected as open space and countless miles of new trails built in existing parks. These numbers are possible largely because some communities have set aside funds to preserve open space and land trusts have been established to protect land through conservation easements or purchases. Taking a hike takes on a new meaning.

---

trail loops around and passes it again at 0.6 mile. The blue trail reaches white trail #1. Passing through a Norway spruce grove severely damaged by Hurricane Sandy in 2012, the blue trail ends in 0.9 mile at a service road into the soccer field. Parking is a short distance to the left.

DRIVING: From I-684, take Exit 4 (Route 172) and follow it east to where it ends at Route 137. Turn left and drive 0.3 mile to a parking area to the left [41.213603N 73.576897W].

PUBLIC TRANSPORTATION: None available

For contact information, see Appendix, Pound Ridge Land Conservancy.

Crawford Park and Rye Hills Park

Rye Brook • 0.8 mile, 43 acres

S eparated by an ivy-covered concrete wall, Crawford Park and Rye Hills Park sit side by side on top of a hill in Rye Brook. The grounds of Crawford Park have gardens, benches, and a wildflower area. Paved paths are handicapped accessible.

Shanarock Farm was once the main family home of Edna and Everett Crawford, who purchased the 35.6-acre estate in the early 1900s. With development surrounding them, the Crawfords wanted to protect open space. So, in 1955 they bequeathed their estate to the Town of Rye. In keeping with their wishes, no announcement of the gift was made until

Stone story circle.

Mrs. Crawford's death in 1974, when the estate became a park. The mansion is an example of a big house of that era, surrounded by landscaping, formal gardens, and outbuildings. Mature trees line the vast expanse of lawn and the mansion is used for community events.

A 0.5-mile walking path is along most of the park's length, as well as along the ball fields. There is pedestrian access from Rye Hill Park and adjacent neighborhoods. Rye Hills Park has a wide 0.3-mile loop trail with a story circle and a belvedere (a scenic overlook).

DRIVING: From the northbound Hutchinson River Parkway, take Exit 29 (North Ridge Road) and turn right. If southbound, turn left onto North Ridge Road. It is a mile from the intersection of the northbound exit and North Ridge Road to the Crawford Park entrance to the right [41.014556N 73.68150W]. The road is one-way only through the park, with parking at the hilltop to the right of the mansion, and near the exit to Lincoln Avenue.

Anyone with handicapped permits may continue past the entrance to Crawford Park and turn right onto Long Ledge Drive (Hidden Falls entrance). Turn left at Parkridge Court and take the next left into Rye Hills Park [41.013973N 73.685130W].

PUBLIC TRANSPORTATION: None available

For contact information, see Appendix, Rye (Town), Rye Brook.

Croton River Gorge Trail

Croton-on-Hudson • 0.9 mile, 34.4 acres

Beginning in the parking lot for Silver Lake Park (at the end of Truesdale Drive), the Croton River Gorge Trail follows what is known as a 'paper' road, a road that appears on maps, but in this case has never been paved. The wide trail is basically level, but at 0.3 mile, a narrow unmarked trail to the right descends steeply to reach Quaker Bridge Road. It is a 0.2 mile road walk to Black Rock Park, (Croton resident permit required during the summer). Just past the trail which descends into the gorge, an unmarked trail heads uphill 0.2 mile to the parking lot behind the Carrie E. Tompkins Elementary School. A round trip from the end of Truesdale Drive to Cleveland Drive is 1.2 miles.

DRIVING: From Route 9, take the Croton Point Avenue Exit and turn away from the river. After one block, turn left at a traffic light and take the first right onto Benedict Boulevard. When Benedict Boulevard reaches a traffic circle, take the second exit onto Truesdale Drive. Follow Truesdale Drive to its end for parking at Silver Lake Park [41.207014N 73.872222W]. Or, take the third exit from the traffic (Cleveland Drive) for 1.5 miles for parking [41.214626N 73.868167W].

PUBLIC TRANSPORTATION: None available

For contact information, see Appendix, Croton.

East Irvington Nature Preserve

East Irvington • 0.5 mile, 32 acres

No climbing is necessary to reach the views at the East Irvington Nature Preserve which sits atop a ridge. From the entrance, it is 0.1 mile along the Wecquasgeeks Trail to reach a viewing platform that overlooks a pond. From the pond, turn right along the gravel road and in another 0.1 mile, pass a 0.3 mile orange-blazed trail which eventually loops downhill and back up to the gravel road.

DRIVING: From Route 9 at the Irvington/Tarrytown line, turn east onto Sunnyside Lane, which is 1.0 mile south of I-287 and 0.5 mile north of Main Street in Irvington. Follow Sunnyside Lane for 0.6 mile which bears left to become Taxter Road. Continue 0.7 mile further to the preserve entrance to the right [41.048322N 73.840129W].

PUBLIC TRANSPORTATION: None available

For contact information, see Appendix, Greenburgh.

A gateway to the preserve.

East Rumbrook Park

Greenburgh • 0.5 mile, 51 acres

Ball fields dominate East Rumbrook Park, itself somewhat a diamond in the rough. This little slice of field and forest provides a short walk and a way to escape suburban sprawl.

At the far end of the parking lot, the lone trail passes a dog park with separate fenced areas for large and small dogs. The paved path is along the edge of a power line right-of-way and leads into a mixed hardwood forest. Turn right off the road and cross Rum Brook at 0.4 mile on stones, which in high water might not be sufficient to keep feet dry. The path turns away from the stream and passes behind houses. Numerous tracks lead to a set of wooden steps ascending into private property. The trail turns away from the houses and recrosses the stream. It closes the loop at the road.

DRIVING: From the Sprain Brook Parkway, take Dobbs Ferry Road/100B Exit and turn east. The entrance to the park is adjacent to the southbound exit ramp [41.040142N 73.818867W].

PUBLIC TRANSPORTATION: None available

For contact information, see Appendix, Greenburgh.

Eastwoods Preserve

East Woods • 0.9 miles 48 acres

More than just charming, Eastwoods Preserve is a sanctuary of high quality habitats. Small streams wend their way through the property and feed the central wetlands. Vast arrays of New York ferns carpet several areas and rock outcroppings are spattered with lichen, moss, and ferns. As of 2013, several healthy hemlocks have avoided infestation by the wooly adelgid and the noticeable absence of invasive plants adds to the primal feel of this preserve.

The town purchased the property in 2007 from the estate of C.C. Wang, the father of Vera Wang, the fashion designer. Preserved as Town of Pound Ridge open space in 2007, it protects the headwaters of Stamford's Siscowit Reservoir. It is a key connecting tract in the Eastern Westchester Biotic Corridor that includes Ward Pound Ridge Reservation.

The lone trail (green) loops 0.9 mile through the forest off and on wood roads, over streams, through small ravines, and along rock outcroppings. From the parking area, the trail splits. Heading left, it turns to parallel a stone wall and passes percolation pits, evidence that the property had been considered for development. The trail crosses stone walls and then joins and leaves wood roads. At 0.3 mile, it crosses a stream on a causeway and goes downhill into a ravine. After crossing several streams, the trail winds through a valley. It heads uphill at

A rocky wrinkle.

0.6 miles as it rounds the end of a rock outcropping. At 0.8 mile, there is so much moss and lichen on the rock outcroppings that it looks as if it were painted on. The trail closes the loop at 0.9 mile in sight of the road and parking.

DRIVING: From I-684, take Exit 4 (Route 172). Turn east and follow Route 172 through Bedford Village to where Route 172 ends at Route 137. Turn right and go 0.7 miles. Turn left onto Westchester Avenue and, in 0.2 mile, make a slight left onto Fancher Road. In 0.5 mile, go straight onto Eastwoods Road when Fancher Road turns right. Stay on Eastwoods Road for 1.4 miles ignoring the signs when it when it is co-aligned with Trinity Pass Road. The preserve is to the left with a small spot that can accommodate two cars carefully parked [41.210882N 73.540142W]. The nearest house before the preserve is #125.

PUBLIC TRANSPORTATION: None available

For contact information, see Appendix, Town of Lewisboro.

Fort Hill Park

Peekskill • 0.8 mile, 52 acres

Located on a hill near the center of Peekskill, Fort Hill Park is a refuge from the hustle of downtown. Stone steps at the entrance and some paths attest to a time when the park was more formal. The area is also rich in American history; during the Revolution, Fort Hill was the site of a redoubt and five large barracks. An interpretive sign gives a brief history of the role the area played in the conflict. A trail marked intermittently loops through former pastures and along old farm roads. There is a viewpoint with a seasonal view over the Hudson River. The park increased in size in 2007, when the Ginsberg Development Companies donated 40 acres in exchange for the rights to build townhouses on adjacent property.

DRIVING: From Route 9, take the Route 6/202 Exit to Peekskill. Turn left onto Main Street. After a short distance, turn left onto Hadden Street, adjacent to a playground, and follow it to the end. Turn right, drive one block to Decatur Street, and turn left. The park entrance is to the left just before Orchard Street. Curbside parking has limited hours [41.294141N 73.923904W].

PUBLIC TRANSPORTATION: Beeline Bus #17 on Main Street

For contact information, see Appendix, Peekskill.

Guard Hill Park

Mt. Kisco • 0.5 mile, 17 acres

A short stiff climb is necessary to reach the high point in Guard Hill Park, which is overgrown with trees. During the American Revolution, observation patrols were stationed on Guard Hill, called a "commanding height" on maps made by Robert Erskine, General George Washington's cartographer. In 1981, Wilhelmine Kirby Waller donated the property to the Town of Bedford.

From the parking area, the yellow trail begins between a fence and a stone marker. Logs and branches delineate the path in the open mixed hardwood forest. At 0.1 mile the trail splits, follow the left branch, and pass a view of a farm field. At 0.3 mile the trail turns right; the unmarked trail straight ahead leads into private property. The trail continues to climb and reaches a red trail which ascends 0.1 mile to reach a radio tower. The only view at the top is to the left, along the access road to the tower at the property boundary at 0.1 mile, where there is a sweeping view of a horse pasture. Retrace your steps to the yellow trail and turn left at the junction. Continuing steeply downhill, the trail at 0.4 mile joins the access trail from the parking lot. A hike to the top and back to the parking lot is 0.7 miles and 0.9 miles if the side trip to the view of the horse farm is included.

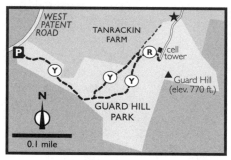

DRIVING: Take I-684 to Exit 4 (Route 172) and turn west toward Mt. Kisco. Turn right onto West Patent Road and head north for 0.4 mile. Pass John Cross Road to the left; just beyond the stone walls of the entrance to #284 to the right, there is a small unmarked parking area. The only sign is a plaque on a rock, not noticeable from the road [41.205832N 73.705859W].

PUBLIC TRANSPORTATION: None available

For contact information, see Appendix, Bedford.

Haas Sanctuary

Armonk 0.9 mile; 14.5 acres

Within tiny Haas Sanctuary, there is a surprising range of habitats: field, edge environment, vernal pools, forest, and rocky outcroppings. The first seven acres were a donation by the Haas family in memory of George C. Haas, a World War I veteran who owned and exhibited hackney horses. Because of the Betts family's gift of an additional seven acres to Saw Mill River Audubon in 2007, there is better access, parking, and additional trails.

The names of the trails in Haas Preserve indicate a habitat or destination. The 300-foot climb from the entrance on Sheather Road to the ridge is sufficient to provide a real aerobic workout. From the entrance, the Hillside Trail (yellow) heads uphill and passes the Blue Bird Trail (blue) to the left. They meet again 0.2 mile later. The Valley Trail (white) is located in the original sanctuary property and passes rocky cliffs along its 0.3 mile loop. The Blue Bird Trail (blue) forms a 0.3 mile loop through the meadow and along the forest edge. The 0.1 mile Cliff Trail (red) is the original entrance trail from Tripp Street.

DRIVING: Take the Saw Mill River Parkway to the light at Readers Digest Road and cross the railroad tracks. Stay on Readers Digest Road until it ends at Route 117 (Bedford Road). Turn left, head north for 1.5 miles, and turn right on Armonk Road (Route 128). It is 0.9 mile to a left turn onto Sheather Road. Follow Sheather Road 1.1 miles to the sanctuary's entrance to the right [41.166233N 73.721139W].

PUBLIC TRANSPORTATION: None available

For contact information, see Appendix, Saw Mill River Audubon.

Along the ridge line.

Halsey Pond

L ike a sentinel, the Beltzhoover Teahouse overlooks Halsey Pond. This stone building is the largest remaining structure of Rochroane, the Beltzhoover estate built in 1905. After the property was sold to a developer, The New York State Office of Parks, Recreation and Historic Preservation deemed it "architecturally and historically significant as rare examples of Gothic stone architecture associated with mid-nineteenth century picturesque landscape." It makes the perfect setting for a very small wedding. Surrounded by houses and adjacent to a golf course, this tiny park has a wide variety of trees, shrubs, and wildflowers.

From the parking area at the end of Hamilton Road, an unmarked path heads uphill to Halsey Pond. The left hand fork leads to the teahouse with views over the pond. A wide level path circles the pond which has a catch and release policy. Birch Lane, Havermeyer Road and Palister Road are pedestrian entrances, all without parking.

NEARBY PARKS: Old Croton Aqueduct, Juhring Estate

DRIVING: From Broadway (Route 9) just north of Mercy College in Dobbs Ferry, turn right onto Hamilton Road. Park at the end of the street, but take care not to block nearby driveways [41.029814N 73.861165W].

PUBLIC TRANSPORTATION: Beeline Bus #1W or #1T along Broadway at Ardsley and Clinton avenues.

For contact information, see Appendix, Irvington.

Beltzhoover Teahouse.

Hemlock Brook Preserve

Huntersville 0.6 mile; 14 acres

Rushing water is the first thing you sense when you enter Hemlock Brook Preserve. The trail leaves Hemlock Brook and skirts the ravine, beginning a loop at 0.1 mile. Going clockwise from a trail junction, it winds south under towering trees. The hemlocks, unfortunately, are being ravaged by wooly adelgid. Accidentally introduced in 1951, this tiny insect now infests hemlocks in states along the eastern seaboard. At 0.3 mile the loop turns downhill to begin the return trip. At 0.5 mile, the trail passes an old stone fireplace beside the trail and heads uphill to close the loop at the access trail.

DRIVING: From the Taconic State Parkway, take the Baldwin Road exit and turn west towards the Mohansic Golf Course. Go 0.9 mile and turn right onto Baptist Church Road. It is 0.3 mile to a pull-out next to the Catskill Aqueduct. Do not block the gate [41.257395N 73.817448W]. The preserve entrance is less than 0.1 mile downhill and diagonally across the street.

PUBLIC TRANSPORTATION: None available

For contact information, see Appendix, Westchester Land Trust.

Hunt Woods Park

Mount Vernon • 1.1 miles, 21 acres

Over the years, countless dogs with their owners and generations of children have enjoyed Hunt Woods Park with Laurel Brook winding its way toward the Bronx River. In the 1920s, Westchester County purchased this land, which is now the park, to be a right-of-way for the Cross County Parkway. However, instead of using the land for the parkway, the county, in a cost saving move, realigned the parkway more directly via a bridge over the Bronx River and the Bronx River Parkway. In December 1967, the land was transferred to the City of Mount Vernon. Tall stately trees, some older than 250 years, grace two unmarked parallel trails. Although the area is densely populated, little road noise can be heard in the park because of its setting in a valley. Because the well-worn paths are often in the flood plain of Laurel Brook, they may not be passable after a rain. The trail begins at the end of a guardrail on Central Parkway in Mount Vernon and goes along a sewer right-of-way. Keep left at the first trail junction. The trail passes a cross trail and then Laurel Brook, which flows out of a culvert and along a course faced with rocks. At 0.3 mile, the trail reaches a wide intersection where a second trail joins and then splits off again with each trail going over a wooden bridge.

Keeping left again, the trail heads slightly uphill, still paralleling Laurel Brook. The trail crosses the stream on concrete block stepping stones and reaches what looks like a dead end at a stone wall at 0.5 mile. However, there are broad steps which go up to Gramatan Avenue. On the other side of the street, a flight of steps heads back down to the stream. This section has considerable evidence of past flooding and the path is narrower. The trail ends at ball fields at 0.6 mile.

For a return trip, retrace your steps to cross Gramatan Avenue and go back down the stairs. At the stream, cross on the concrete stepping stones, keeping left. The sometimes narrow trail hugs the side of the valley. It crosses a wooden bridge to reach a wide intersection. Go left, but almost immediately bear right at a Y junction, staying in Hunt Woods. The left branch continues 100 yards to end at Vernon Parkway. The main trail passes the cross trail mentioned earlier, and then a trail to the left which ends at the corner of Rhynas Drive and Central Parkway, where you can see your starting point to the right.

DRIVING: From eastbound Cross County Parkway, take Exit 8 (Route 22) toward North Columbus Avenue, Mount Vernon. Follow the parkway south, and turn left to head north on Columbus Avenue.** After two blocks, turn left onto East Devonia Avenue at 0.3 mile, then turn right onto Central Parkway. The park entrance is to the left adjacent to #112 Central Parkway (the first house); however, there is a No Parking sign. From westbound Cross County Parkway, take Exit 8 (Route 22). At the end of the exit ramp, turn left onto Columbus Avenue (Route 22). Follow the directions from ** [40.927785N 73.827141W].

PUBLIC TRANSPORTATION: Beeline Bus #40 along North Columbus Avenue. Follow the preceding directions from East Devonia Avenue, above.

For contact information, see Appendix, Mount Vernon.

Leatherman's Ridge

Bedford Hills • 0.4 mile, 33 acres

The efforts of neighbors, the Town of Bedford, and the Westchester Land Trust preserved Leatherman's Ridge. On his route through Westchester County, the Leatherman frequented a cave on the site. (See sidebar about the Leatherman in Ward Pound Ridge Reservation.) The only trail is a loop with a cross trail to allow for a shorter hike. An unmarked path under the power line is quite passable about 0.3 mile northwest of its intersection with the yellow trail.

DRIVING: From northbound Saw Mill Parkway, take the Bedford Hills Exit and turn left onto Route 117. At the intersection where Bedford Road goes right, continue straight ahead on Cherry Street.* In 0.2 mile, turn left onto Dwight Lane to park at the end [41.240702N 73.701502W]. From southbound Saw Mill Parkway take the Bedford Hills Exit. Turn right onto Haines Road, then left onto Route 117 (Cherry Street) at the intersection with Bedford Road. Follow above directions from *.
PUBLIC TRANSPORTATION: Metro-North Bedford Hills Station. Walk south along Adams Street, turn right onto Route 117, and follow the driving directions from the northbound Saw Mill Parkway. It is about a half-mile to the trailhead.

For contact information, see Appendix, Bedford.

Henry Morgenthau Preserve

Pound Ridge • 1.0 miles, 35 acres

Four distinct forest communities (oak-hickory, red maple swamp, sugar maple forest, and white pine plantation) are at the Henry Morgenthau Preserve. Locations of the forest communities are identified in a brochure available at the kiosk, which also has extensive information about Henry Morgenthau. In 1972, Ruth M. Knight donated twenty acres to establish the preserve in memory of her father Henry Morgenthau. He served as U.S. Ambassador to the Ottoman Empire, (1913-1916) and was the father of Henry Morgenthau,Jr, Secretary of Treasury under Franklin D. Roosevelt and grandfather of Robert M. Morgenthau, long-time Manhattan district attorney. The original 20-acre preserve has grown with a purchase in 1973 and a donation in 1984. The Henry Morgenthau Committee of the Bedford Audubon Society manages the site.

Blue Trail
Length: 0.7 mile Blaze: blue

From the entrance at the rear of the parking lot, the blue trail passes a kiosk and heads into the preserve, passing through a grove of young sugar maples. Just past a stone wall at 0.1 mile, it splits. Continue straight and pass the yellow trail to the right, a 0.1-mile side trail loop to a massive white oak. This tree once provided shade to animals pastured in the fields. At the next junction, a white trail heads left providing a 250-foot short cut to the return route.

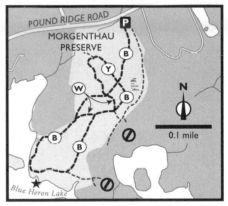

The blue trail goes through a white pine plantation established in the 1940s. It passes a second white trail, which leads 100 feet to the return route. The trail turns, descends, and follows the shore of Blue Heron Lake, enlarged from a marshy pond in the 1920s. It heads away from the lake and passes a deer exclosure, a fenced in area protecting two rare and endangered orchid species. It makes a sharp left at 0.4 mile. This turn is easily missed because the route straight ahead is more heavily trodden and leads to unmarked trails on private property.

As the trail heads back to the parking lot, it passes rock outcroppings and a glacial erratic at the intersection with the southern of the two white trails. After passing the intersection with the northern of the two white trails at 0.6 mile, the blue trail turns and closes the loop at 0.7 mile. The yellow trail is just off to the left. Turn right to return to the preserve entrance.

DRIVING: From I-684, take Exit 4 (Route 172) and head east, passing through Bedford Village. The preserve entrance is approximately 2.9 miles from the Bedford Village Green. Marked with a small sign, the preserve is to the right just past Tatomuck

Road and opposite Meadowbrook Farm [41.201410N 73.588057W].

PUBLIC TRANSPORTATION: None available

For contact information, see Appendix, Bedford Audubon Society.

Old Church Lane Preserve

Vista • 0.6 mile, 31 acres

In Old Church Lane Preserve, lush vegetation surrounds the lone trail which winds its way in and around wetlands and through a moist acidic forest. The preserve was established with a donation to the Open Space Institute (OSI) in the mid 1990s. Subsequently, OSI donated the land to the Westchester Land Trust. The preserve protects the shrubby wetlands and surrounding woodland, habitat for vulnerable amphibians such as wood frogs and spotted salamanders.

Just beyond the entrance, the trail passes four white pines growing together. It enters a wetland, crosses a stream, and heads up to the top of a ravine at 0.2 mile. The trail meanders through the forest with thick understory, which is predominately mountain laurel. It heads downhill and crosses a stream. At 0.4 mile, the trail reaches a T junction with a woods road and turns left. It passes extensive wetlands to the left at 0.5 mile, and ends on Old Church Lane across from #28 at 0.6 mile.

NEARBY PARKS: Levy Preserve, Onatru Farm Park and Preserve

DRIVING: From I-684, take Exit 6 (Route 35) and turn east. Drive 9.1 miles and turn right at the traffic light on Route 123 (just before the New York-Connecticut state line). Follow Route 123 south for 1.8 miles and turn right onto Kitchawan Road. Drive 0.5 mile and turn left onto Old Church Lane. Another half-mile leads to parking to the left, across from #40 [41.232511N 73.531558W].

PUBLIC TRANSPORTATION: None available

For contact information, see Appendix, Westchester Land Trust.

Onatru Farm Preserve

Vista • 0.7 mile, 101 acres

A large white Colonial style farmhouse greets visitors to Onatru Farm Park and Preserve. Starting in 1962, Alice Lane Poor made donations to the Town of Lewisboro which resulted in Onatru Farm Park and Preserve. Her wish was to protect the land and preserve the farming atmosphere of Lewisboro. Onatru is derived from "on a true farm" and is a word made up by Mrs. Poor's father, Edward Lane, who purchased the property in 1904 map as a country house. The farm fields are now ball fields and her original donation of the woodlands across the street is the preserve. The farmhouse serves as a town office building. Camping,

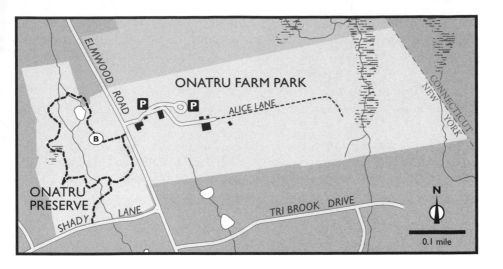

with some restrictions and a permit, is allowed at the preserve. Applications are available through the Town Clerk's office, 914 763-3511.

The blue trail in the preserve starts almost directly across the street from the former farmhouse. Trees are labeled, including a log from an American chestnut. The trail crosses a field and enters the woods on a woods road. Turning right, it heads uphill and begins to wander through the woods, passing a man-made pond to the left. After crossing several streams, it turns left at 0.3 mile, passing several red oak trees growing together. The trail crosses a stone wall to enter a wetland at 0.5 mile. It reaches a trail junction where a trail heads 0.1 mile to end just west of #26 Shady Lane. The trail then ascends steeply, reaches the top and enters a field. After it passes a kiosk, it ends at Elmwood Road.

NEARBY PARKS: Levy Preserve, Old Church Preserve

DRIVING: From I-684, take Exit 6 (Route 35) and turn east. Follow Route 35 for 9.1 miles and just before the New York-Connecticut line, turn right at the traffic light onto Route 123. Continue south for 1.9 miles and turn left onto Shady Lane. At the T junction with Elmwood Road, turn left. Parking for the preserve is available at Onatru Farm Park to the right, 0.1 mile from the last turn [41.242678N 73.515514W].

PUBLIC TRANSPORTATION: None available

For contact information, see Appendix: Lewisboro.

Pinecliff Sanctuary

Chappaqua • 0.5 mile, 7 acres

One might easily overlook tiny Pinecliff Sanctuary, set at the end of a cul-de-sac. Its 0.2-mile long wheelchair accessible boardwalk circles the wetlands and a pond. Both white and yellow trails form loops off the boardwalk for 0.2 and 0.1 mile, respectively.

In 1969, the Stern and Arleo families donated seven acres to New Castle Land Conservancy (which later merged with Saw Mill River Audubon). In 1996, the boardwalk was built with funds from a Westchester Community Development Block Grant and local support including volunteer labor.

DRIVING: From the Saw Mill Parkway, take Route 120 north towards Millwood. At Pinecliff Road, turn right and continue to the end. Parking is limited [41.166866N 73.773083W].

PUBLIC TRANSPORTATION: Metro-North Harlem Division Chappaqua Station. Cross to the west side of the tracks and head north 0.6 mile on the sidewalk along Route 120. Take the third right onto Pinecliff Road and walk 0.2 mile to the end.

For contact information, see Appendix, Saw Mill River Audubon Society.

Purdys Ridge Preserve

Purdys 1.0 mile; 66 acres

High on this hill is not a lonely goatherd, but a lone trail on Purdys Ridge Preserve, purchased in 2005 by the Town of North Salem and North Salem Open Land Foundation. The single trail makes a loop through the property climbing 250 feet to the ridge. Unfortunately the sound of I-684 is always present even when the leaves are on the trees.

Across from the last house on Old School House Road, steps lead into Purdys Ridge Preserve. Marked with red/white square blazes nailed to trees, the trail heads steeply uphill, It winds through woods and past a sea of barberry. At 0.4 mile the trail reaches the top of the ridge where a long, low rock outcropping stretches out like a lizard sunning. Descending through open forest, the trail passes, at 0.6 mile, a large spring fed by a seep in the side of the hill. Continuing downhill, the trail crosses streams, gullies, and stone walls. It ends at the end of Old School House Road.

DRIVING: From north bound I-684, take Exit 7 (Purdys) and at the top of the exit ramp, turn right onto Route 116. Turn left onto Route 22/Route 116 and then make an immediate right hand turn onto Titicus River Road. **Go one block and turn right on Main Street, a left turn onto Mills Road and a right turn onto Old School House Road. The preserve is at the end of the street. From southbound I-684, take Exit 8 Hardscrabble Road/ Croton Falls and turn left at the

Spring fed.

end of the ramp. Take Route 22 south for 1.2 miles and turn left onto Titicus River Road. Continue from ** [41.324396N 73.654391W].

PUBLIC TRANSPORTATION: None available

Ridgeway Nature Preserve

White Plains • 0.4 mile, 16 acres

As a small preserve tucked in behind an elementary school, the Ridgeway Nature Preserve utilizes a sewer line right-of-way which runs along a stream. To reach the preserve, park in Ridgeway Elementary School's parking lot (only if the school is closed) and walk along the east side of the ball fields. At the south end of the parking lot, a path heads along the edge of the school property behind the baseball backstop, then downhill to the park entrance to the left. The wide trail looks down onto a stream with stonework channeling the water. It passes a strange stone structure with steps in the back. At 0.2 mile, the path turns right onto a trail that leads to a stone bridge downstream from a small dam. Continue counterclockwise along the main trail to return to the parking lot.

NEARBY PARK: Jack Harrington White Plains Greenway

DRIVING: From I-287, take the Bloomingdale Road Exit and turn left onto Bloomingdale Road, which becomes Mamaroneck Avenue. Pass Stepinac High School to the right and take the next right onto Ridgeway. Ridgeway Elementary School is to the left and, if not in session, park in the lot. No other parking is available [41.004775N 73.753253W].

PUBLIC TRANSPORTATION: Beeline Bus #60 on Mamaroneck Avenue and walk 2 blocks along Ridgeway to the Ridgeway Elementary School. Beeline #63 on Route 125 (Old Mamaroneck Road) and walk east on Ridgeway to Seeger Drive, a short dead end street just west of #165 Ridgeway. The park entrance is at the end of Seeger Drive.

For contact information, see Appendix, White Plains.

Rock Hill Park

Mohegan Lake • 1.1 mile, 14.5 acres

Tiny Rock Hill Park is being developed on the site of the former Rock Hill Lodge, which had residential buildings and bungalows, along with a casino and dining hall that hosted lively gatherings during its heyday in the early 1900's. From the late 60's until the early 90's, the site was operated as the Holland Sporting Club. Acquired by the Town of Yorktown in 2005 with the intent of converting it into a park, it was neglected and vandalized. In 2012, the remaining buildings were demolished. The stone benches dotting the landscape, hearken back to when visitors came to the "country" to enjoy its rural charm.

Circling the property, the 0.8 mile Lake View Loop (yellow) provides access to Mohegan Lake to enjoy the views or walk along the shore. The Corner Trail (orange) goes 0.1 mile from the corner of Cabot Lane and Horton Road to the tree lined former entrance road. The Rock Hill Trail (green) goes 0.1 mile from parking down to the lake shore where it ends on the Lake View Loop.

DRIVING: From Taconic State Parkway, take the Route 6 Exit and head west. From the traffic light at Route 132, it is 2.3 miles to Lexington Avenue. Turn left at the Lexington Avenue and at 0.3 mile turn left onto ** Decatur Road and go 0.3 mile. Turn right on Cabot Lane and then turn left at the T junction to Horton Road. The park is to your left [41.314133N 73.851833W].

PUBLIC TRANSPORTATION: Beeline Bus #15 to Lexington Avenue. Then follow the directions from **.

For contact information, see Appendix, Yorktown.

St. Paul's Chapel

Vista • 0.8 mile, 32 acres

The trails at St. Paul's Chapel wander through the property giving hikers a chance to enjoy laurel groves, wetlands, vernal pools, a balanced glacial erratic, and a stream. The trails offer walks that can be both physically and spiritually satisfying. From the kiosk beside St. Paul's Chapel, the blue trail makes a 0.3 mile loop through St. Francis Chapel and returns to the parking lot on the other side of the chapel. A 0.1 mile orange trail goes through a rock field, passes a balanced rock, and ends at the white trail. A 0.3 mile loop (white) crosses streams and leads to a second blue trail which has a short steep climb, but there is no view.

Balanced glacial erratic.

NEARBY PARKS: Levy Preserve, Onatru Farm Park and Preserve

DRIVING: From I-684, take Exit 6 (Route 35) and head east for 9.1 miles. Turn right at the traffic light on Route 123, which is just before the New York-Connecticut line. Follow Route 123 south for 2.3 miles. St Paul's Chapel is south of the intersection with Elmwood Road on the left side [41.222449N 73.517657W].

PUBLIC TRANSPORTATION: None available

For contact information, see Appendix, Lewisboro Land Trust.

Art in residence.

Sculpture Garden at PepsiCo

Purchase • 1.1 miles, 168 acres

World class takes on new meaning at the Sculpture Garden located at PepsiCo World Headquarters. The gardens are formally named for Donald M. Kendall, former chairman of the board and CEO of PepsiCo. He imagined an atmosphere of stability, creativity, and experimentation, reflecting his vision of the company. Set on a former polo field, the sculpture garden is also an arboretum with both native and non-native trees and plants. Due to renovations to the building, the garden is closed to the public until the summer of 2015; in the past, a map has been available at the small visitors center.

Edward Durrell Stone, Jr. designed the extensive landscaping, with an understanding and appreciation of the forms, textures, colors, and scents of the flora. The grounds around the formal gardens are on a grand scale and surround the building which was designed by his father. The noted British garden designer, Russell Page, extended the garden from 1980 until his death in 1985. Thereafter, Françoise Giffinet continued to develop the garden.

A path winds 1.1 miles around the building, passing small groves of similar tree species, specialty gardens, and woodlands. The gold gravel covering the paved path is Russell Page's concept of a golden ribbon tying the garden's features together. There are five sets of four-inch-high steps, both wide and long enough to allow the route to be handicapped accessible. The loop around the lake has no steps.

The art collection was begun in 1965. Featuring the work of major twentieth century sculptors, it had grown to include 45 pieces, by 2006. Ten sculptures are in the courtyard of the building, while the others are in continuous view of the path. Benches are placed throughout the route, allowing for reflection, contemplation, and a chance to study the art from numerous angles.

DRIVING: From eastbound I-287, take Exit 8E. Make a gentle left onto Westchester Avenue, and then another gentle left onto the ramp leading towards Anderson

Hill Road. At the fork, continue towards the right on Anderson Hill Road to reach the PepsiCo entrance in 2.5 miles. From westbound I-287, take Exit 10 (Bowman Avenue/Webb Avenue). Follow Webb Avenue to Westchester Avenue. Turn right to follow Westchester Avenue for 0.2 mile, turning left onto Lincoln Avenue and continuing 2.1 miles to Anderson Hill Road. Turn right, and right again, at the entrance into PepsiCo. A security guard at the gate will direct you to parking. Maps are available at the visitors center [41.038703N 73.696289W].

PUBLIC TRANSPORTATION: Beeline Bus #12 can be used to reach or leave the site, weekday mornings and evenings, respectively.

For contact information, see Appendix, PepsiCo.

Sparkle Lake Park

Yorktown • 0.5 mile, 37 acres

Beginning at the north end of the parking lot, the trail runs north above a sewer line right-of-way along the edge of Sparkle Lake with sweeping views that offer ample opportunities to observe wildlife. At times the trail is close enough to the lake to allow fishing. It passes the end of the lake at 0.2 mile and an unmarked track heading 225 yards to private homes. At 0.3 mile, it passes a trail to the right which leads in 250 feet to a playground, accessible from Douglas Drive. The sewer line heads uphill to end at London Road, near Curry Street. A paved handicapped accessible path heads south from the main parking lot along the beach. In summer, this portion of the park is open only to Yorktown residents with swimming permits.

DRIVING: Take the Taconic State Parkway to the Underhill Avenue exit and turn east. At the traffic light at Route 118, turn left and go 1.1 miles to Broad Street. Turn left and pass at 1.0 mile, a large sign (Yorktown Parks and Recreation) and 0.2 mile later. turn left at the next entrance (with a smaller sign) [41.304259N 73.781452W]. The trail begins at the north end of a larger parking lot adjacent to the Parks and Recreation office

PUBLIC TRANSPORTATION: None available

For contact information, see Appendix, Yorktown.

Turtle Rock in Armstrong Preserve.

SECTION II

POCKET PARKS

- ◆ Have one to two miles of trails
- ◆ Provide perfect opportunities for quick walks
- ◆ Are in nearby communities

Armstrong Preserve
Richards Preserve

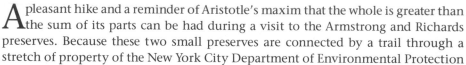

Cross River • 1.7 miles 43 and 15.5 Acres

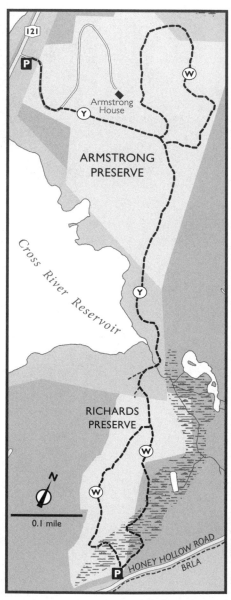

A pleasant hike and a reminder of Aristotle's maxim that the whole is greater than the sum of its parts can be had during a visit to the Armstrong and Richards preserves. Because these two small preserves are connected by a trail through a stretch of property of the New York City Department of Environmental Protection (DEP), the combined length can make for hikes of more than two miles.

In 2001, a gift from the estate of Dr. Catherine Armstrong (1915-1999) to the Pound Ridge Land Conservancy established the Armstrong Preserve. A pediatrician in Carlsbad, New Mexico, Dr. Armstrong and her sister had purchased the property in 1961 from a nephew and heir of John Corbin, who had owned the property and in 1912 built the house there as a three-season retreat. He had been a drama critic, editor and author who had worked at *Harpers Magazine* and *The New York Times*.

Richards Preserve was established when Richard Richards donated the property to the Pound Ridge Land Conservancy in 1979. The trail was opened in 2009.

TRAILS

Massive rock outcroppings tower above the trails in the Armstrong Preserve. The loop trail in the Richards Preserve goes through a mixed hardwood forest, a wide watershed strewn with boulders, and former farmland on an elevated plateau. Starting from the Armstrong Preserve, a round trip through all three properties is 2.5 miles. From Richards Preserve, it is a 2.1 mile round trip.

Yellow Trail
> *Length: 0.7 miles Blaze: yellow*
Serving as the entrance trail to the

Armstrong Preserve, yellow trail follows the driveway uphill. At 0.1 mile, it veers to the right onto a woods road. It passes a rock outcropping topped with the array of solar panels which supplies power to the Armstrong House. In quick succession the trail enters a meadow, leaves it and briefly joins the white trail only to split off.

The yellow trail crosses a seasonal stream and, at 0.4 mile, it goes through a flat topped stone wall marking the boundary of DEP property. After passing seasonal views over the Cross River Reservoir, the trail heads downhill, crosses a stream on a wooden bridge, goes through a stone wall, and ends at the white trail in Richards Preserve.

White Trail – Armstrong Preserve   *Length: 0.5 miles Blaze: white*
Just past the stone wall at the end of the meadow on the yellow trail, turn left onto the white trail. It heads uphill with a massive rock outcropping towering overhead and turns left. The trail swings in an arc past a rock outcropping called Turtle Rock which is the shape of a giant turtle, and continues its ascent. At 0.2 mile, it heads downhill and then uphill once again. It goes over the crest of the hill and when it reaches a woods road, turns left. Armstrong House and the demonstration garden are to the right. The white trail leaves the woods road and ends at the yellow trail.

White Trail – Richards Preserve   *Length: 0.5 miles Blaze: white*
A short access trail leads from the parking spot on Honey Hollow Road and soon splits into a loop. The white trail to the right briefly follows a woods road and heads downhill through a rocky area. It passes large boulders and a small spring to the right and then heads steeply uphill. It reaches the top of the rise at 0.2 mile and heads downhill. After passing the junction with the yellow trail which comes from the Armstrong Preserve, the white trail turns left and heads uphill. The view to the right at 0.4 mile is of former flat farmland with stone walls stretching outward across the field. The trail continues parallel to a stone wall, then slowly descends the ridge to close the loop near the entrance of the preserve.

LIFE OFF THE GRID

The Armstrong House, once the country house of a prominent drama critic, has become a stage for showcasing conservation and sustainability. It also serves, as a high-tech education center and a residence for the Pound Ridge Land Conservancy's land steward and educator.

When PRLC received the bequest in 2001, the house had not been used for many years and required extensive restoration. Hundreds of hours donated by volunteers, including high school students, supplemented the work of subcontractors who utilized recycled materials whenever possible and installed state-of-the-art technologies. These innovations allow the center to function "off-the grid." At the same time it serves as an education and research center to study alternative energy systems such as biogas generation, wind, and solar power. Other green projects include gray-water recycling, integrated local food production, and conservation techniques. Visits to the Armstrong House are possible through prearrangement by e-mailing a request to info@prlc.org.

NEARBY PARKS: Ward Pound Ridge, Palmer Lewis Memorial Sanctuary

DRIVING: From I-684, take Exit 6 (Route 35) and turn east onto Route 35. Drive 3.8 miles and turn right onto Route 121. For Armstrong Preserve, continue 1.1 miles to #1361, just before the causeway over the Cross River Reservoir. There is parking for one or two cars on the side of the driveway before the gate [41.246862N 73.616962W]. Parking is also possible across Route 121 in pull out areas.

For Richards Preserve, stay on Route 121 for 0.8 miles past the Route 35 intersection and turn left on Honey Hollow Road. Go 1.4 miles to the trailhead to the right, shortly after #134 [41.238167N 73.60905W]. There is parking for one or two cars on the side of the road.

PUBLIC TRANSPORTATION: None available

For contact information, see Appendix, Pound Ridge Land Conservancy.

Bloomerside Preserve

Peach Lake • 1.8 miles, 64 acres

Prime real estate on Bloomer Road became Bloomerside Preserve when the North Salem Open Land Foundation, the Town of North Salem, and town residents purchased the property from the Bloomerside Cooperative in 2006. Trails for hikers and equestrians wind through forests, meadows, and rolling hills. Other than an occasional piece of trash peeking out from under the deep layer of woodchips, one would not realize that a former (and now capped) dump was on the site. Except for an occasional North Salem Bridle Trail Association blaze nailed to a tree at crucial places, the trails winding though Bloomerside Preserve are unmarked.

NEARBY PARKS: Baxter Tract

DRIVING: From I-684, take the Croton Falls/ Hardscrabble Road Exit and head east. When Hardscrabble Road ends at a Y junction at June Road, turn left. Make the first right turn at Bloomer Road where there is parking across from Star Ridge Road[41.356373N 73.591157W]. Or continue to parking for one car opposite #57 for one car [41.355995N 73.584491W].

Apartment house.

PUBLIC TRANSPORTATION: None available

For contact information, see Appendix, North Salem Open Land Foundation.

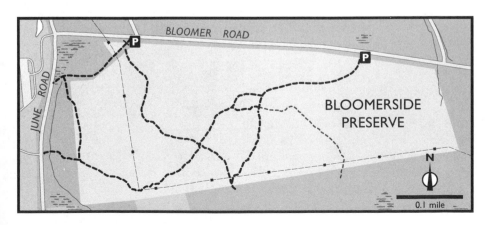

Choate Sanctuary

Mt. Kisco • 1.3 miles, 32 acres

Wetlands greet visitors as they enter Choate Sanctuary, but once inside, tall trees and rock cliffs dominate the terrain. The original 23-acre sanctuary was established in 1972 by the heirs of Joseph H. Choate, Jr., the chair of a self-appointed committee to repeal the 18th Amendment (Prohibition). After the amendment's repeal, Choate was the first head of the Federal Alcohol Control Administration. In 1974, an additional three acres were added when Geoffrey Platt donated the property in memory of his wife, Helen Choate Platt. Four more acres were added in 1997 under a 99 year lease from the Town of New Castle. These additional acres include the Swamp Loop Trail.

TRAILS

Three short trails loop their way through Choate Sanctuary with elevation gains and losses. Although the sanctuary is located near a main road, portions of the trails have relatively no road noise. The Hickory Trail (yellow) is a 0.2 mile loop which passes a ravine. Along the way four species of creeping cedar (Lycopodium) can be seen; they are ground pine, running pine, shining club moss, and ground cedar.

White Oak Trail

Length: 0.6 mile Blaze: white Beginning on Crow Hill Road, the White Oak Trail enters an extensive wetland and crosses a bridge. At 0.1 mile at a T junction with the Hickory Trail (yellow), the White Oak Trail turns right to head uphill and splits at 0.2 mile. Heading clockwise, the trail continues to ascend. It turns right at a large erratic and passes a rock outcropping to the left. At 0.5 mile, the trail reaches the Swamp Loop Trail (blue), turns and closes the loop.

Swamp Loop Trail

Length: 0.5 mile Blaze: blue From the White Oak Trail (white), the Swamp Loop Trail splits to form a

Twin tulip trees.

loop. Going clockwise through an upland forest, the Swamp Loop Trail passes a white-blazed shortcut. At 0.2 mile, it descends to enter a red maple swamp. It goes through banks of Christmas and New York ferns and passes the other end of the side trail. Turning right, it ascends to close the loop at 0.5 mile.

DRIVING: From the Saw Mill Parkway, take the Route 133/Mt. Kisco Exit. Head west on Route 133 for 0.5 mile to the Mt. Kisco Presbyterian Church to the left, opposite Crow Hill Road. Parking may be available in the church lot [41.207283N 73.746266W]. Use caution when crossing Route 133 and walking along Crow Hill Road. From the church parking lot, Choate Sanctuary is 100 feet up Crow Hill Road to the left. It is illegal to park along Crow Hill Road.

PUBLIC TRANSPORTATION: None available.

For contact information, see Appendix, Saw Mill River Audubon Society.

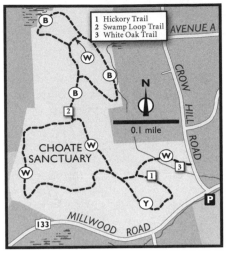

Clark Preserve

Although one could say that the Clark Preserve majors in stone walls and minors in benches, visitors here are treated to a full curriculum with ponds, wetlands, meadows, towering trees, and rolling terrain. Even a short hike offers variety. Donated to the Pound Ridge Land Conservancy in 1997 by Ben and Charlotte Clark, the preserve is part of the biotic corridor extending along the eastern portion of Westchester County that includes Ward Pound Ridge Reservation to the north.

TRAILS

In the Clark Preserve, most trails have more than one color blaze, except for three red trails, two of which are loops leading 0.1 and 0.3 mile from the red-blue trail to the edge of the property. The third red trail is a 0.1-mile connection between the yellow-blue trail and the red-blue trail. It is possible to follow either yellow or blue blazes for a loop hike. A 0.1 mile yellow-blue trail connects the red-blue with the entrance trail (red-yellow-blue).

From Autumn Ridge Road, the 0.2 mile entrance trail (red-yellow-blue) leads into the preserve. The yellow trail heads uphill to the left, while straight ahead the entrance trail goes through the first of many stone walls and turns right. At 0.2 mile, the entrance trail ends with the yellow-blue trail going to the left and the red-blue to the right.

Red-Blue Trail
Length: 0.7 mile Blaze: red-blue

From the end of the entrance trail, the red-blue trail turns right and the character of the preserve changes; there are fewer large trees. At 0.1 mile, the red-blue trail turns right and a red trail heads left to connect to the yellow-blue trail. A 0.1-mile red trail to the right leads to the town park on Brook Farm Road East

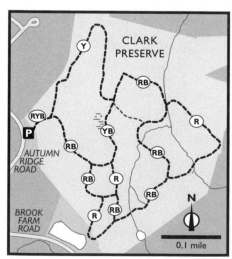

and then loops back. The red-blue trail passes the other end of the 0.1mile red trail and heads downhill to cross a stone wall. After crossing a wetland on a low bridge, the trail skirts it. Once across a stream on large rocks at 0.4 mile, the trail turns right. The red-blue trail passes a 0.3-mile red trail to the right and a 0.1-mile unmarked trail to the left leading to the yellow-blue trail. At 0.5 mile, the red-blue trail passes a bridge to the right, which is the other end of the previously mentioned red trail. The trail crosses a wet area on puncheon (wood planking) and a second bridge. It goes through a small field, enters another field at 0.6

mile, and follows its left edge. The red-blue trail ends at a wide intersection with the yellow-blue continuing straight and the yellow trail to the right.

Yellow Trail   *Length: 0.3 mile Blaze: yellow*
There are more elevation changes on the yellow trail than on any of the other trails. From the access trail, the yellow trail heads uphill. Cresting the hill, it turns right to go through a chain link fence and joins a woods road. From a rocky knob, it descends steeply and enters a cedar grove. It ends at a wide intersection with the yellow-blue and red-blue trails.

DRIVING: From I-684, take Exit 6 (Route 35) and turn east. In 3.8 miles, turn right onto Route 121 and go 2.9 miles to Route 137 (Stone Hill Road). Turn left, continue 1.4 miles, and turn right onto Autumn Ridge Road. It is 0.7 mile further to the entrance and parking to the left [41.214127N 73.598466W].

PUBLIC TRANSPORTATION: None available

For contact information, see Appendix, Pound Ridge Land Conservancy.

A HARVEST OF STONES

Stone fences may have helped to make good neighbors, as the maxim goes, but their primary reason for existence was a dump for rocks cleared from the fields. Early farmers had to pull up the rocks before tilling and then piled them in walls at field's edge. Later as wood was not readily available for fences, stone walls became more commonplace. By the mid 1800s, farmers were moving west to cheaper, more fertile lands and livestock farmers replaced them. Their stone fences were piled higher to keep herds enclosed.

The stone walls in Clark Preserve are "dry," just carefully laid stones, yet with excellent stability and drainage. Cemented or "wet," walls are easier to build but do not drain well and are prone to cracks and shifting.

Croton Gorge Park

Croton-on-Hudson • 1.3 miles, 97 acres

The massive dam at the entrance to Croton Gorge Park never fails to impress whether there is a delicate trickle barely covering the ledges or water roaring down the spillway. And, sometimes visitors are treated to a rainbow. The New Croton Dam is also called the Cornell Dam because it was built on property purchased from A.B. Cornell in 1893. Completed in 1907, the dam stands over 200-feet high. In 1964, New York City, which controls the reservoir system, sold 97 acres to Westchester County to use as a park.

It is possible to take several different long hikes starting in the park. The Briarcliff Peekskill Trailway crosses the top of the dam. Two side trails on the River Trail connect to the Old Croton Aqueduct. There are also unmarked woods roads in the adjacent county-owned Stokes-Green property, a former private estate.

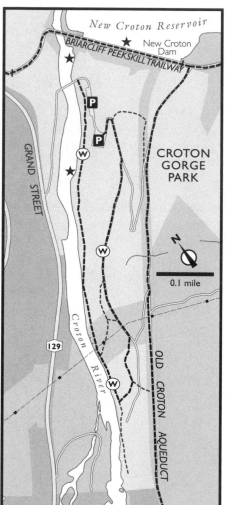

River Trail

Length: 1.2 miles Blaze: white
Beginning by the bridge at the base of the dam, the River Trail heads downstream along the south side of the Croton River, with the sound of rushing water accompanying hikers along this first stretch. Almost immediately after starting, a side trail leads to the river, but then returns to rejoin the main trail. At 0.2 mile, the trail crosses a stone-lined channel, long unused, and then, at 0.4 mile, it crosses the flood plain of the Croton River. It heads away from the river's edge to go under power lines at 0.5 mile, passing a trail which leads 0.1 mile uphill to the River Trail's return portion. It crosses a stone wall and turns left at a telephone pole. Straight ahead, the unmarked path leads to a springhouse and the end of the property.

At a driveway, a sign directs walkers to the Old Croton Aqueduct. The River Trail follows a gravel road and goes under the power lines at 0.9 mile. It passes two trails heading downhill to join the section of River Trail along the river.

After passing through a white pine plantation at 1.1 miles, the River Trail crosses the stone-lined channel again. It crosses a bridge and passes between white pines lining the road. On the right at 1.2 miles, the trail ends at a sign for the Old Croton Aqueduct. Close the loop by walking 0.2 mile past the Authorized Vehicles Only sign and through the parking lots to the bridge at the base of the dam.

NEARBY TRAILS: Briarcliff-Peekskill Trailway, Old Croton Aqueduct

DRIVING: From Route 9, take the Croton Avenue Exit. At the end of the ramp, turn away from the river. Head uphill towards a traffic light at a T junction with South Riverside Avenue/Route 9A (not labeled) and turn left. Go 0.6 mile to turn right at

The spillway at the New Croton Dam.

Route 129 and continue 2.2 miles to the park entrance to the right. Alternately, from the Taconic State Parkway take the Underhill Avenue Exit and head west toward Croton. Underhill Avenue ends at a T junction with Route 129. Turn right and go 3.4 miles to the park entrance to the left, which is downhill from the road over the New Croton Dam (closed to vehicles) [41.226248N 73.85749W].

PUBLIC TRANSPORTATION: None available

For contact information, see Appendix, Westchester County Parks.

Five Ponds Trail

Primarily used by equestrians, the Five Ponds Trail is an unmarked trail on a North Salem Open Land Foundation easement and on private property. A sign at the Grant Road entrance requests riders to stay off the trail when wet, implying that hikers should do the same. Adjacent property owners have established trails to connect with the Five Ponds Trail but they are not open to the public.

From the entrance on Five Ponds Drive, the Five Ponds Trail descends on a woods road along a narrow right-of-way and passes a large storm water retention pond. At 0.2 mile, it goes under a power line on a causeway and then heads uphill. The trail passes at 0.3 mile an unmarked trail to the left which traverses the ridgeline. At the next intersection, the Five Ponds Trail turns right and a 0.1 mile unmarked trail goes straight ahead to connect with the trail on the ridge. From the turn, the Five Ponds Trail heads downhill, paralleling a stone wall with wetlands to the right. To the left, at 0.4 mile, is the end of the first unmarked trail mentioned above. After crossing an AT&T line, the trail enters private property. It parallels a stone wall and wetlands. Reaching a T junction at 0.8 mile, the Five Ponds Trail turns right. After crossing two branches of a stream, it reaches Grant Road (no parking) almost directly across from Turkey Hill Road.

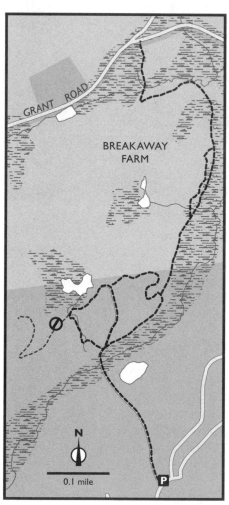

DRIVING: From I-684, take Exit 6 (Route 35) and turn east onto Route 35 for 4.5 miles. Turn left onto Route 121. At 2.5 miles, turn right onto Chapel Road and drive 0.5 mile. Turn left onto Chapel Court. Take the first right onto paved Five Ponds Drive and drive to the end. The entrance is to the left, just before the cul-de-sac [41.304476N 73.602828W].

PUBLIC TRANSPORTATION: None available

For contact information, see Appendix, Lewisboro.

Greenburgh Nature Center

Scarsdale • 1.4 miles, 33 acres

An island of green rising inside a dense commercial area of central Westchester County, the Greenburgh Nature Center is home to an array of flora and fauna in its woodlands, wetlands, and orchard. Because the center is on both the Atlantic and Hudson River flyways, there are over 140 species of birds that either visit or nest on the property. Mushrooms and other fungi compose an integral part of the identified biota because of the efforts of Sylvia Stein, an amateur naturalist and mycologist who was active at the center before her death in 2001. There is an admission fee to the Manor House with a live animal display, discovery room, greenhouse, and changing nature-arts exhibit.

Dr. Lewis Rutherford Morris, a direct descendant of Lewis Morris, a signer of the Declaration of Independence, acquired the property as farmland in 1918. He named his estate "Nunataks," from the Inuit word used to describe rock outcroppings that emerge from ice fields. Some of the stone used to build the Manor House was quarried on-site. When the property came up for sale, money from a 1973 bond issue authorized by a referendum was used to purchase the property. Federal matching funds that stipulated its use for nature education and preservation of its "wilderness state," were also used in the purchase. The group that rallied for protecting the property became Greenburgh Nature Center, the nonprofit, which now manages the center on town-owned land.

TRAILS

Except for the Forest Trail, all trails are unmarked in this compact trail system.

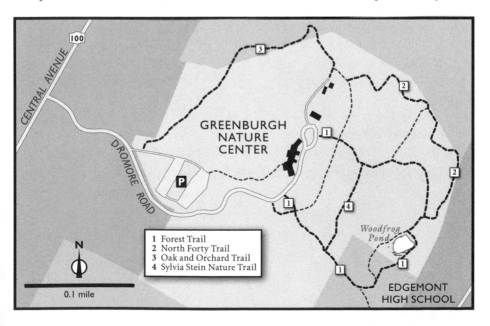

1 Forest Trail
2 North Forty Trail
3 Oak and Orchard Trail
4 Sylvia Stein Nature Trail

Manor House.

There are many cross trails, narrow paths in the rock garden, and trails that connect to a trail system at adjacent Edgemont High School.

    The 0.4-mile Forest Trail (blue) starts by the Birds of Prey exhibit, goes through the forested area of the center to a pond and loops back to the Manor House by the animal cages. The North Forty Trail is 0.3 mile link across the northern part of the property connecting the Oak and Orchard Trail to the Forest Trail. The Sylvia Stein Nature Trail features fungi. The Oak and Orchard Trail starts at the entrance road, heads uphill passing a turtle nesting area and ends at 0.2 mile on the North Forty Trail.

DRIVING: Take northbound Central Park Avenue (Route 100) to Dromore Road, one mile north of Ardsley Road and across from 455 Scarsdale Plaza. Follow Dromore Road to the visitors parking lot [41.004735N 73.808611W].

PUBLIC TRANSPORTATION: Beeline Buses #20 and #21 from the last stop (242nd Street/Broadway) of the #4 subway line in the Bronx and get off at Dromore Road. From the business district in White Plains, exit the bus at South Healy Avenue.

For contact information, see Appendix, Greenburgh Nature Center.

Halle Ravine Nature Preserve
Pine Terrace Preserve

Pound Ridge • 1.4 miles, 38 acres

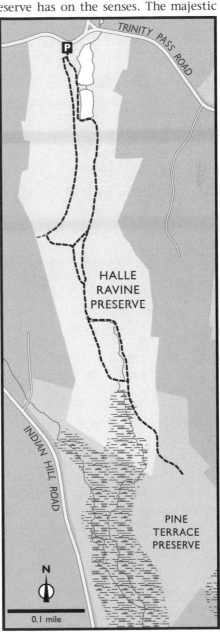

Words like "scenic" or "picturesque" are hardly adequate to describe the effects that Halle Ravine Nature Preserve has on the senses. The majestic trees, flowing waters, and craggy ravine provide a restful and invigorating setting for a walk along the unmarked paths through the preserve's hardwood forests and wetland habitats. The steep-sided ravine keeps visitors and the stream on course. Unfortunately, the woolly adelgid is slowly killing off the old growth hemlocks here.

In 1928, Hiram Halle purchased the property because of the ravine. Halle was a conservationist, philanthropist, inventor, businessman, and part owner of the Gulf Oil Company. He was instrumental in attracting businesses and wealthy residents to Pound Ridge in the 1930s. In 1968, the Halle Properties Corporation sold the land to The Nature Conservancy, which in 2004, transferred the property to Pound Ridge Land Trust with the supporting conservation easement held by Westchester Land Trust.

There is only one trail at Halle Ravine Nature Preserve. But there are places where it splits and offers the option to hike along the side of the ravine or travel along the stream. From the entrance, the trail is along a woods road. It passes a trail to the left leading into the ravine and then a kiosk. At a quarter-mile, where the woods road continues into private property, the trail heads down log steps into the ravine. When it reaches a T junction, turn right, then right again following the stream through the narrow ravine. At the next junction, go straight. The two segments join again at 0.5 mile at a T junction after crossing a bridge.

Cascade.

Follow the trail that is on your right along the stream. The trail becomes narrower and less worn. At a brief steep ascent, cross a stone wall and enter a section of Pine Terrace Preserve.

For the return trip, bear right whenever offered a choice and keep the stream to your left. Follow the trail as it crosses a bridge and joins the original trail at the left fork of the Y junction. Go through the narrow portion of the ravine and at the next intersection, cross the bridge to the right. Pass through another narrow portion of the ravine. After crossing the creek, head uphill on log steps with New York ferns lining both sides of the trail. The valley widens and the footpath becomes a woods road. Below, a small, high dam is visible. At 1.8 miles, cross a dam on a stone bridge where knotted roots of a black birch drape over a portion of the dam. After passing the upper pond, continue uphill and, at 1.9 miles, reach the woods road near the kiosk.

DRIVING: From I-684, take Exit 4 (Route 172). Follow Route 172 through Bedford Village to Route 137 Turn left onto Route 137 and turn north onto Route 124. At Trinity Pass Road, turn right. It is 0.6 mile to parking (3-4 cars) at a white gate, just before the intersection with Donbrook Road [41.216913N 73.562457W].

PUBLIC TRANSPORTATION: None available

For contact information, see Appendix, Pound Ridge Land Conservancy.

Jack Harrington Greenway
City of White Plains Walking Trail

White Plains • 1.2 miles, 21.3 acres

No ribbons of track remain and the last time a train whistle pierced the air along what is now the Jack Harrington Greenway was in 1937, but there is no doubt that it was once the route of a railroad. The New York, Westchester & Boston Railroad from 1912 ran from the Bronx to Mount Vernon with spurs continuing to White Plains and Port Chester. The section in White Plains is preserved but after the line closed, evidence of the line disappeared: features were removed, underpasses were filled in, stations were razed, and the railbed was built upon or became roads. One section in the Bronx became part of the subway system. A few existing portions can be found in Ward Acres and Nature Study Woods. In 2012, what was known as the White Plains Greenway was renamed to honor Jack Harrington, an activist who was the driving force in creating it.

THE GREENWAY

From Gedney Way, Harrington Greenway heads south on a deep layer of wood chips. At 0.1 mile, the trail curves to what initially looks as if it might the have been

NEW YORK, WESTCHESTER AND BOSTON RAILROAD

From the beginning, the New York, Westchester & Boston Railroad, "The Westchester" to its riders, had financial problems. Originally incorporated in 1878, construction did not start until 1909 after it had been acquired by the New York, New Haven and Hartford Railroad Company and after parts of its Westchester routing had become areas annexed by the Bronx.

The railroad was well built from the beginning with elaborate stations made of concrete instead of wood and grades were kept level and straight for speed. Platforms were made level to the floor of the cars and doors were in the middle as well as the ends of the cars facilitated quick entry. The all electric line was quiet, comfortable and fast. Because the line did not go into Grand Central Terminal, Manhattan-bound passengers had to switch to the subway at 133rd Street.

The line did not handle freight at a time when freight lines were more lucrative and commuter lines were less profitable. Debt, too few passengers, and heavy investment lead to financial difficulties which were compounded by the Depression. Service ended on December 21, 1937. Even after the line shut down, it was hoped that service could eventually be restored. Those hopes were dashed when demand for scrap metal during World War II resulted in the removal of remaining wire gantries and tracks and the rolling stock was shipped off elsewhere for the war effort.

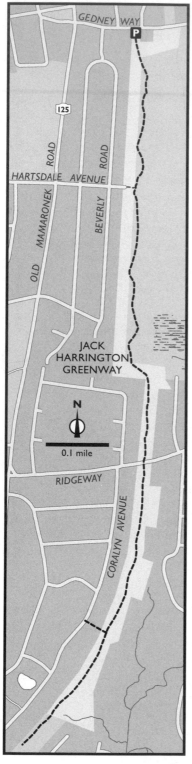

a railbed. The pathway continues through the woods amidst invasive vegetation including pachysandra which has escaped from neighboring gardens. To the right at 0.3 mile, the Greenway passes a side trail heading out to Hartsdale Avenue. The Greenway turns right at 0.6 mile onto the former railbed. Continuing at-grade and above the wetlands, it passes the first of several concrete bases which had supported the electrical lines for the railroad. At 0.7 mile it heads downhill, crosses Ridgeway and passes an interpretive sign. Abutments for a long-gone bridge still stand sentinel.

At the site of the former Ridgeway Station, concrete footings that once supported the station platform line the wide path. The trail is situated high above houses to the right, with woodlands to the left. It crosses a now filled in underpass. Just before a second underpass at 1.0 mile, a path to the right leads down a trail out to Coralyn Avenue. The path continues along the high embankment. It ends abruptly at 1.2 miles at the Scarsdale-White Plains town line, where brush and wet soil fill a rockcut. The filled-in overpass at Reynal Crossing is barely visible.

DRIVING: From I-287, take the Bloomingdale Road Exit and turn left onto Bloomingdale Road, which becomes Mamaroneck Avenue. After passing Burke Rehabilitation Center to the left, turn right onto Gedney Way. Continue two blocks and cross a bridge. An entrance sign faces the road on the south side of the street [41.013565N 73.758894W].

PUBLIC TRANSPORTATION: Beeline Bus #60 on Mamaroneck Avenue and walk two blocks west on Gedney Way; Beeline Bus #63 on Route 125 (Old Mamaroneck Road) and walk two blocks east on Gedney Way.

For contact information, see Appendix, White Plains.

Juhring Estate

Dobbs Ferry • 1.4 miles, 76 acres

Tucked behind a residential area, the Juhring Estate-Shirley Elbert Memorial is a popular place for neighbors to walk. The park is named for John C. Juhring, III, a landscape architect who purchased the property in 1909. The Village of Dobbs Ferry purchased the property through state and federal grants in 1968 to prevent it from being developed and was not designated as parkland until 1996.

TRAILS

From the entrance at Briary Lane, a blue-blazed trail leads 0.1 mile to paths which wind through the woods. The red trail leads 0.1 to Summit Terrace and a white with blue dot trail stops shy of reaching private property. Little road noise penetrates the forest during leaf-on seasons even though the property is near the Saw Mill River Parkway. Parking is only available at the Briary Road entrance.

White Trail   *Length: 0.6 mile Blaze: white*
As the main trail in the park, the white trails stretches 0.2 mile from the entrance

THE ROOTS OF INVASIVES

Garlic mustard

Like house guests that never leave, exotic invasives have taken firm root in many of the parks of Westchester. Some of these plants were originally brought to the country as decorative flora, while others hid in the ballast of ships or the mulch of plantings, hitchhiked on the fur of animals, or were used as cargo packaging.

Japanese stilt grass was first identified in Knoxville, Tennessee in 1919. The grass is thought to have been introduced accidentally while being used as packing for Chinese porcelain. This fast growing grass which forms deep rooted dense stands, is native to Japan, Korea, China, Malaysia, and India. Introduced as an ornamental plant in the 1800s, Japanese knotweed is extremely hard to eradicate. Digging it up only encourages more growth from any portion, however small that is left behind. Garlic mustard was introduced into the country in the 1860's as a culinary herb, but with few natural enemies, began to dominate the understory of many natural settings.

Purple loosestrife's tenure here dates back to Colonial times: a native of Europe, it was brought here as a medicinal plant and cultivated varieties were also brought to enliven Colonial gardens. Mile-a-minute-weed, a native to East Asia, was imported into the country by a nursery in York, Pennsylvania in the 1930's. It escaped the confines of its plantings and has been spreading outward ever since. Porcelain berry, a native to the Far East was originally brought to the United States around the 1870's as a landscape plant.

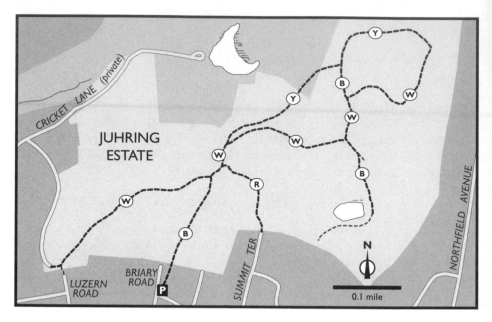

at Luzern Road to the blue trail from Brairy Road. After passing the yellow and red trails in quick succession, it turns left at the junction with the blue dot trail at 0.4 mile. A short blue trail at 0.5 mile connects to the yellow trail. The white trail ends at the yellow trail which immediately heads steeply uphill.

Yellow Trail

Length: 0.4 mile Blaze: yellow

Beginning 0.2 mile from the entrance at Briary Road, the yellow trail completes the loop around the high point with the white trail. It also offers a short-cut via the blue trail to avoid the ascent and descent around the high point.

DRIVING: From the Saw Mill River Parkway, take the Ashford Avenue Exit. Head west for 0.3 mile; turn right onto Briary Road to reach the entrance in 0.3 mile. [41.017863N 73.855056W].

PUBLIC TRANSPORTATION: Beeline Bus #1C, 6, or 66 along Ashford Avenue to Briary Road. The park entrance is 0.3 mile uphill on Briary Road.

For contact information, see Appendix, Dobbs Ferry.

Koegel Park

Somers • 1.7 miles, 77 acres

Along curving driveway lined with stately trees is evidence that Koegel Park was once an estate. Although the pavement ends at a gate, it seems clear that the road had once continued further. Now called Green Way, it is a 30-foot-wide level, grassy path. At the end of Green Way is an open area with a chessboard table, so bring a friend and a chess set when you visit.

Most of the land for the park was donated to the Town of Somers in 1968 by Otto Koegel, a lawyer active in local politics and the town historian from 1955 to 1975, He had tried unsuccessfully to have the United Nations headquarters located in Somers on land he owned. An attempt 25 years later to establish a multi-million dollar airport also failed. His home was located on Richard Somers Drive, but his estate and farm were on Mahopac Avenue.

Tomahawk Chapel is adjacent to the park. The Putney family donated a half-acre plot on which the chapel was built in 1837 by Tom Miller, a local farmer. Many of the early residents of the area are interred in either the public burying ground to the west of the chapel or the Union Church Cemetery to the north.

TRAILS

A tiny network of trails wanders through mature upland forest with large deciduous trees. Koegel Park is at the top of a hill that slopes 140 feet down to the North County Trailway. Two short blue trails connect the red trail and the 0.2-mile Green Way, which, in dry weather should be handicapped accessible. From the parking lot, the white trail heads downhill, passes first the yellow trail to Tomahawk Chapel and then the blue trail to the North County Trailway. It turns, parallels the trailway

The Green Way.

and ends at 0.2 mile at the red trail.

Red Trail   *Length: 0.7 mile Blaze: red*
Beginning by the signboard at the parking lot, the red trail leads into a picnic area on a wide woods road. It passes a blue trail which heads over to Green Way. It drifts downhill and, at 0.2 mile, passes a second blue trail also leading to the junction with the white trail to the left. The red trail turns right, continues uphill to the parking lot, and ends beside the gate on the Green Way.

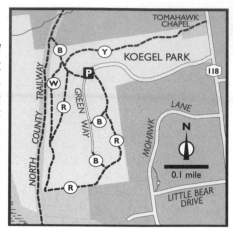

Yellow Trail   *Length: 0.4 mile Blaze: yellow*
Beginning on the white trail, the yellow trail contours around the hill. It crosses stone walls and, at 0.3 mile, reaches a woods road behind houses. Passing between two cemeteries, the trail ends at Tomahawk Chapel.

CONNECTING TRAIL: North County Trailway

DRIVING: From the Taconic Parkway, take Route 6 east to Baldwin Place. Turn right onto Route 118 and go 1.3 miles to Koegel Park to the right [41.329478N 73.755686W].

PUBLIC TRANSPORTATION: Beeline Bus #16 or Putnam Area Rapid Transit (PART) to Somers Commons in Baldwin Place. Go to a small parking lot on the east side of the shopping center near Route 118. The entrance to the North County Trailway is on the far side of this parking lot. Turn right and head south on the trailway for a mile. To the left, shortly past a large rock, a paved path leads up to the blue trail in Koegel Park. (If you reach a bench on the right side of the trailway, you have gone too far and missed the path to the park.)

For contact information, see Appendix, Somers.

North Highland Loop Trails

Croton-on-Hudson • 1.83 miles, 97 acres

Wooded, open spaces or a scenic route to the Hudson River and Croton Landing are easily accessible for residents of Upper Village and other areas in Croton via the North Highland Loop Trails. All the trails on this loop are blazed white: road walks, marked with a white tag blaze, connect residential streets with wooded open space.

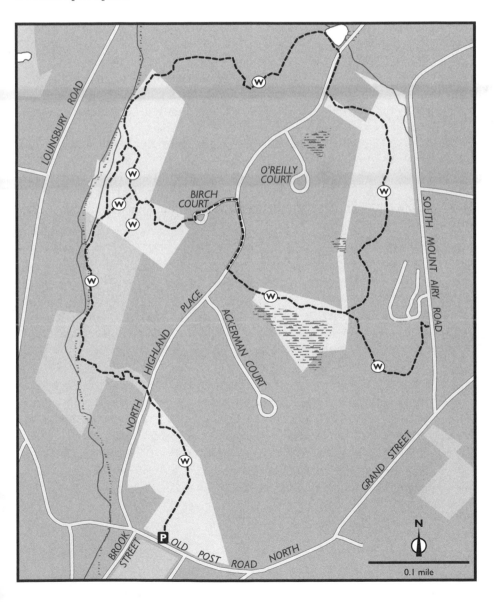

These trails and others in Croton-on Hudson are the result of a unique hiker-friendly approach to planning that began in 1992 with the creation of the Croton Trails Committee. Headed by Jan Wines, this committee of volunteers created a master plan for a network for all the trails in the village and then oversaw its implementation. New trails, both off-road and on, were built, blazed and mapped and links to other open spaces and neighborhoods created. This network of trails stretches more than a dozen miles into county, state, village, and nonprofit parks within and adjacent to the village.

North Highland Loop
Length: 1.6 miles Blaze: white

Across Grand Street from the municipal building, the main North Highland Loop heads steeply uphill into the woods and in 0.2 mile crosses Lower Highland Avenue. It reenters the woods and heads downhill. After crossing two stonewalls, the trail turns to parallel a stream and heads uphill. At 0.4 mile, the trail to the right goes uphill to Birch Court in 0.2 mile. The North Highland Loop follows the stream and at 0.6 mile turns away from it. After crossing a small wash gully, the trail turns to parallel a fence. At 0.9 mile the trail reaches Upper North Highland Avenue and turns right. It turns left just past underground telephone and electricity boxes and reenters the woods. At 1.2 mile it reaches a trail junction, where to the left, it is downhill 0.2 mile to Mt. Airy Road. Turning right the trail passes wetlands to the left and then reaches Upper North Highland Avenue at 1.3 mile. Turn right and at Birch Court, turn left. Head towards the fire hydrant and reenter the woods. Heading steeply downhill, the trail reaches a T junction. To the left is a short side trail to Rubin's Ridge. Turn right and continue downhill to close the loop at 1.6 miles. A left turn is 0.4 mile back to the municipal building for a hike of 2.0 miles.

NEARBY PARKS & CONNECTING TRAILS: Brinton Brook Sanctuary, Croton Gorge Park, Croton Point Park, Croton River Gorge Trails, Croton Waterfront

DRIVING: From northbound Route 9, take Route 9A exit and turn right onto Route 9A and ** in 0.3 mile turn left onto Brook Street. Follow Brook Street for 0.5 mile. At a T junction with Old Post Road North turn right and then right on to Van Wyck Street to park in the Municipal building parking lot. The entrance to the trail is across Old Post Road North [41.208841N 73.887474W]. From southbound Route 9, take Route 9A/Senasqua Road exit and keep right at the fork to Route 9A. Follow the directions above from **.

PUBLIC TRANSPORTATION: No direct public transportation is available. However, there is access to the North Highland Loop Trails by walking north from the Metro-North Hudson Line Croton-Harmon Station 2.1 miles along the waterfront (see Croton Waterfront in Along the River) to cross the pedestrian bridge. At the end the bridge, turn right on Brook Street. It is 0.4 mile to the trailhead.

For contact information, see Appendix, Village of Croton-on-Hudson.

Frederick P. Rose Nature Preserve
Rockshelter Preserve

Waccabuc • 1.9 miles, 105 acres

Each of the three entrances to the Rose Nature Preserve give a different impression of what is beyond. A kiosk at the main entrance welcomes visitors with a walk along a gravel road through woodlands. An entrance across from Todd Road has large cinnamon ferns in wetlands, creating a sense of the primordial, almost as if a pterodactyl might fly by. The third entrance, on Chapel Road, is along a paved driveway.

The preserve is named in honor of the late Frederick P. Rose, head of one of New York City's oldest construction and real estate management firms and a philanthropist who supported Yale University and various cultural institutions in New York City. He and his wife Sandra funded the Rose Center for Earth and Science at the American Museum of Natural History. Their youngest son, Adam, in 2000 donated 20 acres adjacent to several parcels of sensitive wetlands and hilly woods preventing fragmentation of this valuable habitat.

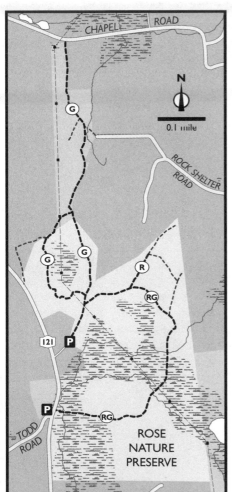

TRAILS

All the trails in Rose Preserve are blazed green and when part of the Lewisboro Horsemen's Association's trail system, they have a red metal tag as well. The 0.3 mile Wetlands Loop goes through more rugged terrain and wetlands.

Green Trail (main entrance)

Length: 0.7 miles Blaze: green
At the end of the paved shared driveway, the green trail leads past a kiosk and crosses under a power line. It reaches the trail coming from the Todd Road entrance and turns left. Just past the turn at 0.1 mile, the green trail passes the Wetlands Loop (green) to the left. The trail parallels the power line, passing stone walls and rock outcroppings. Drifting downhill, it passes the other end of the Wetlands Loop at 0.4 mile and enters the Rockshelter Preserve at 0.5 mile where a 200-foot trail leads to Rockshelter Drive (a private road, no parking). The green

trail reaches a paved driveway at 0.7 miles and follows it to end at Chapel Road.

Green Trail (Todd Road entrance)
Length: 0.7 miles Blaze: green

From the entrance opposite Todd Road, the green trail winds through extensive wetlands. Even though the trail is on a raised bed, the trail might be impassable after heavy rains. The trail continues along a woods road and turns left at 0.2 mile. Just before the trail crosses a stone bridge, Lewisboro Horsemen's Association (LHA) red blazes are on trees along with the green ones. Equestrians from adjacent properties use these trails.

Ancient flora in a current setting.

The green-red trail goes under a power line on a wood bridge. It enters woods and goes through dense barberry understory. Crossing another stream, the trail heads uphill through open woods and then descends. At 0.4 mile, it passes percolation pits, rectangular open pits with a mound of dirt beside each, indicating that at one time this area had been considered for development.

The trail crosses a stream and reaches a Y junction where an unmarked trail leads 0.1 mile to private property. Turning left, the green-red trail continues on a woods road and crosses a stream at 0.6 mile. At a T junction, a red trail to the right leads to private property. Heading left, the green-red trail reaches another T junction at 0.7 mile. To the left is the entrance trail from the main entrance.

NEARBY PARKS: Five Ponds Trail, Long Pond Preserve, Old Field Preserve, Pine Croft Meadow

DRIVING: From I-684 take Exit 6 (Route 35) and go east for 4.3 miles to a traffic light where Route 121 turns left and leaves Route 35. Follow northbound Route 121 for 1.7 miles to a shared driveway for #191 and #195. Parking is at the end of the driveway. [41.292556N 73.611088W]. Another entrance is across from the intersection of Route 121 and Todd Road (parking for 2 cars) [41.290420N 73.611808W]. A third entrance is along the driveway of 90 Chapel Road, immediately past the power line (no parking).

PUBLIC TRANSPORTATION: None available

For contact information, see Appendix, Westchester Land Trust.

Sleepy Hollow Cemetery

Sleepy Hollow • 90 acrcs

Washington Irving not only left his mark in the lore of the area, but he also left his earthly remains in Sleepy Hollow Cemetery. He is joined by Samuel Gompers, the labor leader, Andrew Carnegie, the industrialist, Boyce Thompson, the philanthropist, and almost 40,000 others who are interred here.

The roads in the cemetery are narrow and twisting particularly in the older sections. Vehicles usually move slowly through the grounds and strollers have little worry about the traffic. Dog are permitted if on a leash. Visitors are asked to respect services being held and those visiting graves.

Cemetery maps are available at the office at the main gate and in a box at the south gate. The cemetery, which is listed on the New York and National Registers of Historic Places, offers both daytime and evening tours, but advance registration is required. Tickets can be purchased online. For more information, see www. sleepyhollowcemetery.org.

Mausoleums with ornamental trees are in the northern section of the cemetery. Sleepy Hollow Avenue parallels the Pocantico River; a walk along it provides a chance to enjoy the sight and sound of flowing water. The modern cemetery is behind this area.

The oldest section of the cemetery is adjacent to the Old Dutch Church of Sleepy Hollow, a separately administered non-profit entity. Both the church and the surrounding burial ground of roughly three acres are owned by the Reformed Church of Tarrytown, which still holds services in the church. Friends of the Old Dutch Church offer free guided seasonal tours of the Old Burial Ground.

DRIVING: From northbound Route 9 in Tarrytown, head north toward Sleepy

Old Dutch Burying Ground where a legend was born.

Hollow. The cemetery's south entrance is on the right just past Philipsburg Manor, an historic site. A walk-in gate is across the street from Palmer Avenue; the main gate is at the cemetery office 0.4 mile north of the south entrance [41.097000N 73.861759W]. Parking is at the south entrance [41.090000N 73.861759W].

PUBLIC TRANSPORTATION: Metro-North Hudson Line Philipse Manor Station; walk east on Palmer Avenue, cross Broadway, and enter the cemetery at the walk-in gate. Beeline Bus #13 runs along North Broadway.

For contact information, see Appendix, Sleepy Hollow Cemetery.

A LEGENDARY SETTING

Ichabod Crane of Washington Irving's *The Legend of Sleepy Hollow* couldn't get away from the cemetery fast enough. But for the not-so-hurried or harried visitor, the Old Dutch Burying Ground and the surrounding Sleepy Hollow Cemetery make an enchanting place to walk. And there is little fear from the Headless Horseman: he hasn't been seen in generations and then only in "the gloom of night."

The Old Dutch Burying Ground is the area around the Old Dutch Church and dates to the mid 1680's; the rest of cemetery, about 85 acres, opened in 1849 as "Tarrytown Cemetery." In a letter written at the time, Washington Irving had remarked that he hoped the new cemetery would keep "that beautiful neighborhood sacred from the anti-poetical and all-leveling axe." He said that although he hoped to "one day lay my bones there" the name was a blunder. He thought it should be called, "Sleepy Hollow Cemetery," a name that in itself would "secure the patronage of all desirous of sleeping quietly in their graves."

When Irving died in 1859, he was buried here. After his death, the cemetery's name was changed to "Sleepy Hollow" to honor his request. Irving is buried in a plot overlooking and just north of the Old Burying Ground and Old Dutch Church. It is but a short stroll from the site where Crane is said to have had his fateful encounter with the legendary phantom horseman.

Van Cortlandtville Woods

Van Cortlandtville • 1.7 miles

What's in a name? If protected open space doesn't have a name, how can it exist in an alphabetical listing? Although the Parks Division of the Town of Cortlandt knows about the park, they have no formal name for the property. To forestall any conundrum, the authors of this book felt obligated to provide the space with a name. Given its location in the hamlet of Van Cortlandtville and its proximity to the Van Cortlandtville School, they decided on Van Cortlandtville Woods. Happy "Name Day!"

Van Cortlandtville Woods with its unmarked trails is easily accessible from residential streets. The trails pass tall trees and wetlands as they wander from the town's property onto that of the Lakeland School District. These trails have proved ideal for residents wanting to walk the dog or take a long or short stroll, and for children to walk to school.

This park area may seem limited to an outside visitor but is an example of an accessible open space being used frequently and thoroughly by local residents.

DRIVING: From Bear Mountain Parkway take the Route 6 Exit and head east. Go 0.7 miles to Westbrook Drive and turn left at the light. In 0.4 mile turn right on Fawn Ridge Drive and ** then an immediate right on Jo Drive. It is 0.2 mile to the entrance is at the end of the cul-de-sac [41.315432N 73.876248W]. There are entrances with no parking on Cynthia Road [41.313681N 73.875865W] and limited parking on Laurie Road [41.312207N 73.874024W].

PUBLIC TRANSPORTATION: Beeline Bus #16 to Westbrook Drive and Fawn Ridge Drive. Then follow the directions from **.

For contact information, see Appendix, Cortlandt.

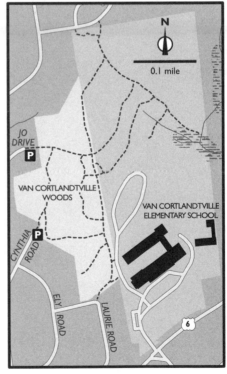

Westchester Community College

Valhalla • 1.5 miles, 36 acres

In 1957, Westchester County acquired the former 350-acre Hartford estate and set aside 218 acres to become Westchester Community College. Known as Buena Vista Farm, the estate was the weekend and summer retreat for John Augustine Hartford, who had been president of A&P. Many of the original buildings are still used and the mansion was declared a national historic landmark in 1979.

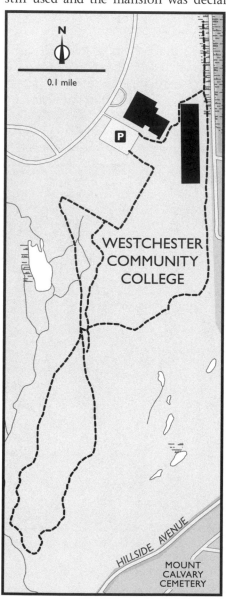

As president of A&P from 1916 until to his death in 1951, Hartford helped to shape the company into the largest retail grocery chain in the world. By lowering the price of food and expanding the diet of the average American, he has been credited with improving the country's nutrition.

On the campus is a woodland sanctuary with trails, located south of the gymnasium, and the Native Plant Center, located near the northeast entrance to the campus.

TRAILS

The unmarked trails in the woodlands are part of a 36-acre college-designated sanctuary. They were developed by the biology department and built by the ecology club in the late 1960s and 1970s. At various times, the trails have served as a cross country running course and an outdoor classroom. The rolling topography contains a mixed hardwood forest, stream and a pond. Much of the area is heavily degraded with erosion, fallen trees, and invasive species, but these conditions have not stopped people from using the trails.

To reach the woodland trails, go to the parking lot south of and adjacent to the gym. Walk around to the south side of the field. A path into the woods is about halfway around the field and another is near the southwest corner. A third trail can be accessed from the other side of the

Springtime on campus.

physical education building by walking east past the tennis courts and turning right; this trail ends at the center of the figure 8 formed by the woodland trails.

DRIVING: From the Sprain Brook Parkway, take the 100C Eastview Exit and turn east. It is 0.4 mile from the northbound exit ramp to the entrance to Westchester Community College. Drive around the loop to the southern part of the campus near gym and across the street from parking lot 8 [41.064891N 73.786849W].

PUBLIC TRANSPORTATION: Beeline Bus #1C, 1X, 15, 40, and 41

For contact information, see Appendix, Westchester Community College.

RETURN OF THE NATIVE (FLORA)

The buildings sprouting up on campus of Westchester Community College are certainly not native to the terrain, but many of the plants on campus are, largely because of the Native Plant Center. The center, which promotes the study and use of native flora, is a program of the Westchester Community College Foundation. It began in 1998 as the first affiliate of the National Wildflower Research Center in Texas, now the Lady Bird Johnson Wildflower Center, a group founded by the former First Lady and Helen Hayes, the actress.

The center offers education programs and seminars in landscaping and gardening with native species for both amateurs and professionals through the college's continuing education division. In addition to advising the county and municipalities in the use of native plantings, the center has established demonstration gardens on campus: butterfly, ground cover, foundation plantings, and one of winter interest. The Linda Bird Johnson Demonstration Garden has meadow plantings and shrubs and trees beneficial to birds. One long-term projects is to restore the trails on the campus and include native shade loving plants in the woodlands through which the trails go.

A stroll through the meadow at Old Field Preserve.

SECTION III

MORNING STROLLS

- ◆ Have two to three miles of trails
- ◆ Provide more choice of trails
- ◆ Offer an hour or more of walking or hiking
- ◆ Are within a 10-15 minute drive

Burden Preserve

Mt. Kisco • 2.6 miles, 124 acres

Six ecosystems are packed in the Burden Preserve: wetland, pond, stream, meadow, upland forest, and rock outcropping. The trails are laid out so that a hiker passes from one habitat to another, providing many different opportunities for birding.

This preserve was once part of the estate of William A. M. Burden (1906-1984), an aviation finance consultant whose public service included a stint as U.S. ambassador to Belgium (1959-1961). In 2004, the Town of New Castle's plan to build affordable housing failed when the Village of Mt. Kisco would not permit a development of that density to connect to its sewage system. The town purchased an additional 12 acres to connect the two pieces they already owned. The preserve opened in 2008.

TRAILS

Extensive wetlands are adjacent to the entrance to Burden Preserve. After it rains, this area is waterlogged, with lots of rivulets. But other sections of the preserve have better drainage. The preserve has many loops, so that a hiker rarely has to retrace steps. The orange trail is a 0.2 loop off the blue trail along a stream. At the beginning of the yellow trail's 0.2 mile clockwise circle of a pond, it passes an expanse of horsetails (*Equisetum*) which looks like a large green hair brush.

Blue Trail   *Length: 0.7 mile Blaze: blue*
From the parking area on Sheather Road, the blue trail passes a kiosk and heads

---

A BOTANICAL DINOSAUR

Often referred to as a living fossil, this fern-like plant once dominated the undergrowth of primitive forests. Although it gets its name, horsetail (*Equisetum*, from the Latin *equus* for horse and *seta* for bristle) from a resemblance of the stalk to a horse's tail, it predates the horse, or any other mammal, by more than

100 million years. It was a major component of the swamp forests of the Carboniferous or coal age.

The plant does not produce seeds, but reproduces by spores or though root growth. Because of its high silicon content, it has been used for polishing metals and campers have been known to scrub pots with it. The plant is a diuretic and has been used as a traditional medicine for many ailments in various cultures, although its medicinal usefulness is still being researched.

into the wetlands along a path lined with logs. At an intersection, turn left to follow the loop clockwise. When necessary to protect wetlands, the pathway is crushed stone. The trail follows several stone walls before reaching a T junction with the white trail at 0.4 mile. Turning right, it heads into the woods. Going uphill, it passes a cement structure and then a stone foundation. The blue trail gradually turns and heads downhill. It passes the orange trail to the left, reenters the wetlands, and closes the loop.

Magenta Trail
Length: 0.5 mile Blaze: magenta

Beginning on the red trail, just below the top of the hill, the magenta trail crosses a stone wall on a narrow path. Initially flat, it soon heads steeply downhill and descends even more steeply on a series of switchbacks. When the trail reaches a pond, it turns right to follow the shore, sometimes more closely than at others. The trail heads away from the pond along the berm of a breached dam. It turns away from the dam and the site of a former pond and ends at the white trail at 0.5 mile.

Red Trail
Length: 0.6 mile Blaze: red

At the end of the white trail at a stone wall, heading clockwise, the red trail heads left to cross a field. Following a wide path, it reaches a kiosk and a 100-foot trail to intersection of Route 128 and Horseshoe Road. The red trail turns, passes a stone foundation, and heads uphill along a path lined with multiflora rose and barberry bushes. Ascending more steeply, it goes over rock slabs and through a grove of large old red cedars. Immediately, the trail heads downhill, passing the magenta trail to the left. The trunks of slender trees to the right are spattered with lichen. After passing through parallel stone walls, the redtrail reaches the white trail and closes the loop.

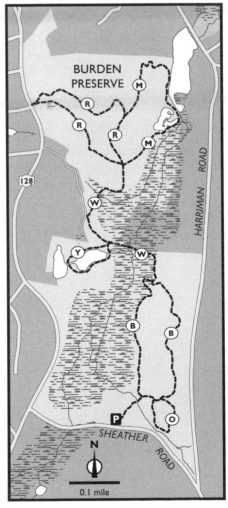

White Trail
Length: 0.4 mile Blaze: white

From the junction with the blue trail, the white trail continues through the wetland. It turns at the end of cement fence posts and crosses a stream on a wooden bridge. The white trail reaches an intersection with the yellow trail and turns right. At 0.3 mile, the trail skirts the edge of a field and heads uphill, passing several scotch pines. After crossing a

Keeping your feet dry in wetlands.

stone wall, it enters a second field. The trail ends with the red trail to the left and straight ahead. The magenta trail is to the right.

NEARBY PARK: Haas Sanctuary

DRIVING: Take the Saw Mill River Parkway to the light at Readers Digest Road and cross the railroad tracks. Stay on Readers Digest Road until it ends at Route 117 (Bedford Road). Turn left, head north for 1.5 miles, and turn right on Armonk Road (Route 128). It is 0.9 mile to a left turn onto Sheather Road. Drive 0.1 mile to the parking area to the left [41.1763N 73.7270W].

PUBLIC TRANSPORTATION: None available

For contact information, see Appendix, New Castle.

Ruth Walgreen Franklin and
Winifred Fels Memorial Sanctuary

North Salem • 2.7 miles, 204 acres

Tucked into a residential neighborhood, Franklin-Fels Sanctuary with its red maple swamp, shrub swamp and deciduous woodlands is the perfect place for morning birding or evening walks. In 1974, Ruth Franklin's bequest and Winifred Fels' donation to the National Audubon Society established the sanctuary which was subsequently deeded over to the Bedford Audubon Society. It is not known whether Ruth Walgreen Franklin and Winifred Fels knew each other.

TRAILS

The trail system consists of a main loop, a side loop, and a shortcut. Unmarked woods roads lead into private property. Two short orange trail totaling 0.2 mile head out to the edge of the property.

White Trail   *Length: 1.6 miles Blaze: white*
Beginning at Lakeview Road, the white trail heads through wetlands to a bridge.

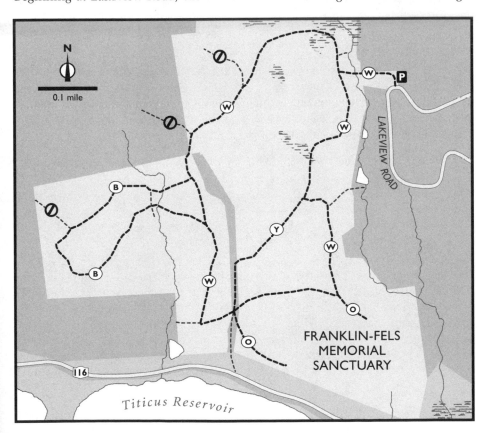

At a T junction with a woods road, turn left to go clockwise. At 0.3 mile, the white trail crosses a stream on a causeway. It turns left at 0.4 mile where the yellow trail goes straight (a 0.2-mile shortcut). When the white trail makes a right turn, an unmarked trail leads left into private property. The white trail makes another right turn and straight ahead an orange trail ends in the woods. At a five-way intersection at 0.8 mile, the white trail passes the yellow trail to the right, an orange trail to the left which ends at a wooden platform, and an unmarked trail which goes downhill to Route 116. The white trail continues straight and turns right at the next intersection where an unmarked trail leads to private property. After climbing steadily uphill, the white trail passes first one end of the blue trail to the left at 1.0 mile and then the other end. Continuing uphill, the white trail passes, to the left, a large rock outcropping and two unmarked trails into private property. The white trail closes the loop at the junction with the entrance trail.

Blue Trail   *Length: 0.7 mile Blaze: blue*
From the west side of the white trail loop, beside a stone wall, the blue trail on its narrow, infrequently used path is easy to miss. It crosses a stream and then immediately a woods road which connects to the other leg of the blue trail. Heading uphill steeply, it reaches a second woods road, turns left onto it, and immediately leaves to the right. At 0.3 mile, the blue trail goes over a rock outcropping with seasonal views of the reservoir. Continuing to head uphill, it curves away from the reservoir, reaches a woods road, and turns right. To the left, a woods road leads to private property, while the blue trail continues downhill, passes the woods road, and ends at the white trail.

DRIVING: From northbound I-684, take Exit 8 (Hardscrabble Road) and turn right. From southbound I-684, take Exit 8, turn right, cross over I-684, and head east. Follow Hardscrabble Road for 2.4 miles and turn right onto Delancy Road. Continue 0.6 mile to Lakeview Drive to the right. Parking for 2 cars is to the right, opposite #23 [41.3432N 73.6145W].

PUBLIC TRANSPORTATION: None available

For contact information, see Appendix, Bedford Audubon.

BEHIND THE NAMES

Ruth Franklin, born in Chicago in 1910 to the Walgreen drug store family, was a writer, editor, and translator. Known as Ruth Stephan, the surname of her second husband, the painter John Stephan, they founded *The Tiger's Eye*, a literary and art magazine published in the late 1940's. Her papers are stored at Yale University Library. She lived in Westport and Greenwich prior to her death. Her bequest forms most of the sanctuary.

Winifred Fels was born in the Bronx, but lived most of her life in Croton Falls. She and her husband, Rene, ran a garment company in Manhattan. After his death in 1974, she donated land to the National Audubon Society. She retired in 1988 and moved to Saratoga Springs where she died in 2007.

Glazier Arboretum

Chappaqua • 2.2 miles, 48 acres

The long narrow trail system in Glazier Arboretum offers options of short or long hikes, in a valley, or along a ridge. Well-trod paths along the blue and red trails attest that Glazier Arboretum is a popular place to walk. On a mild, sunny winter day, hikers can enjoy exercise, sunshine and fresh air and take their dog along as well. Mid-week days in summer provide the chance to enjoy the arboretum without seeing another person.

In 1919, Henry S. Glazier, Sr. purchased 85 acres from the George MacKay Estate. The property included a 1785 farmhouse, part of the original Quinby family property. Upon the death of Mr. Glazier Sr., each of his two sons inherited half the property. Henry, Jr. donated his share to establish the arboretum in 1976. The Town of New Castle's Town Conservation Board now manages it and uses it to demonstrate how homeowners can live harmoniously alongside local wildlife. Even though the property is an arboretum, the only labeled tree is the giant sequoia, which is not native to the area and stands at the edge of the meadow next to Whippoorwill Road.

TRAILS

The view from the gate at the parking lot is a spreading open meadow. Trails form loops and can be followed in different combinations. A 0.1 mile route through the meadow may vary from year to year. Some years it is brushhogged to remove

Giant sequoia.

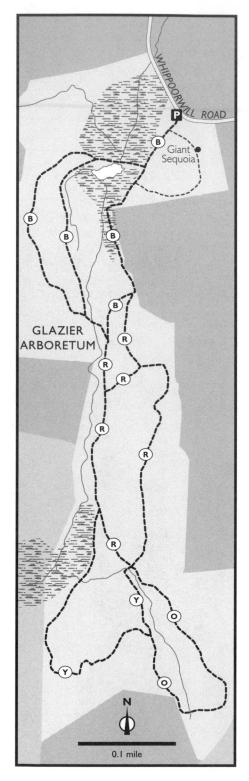

GLAZIER
ARBORETUM

N

0.1 mile

the woody vegetation and in other years
only a path is cut.

Blue Trail

Length: 0.8 mile Blaze: blue
From the road beyond the gate, the blue
trail reaches a kiosk and splits to form
a loop. The piece straight ahead is the
shortest access trail to the interior. The
section to the right offers two choices: a
trail on a ridge or another along a woods
road.

Take the section of the blue trail
that goes straight ahead. It reaches, at
0.1 mile, a long boardwalk lined with
tussock sedge and royal and cinnamon
ferns. At 0.2 mile, it passes a junction
with the red trail going off to the left.
Shortly, the blue trail reaches the other
end of the red trail and turns right to
cross a stream on a causeway. In 75 feet,
the blue trail splits. Take the left branch.

This branch of the blue trail gently
ascends a ridge and, at 0.3 mile, passes a
high rocky slope on the left. Descending,
it reaches a grassy open area, where in
August, goldenrod, black knapweed,
and yarrow bloom in profusion. At 0.5
mile, it passes by the middle section
of the blue trail and joins a wood road
ending at the kiosk at 0.6 mile.

The middle section of the blue trail
is a level former farm road lined with
barberry and multiflora rose bushes,
which, unfortunately, obscure views of
the pond. It provides a 0.2-mile-long
shortcut that avoids the climb to the
ridge mentioned above.

Red Trail *Length: 0.6 mile Blaze: red*
The red trail is a large loop beginning
at the blue trail and ascends to a T
junction. The split to the right is the
shortcut to the other side of the loop
and runs along 200 feet of washed-out
woods road. Turn left and follow the
woods road. The trail crosses a stream,

reaches the orange trail at 0.3 mile, and, 10 feet further, the yellow trail.

Turning downhill, the red trail passes the other end of the yellow trail at 0.4 mile. It follows a stream with wetlands on the far side. At 0.5 mile, the red trail passes the cross trail mentioned above, to end at the blue trail.

Orange Trail   *Length: 0.4 mile Blaze: orange*
From the red trail, the orange trail heads steeply uphill along a rocky treadway paralleling a stream. At 0.2 mile, the orange trail descends into a valley. It crosses a bridge, turns right to go through a stone wall, and parallels the stream in the valley below, ending at a junction with the yellow trail.

Yellow Trail   *Length: 0.4 mile Blaze: yellow*
Heading into the far reaches of the arboretum, the yellow trail is a loop accessible from the red trail. From the junction of the red and orange trails, it goes steeply downhill and crosses a stream. Briefly in sight of the orange trail on the other side, the yellow trail follows the stream. After passing through a disturbed area, the trail crosses a bed of New York and cinnamon ferns. It parallels a stone wall and, at 0.2 mile, descends steeply. Crossing a stream, the yellow trail ends at a T junction with the red trail, at 0.4 mile.

NEARBY PARK: Whippoorwill Park

DRIVING: From the Saw Mill River Parkway, take the Roaring Brook/Readers Digest Exit east to Route 117 (Bedford Road). Turn right onto Route 117 and take the next left turn onto Whippoorwill Road. Continue 1.2 miles to the arboretum [41.157859N 73.741654W].

PUBLIC TRANSPORTATION: None available
For contact information, see Appendix, New Castle.

Hunter Brook Preserve

Huntersville • 2.0 miles, 56 acres

With plentiful shade from towering trees and the cool effects of swiftly flowing water, Hunter Brook Preserve is the perfect respite from a scorching summer day. But no need to limit a visit to the dog days of August, for this preserve is a pleasure in any season. Hunter Brook is also home to mink, muskrat, native brook trout, sunfish, frogs, and salamanders.

An agreement between the developer of adjacent housing and the Town of Yorktown, in conjunction with the Westchester Land Trust and the Yorktown Land Trust, has made the preserve possible. The portion owned by the Town of Yorktown has been renamed Jerry Dineen Hunter Brook Linear Park in memory of a long time resident and former Planning Board member.

TRAILS

The trails in Hunter Brook Preserve wind along the banks of a tributary of the Croton Reservoir and through a wooded area composed of stands of beech, oak, maple, and tulip trees.

White Trail
Length: 0.8 mile Blaze: white

From the trailhead on Fox Tail Lane, the white trail curves downhill along a grassy strip through an open area. At 0.2 mile, it gradually turns left and then parallels Hunter Brook. Veering away from the stream, the trail crosses a stone wall, passes a triple tulip tree, and parallels the stream once again. Now on a woods road, it reaches a large bridge over Hunter Brook to the right. Straight ahead a white trail goes 0.1 mile to Beekman Court (parking).

Green Trail
Length: 1.2 miles Blaze: green

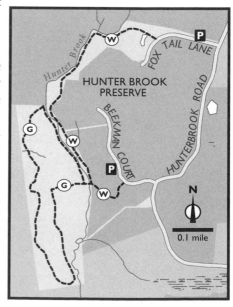

From the west side of the bridge, follow the green trail clockwise. It crosses stone walls and briefly parallels Hunter Brook. Baying hounds on the adjacent Southern New York Beagle Club can be often be heard as the trail parallels that property. It turns to head north. After crossing a big trench, the trail heads through an area with deep gullies and descends steeply. Turning to parallel Hunter Brook, the green trail goes through a stone wall and passes through a grove of Norway spruce with drooping branches. It closes the loop at the bridge.

Along Hunter Brook.

DRIVING: From the Taconic State Parkway, take the Route 202 Exit and head west. At 0.6 mile, turn left onto Pine Grove Court. Immediately turn right onto Old Crompond Road. Go 0.3 mile and turn left onto Hunterbrook Road. It is 1.1 miles to a right turn onto Fox Tail Lane. Park by the kiosk [41.274575N 73.84054W]. An alternate entrance is on Beekman Court, 1.5 miles from the intersection of Old Crompond and Hunterbrook roads. Parking is to the left at 0.1 mile in a small pullout beside a small sign Trail Head Parking Area [41.269427N 73.842428W]. The trailhead is 200 feet back along the road at a sign between two driveways.

PUBLIC TRANSPORTATION: None available

For contact information, see Appendix, Yorktown.

Larchmont Reservoir

Wykagyl • 2.2 miles, 62 acres

The waters of Larchmont Reservoir draw birds of many varieties and also attracts birders of all sorts with necklaces of optics in every focal length. So for birds, and their watchers, Larchmont Reservoir is a good place to be. The reservoir and the surrounding land straddle the City of New Rochelle and the Town of Mamaroneck, but belong to the Village of Larchmont.

TRAILS

Co-aligned trails are the name of the game at Larchmont Reservoir. The Colonial Greenway is co-aligned with three different trails as it goes through the park. The Cliff Emanuelson Trail is named for the environmental consultant who designed the trails and bridges in the 1970s. It is co-aligned with the Colonial Greenway for

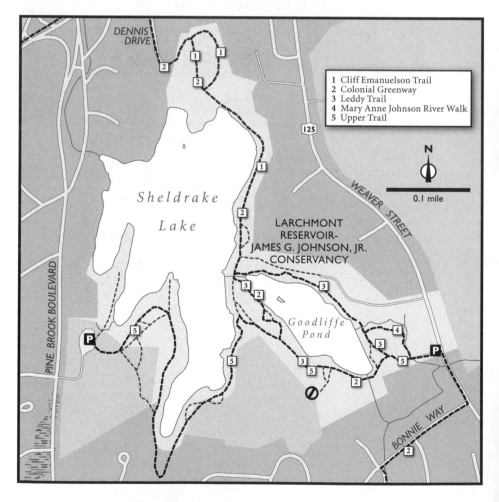

From Mills to Migrating Birds

The Larchmont Reservoir is not part of the natural landscape: It was created in the eighteenth century when mills harnessed water power along the Sheldrake River and eventually it evolved into a protected area for recreation, flood control, and conservation.

A saw mill and a grist mill were built in the 1750s and by 1800, a cotton mill was operating there as well. In 1876, John T. Goodliffe constructed a dam to create a pond for his ice business. When wells in the area became inadequate by the 1880s, the Larchmont Water Company purchased the pond as a water source.

Flood control of the Sheldrake River and the increasing demand for drinking water resulted in construction of a dam to create what is now Sheldrake Lake. The first dam was completed in 1903 and a second was built in 1920 to increase capacity. By the 1960s, however, its water had became costly to purify and a linkage to the Delaware Aqueduct through the Westchester Joint Waterworks allowed Larchmont to buy water from the New York City system. By 1975, drinking water was no longer being taken from the reservoir, which was still used for flood control.

Even though the reservoir was closed to the public, walkers and birders continued to use the site. In 1979, the property was placed on the market by the village. Local Involvement for Environment (LIFE) and Friends of the Reservoir opposed the sale successfully and in 1984 it was dedicated as a conservation area in perpetuity. It was renamed the Larchmont Reservoir— James G. Johnson Jr. Conservancy, although local still call it "The Reservoir." In 2001, LIFE and Friends of the Reservoir merged to become the Sheldrake Environmental Center.

all but 0.1 mile. A 0.2 mile paved road connects the Westchester Joint Waterworks and the abandoned Larchmont Pump Station and Chemical Feed building to the former house of the reservoir superintendent and the LIFE Center Field Station. The Mary Anne Johnson River Walk follows the Sheldrake River for 0.1 mile. Walking around the reservoir is possible utilizing a 0.6 mile road walk from Dennis Drive to the Pinebrook Tennis Court.

There many secondary paths. Many have paint blazes which were never removed, so pay attention to the tags nailed to the trees. These alternates to the Upper Trail (red) and short connecting trails add about 0.5 mile of trails.

An all-terrain wheelchair is available upon request; contact the Engineers Office, Village of Larchmont, 914-834-6210.

Colonial Greenway   *Length: 0.7 mile Blaze: blue with a white star*
Entering the property at Weavers Street, the Colonial Greenway crosses a small bridge, and enters in the parking lot to be co-aligned with the Upper Trail (red). The Leddy Trail joins them at Goodliffe Pond and they pass a stone gatehouse now a bird blind, a wildlife map, and a millstone before following the edge of the pond. At 0.1 mile, they go up steps to a viewpoint and then go over slab rock. Heading downhill, the trail passes an unmarked trail leading to a private swim club. The co-aligned trails go along the shore of Goodliffe Pond. The Upper Trail leaves

to the left and the Leddy Trail and Colonial Greenway reach a viewing platform at 0.3 mile. At the base of the dam, the the Cliff Emanuelson Trail (red) joins and the Leddy Trail turns right. This new co-alignment passes in front of houses overlooking the reservoir and cross a wetland on a boardwalk. Heading uphill, they pass unmarked trails to the left which go to the edge of the reservoir. At 0.6 mile, the Cliff Emanuelson Trail (red) splits with one piece turning right and the other continuing straight with the Colonial Greenway. Just before heading steeply uphill, the Colonial Greenway leaves the Cliff Emanuelson Trail. It passes a large stone structure resembling an extra large fireplace before reaching Dennis Drive. Turn right at the cul-de-sac. Walk out to and then cross Quaker Ridge Road. Turn left follow the sidewalk and turn right at Broadfield Road to reach Ward Acres Park across from William Ward Elementary School.

Leddy Trail
Length: 0.6 mile Blaze: green

Circling Goodliffe Pond, the Leddy Trail honors Tom Leddy, a longtime public works chief and fan of the Reservoir. The Leddy Trail and the Colonial Greenway are co-aligned for the first 0.4 mile. When they reach a T junction at the base of the dam, they turn right to cross a bridge over the spillway. At the end of the dam, they split with the Colonial Greenway continuing straight and the Leddy Trail turning right again. Following the edge of the pond, the Leddy Trail turns onto a paved area and then continues to follow the shore. It crosses the Sheldrake River, the outflow from Goodliffe Pond, on a wooden bridge. The Leddy Trail turns left and closes the loop at the kiosk.

Goodliffe Pond.

Upper Trail *Length: 0.7 mile Blaze: red*

From the parking area on Weaver Street, the Upper Trail is co-aligned with the Colonial Greenway (blue with white star) and the Leddy Trail (green) and leaves those trails at 0.2 mile. The Upper Trail heads uphill to the base of the dam and turns left. It continues more or less above the shore and at 0.4 mile, crosses a bridge over an arm of the reservoir, and heads back uphill. Trails with blazes of varying vintages crisscross the Upper Trail. At 0.5 mile, the trail bears left at a Y junction and heads down to the parking lot for New Rochelle tennis courts on Pinebrook Boulevard, where it ends. A 0.1-mile extension starts at the Lower Trail sign, passes a rock cliff to the left, and ends at an enclosed area which protects nesting water fowl.

NEARBY TRAIL & PARK: Leatherstocking Trail, Ward Acres Park

DRIVING: From the southbound Hutchinson River Parkway, take Exit 20 (Route 125) and turn left onto Route 125. **It is 0.7 mile from the traffic light at Hutchinson Avenue to Quaker Ridge Road on the right and another 0.6 mile to the parking lot entrance on the right just past the Sheldrake Environmental Center sign [40.950483N 73.768608W]. If northbound, take Exit 21 and turn right onto Hutchinson Avenue. At Route 125, turn left and follow the directions from **.

PUBLIC TRANSPORTATION: None available

For contact information, see Appendix, Sheldrake Environmental Center.

Lenoir Preserve
Untermyer Park

Yonkers • 2.5 miles

Two former estates, Lenoir Preserve and Untermyer Park, might seem too small for a lengthy walk, but with a network of their own trails and with their connection to the Old Croton Aqueduct State Historical Site, the options are many and river views expansive.

Lenoir Preserve

Yonkers • 1.3 miles, 39 acres

Like many former estates, Lenoir Preserve has benefited from the common practice of wealthy landowners to import and plant specimen trees. Portions of the formal gardens have been converted to a butterfly garden and community gardens. From the front of the mansion facing the river, birders can watch bird migrations. The former carriage house is a nature center and headquarters for the Hudson River Audubon Society.

The Lenoir mansion dates from the 1850s when it was built for Samuel Tilden, a former Governor and Presidential Candidate in 1876, who also owned a home at what is now Untermyer Park. Aldenwold, another old mansion nearby, burned down in 1979. Westchester County purchased the Lenoir parcel in 1976 and then bought the site of Aldenwold after the 1979 fire.

TRAILS

A 0.4-mile handicapped accessible pathway which connects the Hawk Watch, Dragonfly Pond, Butterfly Garden, and stone gazebo. From the gardens, the yellow trail descends on 73 steps to reach the Old Croton Aqueduct at 0.1 mile.

Gate in stone wall.

White Trail
Length: 0.8 mile Blaze: white
Beginning at the nature center, the white trail follows a path with some remnants of pavement. It turns left along the paved path, passes European beeches, and enters a field. The white trail turns left onto a woods road at 0.2 mile and crosses the driveway to the mansion.

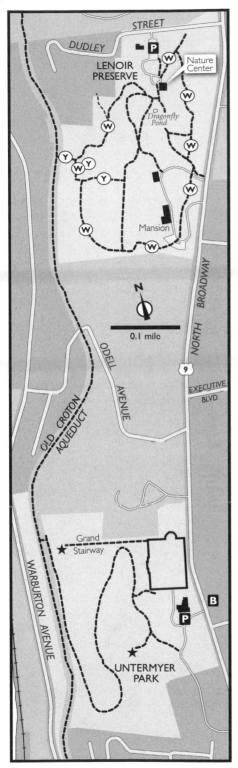

It crosses the lawn and driveway again, and upon reaching a gate in a wall, turns right. Paralleling the wall, the white trail heads downhill, crosses a paved path at 0.4 mile, and descends on steps. It levels out and at 0.6 mile, joins the yellow trail coming from the right. The two trails are co-aligned for 130 feet until the yellow trail continues downhill to end at the Old Croton Aqueduct; the white trail turns right and heads steeply uphill. It passes a trail to an adjacent apartment building and a man-made pond. Ascending more steeply, it ends at an outdoor classroom near the paved path.

DRIVING: From the Saw Mill River Parkway take Exit 9 (Executive Boulevard). Follow Executive Boulevard west for 0.9 mile to North Broadway. Turn right, continue 0.3 mile to Dudley Avenue, and turn left. The park entrance is to the left shortly after the turn [40.977645N 73.882498W].

PUBLIC TRANSPORTATION: Beeline Bus #6 to Dudley Avenue

For contact information, see Appendix, Westchester County Parks-Lenoir Preserve.

CONNECTING THE PARKS

To reach the Old Croton Aqueduct from Lenoir Preserve, take the paved path to the right of the nature center and turn right. Pass the Butterfly Garden and head toward the former formal garden. Follow the yellow trail down to the Old Croton Aqueduct. Walk south on the Aqueduct 0.6 mile to Untermyer Park and take a stroll through that property. An alternate return route is along North Broadway, thus avoiding the steep descent to the Old Croton Aqueduct and corresponding ascent into Untermyer Park.

Untermyer Park

Yonkers • 1.2 miles, 33 acres

Set high on a bluff overlooking the Hudson River, Untermyer Park still bears the remnants of what had been an elegant estate. The mansion is long-gone, but the park offers visitors a stroll through Grecian Gardens of a Beaux Arts landscape design. Plan your hike so that you can picnic and attend Untermeyer Performing Arts Council events during summer months. The gardens are handicapped accessible.

The Untermyer Estate was known as Greystone when it was built in 1892 by John T. Waring, industrialist and philanthropist. The second owner was Samuel J. Tilden and the third owner, Samuel Untermyer, a lawyer, lived there for over 40 years. He bequeathed the estate in 1946 to Yonkers to be a public park. The original villa was where St. John's Riverside Hospital is now.

The major trail is a wide woods road from the left entrance of the parking lot. It passes a stone gazebo which was built for the wedding of Untermyer's daughter. After a switchback downhill, the trail ends at the stone pillars at the Old Croton Aqueduct in 0.8 mile. Nearby, a broad stone staircase leads down from the gardens toward the river. The staircase and gazebo offer settings where a child's imagination can run wild.

DRIVING: From the Saw Mill River Parkway, take Exit 9 (Executive Boulevard). Follow Executive Boulevard west to North Broadway and turn left. The park is to the right, just south of St. John's Riverside Hospital [40.965594N 73.886084W].

PUBLIC TRANSPORTATION: Beeline Bus #6

For contact information, see Appendix, Yonkers.

Stone staircase.

Marshlands Conservancy

Rye • 2.7 miles, 170 acres

Packed into the 170 acres of Marshlands Conservancy is a network of unmarked trails through a mowed field, a deciduous forest, and a salt marsh. There are opportunities to watch wildlife as the trails loop through woods and along the shore. Given the number of cross trails, there are many possible hikes. The trails

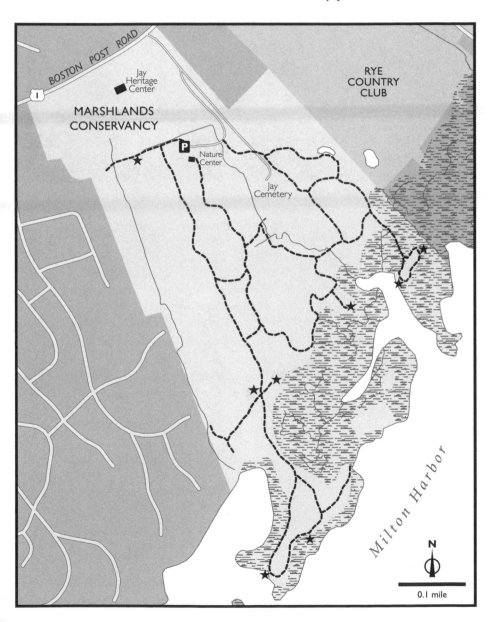

Greenhaven Channel.

leading to the spits of land jutting into Long Island Sound have many birding opportunities. Waves lapping the shore encourage meandering. Because the shore and Route 1 keep walkers from going astray, Marshlands is a good place to practice navigational skills.

The Jay Heritage Center is the large white house overlooking the meadow. John Jay, the first chief justice of the United States, grew up on the farm on the property. He is buried in the adjacent fenced-in Jay Cemetery on land still owned by his descendants.

DRIVING: From the New England Thruway, take Exit 19, Playland Parkway. Take the first right off the parkway, turn left, and then right at the next intersection. In 0.3 mile, merge with the Boston Post Road. Continue 0.5 mile just past the Rye Country Club to the entrance to Marshlands Conservancy to the left [40.95615N 73.703974W].

PUBLIC TRANSPORTATION: Metro-North New Haven Line Harrison Station. Cross Halstead Avenue and walk down Purdy Street. Turn left onto Park Avenue and at the end turn right onto Boston Post Road. The entrance to Marshlands Conservancy is about 200 yards to the left. The total walk is a mile.

For contact information, see Appendix, Westchester County Parks—Marshlands Conservancy.

Merestead

Mt. Kisco • 2.4 miles, 130 acres

The undstated elegance defines Merestead and is reflected in its one word name. It is not referred to as Merestead Park or Merestead Preserve, anymore than either Stonehenge or the Coliseum would be referred to with another name. This Georgian Revival style brick mansion, a listing on the National Register of Historic Places since 1984, overlooks a vast expanse of lawn. A grass tennis court, swimming pool, and croquet court adjoin the house and the spring houses on the farm have distinctive arched openings.

The arts were an important part of the tradition at Merestead. Mrs. Robert L. Patterson, Jr., who inherited the house from her mother, held concerts in the mansion. That tradition continues through a partnership with Copeland House established in 2009 for performances with other musical events and educational activities envisioned.

TRAILS

In 2003, the hiking trails at Merestead were restored and new trails built. The unmarked trails are mainly on farm roads, add 0.5 mile to the trail system, and have the only views in the park which provide birding opportunities. The blazed

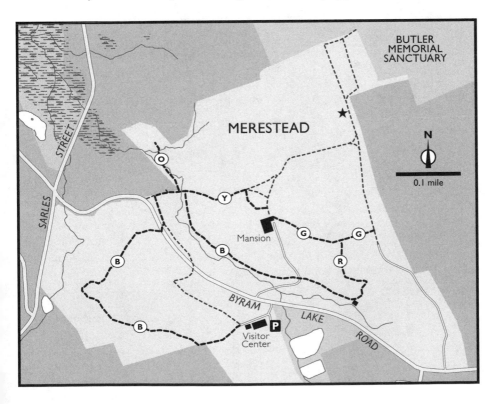

trails often pass through fields which, without a recent mowing, have tall grass obscuring the treadway making it hard to follow.

The green trail is a 0.2 mile connection from the back of the mansion to the unmarked trails on the ridge. Enroute, it passes a pet cemetery with a decorative fire hydrant and then Chinese lanterns along the path through gardens. A 0.2 mile yellow trail connects to the Long Trail (blue) to the mansion.

Long Trail
Length: 0.9 miles Blaze: blue

From the far end of the front of the Carriage House, the Long Trail turns left. It heads uphill along the right edge of the field to the far corner. The trail enters the woods. It turns right through an opening in a stone wall, and heads downhill. After crossing a stone wall at 0.3 mile, it turns left and descends to follow another stone wall. It turns left over a crumbling section of the wall it had been following. After crossing a stream on a bridge, the trail turns right, crosses a second bridge over a seasonal stream and then a third stream on large rock slabs. At 0.6 mile, the Long Trail reaches two fence posts and turns right to contour along the base of a low ridge. After gaining some elevation, it turns left and goes to the top of the ridge. At 0.5 mile, it enters a field and heads towards a tree in the middle of the field. It passes a cedar tree and heads down toward Byram Lake Road.

The Long Trail turns left onto Byram Lake Road and heads forty feet to an opening through the stone wall. It descends stone steps, turns left along the left edge of the field. A BRLA trail coming from the east merges onto the track. Frequent

---

A DISPLAY OF AFFLUENCE

Merestead, from the Scottish word for farmland, was an estate of woods and rolling fields. It was the working farm and county manor of William Sloane II of the W & J Sloane home-furnishings store. He purchased the property in in 1905 and hired the architectural firm of Delano and Aldrich to design the 28-room manse, built the following year. Its furnishings came from his store. Although the Sloanes lived there only only part time, it was their legal residence and they established close ties to the community. Francis Crocker Sloane, his wife, helped to create Northern Westchester Hospital (1916) and to establish Leonard Park (1917). After Mr. Sloane's death in 1922, his only child, Margaret, convinced his widow to keep the property.

When Mrs. Sloane died in 1962, her daughter, now Mrs. Robert L. Patterson, Jr. inherited the property. Her family moved there permanently in 1983. Mrs. Patterson contacted the Westchester Department of Parks about bequeathing her property for preservation as a park and historic house museum and a green link connecting the Butler Memorial Sanctuary, Marsh Sanctuary, and Leonard Park. Upon her death in 2000, the county began the transformation. Reserved tours of the house are available.

The bequest preserved open space and a house that had had only two owners. The contents of the house reflect life of the affluent in the early twentieth century. Servants' quarters were essential for a house that required 12 people to run it. To learn more about Merestead and the people who lived there, see: www.westchestergov.com/parks/naturecenters05/merestead.htm.

Carriage House.

horse traffic makes the route more visible. At 0.6 mile, the Long Trail reaches a woods road and turns right. Just before a bridge over a stream, a BRLA trail leaves to the left across the north edge of a field to end at Sarles Street. Soon after, the orange trail begins to the left, heading along the brook for 0.1 mile. The Long Trail, co-aligned with a BRLA trail, continues straight and crosses a stone arch bridge where it turns right. The BRLA and yellow trails go straight. Paralleling the stream, the Long Trail heads uphill. At 0.7 miles at a Y junction, an unmarked trail goes left uphill to the gardens south of the main house. The Long Trail veers right within sight of the brook and ends at the paved driveway which goes downhill to Byram Lake Road and the parking lot. Ahead, the red trail leads 0.2 mile through a shallow valley to connect to the green trail near a utility line.

NEARBY PARKS: Butler Memorial Sanctuary, Marsh Memorial Sanctuary, Meyer Preserve

DRIVING: Take I-684 to Exit 4 (Route 172) and head west. In 1.5 miles, turn left onto Sarles Street. Continue 1.5 miles to the stop sign at Byram Lake Road, then turn left for 0.4 mile. Parking is across the street from the main driveway [41.176447N 73.704383W].

PUBLIC TRANSPORTATION: None available

For information, see Appendix, Merestead.

Herbert L. Nichols Preserve

Armonk • 2.4 miles, 87 acres

E asy describes the trails in the Nichols Preserve. But varied would apply describe them as well. The preserve has forests, meadows, wetlands, man-made ponds, and abandoned roads, all of which create a landscape perfectly suited to rambling leisurely and watching wildlife. These ecosystems are typical of those found in southern New York and southwestern Connecticut. In season, the ponds harbor turtles, frogs, and water fowl. The abandoned roads, broad meadows, and former orchards provide many opportunities for birding. Over a hundred varieties of wildflowers fill the fields.

Prior to European settlement in 1640, the Siwanoy tribe of the Wappinger Nation lived in what is now the Town of Greenwich. By the early 1700s, Quakers settled in the area around what is currently Nichols Preserve. The close proximity to New York City assured a ready market for local produce. The area was farmed until the 1870s when opportunities for farming moved west. From 1908 to 1910, Herbert L. Nichols, Sr. purchased property. He and his son Herbert, Jr. dug ponds and planted trees and wildflowers. In 1968, his son, Henry Metcalf, and Harriet Underhill donated 44 acres to The Nature Conservancy in honor of the senior Mr. Nichols. Subsequent donations by Mr. Nichols, Jr. in the 1970s and 1980s increased the preserve to its present size. In 2002, The Nature Conservancy transferred the preserve to the Greenwich Riding and Trails Association.

Nichols Preserve is a good place to learn to follow a map, because none of the trails are blazed and it is bounded by I-684 and private property. Unfortunately,

A meadow is just ahead.

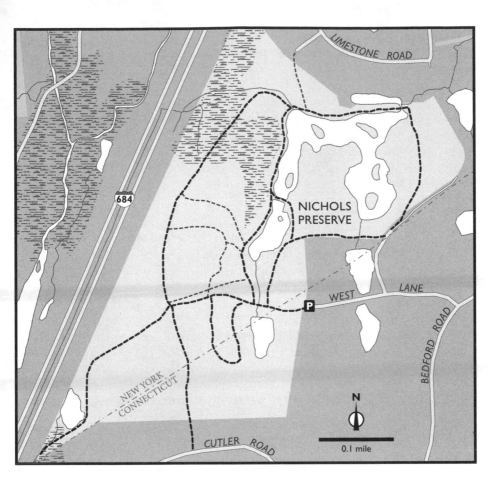

noise from I-684 is ever present. With sufficient snow, the wide woods roads and open fields are suitable for cross-country skiing.

DRIVING: From I-684, take Exit 3 and head north on Route 22. Turn right onto Route 433 and drive 0.7 mile. Just before the Greenwich Connecticut sign line, make the first right turn onto Bedford Road. Turn right onto West Lane (a private road) and continue to the end with parking in front of the gate [41.110925N 73.704709W]. There is an neighborhood entrance on Cutler Road near #115 (no parking) [41.108158N 73.707776W].

PUBLIC TRANSPORTATION: None available

For contact information, see Appendix, Greenwich Riding and Trails Association.

Old Field Preserve

Waccabuc • 2.5 miles, 110 acres

In Westchester County, open fields in which to walk are scarce, but Old Field Preserve has five. The preserve is part of a 22,000-acre biological corridor stretching from North Salem through Lewisboro to Pound Ridge. The open space in the preserve is particularly important for wildlife because of its combination of meadows, old fields, wetlands, and woodlands.

TRAILS

Easy walking is the name of the game on the trails at Old Field Preserve. An open field greets hikers and a mowed farm road follows the edges of the fields. Because of the high water table in the woods, the trail can have many wet spots. Several sections of the fields are suitable for cross-country skiing. The section of the blue trail from Waccabuc River Lane to Bouton Road has steep sections and is likely to be used by horses even in winter.

From 1679 to 1776, Old Field Preserve was part of Van Cortlandt Manor. In 1776 Enoch Mead settled in the area. His descendants farmed until 1974 when Arthur Houlihan purchased the property and farming ceased. In 2003, this open space was preserved thanks to the efforts of Westchester Land Trust, the Town of Lewisboro, Wolf Conservation Center, New York State, and Westchester County.

A clear path - an open invitation.

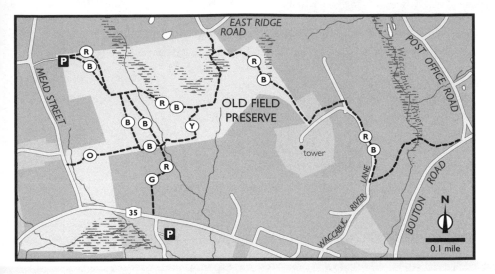

It is jointly owned by the town and the county, with New York State holding a conservation easement. Westchester Land Trust created a management plan to maintain the fields.

The preserve has two trails blazed blue. One of them is also blazed red, indicating that it is also part of the Lewisboro Horsemen's Association (LHA) trail system, it will be referred to as the blue-red trail.

Blue-Red Trail (to Bouton Road)   *Length: 1.7 mile Blaze: blue-red*
Serving as the main trail through the preserve and crossing private property, the blue-red trail begins at the kiosk at the entrance on Mead Street. The red blazes are along the edge of the field while the blue blazes follow a mowed path. They join at 0.1 mile and are co-aligned except for a short split. Leaving the field, the trail crosses through a stone wall at 0.2 mile, and turns left at a woods road. After passing the orange trail, the blue-red trail passes the blue trail to Route 35 in 100 feet. The blue-red trail enters a field on a mowed path. To the right, a 0.2-mile yellow trail heads into a field and an orchard to join the blue trail.

The trail enters the woods again at 0.5 mile and veers left crossing a wet area. It makes a sharp right turn at 0.7 mile as it passes an orange-blazed side trail to the left leading 330 feet to East Ridge Road (no parking). At 1.0 mile, the blue trail reaches a road to an omni (communication) tower, part of the Federal Aviation Administration navigation system. Turning left, the blue trail descends as it crosses a field and turns right to follow Waccabuc River Lane. At 1.3 miles, the blue trail leaves the road and descends, sometimes steeply. After crossing the driveway to Hazelnut Farm, the blue trail turns right only to join the red trail again in 60 yards. At 1.5 miles, the blue trail crosses a bridge and a driveway to end at the corner of Bouton and Post Office roads.

Blue Trail (to Route 35)   *Length: 0.4 mile Blaze: blue*
Starting on the blue-red trail 0.2 mile from the kiosk, the blue trail to Route 35 heads south on a mowed path. In winter, the many shrubs harbor small mammals.

Occasional deer tracks may be seen. Club mosses are hidden in the grass. The blue trail passes the yellow trail to the left at 0.2 mile. Now marked with Westchester Land Trust and LHA blazes, the blue trail heads steeply downhill above a stream. It ends at Route 35 across from the Lewisboro Town Park.

Orange Trail *Length: 0.4 mile Blaze: orange*

Beginning at the blue trail, the orange trail heads south into a field. At a T junction, the orange trail turns right while a blue spur trail to the left leads to the blue trail (to Route 35). The orange trail enters the woods at 0.3 mile, descends steeply to cross a stream, and ends at Mead Street (no parking).

NEARBY PARKS: Lewisboro Town Park, Long Pond Preserve, Pine Croft Meadow Preserve, and Ward Pond Ridge Reservation

DRIVING: From I-684, take Exit 4 (Route 35) and head east 5.6 miles to Mead Street. Turn left and drive 0.4 mile. Schoolhouse Road is to the left across the street from a grass and gravel road into the parking area, which is often muddy. [41.283600N 73.593226W]

PUBLIC TRANSPORTATION: None available

For contact information, see Appendix, Lewisboro.

Pine Croft Meadow Preserve

Waccabuc • 0.4 mile, 9 acres

"Summertime and the livin' is easy" is a tune that comes to mind on a visit to Pine Croft Meadow Preserve during the warmer months. Yet for an insect or butterfly, nothing could be further from the truth. They are busy gleaning sustenance from flowers and plants and in turn, they are the prey of birds and other insects. The preserve is home to songbirds, American kestrels, small mammals, and thousands of non-bothersome insects. This small preserve demonstrates that landscape management practices make a real difference in protecting a scarce habitat and the rural character of northeast Westchester County. The family of L. Emery Katzenbach, a prominent investment banker, donated this land in his memory in 1998. The trails are mowed paths through the meadow and change from year to year. The quarter-mile gravel road is included as a trail for observing birds and insects.

DRIVING: Follow the directions for Old Field Preserve; continue 0.6 mile further to Pine Croft Meadow Preserve, to the left, just past the Waccabuc Country Club [41.291112N 73.595936W].

PUBLIC TRANSPORTATION: None available

For contact information, see Appendix, Westchester Land Trust.

Meadow.

Long Pond Preserve

Waccabuc • 0.7 mile, 39 acres

Bring a budding naturalist with nature guides and plan to spend several hours at Long Pond Preserve. The five ecosystems (meadow, lake, forest, stream, and wetland) are teeming with samples to identify. It is particularly appealing on a hot summer day when the meadows are alive with butterflies, and the cool forest beckons with access to the lakeshore. The property had been in the Mead family from 1650 to 1970, when a group of local residents and the Studwell Foundation, representing the family, donated it to The Nature Conservancy (TNC).

From Mead Street, the single trail marked with green TNC tags on trees enters the preserve. It descends to follow a berm which had supported a power line through wetlands. The trail turns south along the edge of a wet meadow and then enters the forest at 0.2 mile. It parallels the lakeshore and passes the remains of ice-cutting operations at 0.4 mile. It ends at 0.5 mile at the edge of the property. A loop in the preserve and unmarked paths add another 0.2 mile of trails.

DRIVING: Follow the directions for Old Field Preserve, but continue an additional 0.9 mile to the preserve located to the right across from the Mead Memorial Chapel. The entrance is to the right of a wood gate marked Private. From the entrance, a welcome sign is visible down the hill. Parking is on the west side of the road in several pullouts, just south of the entrance before reaching the chapel [41.29571N 73.598389W].

PUBLIC TRANSPORTATION: None available

For contact information, see Appendix, The Nature Conservancy.

Pound Ridge Town Park

Pound Ridge • 2.2 miles, 342 acres

A network of unmarked trails connects the recreation facilities at Pound Ridge Town Park and a 0.1 unmarked trail connects the park to the cul-de-sac at Beech Hill Lane. Shelley's Walk is a 0.4 mile handicapped accessible path along the shore of a rehabilitated pond with interpretive signs. Named in memory of Shelley Satin, a long-time Pound Ridge resident and community advocate, it links the park to the access road to town hall and a 1.1-mile bike path which extends south to Scott Corners. There is no visible boundary between the park and Pine Terrace Preserve, which extends to the east through wetlands towards the Halle Ravine Preserve.

NEARBY PARK: Eastwoods Preserve

DRIVING: From I-684, take Exit 4 (Route 172). Head east through Bedford Village on Route 172 to where it ends at Route 137. Turn right and continue 0.5 mile to the park entrance to the left [41.20133N 73.571196W].

PUBLIC TRANSPORTATION: None available

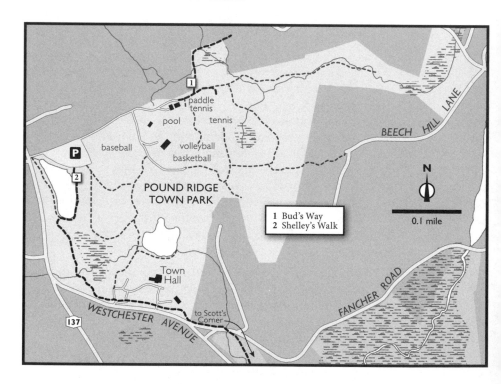

Pruyn Sanctuary

Chappaqua • 3.0 miles, 92 acres

Woodlands, wetlands and hilltops crowned in granite at Pruyn Sanctuary invite the hiker to take their time for their visit here. In 1966, Dr. F. Morgan Pruyn, one of the founding physicians of the Mt. Kisco Medical Group, and his wife, Agnes, donated 16 acres to the Saw Mill River Audubon Society to establish Gedney Brook Sanctuary, as it was then known. In 1978, Dr. Pruyn purchased an additional 31 acres to prevent its being developed and then donated it to the Audubon Society. Later the Pruyns bequeathed their house and its surrounding property, further enlarging the sanctuary. Their modest white house is now the office of Saw Mill River Audubon. In 1990, the sanctuary was renamed in the Pruyns' honor.

TRAILS

Visitors to Pruyn Sanctuary will find wide woods roads, boardwalks, narrow trails, and former gardens. The gentle terrain fosters strolling as well as brisk walks, but there are steeper sections that provide a good workout. In addition to the cross trails, there are four short trails. The Ridge Walk Trail (blue) and the Deer Loop Trail (yellow) in the more rugged section of the sanctuary are 0.2 mile and 0.3 mile respectively. The Swamp View Trail (red) is a 0.3 mile loop trail which provides access to the 0.3 mile Crystal Spring Trail (orange) with rock outcropping, a stone foundation with intermittent spring and wetlands.

Blue Flag.

Fern Trail

Length: 1.0 mile Blaze: white

Starting out as a woods road from the entrance at Woodmill Road, the Fern Trail is the main route into the sanctuary. The trail passes a kiosk, visible from the entrance, and then the junction with Ridge Walk (blue). The woods road ends at a T junction with the Pruyn Trail (green) on a boardwalk to the right. The Fern Trail turns left. At 0.2 mile, it passes through a section of a felled three-foot diameter tree. The Fern Trail reaches an intersection with the other end of Ridge Walk to the left, and the Pruyn Trail to the right.

At 0.4 mile, the Fern Trail passes to the left a white-blazed side trail which first loops uphill and then back down. At the Y junction with the Swamp View Trail (red) at 0.4 mile, the Fern Trail bears right. It heads uphill along a woods road, crosses through several stone walls, and passes the other end of Swamp View Trail entering from the right. The Fern Trail is now mainly on woods roads. At 1.0 mile it ends at a driveway, which leads to parking for two cars at Seven Bridges Road. A small sign for the sanctuary is near the mailbox for #59 Seven Bridges Road.

Pruyn Trail

Length: 0.9 mile Blaze: green

Although the Pruyn Trail can be reached near the Audubon offices in the former Pruyn home, walking along the boardwalk as it crisscrosses Gedney Swamp is

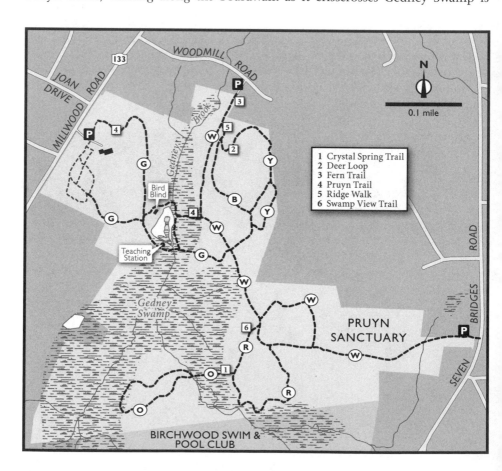

1 Crystal Spring Trail
2 Deer Loop
3 Fern Trail
4 Pruyn Trail
5 Ridge Walk
6 Swamp View Trail

more interesting. The cross trails allow varied routes. Starting at the junction of the Fern Trail (white), 0.2 mile from the entrance on Woodmill Road, the Pruyn Trail is on a boardwalk through most of the wetlands of Gedney Swamp. At the next trail junction, the Pruyn Trail turns right, and, after passing a bird blind, it reaches a T junction at 0.1 mile. Turn left and almost immediately turn right to head uphill. At 0.4 mile, the trail reaches the mowed area of the former lawn where there is a choice of several unblazed routes. Use whichever route to the driveway seems most pleasing and then take the grassy path heading into the woods. At 0.5 mile, the Pruyn Trail turns right, heads downhill, briefly parallels a stone wall, and then descends gradually. At 0.7 mile, the Pruyn Trail passes the trail to the bird blind and continues straight ahead. At the next intersection, turn left. The trail continues on a boardwalk through the wetlands and passes the cross trail mentioned above. The boardwalk ends but soon begins again and winds through the wetlands. The Pruyn Trail ends at the Fern Trail at 0.9 mile.

DRIVING: From the Taconic State Parkway, take the Route 100 Exit. Head north on Route 100 to the traffic light at Station Place at a shopping center and turn right. Continue 0.5 mile further and at the next intersection turn right where Route 133 joins Route 120. In 0.6 mile, when Route 120 bears right, keep left. The Saw Mill River Audubon Society headquarters is to the right at 0.5 mile [41.194596N 73.780605W]. Continue and take the first right for the entrance at the end of Woodmill Road. Park to the right, taking care not to block the entrance or nearby driveways [41.195740N 73.776504W].

PUBLIC TRANSPORTATION: None available

For contact information, see Appendix, Saw Mill River Audubon Society.

Edith G. Read Wildlife Sanctuary

Rye • 2.2 miles, 179 acres

Whether a novice or an experienced birder, take advantage that at Edith C. Read Wildlife Sanctuary sightings are posted daily at the Visitors Center. Recognized as an Important Birding Area by the Audubon Society of New York, it is also a place to stroll through forest, field, and shoreline. Boardwalks allow meandering through wet areas in the forest.

When the property was purchased in 1925 to build Playland, a salt marsh was dredged for landfill and a brackish lake was created. Sixty years later, the county set aside the lake, adjacent shoreline, woodlands, and fields, to establish a wildlife sanctuary. It was named to honor Edith Read, a community and environmental advocate, who worked to save open space and natural habitat in Rye.

Unmarked trails loop around the property, sometimes along the shore of Playland Lake (with a bird blind), and at other times through woods. During growing seasons, trails through fields and meadows are mowed and clearly visible. Benches and boardwalks are strategically placed. A portion of the gravel road near the Education Center is handicapped accessible. The approach to the Long Island

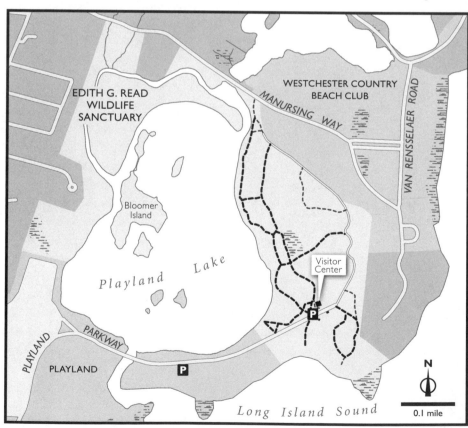

Long Island Sound.

Sound shoreline is a boardwalk south and east of the parking lot and also through a mowed path, if the thick reeds have been cut.

NEARBY PARKS: Playland, Rye Town Park, Oakland Beach

DRIVING: From the New England Thruway (I-95), take Exit 19 (Playland Parkway). Follow the Parkway to the Playland entrance, directly ahead at the third light. Continue around two traffic circles to reach a parking lot. Drive through the lot, head to the far right corner, and turn right. The road ends at the sanctuary [40.9686N 73.66458W]. A parking fee is charged May through September.

PUBLIC TRANSPORTATION: Beeline Buses run seasonally to the Playland bus terminal: #75-Rye Railroad Station; #76-Portchester, Rye; #91-New Rochelle, Mt. Vernon, Yonkers; #92-White Plains Express. An 0.8-mile walk leads to the sanctuary.

For contact information, see Appendix, Westchester County Parks—Read Sanctuary.

Rye Nature Center

Rye • 2.8 miles, 47 acres

Tucked away from busy Boston Post Road, the Rye Nature Center is located on the former Parson family estate. Its original 35 acres were acquired by the City of Rye in 1945. Two additional parcels of land (2 acres, 10 acres), were added through purchase and donation. Rye Nature Center was the first nature center to be designated an Urban Wildlife Sanctuary by the National Institute for Urban Wildlife. Owned by the City of Rye, it is operated by Friends of Rye Nature Center.

TRAILS

A compact trail system goes through rocky outcroppings, wetlands, fields, and streams. The High Point Trail (black) loops 0.3 mile across rock outcroppings to the top of a quarry. The 0.3-mile Hoof Trail (red) starts, passes a neighborhood entrance, and ends at the kiosk. A trail from Central Avenue leads into the park to meet the 0.2-mile Dragon Fly Trail (blue) which parallels Blind Brook. The Tree Trail (white) passes the Parson Mansion ruins to go downhill, briefly joins

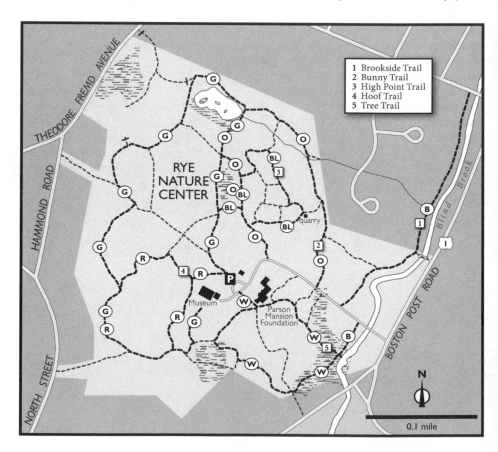

Parson Family Mansion.

the Dragon Fly Trail and heads back uphill ending at 0.3 mile. There is a mile of unmarked connecting and entrance trails.

Bunny Trail   *Length: 0.4 mile Blaze: orange*
From the entrance road, the Bunny Trail heads uphill to join the High Point Trail. At 0.1 mile, it leaves to the right and the Turtle Trail (green) joins from the left. These co-aligned trails cross a bridge and split. The Bunny Trail turns right and passes an unmarked trail to the right. At 0.3 mile, it passes an unmarked trail to private property, an unmarked trail to the quarry, and an unmarked trail to the Dragon Fly Trail (blue). It ends at the entrance road.

Turtle Trail   *Length: 0.6 mile Blaze: green*
From the kiosk, the Turtle Trail goes along the telephone line and turns right. It passes the High Point Trail (black) and then joins the Bunny Trail (orange). They cross a bridge by a pond and the Turtle Trail turns left. It passes a deer exclosure at 0.2 mile and two unmarked trails. The trail turns left onto the telephone line and leaves to the right. At 0.5 mile, the Hoof Trail (red) joins from the left. The trails split to return to the kiosk via different routes.

DRIVING: From I-287, take Exit 11 (Rye) and head south on US 1 (Boston Post Road). Go 1.1 miles to the entrance road [40.975461N 73.686807W] to the right. The buildings are at the end of the road. Pedestrian access gates are on Boston Post Road, Hammond Street, Theodore Fremd Avenue, and North Street.

PUBLIC TRANSPORTATION: Metro-North New Haven Line Rye Station. Walk along Purchase Street to Boston Post Road (US 1) and turn right, a 0.5-mile walk.

For contact information, see Appendix, Rye Nature Center.

Betsy Sluder Nature Preserve

Armonk • 2.0 miles, 70 acres

Anarrow entrance between a gated community and an industrial park is not indicative of what lies ahead in Betsy Sluder Nature Preserve. The beech-maple forest has many vernal pools which, in the early spring are full of frogs singing to attract a mate. Besty Sluder was a conservationist in Armonk and active in the local garden club.

TRAILS

Although the elevation gains are slight, it seems that no sooner does a trail go uphill, then it goes down. Schist outcroppings line the trails. The white and blue trails provide alternate ways to reach the green trail.

Red Trail
Length: 0.8 mile Blaze: red

As the main trail through the preserve, the red trail is on a narrow right-of-way through wetlands. Eventually, the red trail widens and becomes a woods road. Aside from an occasional short level section, it plods slowly uphill for its entire length. At 0.2 mile the red trail passes the white trail, which leads 0.1 mile uphill to the blue trail. Continuing more steeply uphill, the white trail passes the blue trail to the right which leads 0.3 mile uphill to the green trail. The white trail passes under a massive boulder jutting out over the trail. At 0.4 mile, it passes the green trail to the right, then wetlands. The yellow trail is to the left at 0.5 mile and 0.6 mile, respectively, with the other end of the green trail at 0.7 mile, just beyond a large boulder. The red trail ends at a parking area off of Shippen Road.

Green Trail
Length: 0.5 mile Blaze: green

On the red trail, just before it reaches the unmarked trail to Shippen Road, look for a large boulder to the right where the green trail heads downhill on a woods

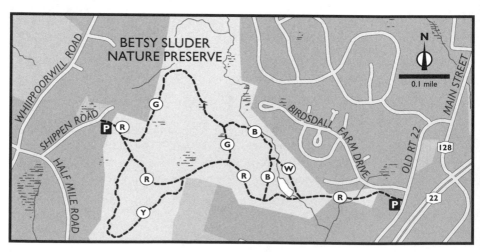

Boulder along the Green Trail.

road. Veering right, it passes a vernal pool where, in wet weather, the trail may be submerged in spots. At 0.2 mile, it curves slowly right, circling a high point of large rocks. It passes the blue trail to the left, flattens out, and ends at the red trail.

Yellow Trail   *Length: 0.4 mile Blaze: yellow*
As it wends its way through open forest, the yellow trail goes up and down. Starting from the east junction on the red trail, the yellow trail passes the first of many vernal pools at 0.2 mile. At the top of a rise, the trail turns right in view of a large house. At 0.3 mile, the trail turns left and heads up over a rise. The yellow trail passes between two vernal pools and ends at the red trail.

DRIVING From I-684, take Exit 3 and head south on Route 22. Turn right onto Route 128 and take the first left, Old Route 22. The preserve entrance is to the right [41.120617N 73.717102W] just past a gated community on Birdsall Farm Drive . An alternative entrance off Shippen Road has parking for 5 to 8 cars. This entrance is 50 feet up the private driveway of 11 Shippen Road [41.122966N 73.728415W].

PUBLIC TRANSPORTATION: Beeline Bus #12 stops near the intersection of Route 22 and Old Route 22.

For contact information, see Appendix, North Castle.

Sunny Ridge Preserve

Ossining • 2.8 miles, 77 acres

Even when the skies are far from clear, a visit to Sunny Ridge will brighten any day. Once there, you will find many reasons to return. First, there are two lovely ponds close enough to the entrance to entice even a timid hiker. And for those who wander farther back into the preserve, there is a view out toward distant hills. Along the trails are many spots to interest budding naturalists, so bring nature guides when you visit.

In 1999, a local resident gave 33 acres to the Town of New Castle to protect wetlands and wildlife habitat. The town later purchased adjacent parcels, one of which had been slated for development. The land in the area was once part of the estate of David T. Abercrombie, founder of Abercrombie & Fitch, a store for outdoorsmen. His stone castle, Elda, still stands on adjacent private property.

TRAILS

The trail system is well laid out in a series of loops off the white trail, making it possible to vary return trips. Many of the trails which are not along woods roads are lined with logs, making it easy to see where the paths lead. Some blazes have white borders, making them more noticeable on trees with dark bark.

Except for the white trail, all trails are short. The two red trails are described southbound so they can be used as the return trip. The blue trail is a 0.1 mile alternate to the southern red trail. The 0.3 mile green trail goes through wetlands. The yellow trail follows a stream and then heads uphill to the ridge. Along its 0.3 mile route, there are rectangular pits that were used in percolation tests for septic fields. The 0.3 mile orange and 0.2 mile purple trails are on the ridge with the latter leading to a short spur to view of an adjacent ridge in the foreground and a distant ridge in Harriman Park across the Hudson River.

White Trail
Length: 0.8 mile Blaze: white

As the main trail, the white trail connects Route 134 to Spring Valley Road. At the preserve's entrance on Route 134, the trail heads north on a woods road and passes a kiosk. The white trail goes by the southern red trail to the left and then a vernal pond to the right. After passing the yellow trail to the left at 0.1 mile, the white trail heads through barberry and wineberry bushes on a woods road. At an old foundation, the trail leaves the woods road to the left. An unmarked trail straight ahead leads to a dam and a pond.

After heading downhill, the white trail crosses a seasonal stream and then climbs steeply up Motts Hill along a path lined with logs. At 0.3 mile, the white trail reaches a T junction with the yellow trail and turns right. The narrow trail soon curves and heads up log steps. Logs line the trail as it becomes a woods road. At 0.4 mile, it reaches a junction with the northern red trail to the left and then passes it again at 0.6 mile. The white trail heads downhill to a Y junction where

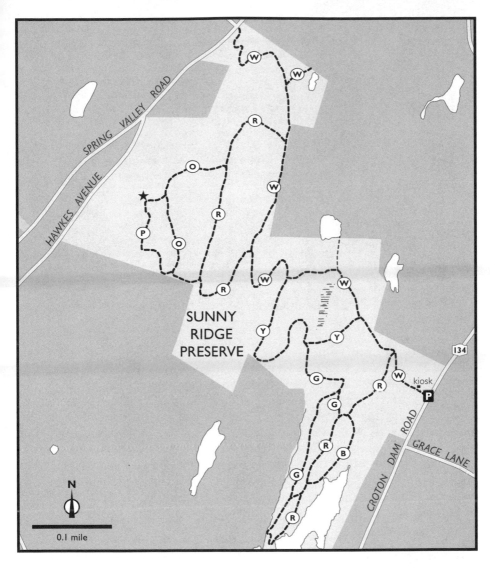

SUNNY
RIDGE
PRESERVE

N

0.1 mile

white blazes go both ways. The right fork ends 200 feet ahead at a crude stone wall. The left fork heads downhill and snakes its way on a series of switchback turns to end at Spring Valley Road across from Glendale Road (no parking).

Red Trail (northern)   *Length: 0.4 mile Blaze: red*

A loop off the white trail, the northern red trail is located near the top of Motts Hill. It heads uphill, shortly joins a woods road, and then goes by, at 0.1 mile to the right, the orange trail. After bypassing the other end of the orange trail, it heads left passing piles of neatly stacked logs. At 0.4 mile, the northern red trail ends at a T junction with the white trail.

Pond on the southern red trail.

Red Trail (southern)
Length: 0.4 mile Blaze: red

Shortly past the preserve entrance, the red trail goes off to the left. It heads uphill to meet the blue trail at 0.1 mile and then descends on steps filled with crushed stone and passes a spur trail (green) that leads 150 feet to the green trail. After crossing a wet area on a boardwalk, the red trail meets the other end of the blue trail at 0.2 mile and arrives at a junction with red blazes in two directions. Take the path to the right which soon passes the green trail, travels downhill on steps parallel to the stream, and then uphill to overlook the pond. After reaching a dam, the trail turns and follows the shore. It reaches the second pond and at 0.4 mile, loops back to the junction mentioned above.

NEARBY PARK: Briarcliff Peekskill Trailway, Teatown Lake Reservation

DRIVING: From Route 9A, take Route 134 east for 0.5 mile. Just past Grace Lane is a parking area is to the left [41.190173N 73.840538W]. This entrance is 2.5 miles west of the Taconic Parkway's Route 134 Exit. Another entrance is at Spring Valley and Glendale roads (no parking).

PUBLIC TRANSPORTATION: None available

For contact information, see Appendix, New Castle.

Taxter Ridge Park Preserve

Tarrytown and Irvington • 2.4 miles, 182 acres

Open space in southern Westchester County is a precious commodity, especially a piece as large as Taxter Ridge Park Preserve. Its preservation is yet another example of how effective concerned citizen can be in rallying to protect open space. Their efforts led to the joint purchase of the property in 2004 by the New York State, Westchester County and the Town of Greenburg from the Unification Church.

The property overlooks I-87/I-287and is managed by the Town of Greenburgh. When the property was acquired, there was hope an abandoned building could serve as caretaker residence. However, the renovations necessary were deemed too expensive and the town abandoned the idea. Hopefully when funding becomes available, the town will demolish the building, opening the possibilities for additional trails.

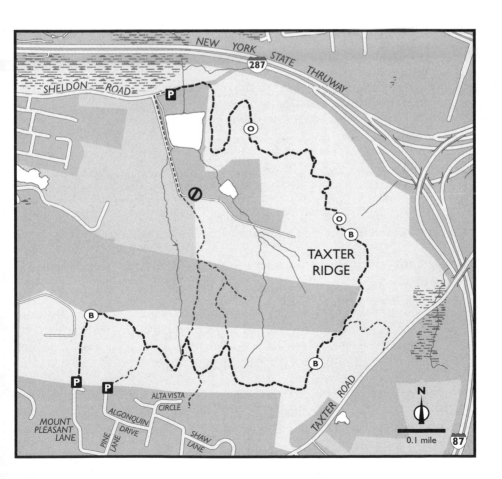

Fungus.

TRAILS

There are three trailheads at Taxter Ridge: one on Sheldon Avenue at the base of the hill and the other two at Mt. Pleasant Lane and Algonquin Drive at the top of the ridge. Starting from one of the latter results is a reverse hike—downhill first and uphill on the return. When the Town of Greenburgh has funds for a parking area, they will complete the yellow trail which will go 0.2 mile from the blue trail and ends in the woods before reaching Taxter Road.

A section of the orange trail is closed and, until negotiations with the developer of an inholding are completed, unmarked ATV tracks can be followed to make a loop hike. Even without a loop, the orange and blue trails make for an interesting linear or out-and-back hike.

There are many unmarked woods roads and ATV tracks that, hopefully, will be utilized once the development in the inholding either materializes or the open space is added to the park. In the meantime, neighbors continue to enjoy the walking opportunities available to them.

Orange Trail   *Length: 0.9 mile Blaze: orange*
For most of its length, the orange trail is along graded woods roads thus making the climb seem less onerous. From the entrance on Sheldon Avenue, the orange trail follows a former road within sight and sound of I-87/I-287. It makes a right turn and overlooks a lake. At 0.2 mile it makes a sweeping 180 degree turn, continuing to ascend on cut and fill construction. It reaches the foundation of a building with only a chimney standing to the left at 0.5 mile. Judging by the size of the trees, the house has been gone a long time. At 0.8 mile, the orange trail passes a balanced rock. The trail flattens out and then descends to reach a trail junction with the blue trail at 0.9 mile. Expect changes at this junction when land and abandoned building issues are settled.

Blue Trail *Length: 1.4 miles Blaze: blue*

Starting at directional signs to trailheads at the end of the orange trail, the blue trail heads uphill, eventually ending at Mt. Pleasant Lane. After crossing stone walls, the blue trail passes the yellow trail, which ends at 0.2 mile, in the woods just shy of Taxter Road. Wandering along the ridge at 0.3 mile, the blue trail passes through open woods with little understory and goes into and out of small valleys. At 0.8 mile, it heads steeply downhill into a valley. At a signpost when the blue turns to go uphill, an orange trail heads 0.1 mile downhill to a construction road. The blue trail passes a vernal pool and crosses a stone wall as it continues uphill. It turns left in a wide open area at 1.0 mile. A woods road comes in from the left; marked with occasional orange blazes, this road leads 0.1 to Algonquin Drive. The blue trail continues right and heads downhill. Turning left, the blue trail once again heads uphill and passes the road to the water tank at 1.3 miles. It ends on Mt. Pleasant Lane.

NEARBY PARKS: Old Croton Aqueduct, East Irvington Nature Preserve

DRIVING: Sheldon Avenue trailhead: From westbound I-87/I-287 take the Route 119 Exit (last exit before toll). Turn left onto Route 119 and when it ends at Route 9, turn left again just past the east bound I-87/I-287 exit-entrance ramp. Turn left on Walter Avenue. **Go left again on Sheldon Avenue and follow it 0.5 mile to the end. [41.059430N 73.845738W]. From east bound I-87/I-287, take Exit 9, Route 9 and turn left at the bottom of the ramp. Take the next left and follow the directions above from **.

The Mt. Pleasant Lane entrance: From Route 9 in Tarrytown, turn east on East Sunnyside Lane which is opposite the road to Sunnyside historic site. Go 0.6 mile and make a slight left onto Taxter Road. Take the first left onto Pine Lane and left again to Mt. Pleasant Lane. Park in the cul-de-sac near the sign [41.050511N 73.849653W].

For Algonquin Drive, follow directions above but continue 0.2 past Pine Lane. Turn left on Eiler Lane, left on Genevieve Drive, and right on Algonquin Drive. Park in the cul de sac near the sign [41.050423N 73.848345W].

PUBLIC TRANSPORTATION: None available.

For contact information, see Appendix, Town of Greenburgh.

Warburg Park

Millwood • 2.4 miles, 32 acres

A wide gravel road greets visitors to Warburg Park, but a walk along it is short, unless there's an interest in examining the Town of New Castle's composting area with its wood chip mountains. Warburg Park is a cooperative venture of the Town's Conservation Board and its Recreation and Parks Commission.

In 1948, James and Bessie Rosenberg donated a 37-acre landlocked parcel to New York State in honor of Felix M. Warburg (1887-1937), philanthropist, banker, and proponent of an Arab-Jewish state. When the Taconic State Park Commission decided the area was not large enough to be a state park, the state transferred it to the Town of New Castle in 1963. The town negotiated with Con Edison and in 1988 acquired an adjoining 57-acre parcel, which gave access from Pinesbridge Road. Part of this additional land is used for town composting operations.

TRAILS

Easy on the feet describes trails in Warburg Park, passing as they do through mixed hardwood forest. To the left of the access road on the Perimeter Trail, a small net work of trails makes many short hikes possible. A 100-foot orange trail connects the white trail to the Ridge Valley Loop.

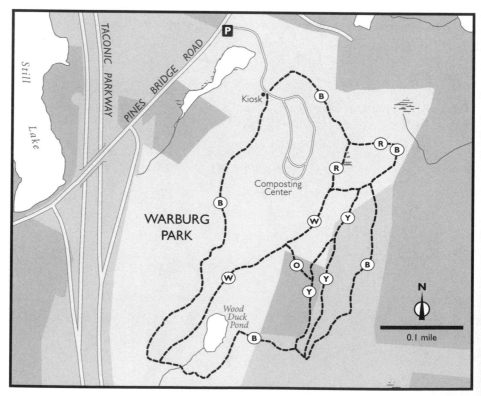

Woodduck Pond.

Perimeter Trail

Length: 1.3 miles Blaze: blue

Where the Perimeter Trail crosses the access road, go counterclockwise and pass a kiosk with a map. The trail heads up to reach a ridge and zigzags as it follows a stone wall. Leaving the stone wall, it follows the edge of the ridge looking down into the valley and at a pond. At 0.3 mile, the trail descends to where road noise from the Taconic State Parkway is audible. Turning away from the parkway, the trail heads steeply downhill to pass the white trail to the left at the end of a stone wall.

The Perimeter Trail crosses a stream and turns away from the pond. At 0.7 mile, the Ridge/Valley Loop (yellow) enters from the left to join the Perimeter Trail for 100 feet before heading to the left up onto the ridge. The Perimeter Trail continues to climb over the flank of the ridge, turns, and goes up a valley. It turns again, away from the ridge, and then heads downhill, passing a vernal pool. The red trail joins from the left at 1.0 mile and together they enter the next valley. The trails go uphill steeply with the town composting site visible. The red trail leaves to the left. The Perimeter Trail reaches a woods road, turns left, and ends at the access road.

Red Trail

Length: 0.3 mile Blaze: red

The red trail is a short loop providing access to the white and yellow trails. For half its length, it is co-aligned with the Perimeter Trail (blue). From the beginning of the red trail on the Perimeter Trail, go right (counterclockwise), following only red blazes. The red trail passes the white trail to the right, then the Ridge/Valley Loop (yellow) at 0.1 mile. At a T junction, the red trail turns left to join the Perimeter Trail which enters from the right. The co-aligned trails circle back to where the red trail started.

VERNAL POOLS

Depressions with no apparent inflow or outflow stream, vernal pools are a special type of wetland. Generally they are quite small, below the size that would insure their legal protection as wetlands. Vernal pools typically have water in late winter and early spring, but are dry at other times, thus the term 'vernal.' They may be wooded or open and have plant life specifically adapted to wetland habitat.

The unique feature of vernal pools is that they have no fish because they dry up in summer. As a result they are ideal breeding places for amphibians and insects. After a pond has dried and the young amphibians have matured, they may range for hundreds of feet. Consequently, large protected space is needed for them to thrive. Frogs, toads, and salamanders return the following spring to the pool in which they were born, to mate and reproduce. In early spring to find a vernal pool, just listen for the songs of wood frogs and spring peepers.

Ridge/Valley Loop   *Length: 0.5 mile Blaze: yellow*

The Ridge/Valley Loop is a trail of contrasts. From the junction with the red trail, head south, and at the point where the trail splits, go left. Almost immediately the trail heads up onto the ridge, narrow enough in places to see both sides. The trail reaches a T junction with the Perimeter Trail (blue) at 0.2 mile. It turns right joining this blue trail for 100 feet before leaving it to head up the wide valley with outcroppings on the ridge just traversed. At 0.3 mile, the trail reaches an orange trail which heads 100 feet straight ahead to join the white trail. The Ridge/Valley Loop, however, turns right and right again to parallel the ridge. It closes the loop at a T junction.

White Trail   *Length: 0.3 mile Blaze: white*

Starting out on the Perimeter Trail (blue), the white trail first leads to a pond, then passes below a high rock outcropping on the left where large pieces of metamorphic rock with contoured bands have tumbled down the hillside. As the trail heads up the valley noise from the Taconic State Parkway abates. After crossing into another valley at 0.2 mile, the white trail passes the orange trail to the right. Within sight of compost piles and with the smell of wood chips in the air, the white trail ends at the Perimeter Trail.

DRIVING: From northbound Taconic State Parkway, take the Pinesbridge Road Exit and turn right. The park is to the right, just past houses [41.201899N 73.803838W]. From southbound Taconic State Parkway, exit at Route 133, turn right, and pass under the parkway. Turn left to go northbound on the parkway, following the directions above.

PUBLIC TRANSPORTATION: None available

For contact information, see Appendix, New Castle

Returning from a hike in Glenville Woods.

SECTION IV

AFTERNOON JAUNTS

- ◆ Have three to five miles of trails
- ◆ Offer varied habitats
- ◆ Provide enough trail miles for aerobic exercise
- ◆ Are within a 15-30 minute drive

Buttermilk Ridge Park
Glenville Woods Park Preserve
Tarrytown Lakes Park

Tarrytown, Eastview • 4.8 miles

Although these three parks are connected, Buttermilk Ridge Park, Glenville Woods Park Preserve, and Tarrytown Lakes Park are all quite different. Buttermilk Ridge Park is a linear path on a ridge that parallels the Saw Mill River Parkway. Glenville Woods Park Preserve is a former quarry and nursery that was part of an area slated for development, and Tarrytown Lakes Park is a paved former right-of-way of the Putnam Division of the New York Central Railroad. The trails on the grounds of Hackley School are closed to the public.

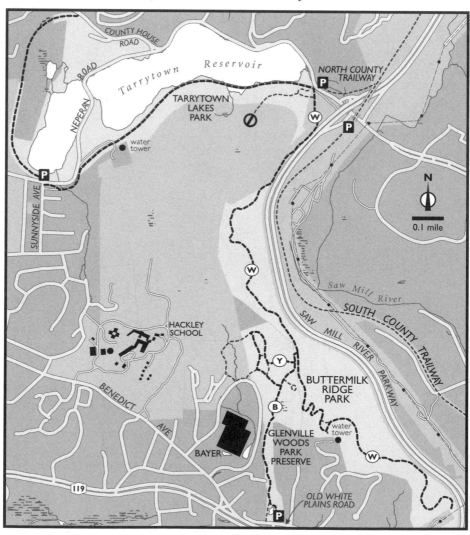

Belvedere.

Buttermilk Ridge Park

Eastview • 2.3 miles, 114 acres

Long and narrow, county-owned Buttermilk Ridge Park parallels the Saw Mill River Parkway, so traffic noise is usually present. Mountain bikes are allowed in Buttermilk Ridge; unfortunately, some bikers consider it necessary to leave their mark in the woods and have spray painted routes on adjacent private property. The park was established in 1924, but the stonework dates from the 1930s.

The white trail on Buttermilk Ridge begins near the road just before the gate at the base of the dam at Tarrytown Lake. It crosses a drainage ditch, heads steeply uphill, and crosses a former railbed. At 0.1 mile, the Buttermilk Ridge Trail turns to parallel the parkway below and then descends to it. The trail is not defined as it crosses a grassy area adjacent to the parkway. Just as the grassy area narrows, the trail heads into the woods. It reaches a built-to-grade road and, at 0.3 mile, heads downhill along a road with wood posts that at one time supported guardrails. The Buttermilk Ridge Trail heads uphill and then downhill once more. On another built-to-grade section, the trail crosses a small stream with a waterfall to the right, at 0.5 mile. The Buttermilk Ridge Trail reaches a stone belvedere (overlook) and then a section of stone pillars with wood railings. Many of these railings have rotted away leaving holes in the pillars. At the end of the pillars, a stream passes under the stonework as the trail continues its ascent. It reaches the top of a rise at 0.8 mile and then heads downhill to reach a second belvedere with an inscription *WCPS 1933* (Westchester County Park System).

The trail continues through open forests, often at-grade. At 1.1 miles, it passes a short unmarked trail leading 60 feet to the right to trails in Glenville Woods. After passing over a stream, the trail is on a raised bed with stonework to the right. It ascends the hill via switchbacks, reaches a water tower at 1.6 miles, turns left and descends. The white trail on Buttermilk Ridge ends at a woods road near a high tension power line.

DRIVING: From the Saw Mill River Parkway, take the Eastview Exit. Turn west toward the park-and-ride lot on the north side of the road. The white trail begins across the street, near the trail up to the dam [41.082530N 73.830628W].

PUBLIC TRANSPORTATION: None available

For contact information, see Appendix, Westchester County Parks.

Glenville Woods Park Preserve

Tarrytown • 1.5 miles, 37.5 acres

The Glenville Community Association, a neighborhood activist organization, worked to prevent the land that is now Glenville Woods Park Preserve from being developed. A narrow right-of-way next to houses would have become a busy access road to a new development. The Town of Greenburgh, Trust for Public Land, and Open Space Institute negotiated with the Ginsburg Development Corporation to limit the number of units in the development and to arrange for some of the property to become open space. In February 2001, this property was protected through purchase by funding from the Town of Greenburgh, Open Space Institute, New York State, Westchester County, and private donations from the Glenville Community Association.

The Town of Greenburgh developed this park so that as a visitor heads further into the park, the more remote it seems. Dense vegetation and the hill block noise from I-287 and the Saw Mill River Parkway, adding to a feeling of isolation.

Blue Trail   *Length: 0.6 mile Blaze: Blue*
From the parking area on Old White Plains Road, the blue trail crosses a rustic footbridge and passes rock faces which were quarried years ago. The wide gravel path parallels the bottom of the hill, eventually becoming a narrow footpath. It passes what was likely the blasting shack of the former quarry and heads uphill at

A Place to Stop

A tavern that was a popular stagecoach stop in Colonial times once stood on the grounds of what was known as Glenville Woods. By the 1800's a small hamlet called Glenville had taken shape in this small valley between Tarrytown and Elmsford. A quarry had been operating in the area.

By 1900 Julian Detmer, a wealthy industrialist, purchased extensive acreage to construct an arboretum. He called his grounds Evergreens and constructed miles of paved drives for visitors to view the extensive plantings, which represented various flora from around the world. The property eventually became a nursery, catering to estates in the area, but its driveways were accessible to the public. Much of Evergreens is now part of Glenville Woods Park Preserve. Leaf duff has accumulated, almost covering the nursery's paved roads that are still lined with curbing. Some left-over nursery stock, including rhododendrons and leafy maples, tower over the former roads.

0.3 mile. After crossing a stream on a stone bridge, the trail continues uphill and heads into the former nursery. At a Y junction at 0.5 mile, the yellow trail begins to the left and leads 0.2 mile to condominiums. The blue trail continues to the right through the former nursery. At 0.6 mile, it passes the other end of the yellow trail and then an opening in a stone wall to the right, where an unmarked path leads 60 feet to the white trail on Buttermilk Ridge. The blue trail ends where heavy vegetation blocks the trail.

DRIVING: From the Saw Mill River Parkway, take the Route 119 Exit and head west. Turn right onto Dunnings Drive (across from 660 White Plains Road) and immediately turn right onto Old White Plains Road. Parking is to the left, next to the playground [41.061981N 73.833842W].

PUBLIC TRANSPORTATION: Beeline Bus #13 on Route 119, across from the parking lot.

For contact information, see Appendix, Greenburgh.

Tarrytown Lakes Park

Eastview • 1.6 miles, 21 acres

Often referred to as the Tarrytown bike path, Tarrytown Lakes Park is a paved path with views of the reservoir in leaf-off season. From the gate by the building below the reservoir dam, the trail goes uphill for a short distance before leveling off. After crossing the access road to the water tank, the pathway approaches Neperan Road. Although the former railbed is visible across the street and the road crossing has poor line of sight, follow the paved path as it parallels the road. The path passes through a grove of white pines. Its surface is littered with pine needles, cushioning the pavement and making a quiet, soft footing. Although the paved path ends at Sunnyside Avenue across from a parking lot beside the reservoir, the path continues on the west side of the parking lot. Now a dirt path, the former rail bed leads 0.6 mile into the woods. A bridge without decking can be bypassed to provide access to Country House Road (no parking).

This right-of-way was part of the Putnam Division as it passed through the Rockefeller estate. John D. Rockefeller, Jr., tired of the noise and soot of the locomotives, paid to relocate the railroad, eliminating stops at Tarrytown Heights, Tower Hill, and Pocantico Hills. A new stop, Graham, was added. When the project was completed in May, 1931, 150 families had been displaced.

DRIVING: From the Saw Mill River Parkway, take the Eastview Exit. Turn west toward the park–and-ride lot on the north side of the road to park [41.082434N 73.830832W]. The bike path begins across the street, just past the gate to the dam of the reservoir. Alternately, from Route 9 in Tarrytown, take Neperan Road 0.7 mile to the parking lot overlooking the reservoir [41.078113N 73.848205W]. The bike path begins at the intersection of Neperan Road and Sunnyside Avenue.

PUBLIC TRANSPORTATION: None available

For contact information, see Appendix, Westchester County Parks.

Franklin D. Roosevelt (FDR) State Park

Yorktown Heights • 4.8 miles, 841 acres

Wide trails, few elevation changes and little chance of getting your feet muddy make Franklin D. Roosevelt State Park (FDR) a large and convenient place to go for a nice stroll or a long walk. But it's a good place for other activities as well, as cyclists navigating the loop road and local high school athletes doing training runs will attest. It's not unusual to see a youngster in the empty parking lot taking a wobbly first ride on a bike.

In summer and on weekends, the park seems like a different place. Visitors arriving by car and buses fill the park's picnic and recreation areas; the air is scented with the fragrant aromas wafting from grills. During weekends in spring and fall, the park hosts walkathons, road races, and other large events.

TRAILS

The most popular walking route in the park is the 1.9 mile loop along the paved road. But there is also the option of walking or running along unpaved surfaces or along a blazed trail. In addition to the roads, there is a 0.7 mile route around the swimming pool area and a 0.6 mile paved path from the entrance to the swimming pool. The green trail and the eastern most portion of the white trail can be used for cross country skiing.

Local entrances give access to the less developed parts of the park. The orange trail goes 0.3 mile from Viewland Drive (no parking) across the white trail. Access to the southern part of the park is from Baldwin Road where the unmarked trails

FROM ASYLUM TO A PARK

A mental hospital was needed to ease overcrowding in the asylums of New York City, so the state purchased over 500 acres on Mohansic Lake in 1909 to build one, with additional acres purchased south of the lake for the New York State Training School for Boys, a home for delinquent youth. Construction had begun and a few cottages were opened. A rail link to the Putnam Division to serve the hospital was begun about the time when concerns arose over pollution to the Croton Reservoir system. A contentious political battle in the state legislature ensued, halting construction and eventually cancelling the project. All that remains is a railbed, some of which is underwater in Crom Pond or in wetlands.

The land was sold to the county for one dollar in 1922. The southwestern portion became the Mohansic Golf Course and the northeastern part became Mohansic Park. The latter was used as a Civilian Conservation Corps camp from 1935-1942. In 1957, Governor Averill Harriman authorized the return of the lands east of the Taconic State Parkway as a state park and part, now Downing Park, was given to the Town of Yorktown. The golf course in the western section continued to be county-owned.

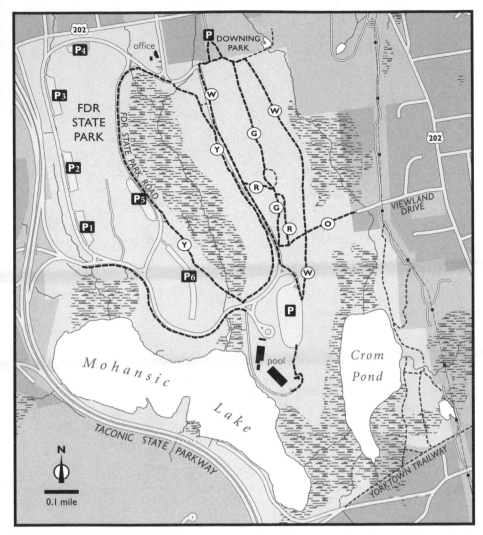

on the east side are through woods and wetlands. Because there is no bridge across the outlet from Crom Pond, these trails do not connect to the blazed trails.

East of the Baldwin Road exit of the Taconic State Parkway, there is access and parking on Mohansic Avenue which was cut off when the Taconic State Parkway was widened to six lanes in the 1960s; it is still used by fishermen to reach their boats on Mohansic Lake. Unfortunately, the Taconic Parkway prevents a trail around the lake.

White Trail
Length: 1.8 miles Blaze: white

Starting at the kiosk just north of the wide intersection with the road to the swimming pool, the white trail heads north along a gravel road. At 0.2 mile, the red trail begins to the right and goes 0.3 mile to the orange trail at the stone buildings. The white trail turns right at 0.6 mile and heads slightly uphill along a a gravel path and parallels a wooden guard rail along the border of Downing

A winter walk with man's best friend.

Park (no trails). At the next intersection, the white trail goes straight and the green trail starts to the right. At 0.8 mile an unmarked trail heads to Yorktown High School and the white trail turns to head south along a woods road lined with wooden guard rail. At 1.4 miles, it crosses the orange trail which goes to the left to Viewland Drive and to the right back to the kiosk. The white trail reaches the swimming pool parking lot at 1.6 miles and turns right on the sidewalk. When the sidewalk ends, the white trail follows the road to close the loop near the kiosk.

Yellow Trail
Length: 1.8 miles Blaze: yellow
The yellow trail follows a former exercise trail along a narrow path and a park road to make a 1.8 mile loop. From parking lot 5, head north along the park road and keep right at the fork. Where the road turns left, continue straight. Turn right into the woods to cross a bridge at 0.6 mile. Bearing right, the yellow trail parallels the white trail which is uphill and to the left along a gravel service road. At 1.1 mile, the yellow trail begins to turn away from the white trail and then heads downhill. It reaches a grassy area and bears right to cross a narrow bridge at 1.5 miles. The trail is along the bed of the former Mohansic railroad spur with massive wetlands to the right. The trail reaches the paved road and then closes the loop at 1.8 miles at parking lot 5.

Green Trail
Length: 0.6 miles Blaze: green
From the intersection on the white trail near Downing Park, the green trail heads south on a woods road and parallels an unmarked trail visible during leaf off season. It passes through an area heavily infested with invasives and crosses a grassy area where, at 0.3 mile, a road leads to the left into the park's stump dump. At a wide intersection at 0.5 mile, the stump dump is more visible. The red trail

joins from the right and almost immediately leaves to the left. The green trail ends at the orange trail which connects to Viewland Drive.

DRIVING: From the Taconic State Parkway, take the FDR Park Exit [41.284528N 73.816886]. There is a daily entrance fee in season and on weekends during spring and fall. Yorktown residents frequently park at Downing Park off Route 202, east of the Taconic State Parkway just past the bus entrance to FDR Park [41.293074N 73.809444W]. The FDR trails are accessible from the southwest corner, just past the swings at the rear of Downing Park.

PUBLIC TRANSPORTATION: Beeline Bus #15 to Route 202 at Strang Boulevard at the blocked off entrance (not on Sundays).

For contact information, see Appendix, New York State Office of Parks, Recreation and Historic Preservation—FDR Park.

THE MEN OF COMPANY 2218V

With military-style discipline, there was an ordered look about the Civilian Conservation Corps camps in Westchester, but the one at Mohansic Park was different. The men here looked older and more hardened, and they were. While most CCC camps were manned by recruits, 18 to 26 years old, this camp was for veterans, many who had who served in World War I. The CCC had restricted recruiting, but when Bonus Marchers descended again on Washington in May 1933, President Roosevelt extended the program to include veterans.

The camp at Mohansic, designated Company 2218V, was opened in 1935. It was considered one of the best in the state; its older and frequently more skilled workers exhibited better workmanship than younger men at other camps. The food was good and morale was high among the 200 workers and they were often invited to social events in Yorktown.

Projects in the camp's early years included building the camp, clearing dumps, razing structures, and building park facilities and trails. In 1938, a crew worked on the Bronx River extension (now the Taconic State Parkway). By 1939, the camp had grown to include headquarters, lecture and recreations halls, infirmary, garage, tool house, mess hall with kitchen and scullery, and canteen. When the camp at Blue Mountain Reservation closed, Mohansic crews took over their work at Crugers Park (FDR VA Hospital since 1945) and Croton Point. The camp closed in 1942.

Mohansic Park was renamed for FDR in 1983 to celebrate the centennial of his birth. It was only in 2012 when a research project conducted by the Friends of FDR Park uncovered the CCC history here that a connection to FDR was cemented. The design, the roads, the many trees planted, Pavilion 1, and the stone structure by the Taconic Parkway entrance are all the work of the CCC. Of their camp, only the flagpole and a fireplace remain. This research project is continuing to keep the history of Company 2218V alive.

Gedney Park

Millwood • 3.7 miles, 126 acres

Do not be misled by the entrance to Gedney Park with its playground, fishing pond, and sledding hills. Having passed the park many times during the first 30 years we have lived in Westchester County, it was only when we started writing the first edition of this book, did we discover the network of interesting trails in this Town of New Castle park. A locked gate prevents access to the southern parking areas when ball fields are closed for the season. Dogs are permitted off leash, but not in the area around the playground.

TRAILS

The trails in Gedney Park form a loop surrounding ball fields, a pond, and playground. They have relatively flat sections with gentle ups and downs and some short steep sections. The 0.4 miles of orange trails either connect trails or are an access trail. A 0.2 mile handicapped accessible paved path goes from the parking

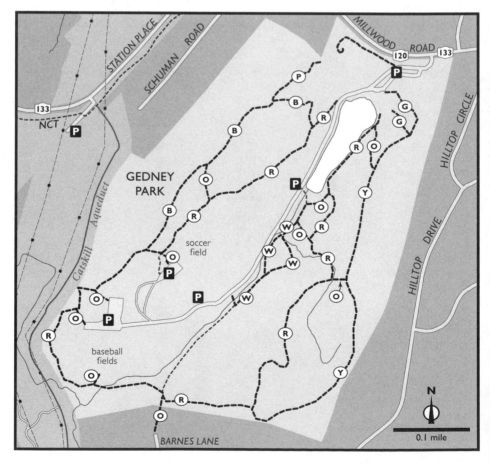

At the pond.

lot to a fishing pier and then parallels the road behind a wooden barrier. It ends at a pull out for 3-4 cars south of the lake. The 9/11 Trail goes 0.1 mile to a memorial to the town residents killed in the attack on the World Trade Towers. An unmarked fire access road goes 0.2 mile to the cul-de-sac at Barnes Lane.

Eagle Scout projects have built three interpretive trails at the park: the 0.3-mile Wetlands Trail (white), paralleling the road along wetlands and a stream, focuses on wetlands; the red trail along the edge of the pond has signs which describe how Native Americans lived, hunted and gathered food; and a 0.1 mile nature trail (green) behind the playground features woodlands.

Blue Trail   *Length: 0.4 mile Blaze: blue*
Beginning on the red trail, the blue trail climbs steeply uphill. At 0.1 mile, it passes the purple trail to the right, which heads 0.1 mile downhill to the top of a hill used for sledding in the winter. The blue trail heads over the crest of the hill and, at 0.3 mile, reaches a junction where, to the left, an orange trail heads downhill to connect to the red trail. Continuing downhill, the blue trail crosses a stone wall and ends at a T junction at the red trail.

Red Trail   *Length: 1.7 miles Blaze: red*
There are many ways to reach the red trail as it circles the park because orange trails provide access from ball fields, parking lots, and other trails. Just past the gate on the road to the ball fields, the red trail heads uphill and passes the blue trail to the right. The red trail continues straight uphill skirting the base of the hill. After passing an orange trail to the right which leads uphill to the blue trail, the red trail heads down steps to parallel a soccer field at 0.2 mile. At the next trail junction, where an orange trail heads left to a parking lot, the red trail bears right. At 0.4 mile, the red trail passes the blue trail and heads steeply downhill. At

a T junction at 0.6 mile, the red trail turns right. The orange trail to the left goes downhill to a parking lot.

At the next intersection, the red trail makes a sharp left. Well inside the woods, the red trail circles ball fields. Passing over a wet area on a bridge at 0.9 mile, the red trail is within sight of baseball fields and passes an orange trail to the back of the ball fields. Turning right, the red trail crosses a stream, and reaches a woods road which leads to the cul-de-sac at the end of Barnes Lane. To the left, it is 0.2 mile along an unmarked woods road to the white trail. Heading uphill, the red trail reaches the junction with the yellow trail at 1.1 miles and turns left. The yellow trail begins straight ahead.

The red trail heads downhill. After crossing a stream at 1.4 miles, it reaches a trail junction where, to the right, an orange trail connects to the yellow trail. At the next intersection at 1.5 miles, the red trail makes a sharp right turn. Straight ahead an orange trail leads downhill to the white trail. The red trail descends to the south of the pond where, to the left, an orange trail heads to the white trail and the red trail curves right. It follows the edge of the pond which has interpretive signs explaining how Native Americans used plants. The red trail ends at an open area near the sledding hill that is next to the playground

Yellow Trail   *Length: 0.5 mile Blaze: yellow*
From behind the playground at the top of the sledding hill, the yellow trail heads up hill at the edge of the woods. At 0.2 mile, it reaches a junction where, to the right, an orange trail goes to the red trail. Bearing left, it follows the base of a hill and crosses stone walls before it climbs steeply uphill. After passing a split rail fence, it ends at the red trail.

NEARBY TRAIL & PARKS: North County Trailway, Pruyn Sanctuary, Warburg Park

DRIVING: From the Taconic State Parkway, take the Route 100 Exit. Head north on Route 100 to the traffic light at a shopping center at Station Place (Route 133) and turn right. Continue for 0.5 mile and at the next intersection turn right where Route 133 joins Route 120 The entrance is in 0.3 mile [41.187924N 73.791507W].

PUBLIC TRANSPORTATION: Beeline Bus #15. The nearest bus stop is at the junction of Station Place and NY 100 in Millwood. Follow the sidewalk to Route 133/120 and turn right to walk 0.3 mile along the road to the park entrance.

For contact information, see Appendix, New Castle.

George's Island Park

Montrose • 2.2 miles, 204 acres

At first glance, George's Island Park appears to be a picnic park and boat launch, but off to the side is a network of wooded trails with interesting features. The trails to the north link to Montrose Point State Forest, making a longer hike possible. Long before the county acquired the property in 1966, Native Americans had come to this shore to feast on oysters from the rich beds in the river. A century ago, brick makers had a major industry in the area harvesting the alluvial clay for their bricks and timber for their kilns.

With the return of bald eagles to the Hudson River, a popular winter-time activity has been watching them when they come to feed along the river and then roost on Dugan Point. The eagles can be viewed from the end of the parking lot farthest from the entrance. Sightings of these magnificent birds are frequent, but never guaranteed.

TRAILS

RiverWalk, Westchester County's portion of the Hudson River Greenway Trail and the winter route are the only marked trails in the park. The entrance road splits RiverWalk. The section to the north is a woodland walk while the section to

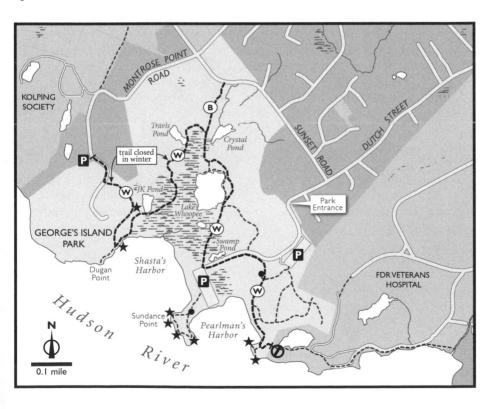

Lake Whoopee.

the south has river views. Both sections have RiverWalk blazes at trailheads and junctions, but are accessed from different parking lots. The connecting piece goes 0.2 mile along the entrance road from the picnic pavilion near the entrance to a mowed path to the right of the parking lot by the river.

To avoid disrupting the eagles roosting on Dugan Point, a winter route to Montrose Point State Forest was constructed. From northbound RiverWalk, a blue trail goes 0.1 mile to turn left to follow Sunset Road for 0.3 mile to a left turn onto Montrose Point Road. It is 0.5 mile to the trail to Montrose Point State Forest.

Southbound RiverWalk begins at the western edge of the parking lot near the entrance. There are shell middens and seasonal views above the river along its 0.3 mile. Unfortunately a locked gate prevents entry to FDR Veterans Administration Hospital.

There is 0.5 mile of unmarked trails in the park, accessible from both parking lots. The trails in and around the pavilion near the boat launch have river views. Although there are no handicapped accessible trails, the parking lots by the river offer broad vistas.

RiverWalk (northbound)   *Length: 1.3 miles Blaze: white*

As the entrance road enters the parking lot nearest the river, there is a post in the grass on the north side indicating RiverWalk. At 0.1 mile, the wide path passes to the right a road leading back to the maintenance building and then Lake Whoopee to the left. The trail winds its way through woods and at 0.3 mile, heads onto a short causeway and up and down several steep hills. At 0.4 mile, RiverWalk makes a sharp left turn where the Winter Route (blue) begins straight ahead. This trail is the 0.1 mile winter route out to Sunset Road, built so that hikers can go to

Montrose State Forest and not disturb bald eagles roosting on Dugan Point.

RiverWalk crosses a bridge and at 0.5 mile, heads through an area littered with bricks. High above a former clay pit filled with water, the trail descends to a bridge over its outlet. Much of this area has a thick understory of invasive plants, indicative of soil that has been heavily disturbed. After a bridge at 0.8 mile, the trail passes large black walnut trees and a pond. It reaches a rock face and the woodland opens up. From the beach, it is tempting to walk back to the parking lot at low tide. Because of the fast-moving outflow from Lake Whoopee, it is likely that feet will become wet and muddy.

The trail follows the shore and, at 1.0 mile, turns right to head steeply uphill. It reaches a woods road along a ledge with views down to a pond. Continuing uphill, it leaves the woods road and goes uphill through an area covered with myrtle and Christmas fern. At 1.2 miles, it turns right onto a closed paved road. To the left, the paved road continues uphill, passes an overgrown side road and ends near the foundation of a house. To see the remains of a formal garden it is necessary to bushwhack from the side road. The white trail heads slightly downhill to parking for three cars on Montrose Point Road. To reach Montrose Point State Forest, follow Montrose Point Road 0.2 mile to the trail through the Kolping Society property.

CONNECTIONS: RiverWalk continues north to Montrose Point State Forest

DRIVING: Take Route 9 to the Route 9A Exit (Montrose). Head north on Route 9A for 1.3 miles. Turn left onto Dutch Street and follow it 0.8 mile to the Park entrance [41.238691N 73.938608W].

HISTORY UNDERFOOT

If you look down, the human history of George's Island Park is right beneath your feet as fragments of shells and chunks of brick. Shell middens are the refuse of oyster harvesting by the Kitchawonks and their forbearers. They likely pre-date the discovery of the New World. Broken or partly vitrified bricks litter the trails in the northern section. They date are from the turn of the 20th century when the area was a center of a brick-making industry.

The Kitchawonks summering in the area harvested large amounts of oysters. The shell remnants left behind can be seen along the trail on the south part of the park and on the trail to Dugan Point. Lake Whoopee, and the park's ponds resulted from commercial mining of clay for bricks; the clay was formed during the last ice age, when glaciers deposited fine clay on the shore of the newly formed Hudson River Valley.

George's Island, which is no longer an island, draws its name from the African-American brick workers brought in, largely from the south. These workers were deprecatively referred to by a common first name. Work in the brick works was arduous; the pay varied by task and, for these seasonal workers, averaged about $50 a month. Changing construction techniques, foreign competition, and depletion of timber to fuel the kilns contributed to the industry's decline. Enjoy the history left behind but leave it where it is: taking artifacts from an archeological site is illegal.

PUBLIC TRANSPORTATION: Metro-North Hudson Line Cortlandt Station. Walk through the parking lot. Turn right and walk about 150 yards north along Route 9A to Dutch Street. Turn left and follow 0.8 mile to the park entrance. Follow RiverWalk north to Montrose State Forest.

For contact information, see Appendix, Westchester County Parks—George's Island.

Montrose Point State Forest

Montrose • 1.2 miles, 50 acres

Your eyes are not playing tricks on you that this open space, Montrose Point State Forest, is a state forest, which seems out of place in a suburban Westchester. Unlike other forests of the New York State Department of Environmental Conservation (DEC), Montrose Point does not allow camping or hunting.

Once the site of the Montrose Brick Company, the land was heavily excavated and little soil was left in the raw clay pits. The exposed black rocks are igneous rocks which are part of the Cortlandt Complex, a bedrock formation rarely seen on the earth's surface. In 2000, the Trust for Public Land (TPL) purchased the site and turned it over to the DEC. Then in 2001, TPL purchased a conservation easement on the adjacent property of the Kolping Society (a Catholic educational and action-oriented organization) to protect the property from development and allow public access to the forest from Montrose Point Road.

TRAILS

The trails at Montrose Point State Forest are part of RiverWalk and wiggle through the woods to interesting destinations and views of the river. Bittersweet and honeysuckle cling to trees and there is dense wineberry and multiflora rose undergrowth. The blue trail is a 0.2 mile short cut to the entrance at Montrose Point Road. There are three branches to the 0.3 mile yellow trail which passes a barrel arched bridge enroute to the views of the Hudson River.

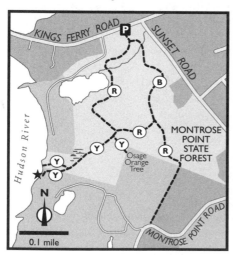

Red Trail *Length: 0.7 mile Blaze: red*
Just past the kiosk at the parking area, the red trail turns right onto an embankment. The trail descends to a bridge and then rounds a pond. It crosses a second bridge and heads uphill on switchbacks as it turns away from the Hudson River. After reaching a seasonal view of the river, the trail heads downhill and turns left onto a woods road. At 0.3 mile it turns left at a T junction and the yellow trail is to the right. It reaches another T junction and turns right.

The blue trail to the left is a return

Barrel arch bridge.

route to the kiosk and parking. After crossing a bridge, the red trail goes uphill. It crosses a wetland on a 100-foot bridge, and enters Kolping Society property. Now on dry land, the trail passes through the easement, delineated by split rail fencing. The red trail crosses a driveway and reaches Montrose Point Road (no parking).

To reach George's Island, turn right and walk 0.2 mile along the road to a small dirt parking lot. Follow RiverWalk (white) along the road for 0.1 mile where it turns off left off the road into the woods.

CONNECTING PARK: George's Island Park

DRIVING: From Route 9, take the Route 9A/Montrose Exit and head north. Just past Roosevelt Veterans Hospital to the left, turn left onto Dutch Street. Go 0.6 mile to Sunset Road, turn right, and continue 0.9 mile to end at Kings Ferry Road. Turn left and head 100 feet to parking [41.249117N 73.948553W].

PUBLIC TRANSPORTATION: See listing for George's island and then follow RiverWalk north to Montrose State Forest.

For contact information, see Appendix, New York State Department of Environmental Conservation.

Mildred E. Grierson Memorial Wildlife Sanctuary
Marion Yarrow Preserve
Mount Holly Preserve

Katonah • 4.0 miles, 147 acres

Three preserves, Greirson Sanctuary, adjacent Yarrow Preserve, and nearby Mount Holly Preserve, make up what The Nature Conservancy calls the Indian Brook Assemblage. The three properties provide ample birding and wildlife watching opportunities in a primarily mixed upland forest.

Mildred E. Grierson Memorial Wildlife Sanctuary
Marion Yarrow Preserve

2.4 miles • 18 and 78 acres

With ponds, wetlands, and a cascade, the Grierson and Yarrow preserves invite multiple visits, especially if one comes with a nature guide. The property was once farmland, as indicated by the many stone walls. With Mount Holly Preserve and Mount Holly Sanctuary nearby, it is easy to have a full day of hiking.

In 1974, Stanley Grierson donated 18 acres to The Nature Conservancy in memory of his mother, Mildred E. Grierson. Two years later, Mr. and Mrs. Wilson P. Foss donated 47 acres in memory of Mrs. Foss's mother, Marian Yarrow, creating the Yarrow Preserve. An additional 31 acres are a conservation easement held by The Nature Conservancy.

TRAILS

The trails in Grierson and Yarrow preserves have dark green diamond markers with arrows indicating the color of the trail. Only the trailhead at the Lake Trail has parking. Horses are allowed on all trails except for the Falls Trail.

Lake Trail   *Length: 0.9 mile Blaze: green*
From the entrance on Mount Holly Road, the Lake Trail (Lake Loop or Maple Trail) heads into the Yarrow Preserve. When the trail reaches a junction at 0.1 mile, turn right at the beginning of a loop. The Lake Trail has numbered posts keyed to a brochure, which may not always be available at the kiosk near the entrance. At 0.2 mile to the right, the Lake Trail passes the Meadow Trail (yellow) which goes 0.2 mile to the Mt. Holly Road (no parking), where it is a 400-foot road walk to parking at the entrance to Mount Holly Sanctuary. The Lake Trail passes the Hickory Trail (white) to the left, which connects in 0.1 mile to the other side of the loop. Continuing downhill, the Lake Trail crosses a rock culvert across a stream. It heads uphill and passes wetlands to the left. At 0.4 mile, the trail skirts the edge of the property and crosses a bridge.

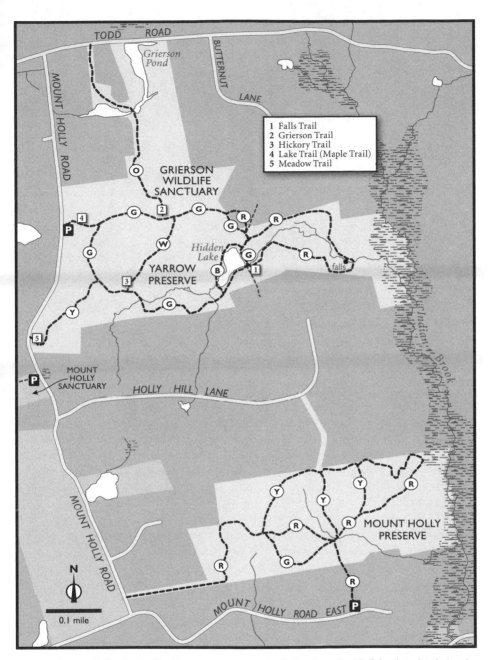

At 0.5 mile, the Lake Trail passes one end of the Bass Trail (blue), which leads 0.1 mile around the other side of Hidden Lake. After passing the Falls Trail (red), the Lake Trail follows a woods road over the dam at the outlet of Hidden Lake. At 0.6 mile it reaches the Bass Trail again to the left and then the Falls Trail to the right. Continuing on the woods road, the trail heads uphill and leaves the woods road leading to the right into private property. The Lake Trail rejoins the woods road and continues uphill. At 0.8 mile, it passes the Hickory Trail to the left and

Hidden Lake.

the Grierson Trail (orange) to the right. Heading downhill, the Lake Trail levels off, crosses a stone wall, and closes the loop where the entrance trail is to the left.

Falls Trail
Length: 0.6 mile Blaze: red

Beginning on the Lake Trail (green) loop, the Falls Trail crosses numerous stone walls and heads downhill. It turns left to cross a stream with the cascade to the left. Heading uphill, it crosses a feeder stream to the left and leaves the main stream. At 0.4 mile, the trail reaches the top of a rise only to head downhill briefly before heading back uphill. Crossing a stone wall, the Falls Trail ascends steeply uphill and ends at the Lake Trail.

Grierson Trail
Length: 0.4 mile Blaze: orange

Beginning on the Lake Trail (green), the Grierson Trail heads north through open forest and then downhill. At 0.2 mile, it descends more steeply and passes through an area blanketed with ferns. The trail enters a wetland and crosses a bridge. After passing a rock outcropping to the right, the trail continues downhill to end at Todd Road (no parking).

NEARBY PARKS: Hunt-Parker Memorial Preserve, Mount Holly Sanctuary

DRIVING: From I-684, take Exit 6 (Route 35) and head east for 1.8 miles. Turn left onto North Salem Road and follow it to Mount Holly Road. Turn right at the Y junction and continue 1.2 miles to where Mount Holly Road makes a sharp left. The preserve is to the right, 0.8 mile past the turn [41.286048H 73.631862W].

PUBLIC TRANSPORTATION: None available

For contact information see Appendix, The Nature Conservancy.

Mount Holly Preserve

Katonah • 1.6 miles, 51 acres

N arrow easements provide access to Mount Holly Preserve, a gift of Mrs. Francis R. Dunscombe to the Nature Conservancy in 1975. Part of the preserve was a dairy farm; less than half is meadow slowly returning to a mixed second growth hardwood forest. Indian Brook and the adjacent wetlands form additional habitats. Rock outcroppings and cliffs of six million-year old Fordham gneiss are along the eastern side. The variety of habitats offer many birding opportunities.

T R A I L S

Trails in the preserve are best hiked using a map and following the signs at most intersections. The 0.1 mile green trail connects segments of the red trail.

Red Trail
Length: 1.0 mile Blaze: red

From the parking on Mount Holly Road East, an access trail leads into the preserve. Turn right and immediately after crossing a stream on a bridge, the trail passes the end of the North Trail (yellow) and then the North Trail Extension (yellow). The red trail goes downhill, passes a large spring to the right and turns sharply left at 0.3 mile. It heads steeply uphill on switchbacks (not open to horses). At 0.5 mile, it ends where the North Trail Extension enters from the left. The North Trail Extension continues straight ahead.

Turn left from the access trail and the red trail heads across an open area and passes the North Trail to the right. It crosses a stone wall and goes through another open area at 0.2 mile. Heading uphill through woods, it turns left and descends. It turns left again and goes behind houses. Entering a narrow right-of-way easement, it heads uphill and descends on steps to end at Mount Holly Road (no parking).

North Trail & North Trail Extension
Length: 0.5 mile Blaze: yellow

To avoid the long climb up to the ridge on the red trail, use the North Trail or North Trail Extension. The former begins to the left immediately after the bridge on the red trail. It heads up to the ridge, turning left at a T junction with the end of the North Trail Extension to the right. Passing through former meadows, it turns to end near a stone wall at the red trail.

The North Trail Extension starts on the Main Trail, 0.1 mile east of the bridge and goes up to the ridge, it turns left at a junction with the red trail and ends at the North Trail.

DRIVING: From I-684, take Exit 6 (Route 35) and head east for 1.8 miles. Turn left onto North Salem Road and follow it to Mount Holly Road. Turn right at the Y junction and go 1.2 miles to where Mount Holly Road makes a sharp left. Continue straight ahead for 0.4 mile to reach parking to the left for two cars with high undercarriage [41.275517N 73.621897W].

PUBLIC TRANSPORTATION: None available

For contact information, see Appendix, The Nature Conservancy.

Hardscrabble Wilderness Area

Pleasantville • 3.8 miles, 235 acres

Nestled on ridges and valleys near the Taconic Parkway, the trails in the Hardscrabble Wilderness Area are a series of interlocking loops allowing several hikes. Although the only view is southwest over the power line, tall trees and shade provide a pleasant place to take an invigorating stroll or a relaxing meander. The heavy use by mountain bikers helps keep paths open and has established numerous unmarked trails paralleling the blazed trails.

The amount of stonework in the park is impressive. With the exception of two wooden bridges, all stream crossings are stone; some are fords while others are stepping stones or causeways. In many places, the trails have logs along the sides. There are beautifully constructed cairns, sculptures rather than just piles of rocks.

TRAILS

The trail system passes through mixed deciduous forest with little understory. There are towering tulip trees and spreading white oaks. Aside from red cedars at higher elevations, there are almost no evergreens. Even in mid-September, wildflowers can be found. In summer, butterflies and bees hover around goldenrod where the red trail crosses under the power line.

Several trails provide ways to shorten or lengthen a walk. The blue trail is a 0.3

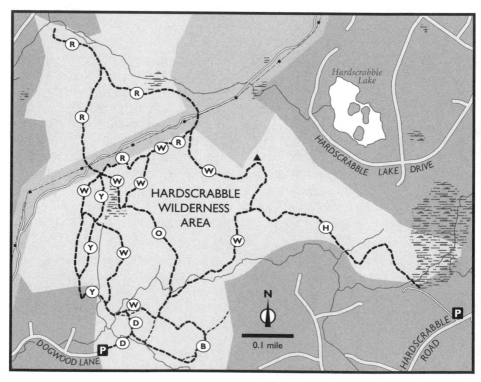

mile loop about 100 yards from the beginning of the Dogwood Trail, just past the stream crossing. The orange trail provides a 0.3 mile shortcut across the white trail eliminating the climb over the high point in the park. It passes a large white oak with gnarled stubs where widely spreading branches once grew and shaded livestock. The 0.3 mile yellow trail is an alternate route to the white trail passing rock outcroppings.

The two access trails into the park are named for their respective access roads. The Dogwood Trail (black D on white) connects the entrance at Dogwood Lane to the white trail in 0.1 mile. Hardscrabble Trail (black H on white) begins at a grassy triangle to the right near the end of the private drive. It heads along a woods road, passing wetlands. It leaves the woods road and skirts a hill. After crossing a stream, the Hardscrabble Trail is on a woods road between stone walls. After going uphill and then down, it meets the white trail at 0.5 mile.

Red Trail
Length: 0.8 mile Blaze: red

Access to the red trail is from the white trail in three places, all near the power line that splits the park. The southernmost point is at the intersection of the red, yellow, and white trails near the power line, reached from either the yellow or white trails. Going counterclockwise, take the red trail uphill, paralleling the power line in the woods. It follows switchbacks up a steep section. When the white trail joins from the right, the trail is blazed both red and white until it reaches another T junction at a quarter-of-a-mile. The trails split, with the white trail going right and the red trail turning left, passing through a stone wall and heading down steps. The red trail then goes under the power line and reenters the woods at 0.3 mile. As it heads downhill, it parallels wetlands. At 0.5 mile, the trail reaches a rock cairn and a red-blazed spur trail, leading downhill 0.1 mile to the edge of the property near houses. The red trail goes uphill, crosses a stone wall at 0.6 mile, and heads under the power line. At 0.8 mile, it closes the loop.

White Trail
Length: 1.5 miles Blaze: white

The longest trail in the park, the white trail is a loop with all trails branching from it. From the end of the Dogwood Trail (black D on white) at a T junction, turn right. The white trail soon heads left at a Y junction and the blue trail continues straight. The white trail then goes uphill and at 0.1 mile, passes the orange trail to the left. Continuing to climb, the white trail crosses a stream. At 0.3 mile, the stream below to the left has a small collapsed dam, now part of a stone wall. Reaching a Y junction with the Hardscrabble Trail (black H on white) at 0.4 mile, the white trail turns left and continues uphill. The trail reaches a stone bench beside a rock cairn sculpture at the high point in the park, which, unfortunately, has no view. Shortly it passes a second rock cairn, massive and not easily missed. The white trail descends, and noise from the Taconic State Parkway can now be heard. The white trail reaches an intersection at 0.8 mile where the red trail is straight ahead. Turning left, the white trail is co-aligned with the red trail but the trails split at 0.9 mile, with the white trail heading left along a ridge and then down to meet the orange trail. At 1.0 mile, the white trail reaches a low point and then ascends to a confusing intersection at 1.1 miles. Going clockwise to the left

Move some rock and look what you get.

are a yellow trail, the continuation of the white trail, the red trail entering from the power line, and finally the red trail heading out and paralleling the power line into the woods. The white trail makes a gentle descent. At 1.2 miles it turns sharply left where a wide unmarked trail continues straight ahead eventually joining the yellow trail.

The white trail crosses the yellow trail, heads into wetland, crosses a stream, and heads uphill. Meeting the yellow trail for the last time at 1.4 miles, the white trail turns left. In this area, there are a number of unmarked trails created by bikers to avoid a rocky section and make their ride easier. After crossing a wooden bridge, the white trail closes the loop at the Dogwood Trail.

DRIVING: From southbound Taconic State Parkway, take the Pleasantville Road Exit, turn left, and head towards Pleasantville. Just after passing under the power lines, turn left onto Dogwood Lane. From northbound Taconic State Parkway, take the Pleasantville Road Exit, turn left and then right onto Dogwood Lane. Go 0.2 mile to the end of Dogwood Lane with parking for 4 or 5 cars near a kiosk [41.143309N 73.810683W].

To reach the entrance on Hardscrabble Road from the Taconic Parkway, take the Pleasantville Road Exit toward Pleasantville. Turn left onto Hardscrabble Road. It is 0.8 mile to #309 to the left, where there is a parking area for 3 or 4 cars. Walk 0.1 mile along the driveway to where the Hardscrabble Trail begins to the right at the end of a grassy area opposite a utility pole [41.144218N 73.797084].

PUBLIC TRANSPORTATION: Beeline Bus #19 stops on Pleasantville Road, 0.5 mile east of Dogwood Lane opposite the Briarcliff schools. Walk up Dogwood Lane to the end.

For contact information, see Appendix, Mount Pleasant.

Hart's Brook Park and Preserve

Hartsdale • 3.2 miles, 123 acres

Imagine the perfect mix of a landscaped park and natural preserve and you have a picture of Hart's Brook Park and Preserve, located in the heart of lower Westchester. The land, once used as a campsite by the French Army of General Rochambeau as they marched south to Yorktown with Washington in 1781, was the former estate of Henry Gaisman, founder of the Gillette Company. A stone building near the pond attests to the opulence of the estate; the barn remains but never housed any horses. A secluded pond, stately woodlands, flowing streams, open fields, and flowering trees entice visitors back for frequent visits. There are interesting geological features along the woodland trails and opportunities for studying a variety of wildlife. Many tulip trees tower over the trails.

In 1932, Mr. Gaisman purchased 135 acres for his estate and later passed the title to the Archdiocese of New York with the provision that he and his wife, Catherine, could remain there as long as they lived. After his death at 104 in 1974, Catherine continued to live on the property until 1995, when she moved to Connecticut. The Archdiocese wished to establish a convent for retired Sisters of Mercy and elderly

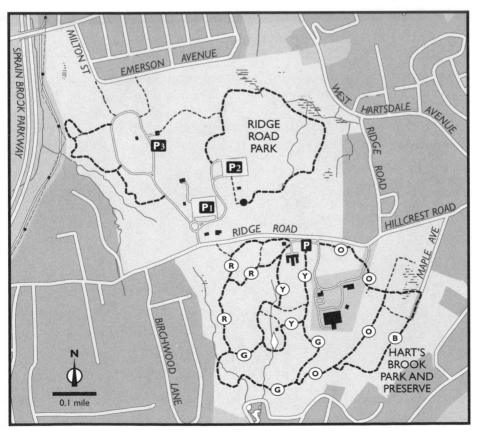

nuns from other orders. Through a cooperative agreement in 1999, the Town of Greenburgh, Westchester County, and the State Office of Parks, Recreation and Historic Preservation purchased 124 acres with the remaining property set aside for the convent named Marion Woods. Currently the Town of Greenburgh manages the park.

TRAILS

For the most part, the wide woodland trails are gently graded and wide enough for walking two or three abreast. Somehow they seem to convey the message, "relax and stroll, there's no need to hurry." Five connector trails add 0.3 mile to the miles of trails in the park. Conditions permitting, the trails are ideal for snowshoeing or cross-country skiing.

Red Trail
Length: 0.6 mile Blaze: red

Paralleling Ridge Road and passing in front of the caretaker's house, the red trail heads uphill. It passes an unmarked woods road to the left leading to another section of the red trail. The one to the right leads 200 feet out to the fence along Ridge Road, where there is a locked gate. Sometimes exposed bedrock peeks up from the grass in the mowed path; at other times a larger slab is visible.

After passing through a field, the red trail reenters the woods on a treadway with remnants of pavement. At a three-way intersection to the left, the red trail heads 0.1 mile back to the yellow trail near a barn and greenhouse. The right branch leads into a field. Straight ahead, the red trail descends through thick understory to end at a T junction with the green trail.

Winter at Hart's Brook.

Yellow Trail   *Length: 0.7 mile Blaze: yellow*

Shaped like a U, the yellow trail loops down to a pond and back up. There are two unmarked connecting trails to provide shortcuts if needed. Starting at the parking lot, the yellow trail heads across the lawn with greenhouses and a demonstration garden to the right. It crosses a short section of pavement before heading into the woods. After passing unmarked trails to the right, it reaches, at 0.2 mile, a Y junction with the green trail to the left. Going right, the yellow trail reaches a second Y junction with the second of the shortcut trails leading to the right. Rhododendrons line the path, splendid in spring when in bloom and in winter when covered with snow. The trail begins its route around the pond and passes a stone warming-house to the right and a short trail to the pond.

Crossing the outlet of the pond at 0.3 mile, the yellow trail passes the green trail to the left. Curving to the right, it passes the ends of the cross trails, the first one at 0.5 mile. The yellow trail reaches the driveway to the barn at 0.6 mile and ends at the parking lot.

Blue Trail   *Length: 0.4 mile Blaze: blue*

Beginning on a wide grassy strip near the orange trail, the blue trail follows a sewer line. It reaches a T junction with a paved road leading 270 feet to a barrier at Maple Avenue (no parking). The blue trail turns right to follow the paved road, which is lined with cut curbstones at 0.1 mile. Passing a fire hydrant, it turns right. Straight ahead, the mowed path is a shortcut to the orange trail. The blue trail jogs left up an embankment, graded to even off the slope. At a quarter-mile, it leaves the pavement to enter an established forest with little undergrowth. After a sharp right turn, it crosses a bridge, heads steeply uphill, and ends at the orange trail.

Green Trail   *Length: 0.6 mile Blaze: green*

Beginning near the southwest corner by the pond, the green trail reaches a Y junction where one branch of the red trail ends. The green trail turns left and heads downhill on a somewhat rough surface. At 0.1 mile, it crosses a bridge and goes uphill only to head downhill at 0.2 mile to cross a second bridge. It flattens out, crosses another stream on a causeway, and heads uphill. After passing the orange trail to the right at 0.4 mile, it continues uphill. At 0.5 mile, it makes a sharp left off the woods road onto a narrow footpath. Winding its way through dense forest, the green trail passes a rhododendron grove and ends at the yellow trail at 0.6 mile.

Orange Trail   *Length: 0.6 mile Blaze: orange*

From the junction with the green trail, the orange trail goes downhill on a woods road, which gradually steepens. It turns and follows a built-up graded path. It goes left at a Y junction with the blue trail and passes a grove of white pines. The orange trail passes a mowed path leading 0.1 mile to the blue trail. At 0.3 mile, it meets a T junction with a sewer line, where to the right is the other segment of the blue trail. The orange trail goes up the steepest grade in the park and reaches a mowed grassy path to the left leading to the convent. The trail heads up stone steps and immediately turns right, passing the broad stone steps of the former

Gaisman mansion. It turns again to head uphill, and reaches the park exit road at 0.4 mile. Turning right, the orange trail leaves the exit road and heads onto grass. It passes overgrown landscaping and continues its way across the lawn. The path is not defined, but the road to the parking lot is visible.

DRIVING: From the Sprain Brook Parkway, take Route 100B Exit. At the end of the ramp, head east. At West Hartsdale Avenue (Route 100A), turn right and continue about 3.0 miles to Ridge Road. Turn right and follow Ridge Road for 0.3 mile to the entrance to the preserve [41.020487N 73.808706W].

PUBLIC TRANSPORTATION: None available

For contact information, see Appendix, Greenburgh.

Ridge Road Park

Hartsdale • 2.0 miles, 236 acres

Where there's a will, there's a way—to find a nearby place to walk. If you live in Hartsdale, Ridge Road Park provides this opportunity. Sounds of picnickers and the smells of treats barbecuing on grills in three picnic areas greet walkers during summer weekends. Off-season and early or late in the day are better times to take advantage of the less-crowded park roads and the small trail system. The gates at parking areas #2 and #3 are locked late in the day, but the exact times are not posted.

The park property was acquired by the county in 1925. Later, in 1942, the Works Progress Administration (WPA) financed and built the stone picnic shelter.

Relatively level unmarked trails traverse dense woods with large tulip trees, including a tree with a 15 foot circumference approximately 120 feet off-the-trail. Logs line the trails. Pallets or boards serve as bridges over wet areas. An 0.8-mile trail circles the area including the octagonal picnic pavilion. On the west side, there is a 0.5-mile trail accessible from the road leading from the gate for picnic area #3. Two 0.1-mile access trails go to Emerson Avenue and Milton Street (no parking). A road walk around the picnic area is 0.5 mile.

DRIVING: From the Sprain Brook Parkway, take Route 100B Exit and at the end of the ramp head east. At West Hartsdale Avenue (Route 100A), turn right and continue about 3 miles to Ridge Road. Turn right and follow the signs to the park entrance to the right [41.021728N 73.812891W].

PUBLIC TRANSPORTATION: None available

For contact information, see Appendix, Westchester County Parks.

Hillside Park and Hillside Woods

Hastings-on-Hudson • 4.9 miles, 98 acres

Situated between residential neighborhoods and two schools, Hillside Park and Hillside Woods are collectively referred to as Hillside. Hillside Park was the property of the Jewish Mental Health Society, acquired by the Village of Hastings in 1941. The Trust for Public Land purchased Hillside Woods in 1993 to prevent its being developed. It is jointly managed as a park by Westchester County and the Village of Hastings. A stone wall which divided the Lefurgy and Birnie/Smith farms is the property line between the parks. The well-trod paths coming from adjacent streets attest to the many feet which have visited these parks over the years. Consider walking because parking is limited. Places to park are at Hillside Elementary School near Lefurgy Avenue and at the tennis courts off Farlane Drive.

TRAILS

The trails in Hillside are not just trails to come for a stroll or to take the dog for a walk. Some are the routes children take to school while others provide access to the park's swimming pool, tennis courts, or ball fields. The trails are sporadically blazed, mostly with yellow paint, so it is best to use a map to navigate. As they wind through the two parks, the wide paths and woods roads allow for walking two or three abreast. In the northeast portion of the park, the trails intersect with the trails of Children's Village, a residential school for children-at-risk. These trails are blazed and have signs, but are not open to the public. The trails at Hillside are

Spring at Sugar Pond.

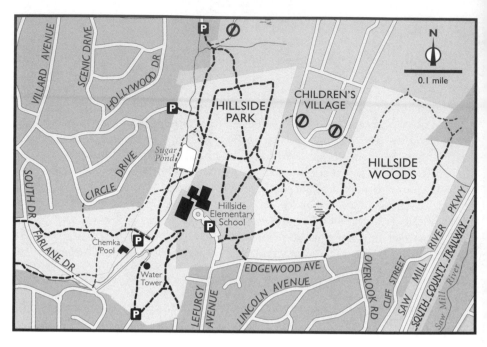

part of the Hastings Trailway, but they are not connected to sections of the trailway in other parks.

Algonquin Trail

Length: 0.5 mile Blaze: occasional yellow

The Algonquin Trail is reputedly to have been once part of a Native American route between the Hudson River and Long Island Sound. Although there is no definitive historical confirmation that this trail was part of that route, it still bears the name. The Algonquin Trail begins just south of a vernal pool, near the unmarked entrance at Edgewood Avenue. At a T junction, the trail goes right, descends, and passes a short trail out to Taft Street and Edgewood Avenue. Continuing downhill, it parallels a ravine to the left. Tree limbs line the steeply descending trail. To the right, rock outcroppings with folded layers are Fordham gneiss. After crossing a third brook, the trail turns left at 0.4 mile at two black birch trees with a large stump at the base of one of them. The trail first descends steeply into a ravine and then ascends towards the bluffs to reach a T junction. To the right, the trail leads to Children's Village. To the left, the red trail with occasional blue blazes heads back to the trails in Hillside Woods.

DRIVING: From the Saw Mill Parkway, take Farragut Parkway west to Hastings. Turn right onto Hillside Avenue which is immediately north of the middle school. Head uphill and at a traffic island, turn left onto Rosedale Avenue. Cross the intersection with Farlane Drive and enter the park by the tennis courts [40.995416N 73.870990W].

PUBLIC TRANSPORTATION: Beeline Bus #6 on Route 9. It is a 0.4-mile walk from the Old Croton Aqueduct to the tennis courts.

For contact information, see Appendix, Hastings.

Hastings Trailway

Three tiny segments of the Hasting Trailway are located between houses in Hastings. Lefurgy Park is a narrow pathway wedged on the side of a hill; it provides a 0.2-mile pedestrian access between Mount Hope Boulevard [40.992022N 73.866466W] and Fairmont Avenue [40.989070 73.868008]. The park is named for Isaac Lefurgy, a tax collector and wealthy landowner who, in 1850, deeded property to establish the First Reformed Church.

Pulvers Woods has 0.3 mile of trails which go through an open forest with little understory. It is two blocks from the intersection of Farragut Avenue and Farragut Parkway at Green and Rose streets [40.986456N 73.873161W]. John Henry Pulver was a farmer, who, in the 1830s, founded a quarry that mined white dolomite marble in the area between the Old Croton Aqueduct and what is now Draper Park.

A quarter-mile of trails wind their way through Ravendale Woods. Accessed through narrow rights-of-way, Ravendale Woods is located one block from the Farragut Avenue Exit of the southbound Saw Mill River Parkway [40.983320N 73.868381W].

Hilltop Hanover Farm and Environmental Center

Yorktown Heights • 3.4 miles, 183 acres

When Westchester County purchased Hilltop Hanover Farm in 2003, it did more than just save the farm, it also protected the quality of drinking water by acting as a buffer to the nearby Croton Reservoir. Only the part of the property on the east side of Hanover Street is also protected parkland. The remaining acres are a community supported agriculture (CSA) farm run by the Friends of Hilltop Hanover Farm and an environmental resource center.

Croton Heights Road and Hanover Street are known to have existed before the American Revolution. The old stone walls both surrounding and within the property indicate early farm field patterns and suggest how the land had been farmed in the late eighteenth century. Dairy operations began about 55 years ago, but when the economy turned sluggish in the early 1990s, the breeding operation was discontinued. In the mid 1990s before attempting to sell the farm, the owners sold the remaining cows.

TRAILS

The parkland portion of Hilltop Hanover contains a trail network through open woods. A 0.1-mile unmarked trail and three short unmarked trails divide the Hilltop Loop. On the west side of Hanover Street, a 1.2-mile mowed path starts north of the barn and winds its way down the ridge to split and go around both

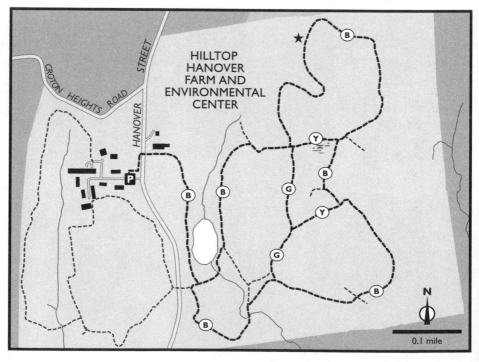

sides of the fenced-in farm fields. On the far side of the farm field, a short trail crosses Hanover Street and connects to the Hilltop Loop.

Hilltop Loop   *Length: 1.7 miles Blaze: blue*

From the kiosk, walk clockwise around the Hilltop Loop and head downhill. The trail crosses a bridge over the outlet stream from the pond and turns left to reach the top of the dam. After briefly hugging the edge of the pond and passing some picnic tables, it turns away. At a T junction, the trail turns left onto a woods road which, to the right, is a 0.1-mile shortcut ending on Hilltop Loop. At 0.2 mile, the trail ascends. At an intersection with the yellow and green trails, the Hilltop Loop turns left. The Vernal Pond Trail (yellow) heads straight to end in 350 feet at the far side of the Hilltop Loop; the Rock Pass Trail (green) goes right for 0.2 mile, also ending at another part of the Hilltop Loop.

Passing under rock cliffs, Hilltop Loop wanders to reach a viewpoint at 0.7 mile. It descends and, at 1.0 mile, passes to the right the Vernal Pond Trail and a vernal pond. The Hilltop Loop heads uphill and turns left as it passes the Campfire Circle Trail (yellow), which leads 460 feet downhill to end at the Rock Pass Trail. Hilltop Loop heads downhill, crossing and joining woods roads. At 1.5 miles, it turns right onto a woods road and passes a breached dam. The trail crosses a stone wall, passes Rock Pass Trail, and an unmarked woods road that leads back to the pond. The Hilltop Loop enters a field and closes the loop. To the left, a short path goes to Hanover Street and the 1.2 mile trail goes through the open fields.

DRIVING: From the Taconic State Parkway, take the Millwood/Route 100 Exit. At the traffic light at Route 100, turn right. Head north for 3.9 miles and turn left onto Route 118. Hanover Street is the first right turn and Hilltop Hanover Farm is 1.4 miles to the left [41.252253N 73.772854W].

PUBLIC TRANSPORTATION: None available

For contact information, see Appendix, Hilltop Hanover Farm and Environmental Center.

Hudson Highlands Gateway Park

Cortlandt • 4.0 miles, 352 acres

The ecology at Hudson Highlands Gateway Park makes it one of the most diverse properties in the county. Ridges, rock outcroppings, slopes, and vales form a variety of habitats. Bordered by Annsville Creek and Sprout Brook, the park also contains meadows, wetlands, and minor and seasonal streams. Birds frequent the more open areas of the former gravel pits, while the core of its intact forest allows migrant birds a place to rest or breed. The vernal pools are home to frogs and salamanders. Reptiles living on the property include eastern box turtles, spotted turtles, worm snakes, black rat snakes, and black racers.

But Gateway, as it is usually called, is also rich in Revolutionary War history. Its viewpoints were once signal hills manned by troops quartered in nearby Continental Village. Some trails are on Revolutionary era roads. In the early 1800s, the Clinton family operated a dairy farm here. During the mid 1900s, parts of its eastern and western edges were quarried for their glacial till and subsequently abandoned. In 2000, Scenic Hudson Land Trust, New York State, and Westchester County together purchased the property which was slated for development. Under a cooperative arrangement, the Town of Cortlandt manages the park.

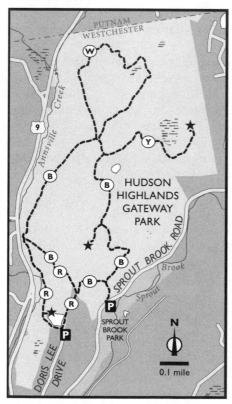

TRAILS

The trail system in Gateway was developed to minimize its impact on wildlife. The trails were designed to utilize existing woods roads and avoid going too close to vernal pools. The four trails pass through a meadow, wetlands, succession forest, and uplands. Unfortunately, illegal ATV use has widened the woods roads and damaged narrow trails.

Upland Trail

Length: 1.8 miles Blaze: blue
Beginning at the kiosk at Sprout Brook Road, the Upland Trail heads uphill crossing a stream to a T junction at 0.1 mile to begin a loop. Going counterclockwise, it passes a bench and heads uphill leaving the former gravel pit. After passing a Revolutionary War era road to the right, it continues uphill. At 0.4 mile, the Upland Trail reaches a side trail leading 0.1 mile to a lookout used during the Revolutionary War. The

seasonal view includes the Hudson River, the Jan Peek Bridge over Annsville Creek, the Sprout Brook Landfill and Indian Point Energy Center (nuclear power plant).

The Upland Trail works its way uphill and down, and at 0.7 mile, passes the Hudson Overlook Spur Trail (yellow) to the right. The Upland Trail goes through a stone wall to join the Vernal Pool Trail (white) to the right. These two trails are together briefly until the Vernal Pool Trail leaves to the right. Heading downhill, the Upland Trail crosses a stream just upstream of a small seasonal cascade. It then parallels a stone wall on a gullied woods road, marked on old maps as Old Revolutionary Road. It passes through laurel at 1.0 mile, leaves an eroded section of the gully, and returns to the old road when the terrain flattens out.

At 1.3 miles, the Upland Trail turns left to join the Annsville Creek Trail (red). It passes a foundation to the left and massive rock outcroppings, some of which have tumbled down the hill. It goes through a rock cut and passes a vernal pool which drains onto the trail further downhill. At a T junction at 1.6 miles, the Upland Trail turns left and the Annsville Creek Trail turns right. The Upland Trail crosses a stream, heads downhill, and closes the loop at 1.8 miles. The return route to the parking lot is to the right.

Annsville Creek Trail
Length: 0.8 mile Blaze: red

From the parking area at the end of Doris Lee Drive, a short access trail goes through a gate in a split-rail fence to reach the Annsville Creek Trail. Going counterclockwise from the sign, the trail passes a pond to the left and then continues through a wet area. At the intersection with the Upland Trail (blue), the Annsville Creek Trail turns left to join it.

Heading uphill, the two trails pass a rock outcropping to the right. At 0.3 mile, the co-aligned trails go over a rise and head downhill. After passing rock outcroppings, the trail reaches an open area with a foundation to the right. At 0.4 mile the Annsville Creek Trail turns left and the Upland Trail turns right. After entering a former gravel pit, the Annsville Creek Trail passes the first of several

Pond on the Annsville Creek Trail.

paths to Route 9. It crosses a wetland on wood chips or puncheons. Turning away from Route 9 to cross a bridge, the trail parallels Annsville Creek at 0.6 mile. It heads uphill on a broad woods road and reaches a side trail leading 60 feet to an overlook of a pond. The Annsville Creek Trail then goes along the shore of the pond and closes the loop at the park sign.

Hudson Overlook Spur Trail *Length: 0.5 mile Blaze: yellow*
From the Upland Trail (blue), the Hudson Overlook Spur Trail heads downhill, sometimes steeply. It makes a sharp right turn, passes a vernal pool to the left at 0.3 mile, and descends to cross a stream at 0.4 mile. Going uphill, the trail passes slab rock to the left. It then turns left to go steeply uphill to a lookout used during the Revolutionary War, where the view of the river valley is now punctuated by the Sprout Brook Landfill and Indian Point Energy Center (nuclear power plant).

Vernal Pool Trail *Length: 1.1 miles Blaze: white*
Reached from the Upland Trail (blue), the Vernal Pool Trail is a loop. It goes through a low ravine at 0.1 mile and a forest with sparse understory. At 0.3 mile, it heads up onto a rock outcropping. Turning left to leave the outcropping, it ascends, slowly curving to the left. After passing a large vernal pool to the left, the trail works its way right and at 0.5 mile, heads steeply downhill. It crosses a stream and then a second stream just above a small seasonal cascade to the right. Paralleling the stream briefly, the Vernal Pool Trail crosses a stone wall, immediately turns left, and heads uphill. It passes through an area covered with mixed ground pine and tree club moss. At a T junction with a woods road at 0.8 mile, the trail turns left. To the right, a woods road heads downhill to Route 9. The Vernal Pool Trail crosses another stone wall and goes gradually uphill. It passes through a former meadow at 1.0 mile, reaches the Upland Trail, and turns left to join it, closing the loop.

DRIVING: From Route 9 at the Annsville Circle, just north of Peekskill, go north 0.6 mile and turn right onto Roa Hook Road at a traffic light. When Roa Hook Road ends at Highland Avenue, turn right and take an immediate left onto Sprout Brook Road. Go 0.3 mile to parking to the right, just past the parking lot for the athletic fields in Sprain Brook Park [41.313854N 73.924137W]. The entrance to Hudson Highlands Gateway is through a gap in the guardrail on the opposite side of the road.

To reach the Annsville Creek Trail from off Doris Lee Drive, follow the directions from Annsville Circle. But instead of turning right, cross Highland Avenue and turn left onto Old Albany Post Road, which parallels Highland Avenue. Turn right onto Doris Lee Drive to end at the parking lot [41.312298N 73.927311W].

PUBLIC TRANSPORTATION: None available

For contact information, see Appendix, Cortlandt.

Hunt-Parker Memorial Sanctuary

Lake Katonah • 4.6 miles, 338 acres

Home to a wide variety of birds, Hunt-Parker Memorial Sanctuary has an array of options for short or long hikes. With the yellow trail into Mt. Holly Sanctuary just 275 yards north on North Salem Road, a full day of hiking is possible at these two sanctuaries. The diverse habitat here includes open meadow, wetland, and upland forest. About 50 species of butterflies live in the meadow at various times from spring until fall.

In the mid 1970's, James Ramsay Hunt, Jr. (a deputy director of the Central Intelligence Agency), his wife Eleanor Pratt Hunt, and their son W. Barnes Hunt donated property to the National Audubon in the name of James Ramsay Hunt, III. Later, gifts from other family members enlarged the sanctuary and in 2001 a bequest by Mary Welsh Parker added another 100 acres. Her 1720s farmhouse, Bylane, is now headquarters for the Bedford Audubon Society, owner of the sanctuary since its transfer in 1990.

TRAILS

With trails of different lengths, it is easy to spend as much time as one would like at Hunt-Parker Memorial Sanctuary, either briskly walking or just quietly observing. Two entrances to the sanctuary have parking, but the short orange-blazed trails that provide neighborhood access do not.

A 0.3-mile access trail starts from North Salem Road and follows a boardwalk next to an 8-foot wide stone wall and ends at the Katonah Ridge and Swamp Maple trails. Starting at the kiosk, the Meadow Trail (white) heads uphill and turns left

A monument to a farmer's toil.

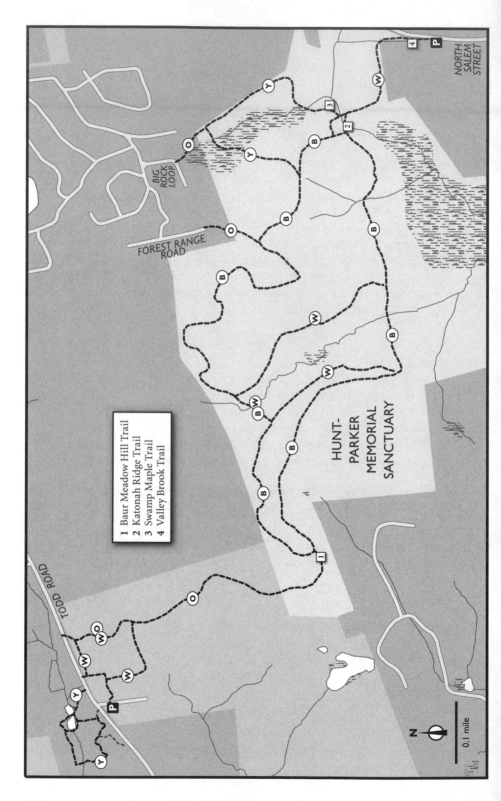

1 Baur Meadow Hill Trail
2 Katonah Ridge Trail
3 Swamp Maple Trail
4 Valley Brook Trail

HUNT-
PARKER
MEMORIAL
SANCTUARY

BIG
ROCK
LOOP

FOREST RANGE
ROAD

TODD ROAD

NORTH
SALEM
STREET

N

0.1 mile

to join the Baur Meadow Hill (orange) at 0.2 mile. Both trails descend through the woods, turn to parallel Todd Road, and end at the kiosk. Behind the house, the Pond Trail (yellow) circles a small pond and goes through woodlands, meadow, and a native plant garden before ending at 0.2 mile at the front door of the farmhouse.

Baur Meadow Hill Trail

Length: 0.6 mile Blaze: orange

Serving as the main access route to the trails on the ridge, the Bauer Meadow Hill Trail starts next to Todd Road where it is co-aligned with the Meadow Loop Trail (white). They parallel the road and turn to head uphill, where at 0.2 mile the Meadow Loop Trail turns right to return to the parking lot. Ascending more steeply, the Bauer Meadow Hill Trail leaves the fields and enters the open woods with no understory. It continues to climb and ends the Katonah Ridge Trail.

Katonah Ridge Trail

Length: 2.2 miles Blaze: blue

To reach the highest areas in the sanctuary, take the Katonah Ridge Trail. From the junction with entrance trail from North Salem Road and the Swamp Maple Trail (yellow), the Katonah Ridge Trail heads straight. At the next intersection, continue straight to go clockwise around the loop. The Katonah Ridge Trail continues through the wetland on puncheon. At 0.4 mile, it passes the White Loop Trail and then its other end at 0.7 mile. Continuing uphill, the trail reaches the Baur Trail (orange) at 1.0 mile. The Katonah Ridge Trail turns first to ascend and then to descend steeply. The White Loop Trail joins from the right at 1.3 miles and the co-aligned trails cross a bridge. At 0.4 mile, the White Loop Trail leaves to the right. From the high point of the sanctuary at 1.7 miles, the Katonah Ridge Trail descends, sometimes more steeply than others. It turns right at 2.0 miles where an orange trail leads 0.1 mile to Forest Range Drive, a local road (no parking). The Katonah Ridge Trail passes the Swamp Maple Trail to the left at 2.1 miles, and closes the loop at 2.2 miles at the entrance trail.

Swamp Maple Trail
Length: 0.5 mile Blaze: yellow
Even though there is wood planking in some wet areas, you still could get wet feet walking along the Swamp Maple Trail. Beginning at the intersection of the White Loop (white) and the Katonah Ridge Trail (blue), the Swamp Maple Trail crosses wetlands on bog bridges. At 0.3 mile, it turns left where a 0.1-mile orange-blazed connector trail heads straight to Big Rock Loop, a local road (no parking). The Swamp Maple Trail ends at the Katonah Ridge Trail.

White Loop Trail
Length: 0.7 mile Blaze: white
Providing an alternate to climbing to the top of the ridge, the White Loop Trail parallels the sides of a valley. At 0.3 mile it turns left to join the Katonah Ridge Trail. Together they cross a bridge and go uphill. At 0.4 mile, the trails split with the Katonah Ridge Trail ascending from the valley. The White Loop Trail turns left to parallel the stream and returns to the Katonah Ridge Trail.

NEARBY PARKS: Grierson-Yarrow preserves, Mount Holly Preserve, Mount Holly Sanctuary, Rose Preserve

DRIVING: For the Todd Road entrance, take I-684 to Exit 6 (Route 35). Turn east onto Route 35. Turn left on Route 22 and go 0.8 mile to Todd Road. Turn right and go 0.7 mile to the parking area to the right [41.282833N 73.670753W].

For the North Salem Road entrance, take I-684 to Exit 6 (Route 35). Turn east onto Route 35. In 1.0 mile, turn left onto unpaved Mt. Holly Road. At the T junction, turn left onto North Salem Road. The entrance is to the left, 0.1 mile from the turn, with parking for three cars [41.275174N 73.650526W].

PUBLIC TRANSPORTATION: None available

For contact information, see Appendix, Bedford Audubon Society.

Kitchawan Preserve

Kitchawan • 5.0 miles, 208 acres

Extremely popular with people who enjoy taking man's best friend on a hike, Kitchawan Preserve is dog heaven, although there's no need to feel out of place if you're without one. The woods roads offer ample opportunities to stroll and chat with other hikers. Although posted signs state that dogs must be kept on a leash no longer then six-foot long, this regulation is, unfortunately, routinely ignored by many dog owners.

Kitchawan Preserve supports a diversity of flora and fauna in a variety of habitats, largely because of its size and its location next to the New Croton Reservoir. Vernal pools grace the preserve, providing breeding habitat for many species of amphibians and invertebrates. The old fields are excellent areas to view butterflies on meadow wildflowers as well as a diversity of field and shrub-dwelling birds. Two prominent riparian habitats are the gems of the preserve.

One stream passes through a beech forest with old trees, where the songs of thrushes reverberate on summer evenings. Local lore reports that the hemlock ravine is original forest where the trees have never been cut. Many majestic old-growth hemlocks are found in the steep ravine of Big Brook and forest birds can be heard overhead in spring. Although many of the native wildflowers have been lost due to deer overpopulation, a few lady's slippers still grow in some sites.

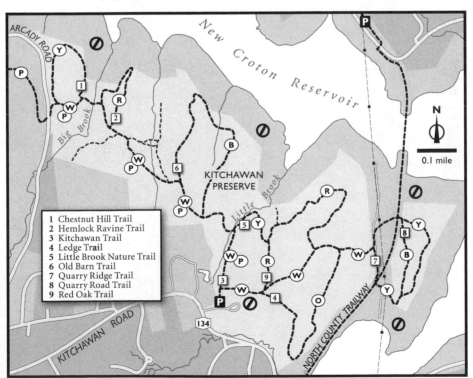

1 Chestnut Hill Trail
2 Hemlock Ravine Trail
3 Kitchawan Trail
4 Ledge Trail
5 Little Brook Nature Trail
6 Old Barn Trail
7 Quarry Ridge Trail
8 Quarry Road Trail
9 Red Oak Trail

TRAILS

Many of the trails at Kitchawan Preserve traverse land that in the 1890s was still pasture. The northern boundary of the preserve is stone walls capped with flat rocks and built around the turn of the twentieth century. Some trails continue into watershed lands of the New York City DEP which border the reservoir, but these trails are open only to those who hold fishing permits.

Two short trails in the western section of the preserve start and end on the Kitchawan Trail. The Hemlock Ravine Trail (red) goes towards the reservoir along a well-worn woods road. It reaches a stone wall delineating the DEP watershed property and makes a U-turn to parallel the wall. It turns right, descends to meet a woods road, and turns left. Heading slightly uphill and avoiding a wet area, the Hemlock Ravine Trail ends at the Kitchawan Trail.

The Chestnut Hill Trail (yellow) loops through open forest for 0.3 miles around Chestnut Hill and ends near Arcady Road.

Kitchawan Trail   *Length: 1.6 miles Blaze: white*

The Kitchawan Trail starts at the parking lot and goes east and west as the spine for all the trails. The section heading west is co-aligned with the Teatown-Kitchawan Trail (TK) (purple) until the white-blazed Kitchawan Trail ends at Arcady Road. At a broad intersection just past the parking lot, the east section of the Kitchawan Trail turns right and ends at the North County Trailway in 0.6 mile; the west section with both white and purple blazes continues straight and ends at Arcady Road in 1.0 mile.

To the right at the end of the access trail, the Kitchawan Trail follows a wide and well-used woods road. At 0.1 mile, it first passes the junction with the Ledge Trail (orange) to the right and then the Red Oak Trail (red) to the left. Continuing

Bridge over Little Brook.

uphill at 0.3 mile, it passes the Red Oak Trail a second time and then the Ledge Trail again. Heading downhill, the Kitchawan Trail reaches the power line right-of-way and its service road at 0.5 mile. To the right is the Quarry Ridge Trail (yellow). The Kitchawan Trail briefly follows the power line access road and then turns right. The access road continues straight to eventually enter watershed lands of the New York City DEP. After passing under the power lines, the Kitchawan Trail reaches the North County Trailway where it ends at 0.6 mile.

At the end of the access trail, the co-aligned Kitchawan and TK trails head straight. They follow Little Brook and reach a bridge. Straight ahead the Little Brook Nature Trail connects to the Red Oak Trail in 0.2 mile. The co-aligned trails turn left to cross Little Brook and turn left again to head steeply uphill. As they enter an orchard and the first of four fields, they pass the Old Barn Trail (blue) immediately to the right. Once in the field which had been the Brooklyn Botanic Garden's demonstration garden, the trails turn right and follow a well-worn path. Entering the next field, at 0.4 mile, they pass the Old Barn Trail and then go into the third field. An unmarked equestrian trail leaves to the left, as does a second one, just past where the trails exit the last field at 0.6 mile. The co-aligned trails turn left at the intersection with the Hemlock Ravine Trail (red). Descending, they turn left to cross a stone wall, while straight ahead is the other end of the Hemlock Ravine Trail. Heading uphill, the co-aligned trails wander through the woods to pass the Chesnut Hill Trail twice and then Arcady Road, at 1.0 mile, where the Kitchawan Trail ends and the TK turns left and continues 5.6 miles to Teatown Lake Reservation.

Ledge Trail
Length: 0.6 mile Blaze: orange

Beginning on the Kitchawan Trail (white), the Ledge Trail gently curves left and passes an occasional rock cairn. It heads uphill onto a ledge where the traffic below on Route 134 is both audible and visible. The Ledge Trail follows a stone wall briefly and heads uphill. At 0.5 mile, it passes through a low ravine and ends at the Kitchawan Trail at 0.6 mile.

Old Barn Trail
Length: 0.7 mile Blaze: blue

From the co-aligned Kitchawan (white) and TK trails (purple), the Old Barn Trail follows along a woods road through open woods and reaches the foundation of an old barn at 0.2 mile. Two large Norway spruces are part of what once was the summer home of Fernando Wood, (see sidebar). It had overlooked the Croton Reservoir before it was demolished years ago. The Old Barn Trail turns left onto a path through barberry bushes. It crosses a narrow stream on stepping stones and heads uphill. Paralleling the stone wall boundary of DEP watershed property, the trail skirts the base of a hill while continuing its ascent. It turns left to join a woods road at 0.4 mile. Passing a stone fireplace to the right, the Old Barn Trail descends into a former orchard. It ends in a field at the Kitchawan Trail.

Quarry Ridge Trail
Length: 0.5 mile Blaze: yellow

Beginning at the power line righ-of-way on the Kitchawan Trail (white), the Quarry Ridge Trail goes under the lines. It crosses the North County Trailway at 0.1 mile while still in the power line right-of-way. At the far side of the right-of-way, the Quarry Ridge Trail turns to enter the woods. To the left at a large sugar maple is the Quarry Road Trail (blue), a 0.2-mile shortcut to the North County Trailway which passes an old quarry, likely to have supplied stone for building the old Putnam Line. The trail follows the quarry rim on top of the ridge and then, at 0.4 mile, heads downhill. The trail passes Quarry Road Trail again and ends at the North County Trailway.

Red Oak Trail
Length: 0.6 mile Blaze: red

Beginning on the Kitchawan Trail (white), the Red Oak Trail goes through a stone wall and along a woods road. It passes the Little Brook Nature Trail and then at 0.2 mile, an unmarked trail into lands that are part of New York City watershed. The Red Oak Trail skirts along the base of a hill to the right and heads uphill. It levels off at 0.5 mile and turns left to end at the Kitchawan Trail.

CONNECTING TRAILS: North County Trailway, Teatown-Kitchawan Trail

DRIVING: From the Taconic State Parkway, take the Route 134 Exit and turn east. The preserve entrance is 1.2 miles past the entrance to the IBM T. J. Watson Research Center. It is to the left just beyond a sharp turn right, where a sign for 712 ARAIM Warren Institute is visible at the entrance to the park [41.220541N 73.786406W].

PUBLIC TRANSPORTATION: None available

For contact information, see Appendix, Westchester County Parks.

Lasdon Park, Arboretum, and Veterans Memorial

Somers • 4.5 miles, 234 acres

Of all the beautiful parks in Westchester County, Lasdon Park may be the most beautiful. To decide for yourself, visit this well-manicured park in the spring when trees and ornamental plants are in bloom and the place is ablaze with color. Located on the former estate of William and Mildred Lasdon, the park has a massive lawn rolling up from Route 35 with a lone sugar maple standing sentinel beside the entrance road.

In 1939, William and Mildred Lasdon purchased what was originally called Cobbling Rock Farm and used it as a summer residence. William Lasdon was a pharmaceutical company executive and philanthropist. Because of his interest in horticulture, Lasdon imported many tree specimens found during his worldwide travels. He had them planted here on his country retreat. As part of its efforts to obtain and preserve open space, Westchester County purchased the Lasdon estate in 1986 for $4.2 million.

Since its acquisition, the county has retained much of the design of the formal grounds and has embellished the collections. In the process Lasdon Park has become the horticultural hub of Westchester County parks with offices for horticultural groups, display space for horticultural and botanical art, and a volunteer-run plant shop offering information and selling garden related items. The park contains special collections of trees, his azalea garden, magnolia grove, and dwarf conifer collection and memorials to the armed forces. A walk at Lasdon Park can be a special interest stroll through these collections or an easy hike along blazed woodland trails.

Manor House.

A portion of the park is fenced to prevent marauding deer from devastating the major tree and plant collections, the formal gardens, and the plantings around the house. The shop, greenhouses, and a Veterans Museum are inside the enclosure because of their proximity to the house, which serves as the park office.

Three groups are active in the park: the Friends of Lasdon Park and Arboretum, the Vietnam Memorial Committee, and the Vietnam Veterans of America, Westchester County Chapter 49.

BLAZED WOODLAND TRAILS

All the blazed woodland trails except for the green trail were part of the equestrian trail system at the Lasdon estate and are suitable for cross-country skiing. A detailed map is available at a pavilion at the upper parking lot. The red, green, and yellow trails can be reached from the lower main parking lot by following the handicapped accessible path past the Merchant Marine Memorial and turning left onto a woods road, a walk of 0.1 mile. The blue trail is accessible from the parking lot at the end of the left fork of the entrance road.

To reach the trail system on the west side of the entrance road from the end of the yellow trail, head uphill directly towards the crown of the sugar maple on the entrance road. After reaching the tree, turn slightly left toward a green sign and a utility line. The Trail of Famous and Historic Trees begins just past the left-most utility pole. Alternately, continue on the paved road to the parking lot for the Chinese Friendship Pavilion and the Famous and Historic Tree Trail.

Yellow Trail   *Length: 0.5 mile Blaze: yellow*
From the handicapped accessible path, the yellow trail continues along a woods road, passing the junction with the red trail to the right. Continuing through open

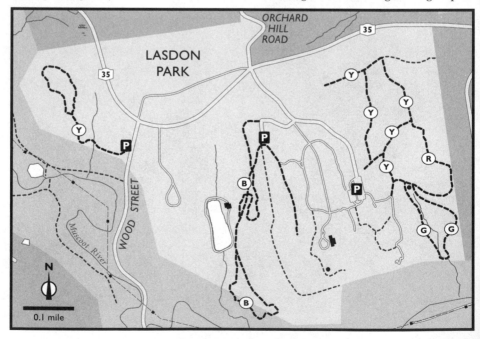

forest it passes an unmarked trail to the left leading to the upper parking lot. At the end of the red trail at 0.2 mile, the yellow trail goes left through a white pine plantation. It passes a trail to the right near a Lasdon Arboretum sign, reaches a T junction with a woods road, and turns left. After passing an unmarked woods road that leads 0.2 mile back to the parking lot, the yellow trail crosses two seasonal streams and ends at 0.5 mile at the lawn.

Blue Trail   *Length: 0.6 mile Blaze: blue*

Starting at the parking lot on the west side of the park, the blue trail follows the outer fence on an unpaved road and crosses the Trail of Historic Trees. Passing through a Chinese arch, it crosses a grassy area beside a pond and heads into the woods. When the trail splits at 0.3 mile, turn right. The blue trail heads uphill through an open forest and passes ruins of two buildings. It turns right off the woods road, descends steeply, and turns onto a woods road. Turning as it heads uphill, the trail crosses a bridge over a seasonal stream, and closes the loop.

Green Trail   *Length: 0.4 mile Blaze: green*

To the right of the gazebo on the red trail, the green trail heads straight downhill through an open area. It parallels a stream and turns to cross it at 0.2 mile. Heading uphill, the green trail reaches a woods road and turns left. The trail passes through an open area to close the loop back at the gazebo.

SPECIALIZED WALKS AND UNMARKED WOOD ROADS

Your favorite plant is likely to be in a collection somewhere in the arboretum. Unmarked trails in or around the special collections encourage a slow pace and offer opportunities for contemplation, reflection, or taking photographs.

The woods road following the west side of the outer perimeter of the fence is 0.4 mile long. A 0.6-mile gravel and dirt road system is inside the fence, as well as the 0.3-mile connection to the American chestnut trees northwest of the mansion. The numerous short paths meander through collections.

The Chinese Friendship Pavilion & Culture Garden has a 0.3 mile trail which circles a pond. This garden recognizes the close ties between Westchester County and Jingzhou in the Peoples Republic of China.

Blue Star Memorial By-Way honors U.S. armed forces as well as veterans of wars fought by the United States. Busts, statues, and memorial trees line the 0.4 mile paved path, which is handicapped-accessible.

The Famous and Historic Tree Trail is a 0.4 mile gravel path lined with trees honoring people and events in American history. Interpretive signs provide information about the person or event, the tree's relevance, and its species.

Just west of Lasdon Park is the Mildred D. Lasdon Bird and Nature Sanctuary, created in 1976, when William Lasdon donated 22 acres to the county to establish it in memory of his wife. It is home to many birds, including 20 species of breeding warblers. To reach the sanctuary from Lasdon Park, head west on Route 35; make the first left turn onto Wood Street. Make a right turn into a small parking area [41.277632N 73.746388W]. From the parking lot, the trail goes along a mowed strip and downhill to cross a causeway. It enters the woods and splits into a loop; head counterclockwise. After crossing stone walls and passing through an expanse of hay-scented ferns at 0.3 mile, the trail closes the loop at 0.5 mile.

NEARBY PARKS: Angle Fly Preserve, Muscoot Farm

DRIVING: From I-684, take Exit 6 (Route 35) west for 3.6 miles to the park entrance to the left [41.280073N 73.741452W].

PUBLIC TRANSPORTATION: None available

For contact information, see Appendix, Westchester County Parks—Lasdon.

Along the Muscoot River

Somers • 1.3 miles

The Muscoot River is the outflow of the Amawalk Reservoir. High or swift flowing water prevents safe river crossings. Just south of the entrance to the Lasdon Bird and Nature Sanctuary on Wood Street [41.277632N 73.746388W], an unmarked fisherman's path heads north along the Muscoot River, passing a non-functioning dam. The quality of the footpath varies over the 0.9-mile walk north to Route 35. Another fisherman's path begins on Pinesbridge Road, a short distance south of the junction with Route 35 [41.285906N 73.765845W]. It heads along the south side of Hallocks Mill Brook and then on the west side of the Muscoot River where the two join. The path leads 0.7 mile to the dam and continues another 0.7 mile further south.

Leon Levy Preserve

Vista • 4.5 miles, 383 acres

T he Leon Levy Preserve is tranquil, scenic, and, since 2005, protected from development. The property contains a ravine with 25-foot high cliffs, extensive wetlands, and hardwood forests. It harbors a variety of wildlife and protects the New York City watershed. A mansion in ruins adds to the charm of the preserve. Old stone walls are located throughout the property.

Formerly known as the Bell property, the preserve is named in memory of its principal benefactor. Leon Levy's love of Lewisboro and for nature came together in the purchase of watershed property that local residents had been trying to protect since 1996. Levy, a Wall Street investor, founder of Oppenheimer Funds, and major philanthropist, died in 2003. A family foundation, his widow, Shelby White, and his brother, Jay, provided $5 million of the $8.3 million purchase, which was completed in 2005.

TRAILS

The carriage roads on the property have become hiking trails and are wide enough to allow walking two or three abreast. Extensive stonework is apparent on the many at-grade raised roadbeds. One mile of unmarked woods roads or illegal ATV tracks traverse the preserve. The 0.3 mile white trail connects two places on the

ABANDONED SPLENDOR

In the late 1800's, the Gilded Age was leaving an imprint on northern Westchester and the complexion of this part of the county was changing. Many farms, some dating to Colonial times, were being bought and transformed into summer estates by the urban wealthy. One of the first of these new part-time residents was James M. Crafts, a chemist, professor, and one-time president of the Massachusetts Institute of Technology. In the 1890s, he purchased about 100 acres and built a mansion on top of one of the highest points in South Salem. He also added other buildings including a cottage, icehouse, coach house, garage and a laboratory for his work.

Crafts died in 1917 and the estate was subsequently purchased by the Kaplan family. Because the mansion was not heated and upkeep difficult, the family gravitated to other buildings that had been converted to living space. The mansion, still furnished and all the household goods in place, sat dormant in its remote location, a modern day Siren to adventurous youth, the curious, and vandals. According to *Lewisboro Ghosts: Strange Tales and Scary Sightings* by Maureen Koehl, it was perhaps around this time that locals began calling it the "Black Mansion." In 1959, the family sold the property to Robert Bell and a partner. The property then became known as the Bell estate. The mansion remained untended until an early morning in January 1979, when it caught fire and was destroyed. The cause of the fire is unknown and all that remains is the foundation and some standing walls.

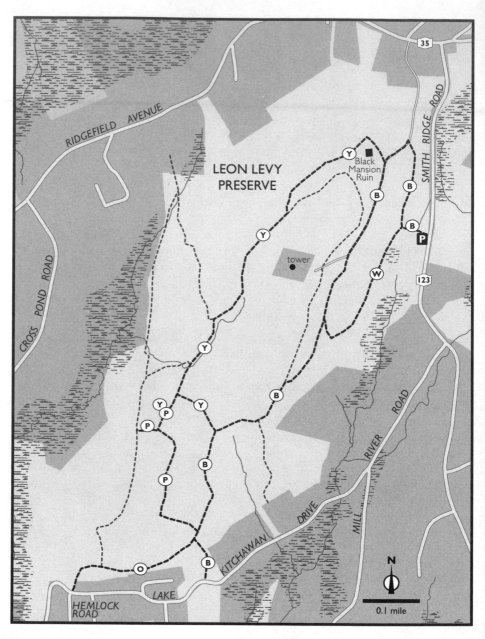

blue trail. It heads south from the entrance parallels wetlands, reaches a hairpin turn with extensive stonework, and ascends to end at the blue trail. On Lake Kitchawan Drive across from Hemlock Road, an orange trail is a neighborhood entrance. It skirts houses as it heads 0.3 mile to connect to the yellow trail.

Blue Trail   *Length: 1.3 miles Blaze: blue*
From the parking lot, the blue trail heads into the preserve and, at a T junction, turns right. It goes uphill and passes the ruins of a stone research laboratory

building to the left. At 0.2 mile, it turns left. It passes the yellow trail to the right which leads up to the site of the Black Mansion. Continuing downhill, the trail passes, to the right at 0.5 mile, the access road to the cell towers. After passing a vernal pool to the left, the blue trail reaches a Y junction with the white trail at 0.7 mile. To the left, just past the intersection, extensive stonework on the white trail is visible below through the trees. The trail passes a rock outcropping, heads downhill, and crosses a ravine on a stone viaduct. At 1.0 mile, the blue trail passes the south end of the yellow trail and continues through open woods.

At 1.1 miles, the trail turns left off the carriage road. Straight ahead the orange trail goes 0.3 mile at Lake Kitchawan Drive (no parking). The blue trail descends, crosses stone walls and a stream to end at Lake Kitchawan Drive (no parking).

Purple Trail *Length 0.3 mile Blaze: purple*
Starting from the blue trail, the purple trail crosses stone walls and, at 0.2 mile, at the top of the rise turns right. After paralleling a stone wall, it reaches a T junction. To the right is the yellow-purple trail which goes to the yellow trail. To the right an unmarked woods road, heads downhill to end at the property line.

Yellow Trail *Length 0.8 mile Blaze: yellow*
From the blue trail, the yellow trail heads uphill towards the site of the former mansion. It goes through the grounds, reenters the woods, and turns right at a Y junction with an unmarked trail 0.1 mile. The yellow trail reaches a small field and goes straight across. The yellow trail reaches a small field and goes straight across. After passing through a narrow row of trees, it crosses a second field with an unmarked trail to the right. The yellow trail enters a wooded area with small trees and heads downhill paralleling a stone wall. At 0.5 mile, it reaches a T junction and turns left through a stone wall. At 0.6 mile, an unmarked woods road to the

Black Mansion - still a lure to the curious.

right heads downhill to end at 0.4 mile in private property. After crossing a stream draining wetlands, the trail turns and goes through a stone wall. At 0.7 mile, it turns left just before reaching a stone wall and continues through open woods. Straight ahead the yellow-purple trail goes approximately 0.1 mile to the purple trail. The yellow trail ends at the blue trail.

DRIVING: From I-684, take Exit 6 (Route 35) and turn east. Continue 9.1 miles and turn right at the traffic light onto Route 123 just before the New York-Connecticut line. Continue south 0.3 mile and just after the sign for the preserve, turn right into the parking lot [41.260874N 73.530020W].

PUBLIC TRANSPORTATION: None available

For contact information, see Appendix, Lewisboro.

Marsh Memorial Sanctuary
Leonard Park

Mt. Kisco • 2.7 miles, 156 acres

Once seemingly devoid of any activity, Marsh Memorial Sanctuary has made a comeback. During the 1970s and 1980s, the sanctuary was a summer camp, but then lay dormant. But with sanctuary signs posted and trails marked, walkers and birders can once again enjoy this preserve. The privately owned sanctuary is open to the public and is managed by Marsh Sanctuary Inc., a nonprofit organization. They partnered with InterGenerate and have established a community garden.

Some of the sanctuary had been Brookside, the home of Martha Leonard, a thespian and gardener, who purchased it before 1900 with the help of her family, who were prominent land owners in the area. She planted extensive gardens and built an amphitheater for plays and concerts she staged there from 1911 into the 1920's. The amphitheater was renovated in 1990.

HONORING A LITTLE GIRL'S LOVE OF NATURE

When Norman and Cornelia Marsh's daughter Cornelia died of a congenital heart ailment at age 10, they wanted to create a memorial to honor her and her love of nature. So, in 1956 they bought a portion of property near the corner of Sarles Street and Byram Lake Road, creating a sanctuary and protecting the wetlands. With subsequent donations of money and land, the sanctuary grew to include the Brookside property.

TRAILS

Trails at Marsh Memorial Sanctuary traverse diverse habitats: woodland, wetland, meadow, stream, and pond. The trails are blazed with a silhouette of a heron on a colored tag. When describing a tag, the background color is first and then the color of the heron. For example, the white/red trail is a white tag with a red heron. The sanctuary has three trailheads: Brookside parking area on Route 172 and the Field and South Trail parking areas on Sarles Street.

BROOKSIDE PARKING AREA

Driving by on Route 172, one does not see the stonework in the amphitheater or the garden. Both give a sense of refinement from a by-gone era. The red/dark blue trail connects to field parking on Sarles Street in 0.4 mile. The 0.3 mile orange/dark blue and the 0.2 mile red/yellow trails wander through the sanctuary in the vicinity of the amphitheater and then up to the red/dark blue trail.

FIELD PARKING AREA

A former chicken coop and a kiosk greet visitors to the 0.7 mile trail system. The 0.4-mile red/dark blue trail connects to trails at Brookside parking. The 0.2 mile

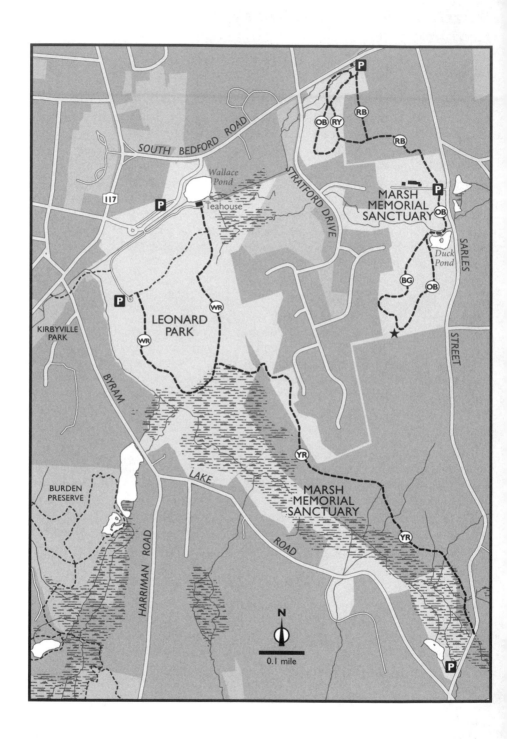

Open air seating for the amphitheater.

light blue/green trail makes a loop with the orange/black trail on the top of a hill. Beginning at the kiosk and chicken coop in a grassy area, the orange/black trail crosses a bridge over a stream. It goes along the shore of a large pond at 0.1 mile and turns left at a junction with the light blue/green trail. Turning away from the pond, the trail enters a field and heads uphill. Entering and leaving fields, it continues uphill and enters woods at 0.3 mile. It heads uphill steeply to reach the top of the hill at 0.4 mile and then a view where it ends with a connection at the light blue/green trail.

SOUTH TRAIL PARKING AREA

Two pullouts across from #286 Sarles Street provide parking for the yellow/red trail that goes 1.1 miles to the white/red trail in Leonard Park. The yellow/red trail enters a mature forest and contours above wetlands. The trail crosses a stream and, at 0.2 mile, leaves the wetlands. It goes through stone walls, crosses a stream and generally drifts uphill. The trail skirts below a house and crosses a stream at 0.8 mile. It is adjacent to a wetland before ending in Leonard Park.

NEARBY PARKS: Merestead, Burden Preserve

DRIVING: Take I-684 to Exit 4 (Route 172) and head west. For Brookside parking (on on Route 172) go 1.5 miles, pass Sarles Street and turn left into the parking area at a barn with a Marsh Sanctuary sign [41.199725N 73.714250W].
Field parking, turn left onto Sarles Street and in 0.3 mile, turn right to park in an open field [41.195603N 73.710566W].
South Trail parking: go another 1.1 miles for roadside parking south of #286 [41.180412N 73.710100W].

PUBLIC TRANSPORTATION: None available

For contact information, see Appendix, Marsh Memorial Sanctuary.

Leonard Park

Mt. Kisco • 1.0 mile, 120 acres

Since 1917, Leonard Park has been a public open space, named after the Leonard family who had an estate in the area. Beginning behind a teahouse on Wallace Pond in the park are one marked and several unmarked trails that co-exist with a disc golf course.

A short unmarked trail called Bellusci Way begins near the playground in Leonard Park and goes to Byram Lake Road. Across the street is Kirbyville Park which had been the site of a grist and saw mill dating to the 1780's. Some stone work and the millstone are still there. The mill had been owned by the Kirby family which gave its name to the area and to a pond it used for the mill. The mill operated into the 1880's, when it was drained in an attempt to control malaria. The Kirby family sold the property to the Leonard family to add to their estate.

White/Red Trail
Length: 0.7 mile Blaze: white/red

Behind the teahouse, the white/red trail begins on a well-trod path and passes an unmarked trail leading to the sledding hill. The white/red trail turns left at a Y junction at 0.2 mile and crosses a ridge. It passes wetlands and follows the base of a hill in open forest. At 0.5 mile, it passes the red/yellow trail which goes 1.1 miles to Sarles Street. Unmarked trails to the right lead to parts of the disc golf course or back onto the main trail. The white/red trail ends near golf basket #9.

DRIVING: From I-684, take Exit 4 and head west on Route 172 for 1.9 miles. The park is located to the left [41.324734N 73.824787W].

PUBLIC TRANSPORTATION: Beeline Bus #19 to Northern Westchester Hospital and walk along Route 172.

For contact information, see Appendix, Mt. Kisco.

The Teahouse at Wallace Pond.

Marx Preserve
Brownell Preserve

Goldens Bridge • 3.8 miles, 228 acres

O ff Route 138 are two preserves linked by an AT&T right-of-way. Marx Preserve, a 110 acre preserve of the North Salem Open Land Foundation (NSOLF), borders the route, while about a half mile west behind private property is the entrance to the 118-acre Brownell Preserve, a Town of Lewisboro park.

Although Marx Preserve has no blazed trails, there are clearly defined pathways, some of which are the result of illegal ATV use. The gentle terrain, woods roads, and tracks make it suitable for snowshoeing and cross-country skiing. The open-forest tracks along the northeast section of Marx are the more pleasurable in both preserves. The path on the AT&T right-of-way links to the blazed trails at Brownell Preserve. The preserve was established in 1976 by the Marx Family.

Lewisboro residents Katharine and George Brownell established the preserves in 1984 with the bequest of open space to be used for wildlife habitat and passive recreation. He was an envoy to Mexico and India during the Truman Administration.

T R A I L S

A 50-foot entrance trail leads into Brownell Preserve and ends at the AT&T cable right-of-way marked with widely-spaced orange posts. The right-of-way connects the two preserves and is the spine of trails in Brownell Preserve. Devastation from Hurricane Sandy in 2012 is evident. Trails in the Brownell Preserve are blazed with colored tags. On many trees along the trails are thick hairy poison ivy vines which are as toxic as the leaves. Touch them at your own peril!

Blue Trail in Brownell Preserve
Length: 1.8 miles Blaze: blue
In order to form a loop through Brownell Preserve, the blue trail uses the AT&T right-of-way which, at times, is not well marked with blazes. From the entrance to the preserve, head clockwise around the loop. At 0.1 mile, it passes a yellow trail to the right providing a 0.2-mile shortcut to the other side of the loop. Just past a stone wall, the blue trail turns left off the AT&T line. After heading steadily uphill, the trail curves into an area with little understory except for barberry bushes. At 0.5 mile, the forest closes in a bit and the trail turns right to join a woods road. The blue trail reaches the AT&T line at 0.7 mile and turns left. Straight ahead is the orange trail which heads downhill, paralleling a stream and stone wall to end in 0.2 mile at the blue trail.

Vines as toxic as the leaves.

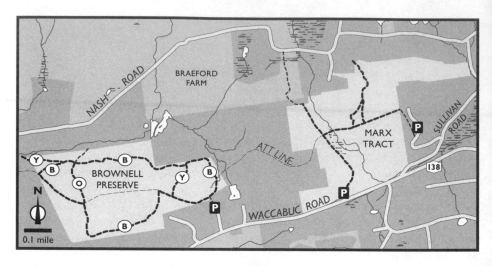

At 0.9 mile, at post #468, the blue blazes reappear on the right-of-way as the trail turns to head downhill. It passes a large sugar maple to the left and then the yellow trail, which descends for 0.1 mile to end at a breached dam. At 1.1 miles, the blue trail intersects the orange trail to the right. Going uphill, the blue trail crosses a series of seasonal streams and passes a large boulder at 1.3 miles. Continuing uphill, the blue trail turns to cross a seasonally wet area. Just beyond a stream crossing at 1.6 miles near the property boundary, it passes the yellow trail to the right which heads uphill 0.2 mile to the AT&T line.

After turning left and crossing a stone wall, the blue trail turns to follow it. The blue trail ends at the AT&T line where, to the right, it is 0.1-mile walk back to the entrance road. To the left, it is 0.5 mile to the Marx Tract.

DRIVING: From I-684 take Exit 6 (Route 35) and head east on Route 35 for 0.1 mile. Turn left onto Route 22 and go 1.9 miles. Make a right turn past a shopping center and follow signs to Route 138. Turn right onto Route 138. To reach Marx Tract continue on Route 138 for 0.7 mile and turn left onto Sullivan Road. Take the first left and drive to the end [41.304760N 73.623446W]. For Brownell Preserve, continue 2.1 miles to Harriet Lane to the left, with parking for two cars at the end [41.300625N 73.638433W].

PUBLIC TRANSPORTATION: None available

For contact information, see Appendix, Lewisboro.

Mt. Holly Sanctuary

Katonah • 3.4 miles, 208 acres

At the Mount Holly Sanctuary, a visitor can be immersed in a symphony of nature, unpunctuated by human noise. Ponds resonate with a chorus of frogs and birds trill against the rolling rustle of leaves. Having the place to oneself in midweek day in season makes it a delight to visit.

Until the twentieth century, except for the steep sections, the land that is now the Mount Holly Sanctuary was farmed. In 1975, the threat of development led concerned citizens to join together to purchase the land from the estate of Edward A. Norman. The numerous stone walls add to the beauty of the place. Mount Holly Sanctuary is not to be confused with the smaller Mount Holly Preserve, located across and south on Mount Holly Road.

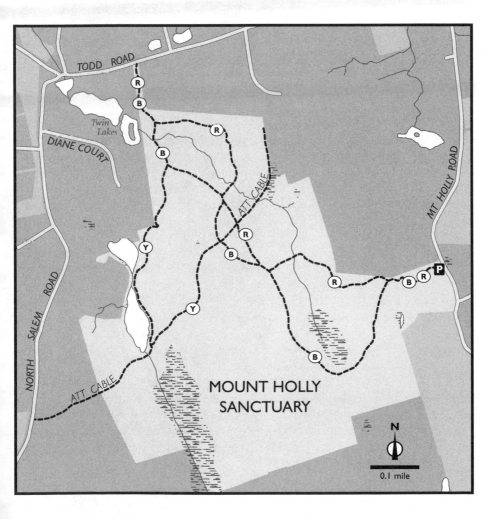

Wetland.

TRAILS

Horses and hikers use the trails of Mount Holly Sanctuary which has a varied topography. The two main trails begin at the parking area on Mount Holly Road. The Pond Trail and the steep portion of the North Main Trail are closed to horses. The entrance to the white trail into Hunt-Parker Memorial Sanctuary is 275 yards south on North Salem Street. A full day of hiking is possible by visiting these two sanctuaries.

South Main Trail   *Length: 1.3 miles Blaze: blue*
From the parking area on Mount Holly Road, the South Main Trail (blue) and the North Main Trail (red) head past the kiosk. At 0.1 mile, they go through a stone wall and split at a T junction, with the South Main Trail heading left. It heads along the edge of the property and then goes gently downhill, crossing numerous stone walls. The trail reaches and briefly joins the North Main Trail at 0.7 mile and continues to descend. At 0.8 mile, the South Main Trail crosses the AT&T right-of-way and heads more seriously downhill.

The North Main Trail briefly joins the South Main Trail for a second time at a stone wall at 0.9 mile; they separate at a Y junction with the South Main Trail going left. Continuing downhill, the South Main Trail passes the Pond Trail (yellow) to the left, crosses the inlet to a lake on stepping stones, and then joins the North Main Trail for the third and last time. They descend together past houses to the entrance at Todd Road (no parking).

North Main Trail
Length: 1.1 miles Blaze: red

From the entrance at Todd Road, the North Main Trail and the South Main Trail (blue) head uphill. At 0.1 mile, they split with the North Main Trail going left and heading steeply uphill. At 0.4 mile, it crosses a stream and is briefly co-aligned with the South Main Trail. Continuing uphill, it crosses the AT&T right-of-way at 0.5 mile and joins the South Main Trail a second time. The North Main Trail goes gradually uphill and through barberry bushes at 0.7 mile. After reaching the crest of the hill, the trail crosses stone walls and skirts the edge of the property. It joins the South Main Trail for the last time at 1.0 mile. Together they go through a stone wall and end at the parking area on Mount Holly Road.

Pond Trail
Length: 0.5 mile Blaze: yellow

Starting 1.0 mile from the entrance at Mount Holly Road along the South Main Trail (blue), the Pond Trail immediately heads uphill, passing a *No Horses* sign. It passes an unmarked trail to the left at 0.1 mile and then descends. The Pond Trail follows the edge of wetlands on a woods road partially paved with stones. At 0.4 mile, the Pond Trail reaches a pond and passes a trail to the left, occasionally marked orange. The Pond Trail reaches the end of the pond at 0.5 mile, turns right, and crosses the outlet on a causeway. The trail has occasional yellow blazes, but can be followed uphill along a woods road. The left branch of a Y junction leads 0.4 mile to the AT&T right-of-way toward North Salem Road.

AT&T Right-of-Way
Length: 0.9 mile Blaze: occasional

The first section starts near 143 North Salem Road on an unmarked route along the AT&T right-of-way. It parallels a driveway and horse fields to the right. Leaving the right-of-way, it goes downhill and reaches the Pond Trail (yellow) at 0.4 mile.

The second section starts at a *No Horses* sign and takes the unmarked trail to the right with occasional orange posts phone line signs. Heading slightly uphill, at 0.2 mile, the trail joins the right-of-way again and skirts the edge of a seasonally wet open area. It passes the South Main Trail (blue) and then the North Main Trail (red). Crossing a stream at 0.4 mile, the right-of-way passes a vernal pool and shortly after, an unmarked trail. At the crest of the hill, it is necessary to retrace steps because houses on adjacent property block the way.

NEARBY PARKS: Hunt-Parker Memorial Sanctuary, Grierson Sanctuary, Yarrow Preserve, Mount Holly Preserve

DRIVING: From I-684, take Exit 6 (Route 35) and head east for 1.8 miles. Turn left onto North Salem Road and follow it to Mount Holly Road. Turn right at the Y junction and continue 1.2 miles to where Mount Holly Road makes a sharp left. The entrance and parking for three cars is just beyond the intersection with Holly Hill Lane [41.281699N 73.632774W]. There is no parking at the entrances on North Salem and Todd roads.

PUBLIC TRANSPORTATION: None available

For contact information, see Appendix, The Nature Conservancy.

Oscawana Island Park

Crugers • 2.9 miles, 161 acres

The two sections of Oscawana Park offer different experiences. The section adjacent to the Hudson River has wetlands, birding opportunities, and in early fall, monarch butterflies resting here during their trip south. From December 1 to March 1, this section is closed because bald eagles roost there overnight.

Away and up(land) from the river on the east and north sides of Furnace Dock Road, the upland section contains the ruins of the former McAndrews estate. If you are interested in learning to identify trees, many of the trees here are identified with both their common and scientific names.

Oscawana takes its name from the local sachem, Askawanes, one of the original signers of the 1682 deed to Teller of Teller's Point, now Croton Point Park.

TRAILS

Views over the river and wetlands are on the section adjacent to the river. The upland section, with its wide trails passing remnants of many structures and many side trails, begs to be explored. A former race track is 0.4 mile around.

White Trail (Riverview)   *Length: 0.5 mile Blaze: white*
From the parking area on Cortlandt Street, the white trail is along a gravel road. It passes a site for hand launch boats and crosses over the railroad track tunnel at 0.2 mile. After cresting the hill, it passes a side trail to a chimney and reaches a view. Turning to parallel the river, the trail loops back to the entrance trail.

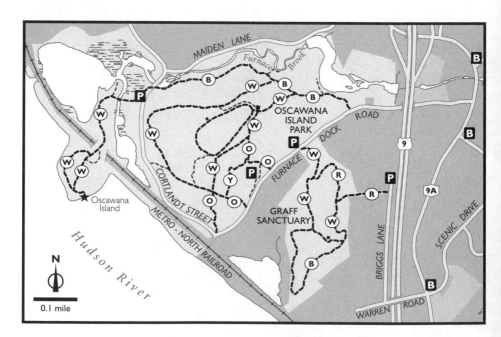

Blue Trail (Upland)
Length: 0.5 mile Blaze: blue

At the gate next to Furnace Brook on Cortlandt Street, the blue trail heads uphill along the Furnace Brook. At 0.3 mile, it turns to ascend more steeply and passes a pump house, more easily seen when heading downhill. At a junction with the white trail, the blue trail heads left. At 0.4 mile an unmarked trail to the left leads 0.2 mile to a view of Furnace Dock Brook. After passing other end of the white trail, the blue trail ends at 0.5 mile at Furnace Dock Road (no parking.)

White Trail (Upland)
Length: 0.6 mile Blaze: white

Many of the remaining ruins of the McAndrews estate are along the white trail. Heading uphill from the second intersection with the blue trail, the white trail passes a stone foundation with pillars and then a former race track to the right. As the trail bears left and leaves the fence, a 0.1 mile orange trail leads to Furnace Dock Road and to a yellow trail which passes ruins of the estate. The white trail heads downhill and reaches an intersection. To the left and straight, two orange trails go to Furnace Dock Road. The white trail continues to the right, passing seasonal views of the Hudson River. While following a fence, the trail curves to parallel the river and then turns away from it. At 0.4 mile, the trail passes below the pump house for the race track. A stone wall supports the race track, which is uphill. The white trail ends at the blue trail.

An Estate in Ruins

McAndrews Estate ruins.

Generations of Westchester residents have been lured to Long View, the McAndrews Estate, a Victorian era estate once owned by Guillaume Reusens, a Belgian-born businessman and racehorse breeder. He assembled the estate from pieces he acquired in the 1880's and built a large house and several other structures on the property, including a race track. When he died in 1915, the property passed to relatives, including Anne and Martin McAndrews. After Mrs. McAndrews death in 1948, her husband moved away and the property fell into disrepair.

Woodlands soon reclaimed the fields and obscured vistas. The ravages of time and vandals added to the destruction of deteriorating buildings. The county sought to condemn the property beginning in 1965 and finalized its purchase from the heirs in 1970. At that time, the derelict buildings were razed, but remnants of them can still be seen: a breeched dam adjacent to wetlands where its pond once existed, a small pump house with remnants of a pump, and a race track. There are miles of fence built with steel pipe. A building best described as 1950s comfort-station architecture was a pump house for the race track. Oscawana Park is managed under an agreement between the County and the Town of Cortlandt.

DRIVING: Take Route 9 to the Route 9A Montrose/Buchanan Exit and turn north onto Route 9A. Turn right onto Furnace Dock Road (west), across from a shopping center and follow it toward the river. At the end of Furnace Dock Road, turn right onto Cortlandt Street, where there is parking [41.224520N 73.920308W]. At 1.1 miles beyond the turn, parking is to the left [41.22732N 73.925721W].

PUBLIC TRANSPORTATION: Beeline Bus #14 stops at the shopping center across the street from Furnace Dock Road.

For contact information, see Appendix, Cortlandt.

Graff Sanctuary

Crugers • 1.1 miles, 30 acres

Tucked behind private homes, Graff Sanctuary is on a wooded hillside with tree-filtered views out over the Hudson River. In 1975, Howard Graff donated the property to the National Audubon Society, which transferred ownership to the Saw Mill River Audubon Society in 1991.

Three trails are through a forest with oak, shagbark hickory and tulip trees. From Briggs Lane, the Jack-in-the-Pulpit Trail (red) goes 0.3 mile into the sanctuary. Access from Furnace Dock Road is steeply uphill via the 0.4 mile Tulip Tree Trail (white). It passes a structure of unknown origin with steps up to a cement platform, which provides a view, probably better when there were fewer trees. The River View Trail (blue) offers limited views along its 0.4 miles.

DRIVING: From Route 9A, just north of Croton-on-Hudson, turn left onto Warren Road, opposite Scenic Drive.** Cross the bridge over Route 9 and immediately turn right onto Briggs Lane [41.226377N 73.912321W]. Parking is at the end of the road beyond the last driveway. Walk up the driveway of #20 to the trailhead into the sanctuary. A second entrance is on Furnace Dock Road, 0.5 mile from its intersection with Route 9A. Limited parking is to the right, across from the sign to Graff Sanctuary [41.227484N 73.91647W].

PUBLIC TRANSPORTATION: Beeline Bus #14 stops at the corner of Route 9A and Scenic Drive. Follow the driving directions from **

For contact information, see Appendix, Saw Mill River Audubon Society.

Structure whose origin is lost to time.

Rockwood Hall

Sleepy Hollow • 3.0 miles, 88 acres

Take a picnic basket, add a sunny day, find the shade of one of Rockwood Hall's many spreading sycamore, maple, or weeping beech trees and you have the recipe for a perfect outing. It has the charm of a small park yet it is large enough to visit many times and still find among its many nooks and crannies new and interesting spots on every visit. Exotic trees, wide paths, and sweeping views make it an enjoyable place to spend the day. Rockwood Hall is managed as a part of Rockefeller State Park Preserve.

TRAILS

Carriage roads of this former estate circle the property, providing a path which overlooks the Hudson River to the Palisades. Although none of the paths are blazed, navigation is easy and there is something interesting around every corner.

The Rockwood Hall Brook Trail goes 0.3 mile from the fields in the north part of the park along Rockwood Hall Brook. After going through small rhododendron groves, it crosses five bridges. It passes a 0.1 mile connection to the Old Croton Aqueduct before ending at an access paved road.

CARRIAGE ROADS AND ORNAMENTAL TREES

In 1886, William Rockefeller (1841-1922), financier and younger brother of John D. Rockefeller, purchased Rockwood, a 200-acre estate overlooking the Hudson, intending it to be his summer home. Accounts vary as to whether he made extensive renovations to the original castle or demolished it to build Rockwood Hall, a 204-room mansion. Frederick Law Olmstead designed the landscape, which includes many unusual ornamental trees. Rockefeller had a carriage road system built. After his death in 1922, his heirs unsuccessfully tried to sell the property to an individual buyer. Eventually, a group purchased the estate and converted it to a country club, which went bankrupt in 1936. A year later, John D. Rockefeller, Jr. bought the estate, leasing the property to another country club, which also was short-lived.

Having no real use for the buildings, Rockefeller had them razed in 1941-1942 and dumped the stones into the Hudson. In 1946, he deeded the property to his son Laurance. IBM purchased 80 acres in 1970 for its world trade center. In the early 1970s, New York State leased the remaining property as a public park for one dollar a year with Laurance underwriting the cost of maintenance. In 1999, he donated the land to the state as part of Rockefeller State Park Preserve. Of the estate buildings, only a gatehouse along Route 9 and the mansion's foundation remain. For more information go to http://rockarch.org/faqs/#miscellaneous and scroll down the page.

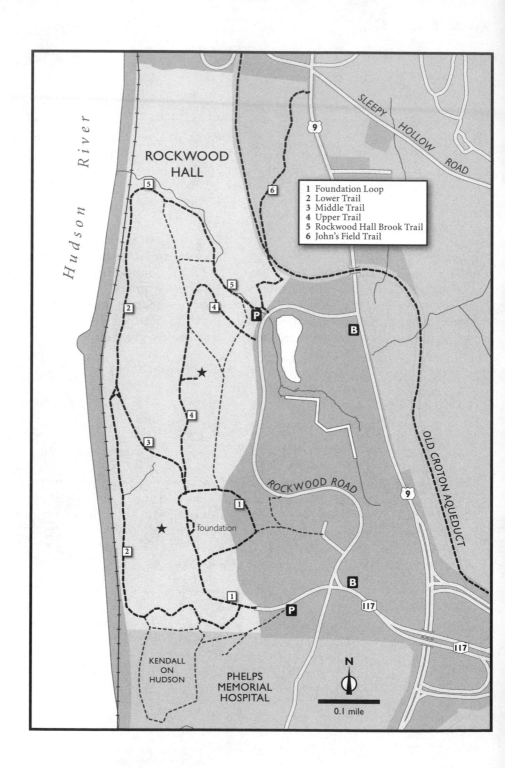

1 Foundation Loop
2 Lower Trail
3 Middle Trail
4 Upper Trail
5 Rockwood Hall Brook Trail
6 John's Field Trail

Hudson River

ROCKWOOD HALL

SLEEPY HOLLOW ROAD

ROCKWOOD ROAD

OLD CROTON AQUEDUCT

foundation

KENDALL ON HUDSON

PHELPS MEMORIAL HOSPITAL

N

0.1 mile

A perfect picnic spot.

Foundation Loop   *Length: 0.6 mile*
Beginning at the end of the parking lot, the Foundation Loop heads uphill. It turns right at a junction where the Lower Trail turns left. Continuing uphill on a surface of paving stones, it passes a massive weeping beech tree to the right at 0.2 mile. Straight ahead are the stone walls that once surrounded the mansion of William Rockefeller. There are sweeping views over the river. On the opposite side of the mansion's foundation, the Foundation Loop turns right, goes downhill along the paved road and curves past copper beeches with an expansive lawn behind them. After passing through stonework that once surrounded buildings, the paved path turns to head uphill. Although the mansion is gone, a sense of grandeur that once flourished is still evident. The Foundation Loop closes the loop at the road near the weeping beech tree.

Lower Trail   *Length: 1.0 mile*
Beginning near the parking lot at the junction with the Foundation Loop, the Lower Trail heads through a rockcut and passes an entrance to Kendall-on-Hudson, a retirement community. At the bottom of the hill, at 0.2 mile, it goes by another entrance and then turns right to parallel the Hudson River with limited views to the Palisades. At 0.6 mile, the Lower Trail passes a junction with the Middle Trail which heads uphill to connect with the Upper Trail. The Lower Trail ends at the Rockwood Hall Brook Trail.

Upper Trail   *Length: 0.5 mile*
From the far side of the foundation of the mansion and off the Foundation Loop, the Upper Trail heads north, almost immediately passing the Middle Trail to the left. Heading uphill on paving stones, it goes through a wooded area which

obscures the view. The path becomes gravel when it reaches an open field. It descends with limited views out over the Hudson River. The Upper Trail passes a large rock outcropping to the right at 0.7 mile. This solid rock platform is just before a mowed path which leads 0.3 mile over the hill and back to the Foundation Loop. To the left 150 feet farther, another mowed path heads downhill for 0.2 mile toward the Rockwood Hall Brook Trail. Both mowed paths offer sweeping views across the Hudson River. The Upper Trail curves to the right, enters the woods, and continues downhill. It ends at a gate on the access road that runs along the border of the property.

CONNECTING TRAIL & PARK: Old Croton Aqueduct, Rockefeller State Park Preserve

DRIVING: From the Taconic State Parkway or Route 9A, take Route 117 west to Rockwood Road where it ends at the parking area [41.111186N 73.861945W]. Alternatively, from Route 9 just north of Tarrytown and south of the junction with Route 117, follow the entrance road to Phelps Memorial Hospital all the way through the hospital facility to a parking area to Rockwood Road.

PUBLIC TRANSPORTATION: Take the Metro-North Hudson Line to Scarborough Station. Walk south for 0.3 mile on River Road to Creighton Lane. Turn right, rejoin River Road briefly. Turn right again to head south on the Old Croton Aqueduct for 0.6 mile to Rockwood Hall. Beeline Bus #13 goes to Rockwood Road, just past the parking areas of Phelps Memorial Hospital.

For contact information, see Appendix, New York State Office of Parks, Recreation and Historic Preservation—Rockefeller State Park Preserve.

St. Matthew's Church Woodlands

Bedford Village • 3.3 miles, 67 acres

Ketchum Sanctuary and The Glebe comprise St. Matthew's Church Woodlands. The sanctuary is former pasture turned woodland and is nestled between ridges and surrounded by private estates. In 1971, Mrs. Kerr Rainsford donated 26 acres to The Nature Conservancy in memory of Arthur Ketchum, pastor of St. Matthew's Episcopal Church from 1923 to 1957. In 2002, The Nature Conservancy conveyed the property to St. Matthew's Church, which cares for the sanctuary and oversees responsibility for the trails on both properties. "Glebe" was traditionally land assigned to a parish priest or pastor for his support.

TRAILS

Some trails in St. Matthew's Church Woodlands are Bedford Riding Lanes Association trails (BRLA) and have yellow blazes. The trails are wide enough to walk two abreast when in The Glebe, but narrow when in the sanctuary. A 0.3 mile Bedford Riding Lanes Association (BRLA) trail links the two parcels. It starts at the bridge and heads uphill on private property. There is 0.9 mile of additional BRLA trails, which either provide access to or crisscross the property.

The Glebe Trail
Length: 0.6 mile Blaze: blue

A large sign welcomes visitors to St. Matthew's Church Woodlands where the Glebe Trail begins. Go clockwise to follow a loop, heading downhill and passing a road to a leaf composting pile. The trail goes by a summer outdoor chapel with a large bell and wood benches. At 0.2 mile, the Glebe Trail passes the access trail to Ketchum Sanctuary, which crosses the bridge over the Beaver Dam River. Heading

Bridging the Beaver Dam River.

upstream on a woods road, the Glebe Trail intersects with BRLA trails. At 0.4 mile, it leaves the woods road, goes through a stone wall, and joins, then leaves, a BRLA trail. The Glebe Trail turns right, paralleling the edge of the parking lot to close the loop at the welcome sign.

Lower Loop Trail
Length: 0.5 mile Blaze: blue
At the end of the BRLA Sanctuary Access Trail, the Lower Loop Trail goes straight and to the right. Continue straight ahead, climbing steeply uphill. The trail curves right and at 0.1 mile at a Y junction, a BRLA trail goes left to reach Route 22 in 0.6 mile. Continuing uphill, the Lower Loop Trail crosses another BRLA trail and turns right at a T junction at 0.2 mile. It passes a rock outcropping and a riding ring on private land to the left. At 0.3 mile, it reaches a Y junction with the Upper Loop Trail (blue) to the left and the 0.1 mile Summit Trail (red) to the right. At the end of the Summit Trail, turn right at the T junction with the Upper and Lower Loop trails. The Lower Loop Trail heads steeply downhill along the parallel stone walls. At a T junction with a BRLA trail, it turns right and closes the loop at the BRLA Sanctuary Access Trail.

Upper Loop Trail
Length: 0.9 mile Blaze: blue
Aside for two small sections, the Upper Loop Trail is off-limits to equestrians. After crossing a BRLA trail, the Upper Loop Trail squeezes through a stone wall. It reaches a road and turns to parallel it. Then it heads downhill at 0.2 mile, crosses a BRLA trail, two seasonal streams and wetlands. After passing two large stones at 0.4 mile, it turns to parallel a stone wall. At a T junction with a BRLA trail, the trail turns right onto a BRLA-blazed woods road and then turns right at 0.5 mile to reenter the wetlands. In quick succession the trail crosses two

1 BRLA Trails
2 Glebe Trail
3 Lower Loop Trail
4 Summit Trail
5 Upper Loop Trail

to Route 22

ARTHUR KETCHUM SANCTUARY

Beaver Dam River

ST. MATTHEW'S CHURCH WOODLANDS

The Glebe

22

N

0.1 mile

A Parish With a Long History

St. Matthew's Episcopal Church has been a fixture of the landscape in Bedford since 1809 when the construction of the Federal-style brick church was completed, but the parish has roots that stretch back to the late 1600's. The area was first settled in 1680 by Puritans when it was still part of Connecticut. When the state line was redrawn in 1693, Bedford became part of New York and the Church of England, (Anglican) was established with the aid of New York's Royal Governor.

After the Revolution, American Anglicans needed to establish a national and autonomous church. The Episcopal Church of America was established and Anglican churches became Episcopal ones. A new state law allowed incorporation of churches by their own determination. The present parish was reformed in 1789 with its church at St. George's, a small building located on what is now Route 117 in Mount Kisco.

When a bequest was left to the parish, the trustees determined they would like a new brick church. In 1803, more than 40 acres were purchased for the site. Because the funds from the bequest were not yet available, John Jay, the former Chief Justice of the Supreme Court and a parishioner advanced the purchase price. The total cost of building it came to $3,012.71 1/2 – somewhat over budget. The burial ground was established in 1812 and the first reference to the parish as St. Matthew's was the next year. Since then, the building has gone through renovations and additions, including a parsonage, assembly hall, church school and, in 1939, the Chapel in the Woods.

bridges and heads to higher ground. Another BRLA trail enters from right and turns right at a Y junction where the Upper Loop Trail goes left. It goes over a stone wall, turns left, and continues right for 100 yards to the Summit Trail (red). Going slightly uphill, it parallels a stone wall and ends at a junction of the Lower Loop and Summit trails at 0.9 mile.

NEARBY TRAILS: Bedford Riding Lanes Association

DRIVING: From I-684, take Exit 6 (Route 35). Head east on Route 35, turn right onto Route 22, and go 3.7 miles to St. Matthew's Church [41.221189N 73.655225W]. Follow the driveway to the parking lots in the rear.

PUBLIC TRANSPORTATION: None available

For contact information, see Appendix, St. Matthews Church.

Silver Lake Preserve

Harrison • 4.8 miles, 236 acres

Established in 1924, Silver Lake Preserve is more than a walk around a lake. It is the site of a Revolutionary War skirmish and of Westchester's first free black community. Fighting at Merritt Hill on October 28, 1776 was part of the Battle of White Plains, when Washington and his army retreated north from New York City. An historical marker erected in the preserve's parking lot on Old Lake Street explains its historical significance.

An African-American community called The Hills was located here. It was founded in the 1770's on land granted by Quakers who had voluntarily freed their slaves. The community existed until 1941, when the last family moved from the area. The 6.5 acre Stony Hill Cemetery is adjacent to the preserve.

TRAILS

Although near a heavily populated section of Westchester County, Silver Lake Preserve, surprisingly, has areas where no road noise can be heard. Stone steps, bridges, and paved areas are along the trails. Even though the stone steps are in disrepair, they add elements of grace and elegance to the preserve. There are 1.3 miles of unmarked trails, not including the ATV tracks near the yellow trail.

Blue Trail   *Length: 0.6 mile Blaze: blue*
Beginning at the north end of the parking lot, the blue trail heads downhill into the woods. At an intersection at 0.1 mile, where the yellow trail goes both ways, the blue trail turns left. The co-aligned trails descend and reach a trail junction at a double tulip tree; the blue trail turns left and the yellow trail goes straight. Heading gradually uphill, the blue trail enters a field and turns left. It follows the

---

MARKING AN HISTORIC COMMUNITY

Just as a tombstone memorializes a past life, the Stony Hill Cemetery adjacent to the Silver Lake Preserve serves as a memorial to the African-American community that once thrived there but is now gone. About 200 residents are buried in the 6.5-acre grounds, some of whom were Civil War veterans who severed with the 29th Connecticut Colored Infantry.

The community had its roots before the Revolutionary War when Quakers in the area freed their slaves and provided the property for the community. The community included houses, a church, school, and the cemetery. Many of the residents were literate and recorded their views and observations in letters to their families. Mt. Hope A.M.E. Zion Church of White Plains, which was founded by members of the Stony Hill community, claims ownership of the cemetery.

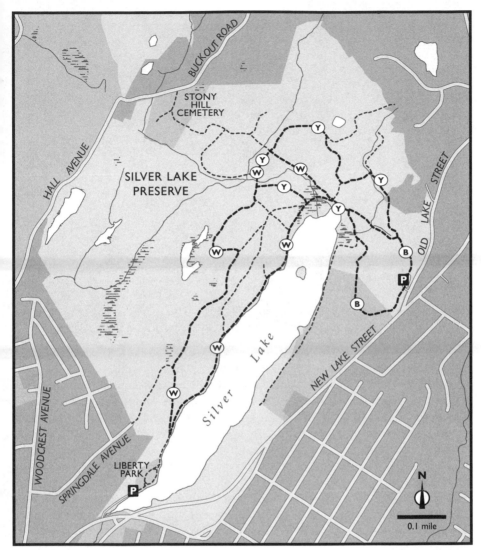

edge of the field as it ascends Merrit Hill. To the right is a cannon marking where a British flank attack was thwarted during the Revolutionary War. The trail reenters the woods on a narrow path at 0.5 mile. It parallels the road and closes the loop at the parking lot entrance.

White Trail
Length: 1.6 miles Blaze: white

At a junction at the bottom of the hill, the blue trail splits to the left and the yellow trail joins the white trail. The co-aligned trails round the end of the lake. At 0.1 mile, the yellow trail turns right and the white trail continues straight and goes up broad steps as it passes an unmarked trail to the right.

The white trail goes along the lake, passing numerous fishing spots. Unmarked trails head uphill to the right. The trail crosses a stream at 0.4 mile and continues along the shore of the lake, until at 0.7 mile, it turns right to head uphill away

More than just a fishing spot.

from the lake. Straight ahead, the unmarked trail leads 0.1 mile to Liberty Park. The white trail heads uphill first gradually and then more steeply, at times on steps. It passes an unmarked trail to the left leading 0.2 mile to Springdale Avenue (no parking). The trail levels off and passes a vernal pool. At 1.0 mile, the white trail crosses a stream and continues uphill. This section contrasts dramatically with the level path along the lake. At an intersection, the trail makes a sharp left; straight ahead the unmarked trail goes 0.1 mile to join an unmarked trail which leads down to the lake.

Curving to the right, the white trail goes through rock outcroppings on both sides of the trail. Descending, it reaches an intersection where an unmarked trail leads 0.1 mile down to the lake. It meets the yellow trail at 1.4 mile, turns left to join it, and crosses a stream. Passing a fireplace, it turns right where the yellow trail continues straight. Descending on steps on a graded path, the white trail closes the loop at 1.6 miles, joining the yellow and white trails coming from the right.

Yellow Trail   *Length: 1.0 mile Blaze: yellow*
Beginning on the blue trail that heads north from the parking lot, the yellow trail is a loop with sections co-aligned with the white and blue trails. To go counterclockwise around the loop, turn right and leave the blue trail. The yellow trail skirts the bottom of a hill and turns left when an unmarked trail heads north into a valley. After descending stone steps, the yellow trail turns right at an intersection where an unmarked trail continues 250 feet downhill to the lake. As the yellow trail ascends on stone steps, it passes, to the right, rock outcroppings with surfaces marked by flowing water. The trail continues uphill and reaches an unmarked woods road leading 0.2 mile through a valley.

Heading downhill, the yellow trail enters a network of former ATV trails. An unmarked trail leads 0.2 mile to the Stony Hills Cemetery. At 0.5 mile, the white trail joins from the left and large flat rocks pave the treadway of the co-aligned trails. The two trails pass a fireplace surrounded by a stone wall and then cross a stream on large flat stones. At a T junction at 0.6 mile, the yellow trail turns left and the white trail continues straight. At 0.7 mile, the yellow trail turns left and joins the white trail entering from the right. Now at lake level, the trails cross two inlet streams and close the loop of the white trail. The two trails reach the blue trail at 0.8 mile, where the white trail ends; the yellow trail joins the blue trail to the left and continues uphill. At 1.0 mile, the yellow trail closes the loop and the blue trail continues uphill to the parking lot.

CONNECTING PARK: Liberty Park at the south end of Silver Lake is an entrance on the trails on the west side of the lake. It was established in 2003 to honor White Plains residents who died in the 9/11 disaster. The City of White Plains has a 30-year lease from Westchester County. The boat launch is open only to White Plains residents. The paved, patterned macadam path is handicapped accessible.

DRIVING: From I-684, take Exit 2 (Route 120) and proceed south for a mile. Turn right onto Lake Street and continue for 1.8 miles; turn right onto Old Lake Street. A parking lot is to the left [41.049487N 73.740436W].

PUBLIC TRANSPORTATION: Metro-North Harlem Line Harrison or White Plains stations. Beeline Bus #5 leaves from those stations and stops at Liberty Park.

For contact information, see Appendix, Westchester County Parks.

Tibbetts Brook Park

Yonkers • 3.3 miles, 161 acres

An historic gazebo and a bathhouse grace Tibbetts Brook Park. The stone and stucco bathhouse with its gabled roof line and neo-classical ornamentation was renovated and modernized in 2012. A woodland buffer surrounds the park's large grassy fields, lake, pond, and brook. The park was opened to the public in June 1927 as Westchester County's first large-scale developed recreational facility. To avoid large crowds using the park to picnic, swim, or play ball, it's best to visit Tibbetts Brook Park either off-season or on weekdays.

The park is named for George Tippet, (other spellings include Tibbetts, Tibbitts, and Tibbit) who settled there in 1668. Along with an adjacent landowner, Jacobus Van Cortlandt, they dammed Tippet's Brook, flooding a portion of both properties to power grist and saw mills, located in what is now Van Cortlandt Park. The mills operated from about 1690 until 1915. Tippet descendants held the property until The Revolution, when it was confiscated due to their Loyalist sympathies.

TRAILS

Walking in Tibbetts Brook Park is along unmarked paved paths and park roads, all easily accessible from the parking lots, neighboring streets, Old Croton Aqueduct, and South County Trailway. A loop around the large lake is 1.1 miles. The loop

Taking advantage of a sunny afternoon.

at the park's north end is 0.9 mile and a loop around the entire park is 2 miles.

There are three access trails from Tibbetts Brook Park to the Old Croton Aqueduct. A paved path at the north end of the park is 0.2 mile; another at the park entrance is 0.1 mile. The third, a 0.1-mile unpaved path is in the southern portion, near restrooms. The 0.8-mile road walk from the entrance booth goes south to the pedestrian entrance at Jervis Road. Several paths on the west side of the park lead to the South County Trailway.

CONNECTING TRAILS: Old Croton Aqueduct, South County Trailway

DRIVING: From the Saw Mill River Parkway, take Exit 4 (Cross County Parkway) and stay in the right lane to get off at the next exit, Yonkers Avenue. At the end of the exit ramp, turn right onto Midland Avenue. The park entrance is 0.5 mile to the right [40.923696N 73.875799W]. A Westchester County resident's pass is required in-season.

From westbound Cross County Parkway, take Exit 3 (Yonkers Avenue East). At the second light, turn right onto Midland Avenue. The park entrance is 0.5 mile to the right [40.923696N 73.875799W].

PUBLIC TRANSPORTATION: Beeline Bus #7 along Yonkers Avenue at the north end of the park, or #4 at McLean Avenue near the Old Croton Aqueduct

For contact information, see Appendix, Westchester County Parks—Tibbetts Brook Park.

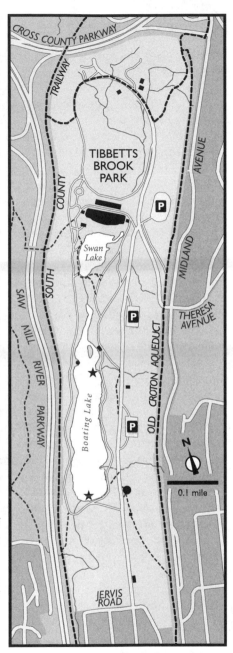

Donald J. Trump State Park

Yorktown Heights and Jefferson Valley • 3.1 miles, 434 acres

Once envisioned as golf courses, two properties adjacent to the Taconic State Parkway and almost 7 miles apart, form the sections of Donald J. Trump State Park. When it was determined they lacked adequate water supplies for golf courses, the projects were abandoned. In 2006, Donald Trump sold the parcels to New York State: the 154-acre French Hill section in the Town of Yorktown and the 282-acre Indian Hill section in the towns of Putnam Valley and Yorktown.

Since the sale, both sections of Trump State Park have been largely ignored. Their development as parkland is hampered by both a lack of funds and a vision of what to do with them. Signs along the Taconic State Parkway indicate what exit to take, but those signs are the only indication that the park exists. However, for the adventuresome, both sections of the park provide opportunities for walking on unmarked and unmaintained farm or woods roads.

Ideas for uses of the French Hill section hinge on cooperative agreements with local groups and could include hiking and mountain biking trails. Those efforts, plus the establishment of the Friends of FDR and Trump State Parks, provide some hope for a better use of the development of the French Hill section.

Aside from abandoned buildings, this section is predominately woodlands. Roads which were made so that test wells could drilled wander through the woods. Posts which supported grapevines are also reminders of how the property had once been used. A plaque honoring William Delavan Baldwin's 1928 donation of 25 acres of his 500-acre estate for the Bronx River Parkway Extension is fixed to a large rock overlooking the Taconic State Parkway [41.2625160N 73.8083870W]. He was the first president of the Westchester County Park Commission and president of Otis Elevator in Yonkers.

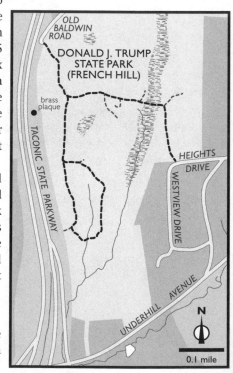

The farm fields in the Indian Hill section are overgrown with invasives, and in places quite dense. It is possible to walk on the property along rutted ATV tracks or on former farm roads. In spring, the flowering apple trees and an occasional dogwood add a splash of color to the vast expanse of green.

NEARBY PARK: Danner Family Preserve

DRIVING: French Hill Section: From the Taconic State Parkway, take the Baldwin

Road exit and turn east. Just past the north bound exit and entrance ramps, turn right onto Old Baldwin Road. The park entrance is at the end of the road [41.266333N 73.806323W].

Indian Hill Section: From the Taconic State Parkway, take the Route 6 exit and turn east. Turn left onto East Main Street after about 100 feet, make a left onto Indian Hill Road. Go uphill for 0.8 mile; the park is to the left [41.339951N 73.806900W].

PUBLIC TRANSPORTATION: None available

For contact information, see Appendix, FDR State Park.

Danner Family Preserve

Jefferson Valley • 0.7 mile, 28 acres

Brer Rabbit would have loved the fields in the Danner Family Preserve which has a myriad of places to hide. Thick with brush and brambles, the fields also provide habitat for shrub-dependent bird species whose numbers have declined. The adjacent forest supports birds that rely on old woodlands to survive. Danner Preserve has no wetlands, which is unusual for protected open space.

As a result of Donald Trump's sale of property across the street to New York State, Eugene and Josephine Danner donated their land to the Westchester Land Trust in 2007. It straddles the border between Putnam and Westchester counties.

The Danner Preserve has three trails, all blazed with Westchester Land Trust green tags. The trail into the property is on a path cut through the brush. Three trails lead from it. Just past a post which indicates the Westchester-Putnam county line, a trail leaves to the right to two small cemeteries and ends at Indian Hill road. Just past the county line, a spur loop trail goes along a wide swath through the brush. It joins the main trail again just before a stone wall which has prevented invasive plants from spreading to the adjacent woodlands. The main trail continues straight where there is a view, unfortunately marred by high-tension power lines. The trail heads downhill, turns to go just below the ridge. It ascends and turns to meet the main trail just before a stone wall.

CONNECTING TRAILS & PARKS: Donald J. Trump State Park – Indian Hill Section

DRIVING: From the Taconic State Parkway, take the Route 6 exit and turn east. Turn left onto East Main Street and in about 100 feet, make a left onto Indian Hill Road. Go uphill for 1.0 mile to the preserve, which is to the right, where there is parking for one car [41.341893 73.803799W]. Please do not park across the street from the entrance.

PUBLIC TRANSPORTATION: None available

For contact information, see Appendix, Westchester Land Trust.

Turkey Mountain Nature Preserve

Yorktown Heights • 3.3 miles, 125 acres

*O*n *a Clear Day You Can See Forever* is the title of a 1965 musical and those words come to mind when enjoying the view from the top of Turkey Mountain, that is of course, if the day is clear. There are few places in Westchester County that have a view to rival the one from Turkey Mountain. Expect to find others enjoying the sweeping view to the west and south toward the Croton Reservoir and the Manhattan skyline in the distance.

From Colonial times until 1917, what is now Turkey Mountain Nature Preserve was owned by members of the Griffen family. Lydia Locke purchased 400 acres and created Loch Ledge, a preserve. In 1951, she sold 125 acres to the Child Services League (Queens) for a boys' summer camp after the Town of Yorktown refused her offer to sell them land for a school. The camp operated from 1957 to 1964, when it closed because of financial difficulties. The following year, the Save Turkey Mountain Committee formed to explore ways to preserve open space. The Town

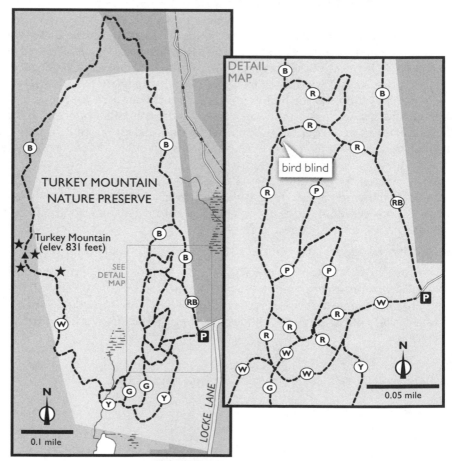

View from the top.

of Yorktown agreed to spend $30,000 to match contributions from two families. In 1969, the property was acquired with a restriction that it was to be used as an outdoor education and hiking facility.

TRAILS

A hike in Turkey Mountain Preserve should include a vigorous hike to the top and a slow amble on the 1.5 miles of intertwined trails adjacent to the parking lot. Many of the trails at the bottom were part of the former camp and wander past the few remaining remnants. For someone interested in plants, there is a lot to see within the woodlands, edge environments, summit, and wetlands.

Blue Trail   *Length: 1.4 miles Blaze: blue*
One of two trails to the summit of Turkey Mountain, the blue trail begins on the north side of the parking lot and initially is co-aligned with a segment of one of the red trails. When the trails split, the red trail leaves to the left. At 0.3 mile, the blue trail crosses a series of seasonal streams. It works its way uphill gradually at first, then more steeply and, at 0.5 mile, begins its assault on the hill. Going over rocks, it reaches the ridge at 0.8 mile. On fairly level terrain, the trail traverses the ridge. Underfoot in some places, is dark gray slab rock which looks like the hide of an elephant, complete with wrinkles. The blue trail reaches expansive views at the top of Turkey Mountain. It ends at three concrete pillar bases where the white trail begins.

White Trail   *Length: 0.7 mile Blaze: white*
As the white trail leads steeply down from the top of Turkey Mountain, there are occasional sections level off slightly. At 0.2 mile, the trail crosses a log bridge. After

NATURE'S FILTERS

Often called swamps, marshes, bogs, or fens, wetlands are ecosystems which must contain some or all of three components: water, wetland soils, wetland flora. Wetlands are found on every continent except Antarctica, from tundra to the tropics. The land must be wet often enough to create wetland soils which encourage the growth of specific water-loving plants. Even when the ground is not obviously wet, the presence of these soils and plants indentifies them as wetlands. Various state and local jurisdictions have their own specific requirements, generally based on U.S. Fish and Wildlife Service definitions.

Inland wetlands are commonly found where groundwater reaches the soil surface or where rainfall saturates the soil and does not drain completely: on floodplains along rivers and streams, in depressions surrounded by dry land, along the margins of lakes and ponds, and in other low-lying areas. Roots of wetland plant species and the soils surrounding wetlands help clean water by processing nutrients and filtering out suspended materials, including pollutants. In addition, wetlands slow the rate of surface water flow, reduce the erosion force of running water, and absorb potentially damaging flood waters. Wetland indicators include cattails, purple loosestrife, tussock sedges, ferns, and reeds (phragmites). Although not actually wetland indicators, frogs, turtles, and red-winged blackbirds are common inhabitants.

The impact of higher density development throughout the county has placed these ecosystems under stress. Fortunately a better understanding of the irreplaceable function wetlands play in the environment has led to stronger regulatory efforts to preserve and protect them.

passing the yellow trail to the right, the white trail is on a boardwalk as it traverses wetlands and a stream. To the right at 0.5 mile, the trail passes the 0.1-mile green trail, which provides an alternate route, and then in quick succession a red trail to the left, the end of a green trail to the right, and a white trail to the left. After a gentle rise, the trail passes, to the right, the trail to the classroom. Now on a woods road, the white trail goes by another red trail to the left, the yellow trail to the right, and a final red segment to the left, before ending at the kiosk in the parking lot.

NEARBY TRAIL: North County Trailway

DRIVING: From the Taconic State Parkway, take the Underhill Avenue Exit and turn east towards Yorktown Heights. At the first light, turn right onto Route 118. Go 1.9 mile, until there are signs for Croton Heights Road on the left and Locke Avenue on the right [41.246646N 73.788895W]. Turn right onto the dirt road to reach parking.

PUBLIC TRANSPORTATION: Beeline Bus #15 on Route 118, but no Sunday service.

For contact information, see Appendix, Yorktown.

Ward Acres Park

New Rochelle • 3.5 miles, 62 acres

Expect to find dogs at Ward Acres. For many years, the wide trails, former farm fields, and woodlands of Ward Acres were a haven for dog owners who liked to exercise their pets off-leash. Because of the excessive number of unleashed dogs, the City of New Rochelle fenced in three acres for a dog park to allow dogs to run freely. It is unfortunate that the same user group that took care of the park by removing litter and curbing vandalism now has to purchase a permit to exercise their dogs there. In spite of the fact that dogs must be leashed, visitors to the park are still likely to find dogs running unrestrained outside of the dog park.

Ward Acres Park was originally part of a 100-acre farm purchased in 1912 by Robert Ward of the Ward Baking Company. His son, William B. Ward, added 300 acres and at his death in 1929, left it to his wife and their five children. One son, Jack, raised thoroughbred horses and by 1940 had established his own company, American Saddle. In 1956 as property was donated or sold, the estate shrank. The final acres with house and barns were sold to the city in 1962, for a passive recreational park, the largest in the city.

The New York, Westchester and Boston Railroad went through Ward Acres in the north part of the park on a level bed often built at-grade. To learn more about the railroad, see Jack Harrington Greenway in Pocket Parks.

TRAILS

Delineated by three roads, Ward Acres Park has marked trails and a network of unmarked mowed paths and woods roads. Although the terrain is flat, the footprints in the snow made by the large number of visitors leave the trails unsuitable for cross-country skiing.

Marked trails are mostly narrow paths rimming the park. The 1.7 miles of unmarked trails crisscross former farm fields that are now overgrown. Frequent traffic on these pathways has kept invasives somewhat at bay. Other unmarked trails follow stone walls or are near the remaining farm buildings.

There are two sections of a blue trail beginning on the wide woods road across the park. The longer one connects the white trail 0.2 mile to the Colonial Greenway. The shorter one connects 0.1 mile to the red trail. A white trail enters the park at Pinebrook Boulevard near an exit ramp and passes a thoroughbred horse cemetery. It turns away from the parkway, crosses a driveway to a vacant house and ends at the blue trail at 0.3 mile.

Red Trail
Length: 0.6 mile Blaze: red

At the main entrance on Broadfield Road just before the dog park, the red trail heads north, enters the woods, and passes access points to Broadfield Road. At 0.2 mile, it makes a sharp left at a T junction. It turns around the end of a stone wall and crosses a wide unmarked woods road leading 0.2-mile across the park. The red trail heads onto the bed of the former New York, Westchester and Boston Railroad, passes a structure thought to be an abandoned power station, and parallels a stream. At 0.3 mile, the red trail turns left to leave the stream and a blue trail goes right for 0.1 mile to end at the wide woods road across the park. It goes uphill, crosses a tiny stream, and reaches a junction where the Colonial Greenway enters from the right. The co-aligned trails cross boardwalks and wetlands, pass backyards, and reach Pinebrook Boulevard at 0.6 mile.

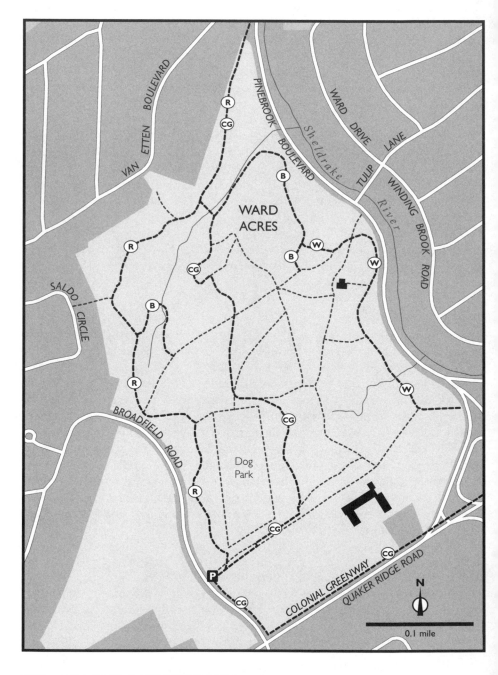

For man's best friend.

Colonial Greenway *Length: 0.6 mile Blaze: blue with white star(s)*
Across from the William Ward Elementary School, at the main entrance there is a Colonial Greenway sign. This section of the Colonial Greenway enters Ward Acres and parallels a stone wall with the dog park on the other side. Turning left to go through the stone wall, the trail enters a field and heads north. Just after entering the woods, the trail turns left to round the corner of a stone wall and at a junction turns right to parallel another stone wall. It crosses a wide intersection and heads down to cross a bridge into a wetland. The Colonial Greenway heads into dense vegetation, crosses a bridge at 0.4 mile and joins the red trail utilizing boardwalks to cross the wetlands. The Colonial Greenway leaves Ward Acres Park at southbound Pinebrook Boulevard and heads north to join the Outer Loop.

NEARBY PARKS & TRAILS: Larchmont Reservoir, Colonial Greenway, Leatherstocking Trail, Hutchinson River Pathway

DRIVING: From the southbound Hutchinson River Parkway, take Exit 20 (Route 125), turn left onto Route 125, and continue for 0.8 mile. **Turn right onto Quaker Ridge Road; go 0.5 mile and turn right onto Broadfield Road. Parking is on the road, across from the William B. Ward Elementary School. If northbound, take Exit 21 and turn right onto Hutchinson Avenue. At Route 125, turn left and follow the directions from ** [40.955272N 73.782364W].

PUBLIC TRANSPORTATION: None available

For contact information, see Appendix, New Rochelle.

Whippoorwill Park

Chappaqua • 3.8 miles, 167 acres

With trails that traverse the glens and ridges of a towering hardwood forest, Whippoorwill Park is a great place to spend part of a day. There are opportunities for wildlife observation along a pond, near a wetland, and in a mixed hardwood forest. Even in winter with significant snow cover, the park's trails are used. There is little or no road noise because the park is in a valley shielded by large wetlands and a ridge bordered by undeveloped private land below road level.

Whippoorwill Park was once part of Henry Berol's 500 acre estate, which included a game preserve. Berol, an avid quail hunter, was head of the Eagle Pencil Company. In 1966 he sold his estate, which was divided into a park and a residential area.

TRAILS

Trails in the park are marked with colored square plastic tags and are accessible from the parking lot via the red trail. Although no parking is available from Whippoorwill Lake Road and Kitchel Road at the blue and white trails, there is pedestrian access. A 0.3 mile unmarked loop is an entrance off Whippoorwill Road. Additional unmarked woods roads lead into private property; please respect landowner's privacy and do not trespass.

Red Trail   *Length: 0.4 mile Blaze: red*
From the parking lot, the red trail heads downhill along a narrow path. Soon after reaching the valley floor, the red trail passes the blue trail to the right and then continues straight when the yellow trail turns left. The red trail climbs uphill, reaches the ridge top, parallels a stone wall, and descends. Leveling slightly, the trail goes through a stone wall. As it descends, it passes barberry bushes to the left and another stone wall to the right. At 0.4 mile, the red trail ends at a T junction with the blue trail.

Blue Trail   *Length: 0.9 mile Blaze: blue*
At the bottom of the descent from the parking lot, the blue trail begins to the right. It skirts the edge of an extensive wetland and contours around the base of a hill. At 0.2 mile, as it rounds the hill which now has steep slopes, there is an unmarked side trail leading 0.2 mile to Whippoorwill Lake Road and, in 180 feet, a 0.1 mile branch of that same trail. To the right at 0.3 mile, at an easily missed intersection, the blue trail splits to form a large loop around a pond. Going clockwise and continuing straight along the base of the hill, the trail has views of the pond. At a Y junction at 0.5 mile, it reaches the yellow trail for the first time. The blue trail heads left, leaves the lake, and passes the red trail to the left next to a stone wall. The blue trail crosses the yellow trail at 0.6 mile and makes a right turn onto a woods road, which crosses an outlet stream of the pond on a rock bridge. Except for an occasional airplane overhead, this area seems completely

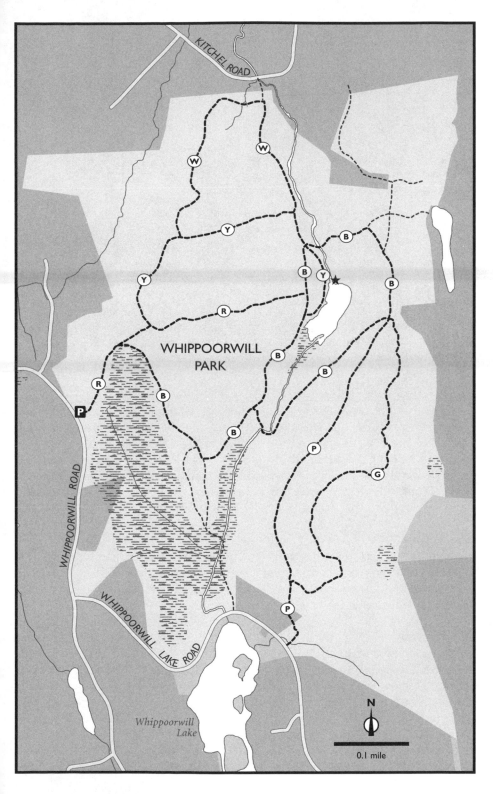

KITCHEL ROAD

WHIPPOORWILL
PARK

WHIPPOORWILL ROAD

WHIPPOORWILL LAKE ROAD

*Whippoorwill
Lake*

N

0.1 mile

Dam on the pond in winter.

removed from the world beyond the park. Heading uphill gradually, the blue trail leaves the woods road and heads to the right. Straight ahead is an unmarked trail into private property. Bearing right, the blue trail reaches a massive downed tulip tree. Turning right, it heads uphill along a woods road, only to turn right again and leave the woods road at 0.8 mile. The trail descends and during leaf-off season the pond becomes visible once more. The trail crosses the inlet stream on a bridge and closes the loop at a T junction.

Green Trail   *Length: 0.6 Blaze: green*
From the purple trail, the green trail heads uphill and then more steeply at 0.1 mile. It reaches a balanced boulder at 0.4 mile and turns left to immediately head steeply downhill. A valley is off to the right, easily seen in leaf-off season. The green trail ends at the junction of the blue and purple trails.

Purple Trail   *Length: 0.5 miles Blaze: Purple*
From the junction with the blue and green trails, the purple trail is along a woods road heading uphill. It goes through laurel at 0.3 mile, continues uphill, and rounds the shoulder of the hill. It passes the end of the green trail to the left at 0.4 mile and heads steeply downhill to end at Whippoorwill Lake Road (no parking).

White Trail   *Length: 0.5 mile Blaze: white*
A sign on the yellow trail indicates that the white trail is a nature trail which focuses on trees found in the area. Signs beside the trees include information

about their uses as well as a map indicating where they are generally found. These whimsical signs make it easy to learn how to identify tree species. From a junction with the yellow trail, the white trail first gradually goes downhill and then crosses a small stream. At the bottom of the hill, an unmarked track leads to a bridge along Kitchel Road. The white trail heads uphill to parallel a cascading stream. It ends at the yellow trail at 0.5 mile near an old earthen and rock dam, a remnant of Colonial times. A short path off the white trail leads to the base of this former dam and spillway.

Yellow Trail

Length: 0.5 mile Blaze: yellow

Heading uphill from a junction with the red trail, the yellow trail joins a woods road and continues uphill. At 0.2 mile, it passes the white trail on the left and descends along a stone wall to the right. At the base of the hill at 0.3 mile, the yellow trail turns right at a T junction with the white trail to the left. At the junction with the blue trail at 0.4 mile, be alert: the blue trail goes either straight ahead or left. The yellow trail crosses the blue trail and follows the stream. It reaches a dam with a breeched spillway, then hugs the lakeshore until meeting the blue trail again at 0.5 mile, where it ends.

NEARBY PARK: Glazier Arboretum

DRIVING: Take the Saw Mill River Parkway to the light at Readers Digest Road and cross the railroad tracks. Stay on Readers Digest Road until it ends at Route 117 (Bedford Road). Turn right onto Bedford Road and head south. At Whippoorwill Road, turn left and continue 1.0 mile to the park [41.168060N 73.744137W].

PUBLIC TRANSPORTATION: None available

For contact information, see Appendix, New Castle.

Woodlands Legacy Fields Park

Yorktown • 3.4 miles, 158 acres

*L**et me count the ways*** describes not only the number of entrances, but also the ways local residents enjoy Woodlands Legacy Fields Park. Wedged between two sections of Strang Boulevard, the park seems to have a split personality. The playing fields are the dominant feature when you enter from the Strang Boulevard off Route 132, but concealed behind the kiosk at the end of the parking lot are alluring trails and the answer to the question, "How do you get to that (pedestrian) bridge over the Taconic?"

To protect the ball fields, the entrance gate is locked when the fields are not being used. With three other entrances plus access over the Taconic Bridge, Woodlands, as it is called by local residents, is a popular place to walk, mountain bike, jog, or take their dog for a stroll.

TRAILS

The trails in Woodlands provide the shortest access to the Taconic Bridge, officially Yorktown Trailway Taconic Parkway Overpass. Anyone wishing to enjoy the view up and down the parkway from the bridge can take the 0.2 mile trail bearing its name. The Taconic Bridge Trail starts from the kiosk at the end of the parking lot at Legacy Fields and heads to the right of the kiosk toward the row of trees. As it heads downhill, it passes the Legacy Trail (green) to the left and then reaches the bridge. On the other side, the trail turns right to join briefly the Yorktown Trailway (green) and then goes through Granite Knolls Park to reach Stony Street and Sylvan Glen Park Preserve.

The Legacy Trail (green) is a 0.3 mile alternate from the Strang Trail to reach the Taconic Bridge Trail. The Manor Street Trail (orange) provides a 0.3 mile route for neighbors to reach the other trails in Woodlands. It begins as a paved path between two houses on Manor Street. A 0.1 mile eroded woods road connects the park to the Taconic Woods Road.

Strang Trail   *Length: 0.7 miles Blaze: white*
There are two Strang Boulevards in Yorktown and the Strang Trail connects them. At the dead end of the Strang Boulevard that is near Mercy College, the Strang Trail heads north and passes the Woodlands Trail (yellow) to the left. It winds through the woods, passes the Hunter Brook Trail (red) before turning left and heading downhill to the brook. At 0.2 mile, it joins the Woodlands Trail as they turn to cross the bridge. The co-aligned trails pass the Parkway Trail (blue) to the left and head uphill. At 0.3 mile, the trails split with the Woodlands Trail going straight and the Strang Trail turning right to head steeply uphill. Leveling off, the trail passes the Legacy Trail (green) to the left. The Strang Trail descends and crosses a bridge over the outflow of a retention pond. At 0.5 mile, it passes the end of the Hunter Brook Trail (red) to the right and heads uphill along a woods road. When it reaches the cleared right-of-way of a gas line, it turns left to follow it and ends at

the entrance road to the park. The kiosk and other trails are 0.1 mile ahead at the far end of the parking lot.

Hunter Brook Trail
Length: 0.4 miles Blaze: red

Starting on the Strang Trail (white), the Hunter Brook Trail crosses a stream on a stone bridge. At 0.1 mile, it passes the Manor Street Trail (orange) which heads uphill 0.3 mile to and entrance on Manor Street. The Hunter Brook Trail begins a long descent towards Hunter Brook. At a T junction with a woods road, the Hunter Brook Trail turns left. To the right, the Taconic Woods Road heads uphill to an entrance (no parking). The Hunter Brook Trail crosses a stone bridge as it passes a pond to the left and ends at the Strang Trail.

Parkway Trail
Length: 0.7 mile Blaze: blue

Beginning at the bridge over the Taconic, the Parkway Trail heads into the woods, crosses the gas line right-of-way to a woods road. At 0.2 mile, it passes the end of the Woodlands Trail (yellow) and turns right. Heading downhill, it turns to

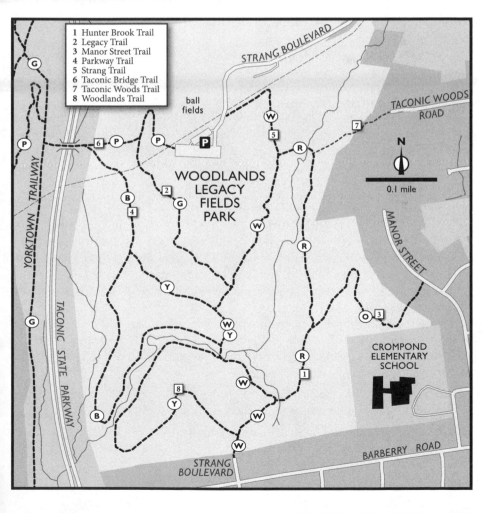

Keeping hikers' feet dry.

parallel the Taconic. At 0.4 mile, the trail turns away from the parkway to parallel Hunter Brook. After crossing feeder streams and boardwalks over wet areas, it ends at the Strang Trail (white) on the north side of the Hunter Brook bridge.

Woodlands Trail   *Length: 0.7 mile Blaze: yellow*
An alternate route down to the bridge over Hunter Brook, the Woodlands Trail starts on the Strang Trail (white) just past the entrance at the end of Strang Boulevard. The trail winds through the woods and at 0.2 mile, descends steeply to meet Hunter Brook and then follows it. After passing a large tree trunk arched over the trail, the Woodlands Trail turns left to join the Strang Trail at 0.5 mile. Together they cross the bridge over Hunter Brook and pass the Parkway Trail (blue) to the left and head uphill. At 0.6 mile, the Strang Trail turns right and the Woodlands Trail continues to ascend. It crosses two stone walls, heads downhill, and ends at the Parkway Trail (blue).

CONNECTING TRAIL: Yorktown Trailway

DRIVING: From Taconic State Parkway, take the Route 202 exit and turn east. For the official entrance to Woodlands Legacy Fields, go 0.7 mile to the traffic light at Route 132 and turn left. Go 1.4 miles and turn left onto Strang Boulevard. The park is at the end of the road. The gate is locked when the fields are not being used [41.309516N 73.821102W].

To reach the neighborhood entrance at the end of Strang Boulevard, turn left at the light on Route 202 at Strang Boulevard and go by Mercy College. It is 0.7 mile to the dead end where parking is limited as to not inconvenience residents [41.303319N 73.819683W].

PUBLIC TRANSPORTATION: Beeline Bus #15 stops on Route 202 opposite Strang Boulevard. It is a 0.7 mile road walk to the entrance at the end of the road.

For contact information, see Appendix: Town of Yorktown.

The Hudson River at Croton Point Park.

SECTION V

DAY TRIPPERS

- Have five to ten miles of trails
- Encompass greater variety of habitats
- Provide sufficient trails for a full day of hiking
- Are worth longer than a half-hour drive

Baxter Preserve

North Salem • 6.8 miles, 167 acres

What were once farm fields in the Baxter Preserve stretch as far as the eye can see as you view them from in the parking area on Baxter Road. Once inside, you'll see they extend even further. The grassy fields close to Baxter Road are mowed, and you can walk anywhere. Deeper into the property, fields are flush with wildflowers in the summer and only a path is kept mowed.

Baxter Preserve is the largest of the properties owned by the North Salem Open Land Foundation (NSOLF), a conservation trust founded in 1974. North Salem is often described as "horsey" and one should expect to see horses and to give them the right of way. Dogs can be off leash, but not on weekends and legal holidays when more visitors frequent the trails. Snowshoeing and cross-country skiing are permitted. Model airplanes may not be flown in the fields.

The rolling terrain and wide sky make for pleasant walking through the Baxter Preserve. However, on hot summer days the sun can be brutal, even with sun screen and a hat. The mowed paths in the fields may vary from year to year and are not always exactly as shown on the map. Sometimes mowed paths are found on both sides of a stone wall. With so many places to walk, varying a route is easy.

The hike around the lake is 1.0 mile and passes evidence of an old steeplechase race track. A stand for viewing the races was perched on the knoll next to a large white oak and a split rail fence along its top. The few distinguishing landmarks on the property make it difficult to describe a hike in detail. The fields are level and it is only in the southern area of the preserve that there are any noticeable elevation changes. Across Baxter Road, an unmarked trail follows the perimeter of the property for 0.5 mile. It passes several jumps whose presence indicate the preserve's equestrian traditions. Those hikers wishing to explore the far reaches of the preserve can use the edge of the property as a guide.

DRIVING: From northbound I-684 take Exit 7, turn right at the end of the exit ramp, and turn left onto Route 22. Once on Route 22, turn right at Route 116 (Titicus Road) and

Grand stand.

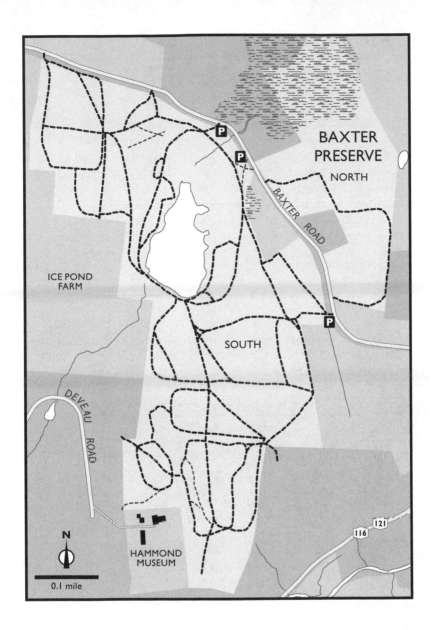

follow it for 3.7 miles. Turn left onto June Road and drive 0.9 mile. Turn right onto Baxter Road and drive 0.4 mile. Parking is available to the right, opposite #107 [41.341000N 73.579683W] and #67 [41.339876N 73.578573W]. If driving from southbound I-684, take Exit 8 and follow Route 22 south. At the intersection with Route 116, where Route 22 heads right, follow Route 116 to the preserve, using the directions above [41.336590N 73.576285W].

PUBLIC TRANSPORTATION: None available

For contact information, see Appendix, North Salem Open Land Foundation.

Beaver Dam Sanctuary

Katonah • 7.8 miles, 171 acres

S cenic paths meander along streams and through mowed fields at Beaver Dam Sanctuary, whose namesake river, a fast-flowing, wide stream, runs through the property, flowing north into Muscoot Reservoir. Expect to see horses because the trails are part of the Bedford Riding Lanes Association (BRLA) trail system.

Established in 1969 with an original purchase of 14 acres containing Broad Brook and Beaver Dam River, this lovely sanctuary has grown through gifts and purchases. Jan and Parker Montgomery and Marilyn and Kelly Simpson, along with other Bedford residents, established a non-profit group to manage it. Marilyn Simpson donated large sections of land including a broad meadow that was later named in her memory.

TRAILS

Hiking at the Beaver Dam Sanctuary is either on flat terrain for a long distance or on short steep sections. Because all trails within the sanctuary are marked with yellow BRLA signs, hikers should pay close attention to their routes. The many fords of the swift-moving Beaver Dam River are for equestrians and almost guaranteed to get hikers' feet wet. Fields are mowed annually so the location and mileage of trails across the fields may vary from year to year. Hikers are asked to stay off those trails open only to BRLA members.

Beaver Dam River.

CONNECTING PARK & TRAILS: John Jay Homestead, Bedford Riding Lanes Association

DRIVING: From I-684, take Exit 6 (Katonah) and travel east on Route 35. Turn right onto NY 22 and head south. Look for an entrance to the sanctuary on the right just past the Harvey School entrance to the left [41.253740N 73.666413W]. An alternate is to drive to Beaver Dam Road, 1.4 miles south of the intersection of routes 35 and 22, where it becomes a dirt road almost immediately. Head downhill and park on the left side, where the road makes a sharp right turn [41.246737N 73.666067W]. More parking is available at the entrance to the northern portion of the sanctuary, 0.2 mile west on Beaver Dam Road [41.245970N 73.669587W].

PUBLIC TRANSPORTATION: None available

For contact information, see Appendix, Beaver Dam Sanctuary.

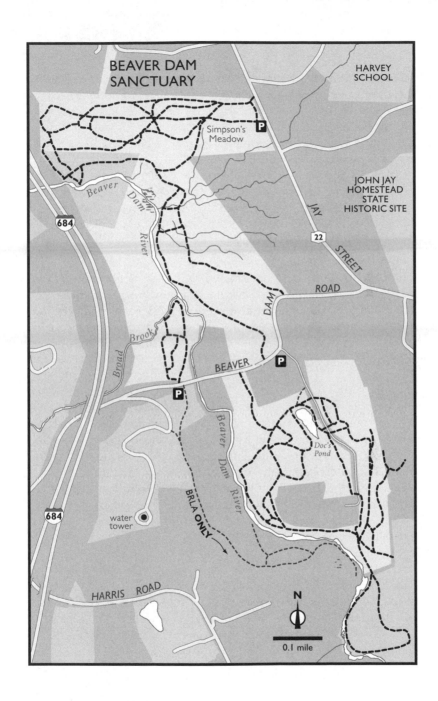

BEAVER DAM
SANCTUARY

HARVEY
SCHOOL

Simpson's
Meadow

JOHN JAY
HOMESTEAD
STATE
HISTORIC SITE

Beaver

Dam

River

684

22

JAY STREET

DAM ROAD

Broad Brook

BEAVER

P

P

P

Beaver Dam River

Doc's
Pond

684

water
tower

BRLA ONLY

HARRIS ROAD

N

0.1 mile

Brinton Brook Sanctuary

Croton-on-Hudson • 4.3 miles, 156 acres

Tucked away from busy Route 9 and inside a ring of development is Brinton Brook Sanctuary, a refuge of open meadows, old orchard and edge environments, red maple swamp, hemlock groves, dry ridge hardwood forest, and rocky slopes. The varied terrain offers opportunities for either easy or vigorous hikes with the change to see a variety of wildlife. The sanctuary's perimeter is surrounded by an apartment complex, a golf course, and power line right-of way.

The tract was originally owned by Laura and Willard Brinton. In 1957, following her husband's death, she donated 112 acres to the National Audubon Society so the land would be permanently protected as a wildlife refuge. After her death, an additional 17 acres were donated by Ruth Brinton Perera, a niece.

TRAILS

A series of loops and connector trails offers many options for exploring the sanctuary. The interconnected 0.2 mile of wide farm roads near the entrance provide an easy stroll. The meadows are mowed to prevent the forest from encroaching on the field ecosystem. Although not considered part of the trail system at Brinton Brook, there is a 0.5-mile path under the high- tension power line adjacent to the property.

Pond Loop Trail
Length: 1.3 miles Blaze: yellow
Heading clockwise from the sanctuary's main entrance, the Pond Loop Trail passes through an open meadow and an old orchard near former farm roads. At 0.3 mile, it reaches Red Maple Swamp and a pond, where an unmarked side trail leads 0.1 mile to building #23 at the Amberlands Apartments. Leaving the woods road, the trail runs along an embankment. It passes the Turkey Trail (blue) to the left at 0.5 mile and again at 0.6 mile. Turning right, the Pond Loop Trail begins its return to the entrance. It passes the Hemlock Springs Trail (red) at 0.9 mile, an unmarked farm road at 1.0 mile, and the Hemlock Springs Trail again at 1.1 miles. The Pond Loop ends at the parking lot.

Coyote Trail
Length: 0.4 mile Blaze: green
From the Turkey Trail (blue), the Coyote Trail heads uphill. At 0.1 mile, it passes an unmarked trail that connects to the Highland Trail (white) and travels between two glacial erratics at the junction. At 0.3 mile, it turns right as it joins the Highland Trail. The Coyote Trail ends at an intersection with the Hemlock Springs Trail (red) at 0.4 mile where the Highland Trail turns left.

Hemlock Springs Trail
Length: 0.5 mile Blaze: red
Beginning on the Pond Loop Trail (yellow), the Hemlock Springs Trail follows above the brook. At 0.1 mile, it passes the Laurel Rock Trail (yellow) at Split Rock Spring, which was designed by Willard Brinton. The trail climbs gradually to the

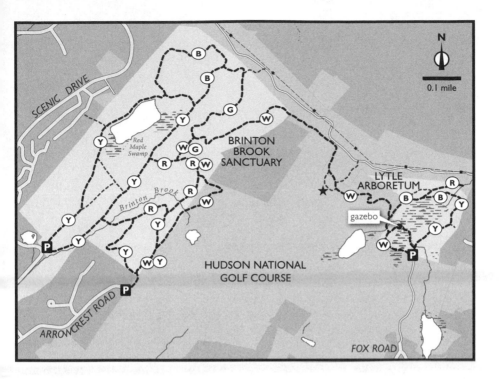

ridge and at 0.2 mile, again passes the Laurel Rock Trail. Continuing to climb, the trail crosses three seasonal streams. The Highland Trail joins from the right and together they pass stone ruins, believed to have been farm buildings dating from the Civil War era, and then the Coyote Trail (green) at 0.4 mile. Continuing downhill, the Hemlock Springs Trail ends at the Pond Loop Trail. To the left, it is a 0.4-mile return to the sanctuary's main entrance.

Highland Trail *Length: 1.1 miles Blaze: white*
From the parking spots on Arrowcrest Road, just outside the entrance to the Hudson National Golf Club, the Highland Trail parallels the golf course and joins the Laurel Rock Trail (yellow) entering from the left. The trails are co-aligned until the Laurel Rock Trail leaves to the left at 0.2 mile. A large sign noting that Lytle Arboretum is 2 miles away is incorrect. The trail had been rerouted to avoid a private holding; it is only 1.5 miles from the entrance on Arrowcrest Road to the arboretum.

The Highland Trail crosses a stream. It turns to descend, passing a massive glacial erratic off to the right just outside the sanctuary. At 0.5 mile, the Highland Trail reaches a T junction with the Hemlock Spring Trail (red) and turns right to join it. Continuing downhill, they pass stone ruins before reaching the end of the Coyote Trail (green) to the right. The Hemlock Spring Trail continues straight ahead and the Highland Trail turns to the right. At 0.6 mile, the Highland Trail turns right again to leave the Coyote Trail. It traverses a ridge and heads downhill. A large glacial erratic is to the right at 0.8 mile. After crossing the power line maintenance road, the trail heads uphill again.

Once across a stream, the Highland Trail enters a Norway spruce grove at 1.0 mile. It climbs uphill steadily between the power line and the golf course. At 1.1 miles, the Highland Trail reaches the power lines. It turns right and continues as the Village of Croton Trail to end at Lytle Arboretum in 0.4 mile.

Laurel Rock Trail
Length: 0.5 mile Blaze: yellow

Starting on the Hemlock Springs Trail (red) at the Split Rock Spring, the Laurel Rock Trail traverses some of the more rugged terrain in the sanctuary. The trail heads uphill sometimes more steeply than at others. At the top of the ridge at 0.3 mile, it turns left to join the Highland Trail (white). To the right, it is 300 feet to the parking on Arrowcrest Road, just outside the entrance to the golf course. The Laurel Rock Trail leaves the Highland Trail to the left at 0.4 mile and heads downhill to end at the Hemlock Springs Trail.

Turkey Trail
Length: 0.5 mile Blaze: blue

From the northeast corner of the pond on the Pond Loop Trail (yellow), the Turkey Trail heads through a hardwood forest of black birch, hickory, and oak. As it nears the edge of the property, the trail reaches the highest point in the park near power lines. At the junction with the Coyote Trail (green) at 0.3 mile, it passes through parallel stone walls to end at the Pond Loop Trail.

DRIVING: From Route 9, north of Croton-on-Hudson, take the Senasqua Road Exit and head north on Route 9A. Pass the Sky View Nursing Home to the left at 0.8 mile and go 0.3 mile to turn right at the sign for Brinton Brook Sanctuary. Follow the gravel road up a private drive to parking [41.222856N 73.905182W]. Alternately to reach the entrance next to the Hudson National Golf Course, Follow the directions above, but turn right onto Arrowcrest Road which is 0.2 mile past the nursing home. Drive to the end of the road [41.221212N 73.901072].

PUBLIC TRANSPORTATION: Beeline Bus #14 stops at Warren Road, 0.2 mile north of the access road. It is a 0.3-mile road walk to the sanctuary from Route 9A.

For contact information, see Appendix, Saw Mill River Audubon Society.

Village of Croton Trail

Croton-on-Hudson • 0.4 mile

The creation of the Village of Croton Trail was possible because of negotiations during the construction of the Hudson National Golf Course. The trail connects Brinton Brook Sanctuary with the Jane E. Lytle Memorial Arboretum. From the Highland Trail in Brinton Brook Sanctuary, the trail continues uphill steadily. At a Y junction, white blazes go in both directions and the segments are of equal length. The trail to the right heads towards the golf course and passes through a stand of phragmite reeds to a view across the golf course to the Hudson River. The chimneys are the remains of a former property owner's mansion. The trail rejoins the main trail as it descends through a series of switchbacks to end at the Link Trail in the Lytle Arboretum at 0.4 mile.

Remnants of the past.

For contact information, see Appendix, Croton.

Jane E. Lytle Memorial Arboretum

Croton-on-Hudson • 0.8 mile, 20 acres

Connected to Brinton Brook Sanctuary via the Village Highland Trail, the Lytle Arboretum is a trailhead for a longer walk. The arboretum can be enjoyed in its own right, as wildlife viewing opportunities are plentiful along its small trail system. The main entrance into the arboretum is along a golf course right-of-way, so remain on the road to avoid being hit by a golf ball. The trail system is a loop with a spur to Brinton Brook Sanctuary and Hixson Road (no parking). Each of the trails in this 0.8-mile trail system has a name, directing visitors to an area of the arboretum which allows them to view a particular type of wildlife. The Beech Trail (yellow) goes 0.2 mile through a beech forest. It finishes at the Marshlands Trail (blue) which continues for 0.2 mile to end at the white trail, the Link, and Village of Croton Trail. Rubin's Trail (red) goes 0.1 mile to a stream. An unmarked mile trail connects the Marshlands Trail to Rubin's Trail. The 0.1-mile Boardwalk Trail crosses wetlands (handicapped accessible to the gazebo).

DRIVING: From Route 9 in Croton-on-Hudson, take either the Senesqua Road Exit or Route 9A Exit onto South Riverside Drive. Turn right, then left onto High Street, ending at a T junction with Old Post Road. Turn right and take the first left onto Lounsbury Road. Continue uphill and go straight onto Fox Road. Pass through the Hudson National Golf Course (gravel road) right-of-way to the parking lot [41.219194N 73.887383].

PUBLIC TRANSPORTATION: None available.

For contact information, see Appendix, Lytle Arboretum.

Butler Memorial Sanctuary

Mt. Kisco • 6.6 miles, 363 acres

Consider Butler Memorial Sanctuary a good place for a nature walk and the best place to watch the fall hawk migration in Westchester. Through the ridge and swale topography of the sanctuary, hikers experience various forest communities, including mixed hardwoods dominated by oak, hickory, or hemlock. Wet areas are mostly red maple swamps.

A hawk watch, erected in 1972 and expanded in 1994, has grandstand-style seating that overlooks a valley at the base of which snakes 1-684. It might lack hot dogs and popcorn, but there is plenty of enthusiasm among the fans during the fall migration. Experts are usually on hand to identify and describe the species being seen and counted. From these bleachers, Long Island Sound is visible 10 miles away.

In 1954 Anna Butler donated 225 acres to The Nature Conservancy in memory of her husband, Arthur, a corporate lawyer. An amateur naturalist and astronomer, he had planted evergreens and laid out many of the trails in what is now the sanctuary. In 1957, the Walter Huber family added 20 acres. The purchase of additional acres increased the sanctuary to its present size.

TRAILS

The trails at the sanctuary are user friendly. Each color plastic blaze is a different shape and intersections display a green arrow showing the shortest route back to the parking lot. There are six short white trails totaling 0.8 mile. Five of them serve as connectors of the other trails and one leads to the viewpoint at Sunset Rock. These are described in relation to the trails they connect. Thus, the white trail which connects the red trail with the yellow trail is mentioned at an appropriate place in the trail description.

Grandstand without the crowds

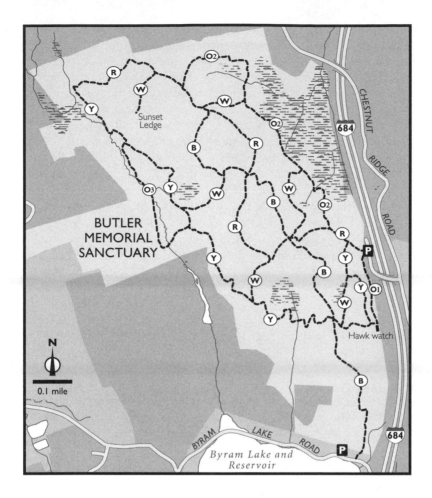

Red Trail

Length: 1.3 miles Blaze: red

Beginning at the kiosk near the sanctuary entrance, the red trail passes, in quick succession, a junction with the yellow trail to the left and one to the orange trail #2 to the right. The blue trail merges from the left at 0.1 mile and, after crossing a stone wall, leaves to the right. Gently contouring around a broad knob, the red trail climbs upward to pass the white trail, which leads down 0.1 mile to the yellow trail. Continuing to contour, the red trail crosses the blue trail at 0.6 mile in a broad saddle, then contours around another. At 0.8 mile, the red trail reaches the end of the blue trail on the left and then immediately passes the white trail leading 0.1 mile downhill to the orange trail #2. The red trail passes the end of orange trail #2 to the right. At 1.0 mile, it passes the white trail to the right and then dead ends in 0.1 mile at the view at Sunset Rock. The red trail continues gently downhill along a woods road to end at the yellow trail, at 1.3 miles.

Blue Trail

Length: 1.3 miles Blaze: blue

Running the length of the sanctuary, the blue trail begins across the road from the northeast end of Byram Lake at Byram Lake Road, where parking for two cars is available 100 yards to the west. The sign at the sanctuary entrance is visible at the stone wall approximately 100 yards from the road.

From the trailhead, the blue trail heads uphill for about 500 feet along switchbacks and through stone walls. At 0.3 mile, it follows the low line of a hollow and gently ascends along a woods road. After crossing the yellow trail at 0.4 mile, it crests a low ridge and descends, crossing a seasonal stream at the bottom. The blue trail continues to descend and follows a stone wall to the right, where the forest floor is covered with grass. It enters a mixed pine and hemlock forest, and then merges with the red trail, entering from the right at 0.7 mile. When the trails split, the blue trail goes right. It soon goes left at a Y junction with the white trail, which gradually descends to reach orange trail #2.

At 0.8 mile, on a path often icy and treacherous in winter, the blue trail climbs steeply at first, then less so. It descends to cross the red trail at 1.1 miles, and the white trail which leads downhill 0.2 mile to the yellow trail. The blue trail ascends out of the hollow and contours around the shoulder of the hill. It heads between rock outcroppings and ends at a T junction with the red trail, at 1.3 miles.

Orange Trails
Length: 1.4 miles Blaze: orange

There are three orange trails: #1 leads to the hawk watch, #2 parallels the red trail as an alternate route, and #3 is a side trail off the yellow trail. From the south end of the parking area, following signs to the hawk watch, orange trail #1 rises steadily to reach the hawk watch at 0.2 mile, where it ends.

Orange trail #2 begins on the red trail 0.1 mile from the parking lot. It parallels wetlands and wiggles through a few sharp turns. At 0.2 mile, it passes a white trail to the left which climbs uphill for 0.2 mile to reach the blue trail. Orange trail #2 passes a rocky crag to the left. It joins a woods road and then contours around the hill. Large ferns line the path and beyond are extensive wetlands. The orange trail passes a junction with a white trail that heads 0.1 mile uphill to the red trail. At 0.6 mile, it reaches a junction with another woods road defined by stone walls on both sides, where it turns left. Wetlands are on the left as the trail heads on a woods road alongside a stone wall. After passing an open meadow to the right, the orange trail ends at a T junction with the red trail, at 0.8 mile.

Well within the sanctuary, 1.3 miles from the entrance via the yellow trail, orange trail #3 is an alternate route along the yellow trail. Descending from the southern junction with the yellow trail, orange trail #3 almost immediately crosses a stone wall. Roots of a large beech tree are visible as they spread outward across the forest floor. Crossing wetland, the trail turns right, crosses a stream, and then parallels it to end at the yellow trail at 0.4 mile.

Yellow Trail
Length: 1.8 miles Blaze: yellow

Starting to the left of the red trail near the entrance kiosk, the yellow trail wanders uphill and down. Heading south, it climbs gradually and passes a white trail which, if taken, eliminates 0.2 mile and the climb up to the hawk watch. The yellow trail contours around a low rock ridge and continues the climb. At a junction, the yellow trail turns right. Be alert here because the short trail to the left is also yellow-blazed and leads to the hawk watch. As the yellow trail drops down the ridge to the west, road noise from I-684 gradually disappears.

At 0.4 mile, the yellow trail passes the other end of the white trail mentioned above. Almost immediately, the yellow trail crosses the blue trail and briefly rises only to descend steeply via switchbacks. At the bottom, the yellow trail crosses an outlet of a wetland, which can be tricky and messy when water levels are high. The trail heads uphill to cross the ridge overlooking a wide wetland strewn with dying hemlocks, victims of woolly adegid infestation, and then descends. At 0.8 mile, it passes the white trail which leads 0.1 mile uphill to the red trail.

The yellow trail ascends and turns right, passing ruins to the right. It reaches a junction with the orange trail #3 on the left at 1.3 miles, and then another white trail to the right that ascends to connect in 0.2 mile to the blue trail. The yellow trail passes through a stone wall and crosses the outlet of the wetlands on stepping stones. It heads uphill and, at 1.4 miles, descends. It passes the other end of orange trail #3 on the left at 1.6 miles. After crossing a small stream on boulders, the trail parallels a larger stream. To the right, a boulder field tumbles down from Sunset Rock. At 1.8 miles, the yellow trail ends at the red trail.

NEARBY PARKS: Westmoreland Sanctuary, Merestead

DRIVING: From I-684 take Exit 4 (Route 172) and turn west towards Mt. Kisco. At 0.3 mile, turn left onto Chestnut Ridge Road. Head south for 1.2 miles, turn right, and cross the bridge. Parking for the sanctuary is at the end of the road, where the entrance is to the left [41.182155N 73.686521W]. More parking is available at the south end of the sanctuary off Byram Lake Road [41.174508N 73.688104W].

PUBLIC TRANSPORTATION: None available

For contact information, see Appendix, The Nature Conservancy.

Camp Smith Trail

Peekskill • 3.7 miles, 216 acres

The most rugged trail in Westchester is, without a doubt, the Camp Smith Trail, and intrepid hikers are rewarded with some of the most spectacular and panoramic views in the Hudson Valley. This strenuous trail which is best done with a car shuttle, has a net elevation gain of 1,100 feet when hiked from south to north. Hikers are more likely to savor the views when hiking in this direction.

Because the state park is narrow as it passes through Camp Smith Army National Guard training site, hikers may see military personnel engaged in training exercises. Although there is buffer land between the trail and the practice ranges, hikers must remain on the trail.

The north end of the trail is the mountain known as Anthony's Nose, which is an excellent spot for watching raptors. Peregrine falcons nest on Bear Mountain Bridge which stretches across the Hudson from the base of the mountain and bald eagles frequent the southern end of Iona Island in winter. It is uncertain whose profile inspired the mountain's name, but its use dates back to the 1690's.

Various environmental groups had long wished to protect Anthony's Nose. Its

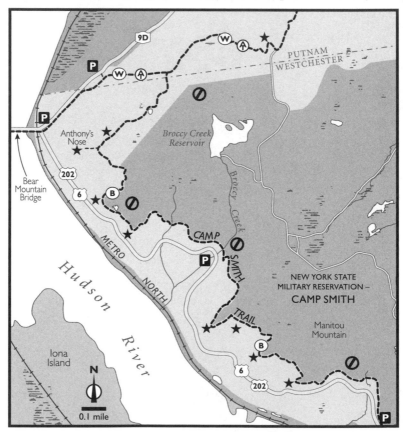

commanding presence at the eastern end of the Bear Mountain Bridge was part of Camp Smith. This National Guard training facility has been in existence since 1882 and, in 1919, was named after Alfred E. Smith, who was then governor. In 1992, negotiations with Camp Smith resulted in permission to build a trail on the property to be part of the Hudson River Greenway. Completed in 1995 while still part of Camp Smith, the trail and its corridor became part of Hudson Highlands State Park in 1998.

The blue-blazed Camp Smith Trail starts behind the historic Bear Mountain Bridge toll house, 0.7 mile north of the entrance to Camp Smith on Bear Mountain Road, Route 6/202. The toll house is the Town of Cortlandt Visitor Center and open in season. At first, the trail parallels the road, climbing steadily. It then drops steeply through a rock field and turns left after passing a massive cliff. At 0.3 mile, the trail goes below a breached earthen dam. Staying within sight and sound of the road, it works its way gradually uphill, crossing small ridges. At 0.6 mile, it begins a serious ascent of Manitou Mountain, climbing very steeply on a series of rock steps. It turns left, climbs more gradually, and reaches a viewpoint to the south. Turning right, it crosses the top of an open rock face.

The Camp Smith Trail drops slightly and resumes its steady ascent of Manitou Mountain, while turning west toward the river. It passes through a gully before it approaches viewpoints on the brow of the mountain. Scrub pines offer a great spot to sit and enjoy the view of Iona Island across the river. At 0.9 mile, the trail turns away from the river. It turns left toward a rock outcropping with views and then turns right and away from the views to begin its descent. The rock steps, switchbacks, and side-hill construction make it possible to safely descend the extremely steep talus slope.

At 1.2 miles, the Camp Smith Trail reaches the bottom of the slope, crosses a flat area, turns gradually left, and arrives at a small rock outcropping with a view. From the viewpoint, the trail leads inland and turns once again towards the river for another westerly view. Leaving the view, the trail continues the gradual descent, crossing intermittent brooks. At 1.9 miles, it reaches a parking area on Route 6/202 at a large bend in the road, 2.2 miles north of the entrance to Camp Smith.

IONA ISLAND

Visitors to the Camp Smith Trail look down on Iona Island with its old buildings and network of roadways. Owned by Palisades Interstate Park, the island, which is part of the National Estuarine Research Reserve, is a bird and habitat preserve. In1849, C. W. Grant, M.D. purchased the island and developed extensive vineyards, which eventually produced the Iona grape. Later, the island was a summer resort, using Dr. Grant's mansion as a hotel. From 1900 until after World War II, the island was a naval arsenal with about 140 buildings. In 1911, the road causeway was built; repairs were made in 1983. Currently, the few remaining buildings are storage facilities for Palisades Interstate Park

A variety of plants and animals live on or visit Iona Island. Bald eagles nest on Round Island, the bump at the island's southern tip. Prickly pear cactus is found on south-facing rocky slopes. Deer, five-lined skinks, wetland birds, and waterfowl make their homes there.

Iona Island from the Greenway Trail.

Continuing north to Anthony's Nose, the trail crosses Broccy Creek and heads gradually uphill, paralleling the road. After turning away from Route 6/202, it joins and leaves woods roads and crosses streams. Rising out of a ravine, the trail turns right, at 2.4 miles, onto a rock outcropping with views of the Hudson River, Iona Island, and Bear Mountain-Harriman State Park. Paralleling the river high over the road, the trail first drops slightly then begins to climb steeply. At 2.7 miles, another rock outcropping with a view offers an excuse to stop before tackling the remaining unrelenting climb to the summit. Along the last 0.4 mile, there are both seasonal and year-round views from open rock slabs. The trail drops down off the summit to join a woods road. Straight ahead, a woods road leads to panoramic views of the Hudson River, the Bear Mountain Bridge, and Bear Mountain-Harriman State Park. A right turn takes hikers to the Appalachian Trail (white), where the Camp Smith Trail ends at 3.7 miles. From that junction, Route 9D is 0.6 mile downhill to the left.

DRIVING: Take Route 6/202 north from the traffic circle located just north of Peekskill. The toll house is on Route 6/202, 0.7 mile north of the entrance to Camp Smith. Parking is available along Route 6/202 at the toll house [41.301444N 73.951272W] and at the hike's midpoint [41.312277N 73.964929W]. Access to the trail's northern terminus is via the Appalachian Trail with parking along Route 9D, just north of the Bear Mountain Bridge [41.320231N 73.979081W].

PUBLIC TRANSPORTATION: Metro-North Hudson Division to Peekskill. A 2.5-mile taxi ride gets you to the trailhead at the toll house. After the hike, follow the southbound Appalachian Trail, 2.0 miles downhill and across the Bear Mountain Bridge to the Bear Mountain Inn, a stop for the Short Line Bus to Manhattan's Port Authority Bus Terminal. For bus schedules, call 1-800-631-8405.

For contact information, see Appendix, Hudson Highlands State Park.

Cranberry Lake Preserve

Valhalla • 6.4 miles, 190 acres

It is not surprising to find visitors at Cranberry Lake Preserve all year round. Here in the midst of suburbia, is a tranquil environment with a glacial lake, cranberry bogs, and abandoned quarrying operations. The portions of the preserve that are sparsely used offer a chance for solitude. All seasons here have their high notes: in early spring, an overture to the opening season erupts from the chorus of spring peepers emerging from the many vernal pools. Hot summer days are tempered in the shade under a canopy of trees. When fall colors are at their peak, a stroll around Cranberry Lake is a feast for the eyes. After a winter snowfall, a clean white stillness is an enticement to intrepid hikers and snowshoers.

TRAILS

The Blue, Red and Yellow trails at Cranberry Lake Preserve are loops which allow visitors to follow only one color when they want to hike. The History Trail is also a loop, often co-aligned with one of those trails. Trails that start at the Nature Center lead downhill to the lake. Many trails are wide with room for walking two abreast. Trail junctions have numbered signs, but unfortunately the county has not put them on the map on their website. When appropriate, there is a sign indicating a return route to the Nature Center. Trails begin and end with a blaze featuring a county park logo. The 1.2 miles of connecting trails, blazed either orange or white, are mentioned where they leave or join one of the major trails.

Yellow Trail   *Length: 1.1 miles Blaze: yellow*
At the Nature Center, the Yellow Trail goes through a gate and heads downhill along a woods road. It passes an orange trail, then a white trail, and a second orange trail to the left, all of which lead down to Cranberry Lake. The trail narrows slightly and, at junction 5 at 0.2 mile, joins the Red Trail which comes in from the right. The Yellow Trail turns left to join the Blue Trail at junction 6. The co-aligned trails go uphill to reach a view over the lake. After passing a white trail which leads uphill to the Nature Center, the co-aligned trails clamber down over rocks to follow the shoreline. They pass orange and white trails which also head uphill to the Nature Center. At 0.6 mile at junction 24, the Yellow Trail turns left while the the Blue Trail continues straight ahead and the Yellow Trail turns left away from the lake to go uphill.

At 0.7 mile at junction 33, it passes an orange trail and then at junction 34, joins the History and Red trails. The three trails are on a woods road and, at junction 35 at 0.8 mile, they separate with the Yellow Trail turning left. It turns right passing a shoulder high rock escarpment to the left at 1.0 mile. The Yellow Trail heads downhill, turns right at junction 31 and ends at the Nature Center.

Blue Trail   *Length: 1.1 mile Blaze: blue*
On the Blue Trail's circuit around two lakes, there are boardwalks, short bridges

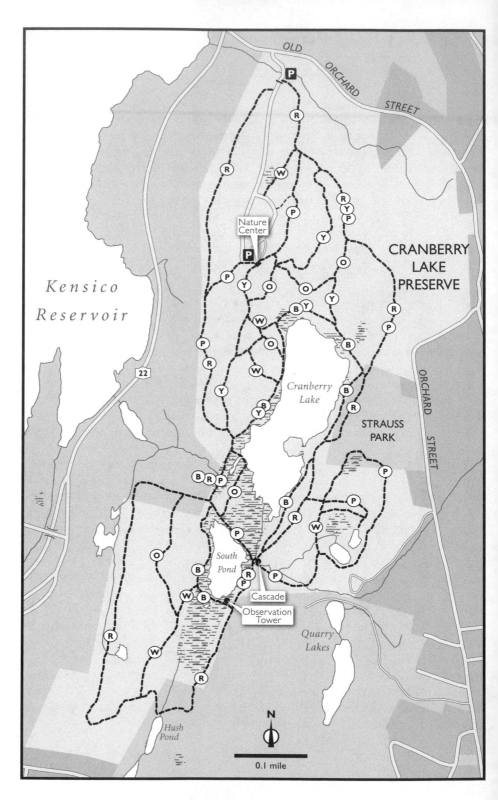

Kensico
Reservoir

Old Orchard Street

CRANBERRY
LAKE
PRESERVE

Nature
Center

Cranberry
Lake

STRAUSS
PARK

Orchard Street

22

South
Pond

Cascade

Observation
Tower

Quarry
Lakes

Hush
Pond

N

0.1 mile

From Crops to Rocks

Stone walls and an abandoned stone cellar are evidence of the agricultural past of what is now Cranberry Lake Preserve. However, the rocky terrain of the area's many small farms was not well-suited to agriculture.

From 1912 to 1917, the preserve was a quarry, furnishing rock and gravel to build the Kensico Dam, a part of New York City's water supply system. The project employed hundreds of skilled laborers, many of whom were recent immigrants from Italy. Seventeen miles of railroad track connected the quarry and rock crusher to the dam construction site. Along the History Trail, hikers can find what remains of the quarrying operations: a rock crushing plant, stone-cutting sheds, railroad beds, and footings for derricks.

Small farms purchased in the early 1900s were merged to form one large estate, which changed hands several times. In the 1940s, Nathan Straus III, owner of WMCA, the last family-owned radio station in New York City, purchased the property. The portion he sold to Westchester County in 1967 became the preserve. It opened to the public in 1973 and became a biodiversity reserve area in 1999.

and an observation tower. At various times, it is co-aligned with the Red and Yellow trails. At junction 6 on the Yellow Trail, turn left to head counterclockwise on the co-aligned Blue and Yellow trails. They go uphill to reach a view over Cranberry Lake and pass junctions 25 and 26 where white and orange trails lead uphill to the Yellow Trail at junctions 4 and 3 respectively. There are views out over the lake. The narrow trail is along the edge of the lake and heads along a boardwalk. It passes, at junction 27, another orange trail which heads 0.1 mile uphill to the Nature Center. At 0.3 mile the Yellow Trail turns left at junction 24 to go uphill.

The Blue Trail turns away from the lake, continues uphill to pass, at 0.4 mile, a large rock with a view. Quarry tailings and the concrete supports of a long-gone structure are uphill to the left. At 0.5 mile, the Blue Trail joins the Red Trail at junction 22 and then splits. The Blue Trail bears right following the shore on a narrow rocky path with rock outcroppings to the left. At 0.7 mile, the trails join for the last time at junction 15, cross a brook, and reach a small scenic cascade with a bench. To the right, the History Trail (purple dot) heads to the Nature Center.

The Red and Blue trails and a purple side trail of the History Trail pass quarry tailings and extensive cement walls which once supported a stone crusher. At 0.8 mile at junction 13, the trails split with the Blue Trail turning right to pass an observation tower. After crossing a wet area on boardwalk, the Blue Trail turns to follow the shore of South Pond. It turns and, at junction 12, a white trail leaves to the left to connect to the Red Trail. The Blue Trail follows the shore, passes through a series of stone wall and turns left at junction 8 to join the Red and History trails. They head uphill on a woods road. At junction 6, the Blue Trail closes the loop and other two trails continue straight ahead with the Yellow Trail.

Red Trail   *Length: 2.4 miles Blaze: red*
Just past the gate into the preserve and to the right, the Red Trail begins a

counterclockwise circuit around the preserve. The trail heads west and turns to parallel a stone wall marking the boundary with New York City watershed lands. At a massive stone outcropping, the red trail turns right to pass through a stone wall. To the left, a large impressive slab looks as if it is glued to the hillside. Now heading downhill, the Red Trail reaches junction 1 at 0.3 mile where the History Trail joins from the right. The co-aligned trails continue through the woods and join the Yellow Trail at 0.5 mile at junction 5. They soon meet the Blue Trail entering from the left at junction 6 where the Yellow trail turns. The Red, Blue and History trails continue downhill. At junction 7, an orange trail goes 0.1 mile on a curved boardwalk out along the wetland and passes an old stone cellar.

At a bend in the road at 0.7 mile, the Blue and History trails curve left and the Red Trail makes a sharp right turn uphill. It follows a stone wall marking the boundary between the New York City watershed lands and the preserve. At junction 9 to the left, an orange trail heads south 0.2 mile to end at a 0.2 mile white trail which connects the Blue and Red trails. After making a sharp left, the Red Trail is along relatively level ground. It turns left again and parallels the bed of the railroad which once moved stone from the quarry to the construction site for the Kenisco Dam. After briefly joining the railbed, the trail descends steeply downhill to turn right where, at junction 11, a 0.2 mile white trail goes left to the Blue Trail. At 1.4 miles, the Red Trail crosses the end of Hush Pond on a large mat of tangled tree roots. It joins a woods road, turns left to head downhill, and then turns right to pass through a seasonal wet area. Reaching a gravel path, the Red Trail turns left and turns left again when it reaches an unmarked woods road. At one time, quarry tailings tumbled down the cement wall. This portion of the Red Trail is a side trail of the History Trail, (purple dot). At 1.6 miles, the Blue Trail joins from the left at junction 13. The co-aligned trails continue on the gravel road. At the cascade, the Red and Blue trails continue straight ahead, while the History Trail is to the left and right.

Crusher Wall.

Just after a small bridge the Red and Blue trails split with the Red Trail bearing right uphill through laurel. At 1.8 miles, it reaches junction 20 where, from the right, the History Trail joins at views of Cranberry Lake. Heading downhill, they join the Blue Trail briefly, and then split off to the right. The Red and History trails go under the cliffs where a derelict tipper (a machine used in quarrying operations) looms overhead. Leaving the quarry area, the co-aligned trails are along a woods road. At junction 34 at 2.2 miles, the Yellow Trail joins from the left and leaves at junction 35 at 2.4 miles. The History Trail turns left at junction 36. Continuing on the woods road, the Red Trail turns right at junction 37, where a white trail heads back 0.1 mile to an overflow parking area near the Nature Center. The Red Trail heads towards the entrance road to close the loop.

History Trail   *Length: 1.9 miles Blaze: purple dot*
A hike along the History Trail is a visit to the quarrying operations which supplied the stone for the Kensico Dam. The trail was also developed to relate the importance of Kensico Reservoir's watershed. It is easiest to follow the History Trail in a clockwise direction. Click on www.westchestergov.com/parks/Trailways. htm for a copy of the Cranberry Lake History Trail map. It is frequently co-aligned with the Red Trail.

From the Nature Center, the History Trail heads north for 0.2 mile and turns right at junction 36 to join the Red Trail. At an open spot with views of Cranberry Lake at junction 20, at 0.6 mile, the History Trail leaves to the left. It crosses a former railbed and passes a 0.1 mile side trail which loops around the quarry floor on a path outlined with rocks and returns to the railbed at junction 18. The History Trail enters the quarry at junction 19 and heads to the top of the quarry. Because there are no paint blazes on the rocks and no signposts, it is tricky to follow the route down from the top of the quarry. Once down from the top at 1.2 miles, turn left near the second of two ponds where at 0.1 mile white trail goes back to junction 18. The History Trail heads left past a decrepit tennis court and crosses a wet area. It heads downhill to a cascade at 1.3 miles at junction 14 and meets the Blue and Red Trails at junction 15. To the left, a spur trail of the History Trail heads south along the remains of the crusher wall for a 0.1 mile round trip.

The History Trail passes junction 15 where Blue and Red Trails go north along Cranberry Lake and then goes along the causeway with views of South Pond. It passes an orange trail at junction 16 which goes 0.1 mile past stone chambers and along a board walk to rejoin the History Trail at junction 7. The History Trail follows the Red Trail until junction 1 at 1.8 miles, when it bears right to return to the parking lot and the Nature Center.

NEARBY TRAIL: Bronx River Pathway

DRIVING: From the Bronx River Parkway at the Kensico Dam in Valhalla, use Route 22 north. Once past the dam, make the first right turn onto Old Orchard Street and again the first right to enter the preserve [41.082023N 73.755758W].

PUBLIC TRANSPORTATION: None available

For contact information, see Appendix, Westchester County Parks—Cranberry Lake Preserve.

Croton Point Park

Croton-on-Hudson • 5.8 miles, 504 acres

Dig into the soil of Croton Point Park and you are likely to find evidence of human history, one that stretches back more than 6,000 years. Shell middens and prehistoric artifacts speak to a Native American presence while remnants of Colonial era farming and brick making from the industrial era are still evident on this peninsula that juts out into the Hudson River.

Croton is named for the sachem (a chief of the Algonquin tribe), Kenoten, whose name means "wild wind." A visit to Croton Point Park on a wind-whipped winter day may explain the use of the name and why the Native Americans did not winter here: but that same breeze blowing in summer offers a refreshing relief on a hot day. Weather aside, the many walking opportunities offer expansive views of the Hudson River, Haverstraw and Croton Bays.

Native Americans harvested oysters, as evidenced by the shell middens located throughout the park. It is possible that they stayed longer or returned to the same sites on a regular basis. Colonial documentation indicates that the Kitchawonks built a palisaded village at the entrance to the southernmost point, which colonialists would first call Teller's Point and later Croton Point. To the right of the entrance road from the bluffs on Croton Neck, they might have seen Henry Hudson's ship, the *Half Moon*, anchored in Haverstraw Bay, which is the north boundary of the peninsula. In 1899, an archaeological study for the American Museum of Natural History found evidence of extensive Native American earthworks on the western portion of the bluffs.

Croton Point Park includes the site of the former Croton landfill. When the county acquired the property in the 1920's, 70 acres in a section of the park that had originally been a wetlands were set aside to be utilized as a landfill. Use of the landfill ended in 1986 and capping of the section was completed in 1995. Before it closed, the landfill was often referred to as the "Croton Dump," a misnomer, because at a dump, garbage is left exposed to weather and scavengers, while at a landfill, garbage deposits are covered daily with a layer of soil.

TRAILS

There are no marked trails at Croton Point and much of the walking is along gravel roads. From the upper parking lot across from the gate to camping, it is 0.8 mile out to Tellers Point. Before reaching a view south to the Tappan Zee Bridge, the road passes English or common yew trees planted by Robert Underhill near his house. They have grown to an impressive size.

The site of the capped landfill now encompasses an 113-acre area and what had once been the feeding ground for thousands of seagulls is now an expansive meadow. With panoramic views out over the Hudson River, it offers opportunities for observing eagles, owls, and other birds, and in summer, butterflies. It is a 1.3-mile walk around the base of the landfill.

The road behind the park office leads up to the picnic area on the bluffs of

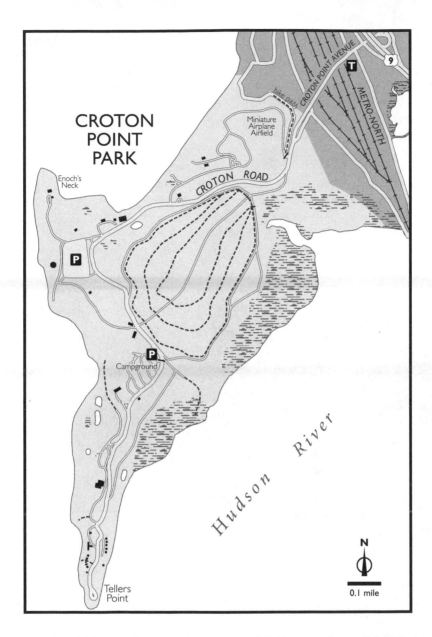

CROTON
POINT
PARK

Enoch's
Neck

Miniature
Airplane
Airfield

bike path

CROTON POINT AVENUE

METRO-NORTH

CROTON ROAD

Campground

Hudson River

Tellers
Point

N

0.1 mile

Croton Neck, which was also a model airplane field for members of the Miniature Airplane Association of Westchester. Signs caution about low-flying aircraft. Although the bluffs are natural, the airfield is a capped landfill. A 0.3 mile path heads down off the landfill to the bike path to Half Moon Bay, and is closed when the airfield is active.

CONNECTING TRAILS: CrOssining Bridge, the bike path to Half Moon Bay

DRIVING: From Route 9, take Croton Point Avenue, turn west towards the river, [41.187601N 73.887092W] and follow signs into the park.

PUBLIC TRANSPORTATION: Metro-North Hudson Line, Croton-Harmon Station. Walk up the entrance road to Croton Point Avenue, turn left, and follow signs to the park. It is a mile walk from the train station to the park office. From there, it is 0.6 mile along the base of the landfill or 0.8 mile along the road to the gate at the campground. The road to the nature center is 0.4 mile from the park office.

For contact information, see Appendix, Westchester County Parks—Croton Point Park.

FROM TRADING POST TO COUNTY PARK

Croton Point, perhaps home to the now Town of Cortlandt's first colonial settlers, was purchased from the Indians in 1682 by Cornelius Van Bursam, who then granted William and Sarah Teller permission to live and run a trading post on the southern point, which became known as Teller's Point. The area was then acquired by the Van Cortlandt estate. By the late 1700's descendants of the Tellers, now linked to the Van Cortlandt family by marriage, owned the point.

Wine Cellar.

Robert Underhill purchased 250 acres in 1804 and at his death, his two sons inherited the property. One son, Dr. Robert Underhill, who acquired an 85-acre tract, gave up his medical practice in New York, took up farming, and eventually established a reputation as an agriculturalist. He developed the high quality Croton grape, with a flavor valued for wine, but, unfortunately, difficult to grow.

In 1837, the second son, William, established a 165-acre brickyard on the point, one of 34 brickyards in Cortlandt. Marked with the imprint W.A.U., the bricks were advertised to have a "fine edge and durable qualities." A village with a store, tavern, and school was around the brickyard which was located in the present-day parking lot near the picnic pavilion. Some buildings remain: two wine cellars (barrel-vaulted brick structures built into the hillside along the exit road), a barn, carriage house, and a school.

About 1900 Croton Point was leased to a club and summer bungalows were built. In 1923, Westchester County purchased it as a park and built baseball fields and a camp for children. The camp was moved to Mountain Lakes Park in 1964.

Graham Hills Park

Pleasantville • 9.8 miles, 431 acres

Wedged between the Taconic State and Saw Mill River parkways, Graham Hills Park is a popular mountain biking destination with narrow trails geared toward expert and advanced bikers. A sign at the entrance warns users that the trails are not for "sissypants." The sign also warns against modifying the trails to suit riding ability. The warning is posted because the trails are deceptively easier closest to the entrance and that they lead downhill making the return trip harder. It is recommended that hikers use the park during weekdays, avoiding weekends and evenings, especially during summer, when bicycle traffic is the heaviest.

The area is named for Dr. Isaac Gilbert Graham, a surgeon's mate in the Revolutionary War who settled in the area in 1785. At one time the hamlet of Graham Hills was a station on the Putnam Division of the New York Central Railroad. The county acquired the property in 1963 and opened it in 1973.

TRAILS

The park is bounded by houses and two parkways, making it hard to accidentally stray off the property. Since the trails were designed and built by mountain

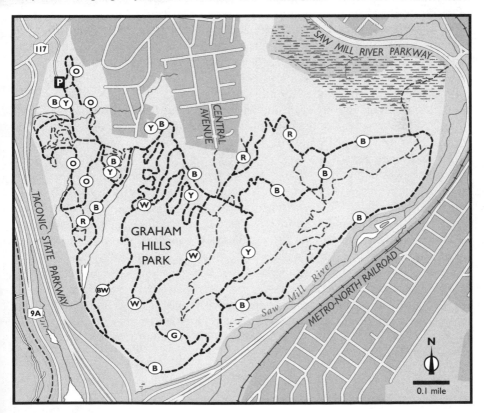

bikers for mountain biking, they meander, undulate, ascend, and descend more frequently than hikers would like and thus provide a more interesting ride.

Three trails go directly up or downhill, making them more challenging than the other trails in the park. Hikers should be especially watchful of downhill riders on these three challenging trails. There are three unmarked trails which are noted in the description of trails where they start or cross.

Blue Trail
Length: 3.6 miles Blaze: blue

The blue trail is the entrance trail and main route through the park. From the parking lot, the blue trail heads downhill and crosses a bridge over a wet area. Immediately after crossing a bridge, it passes the first junction with the pink trail to the right. At 0.2 mile, a pink trail is to the left and another one leaves to the right. The blue trail splits at a trail junction at 0.4 mile. Turn right to go counterclockwise around the loop. The trail crosses the top of a deep ravine and then descends on a woods road. Noise from the Taconic State Parkway is audible. At 0.5 mile, a pink trail heads to the right 0.1 mile connecting with more pink trails.

Continuing downhill, the trail passes a stone foundation with steps leading down into it and then passes through an open area before reentering the woods. It is on a woods road parallel to a fence marking the boundary between the park and the Taconic State Parkway. Leaving the woods road, the trail heads uphill briefly. At 0.9 mile, it passes the end of the blue/white trail which connects, in 0.2 mile, uphill to the white trail. Descending, the blue trail turns to parallel the Saw Mill River Parkway and passes Vinny's Left Collarbone (green) to the left at 1.0 mile. After crossing a stream, the blue trail, at 1.4 miles, passes the junction with the orange trail to the left, which connects to the blue trail on top of the ridge. The blue trail descends steeply and then levels off at 1.5 miles. An alternate to the blue trail is to the left to avoid a seasonal wet area at 1.7 miles. The trail reaches a foundation in a cedar grove at 1.9 miles. After passing a second foundation at 2.2 miles, the trail curves away from the parkway and road noise diminishes. At 2.4 miles, it passes the green trail and then a 0.3 mile unmarked emergency exit to the traffic light on the Saw Mill River Parkway in Thornwood.

The blue trail ascends the ridge and at 2.6 miles, it passes the red trail on the right. It reaches an open old gravel pit and then the other end of the green trail to the left at 2.7 miles. After crossing a stone wall, the trail reaches a high point, leveling off slightly. It then heads steeply uphill. The trail alternately climbs and levels off and passes an orange trail to the left at 2.9 miles. The blue trail passes first an unmarked trail that leads 0.6 miles downhill to the left and then a red trail to the right. Almost immediately an unmarked trail to the right leads to an entrance off Central Avenue (no parking) and the white trail leaves to the left.

After descending sometimes steeply over rocky terrain and passing through an open area, the blue trail again passes the white trail to the left at 3.1 miles and then the yellow trail at 3.2 miles. The blue trail turns left along a woods road with wetlands to the left. Straight ahead a green trail twists and turns 0.4 mile through a section called Disneyland and returns to the blue trail. At 3.6 miles, the blue trail closes the loop.

Green Trail   *Length: 0.4 mile Blaze: green*

The green trail provides an alternate route to the blue trail in the easternmost portion of the park. At 0.2 miles, it passes through an overgrown meadow. It ends on the blue trail at a wide intersection.

Orange Trail   *Length 0.4 miles Blaze: orange*

At the base of the ridge on the south side of the park, the orange trail heads almost directly uphill at a steady grade, passing at first a 0.6 mile unmarked trail to the left and then a 0.8 mile trail to the right. Both unmarked trails join the blue trail on the ridge. The orange trail reaches a flat area and turns left to end on the blue trail.

Pink Trails   *Length 2.2 miles Blaze: pink*

Many pink trails wiggle up, down and around the hill in the northwest portion of the park. While some trails might not actually have a pink blaze, consider that all of them do. Since these trails are likely to change frequently, a description would be fleeting. For some the noise of the nearby Taconic State Parkway is present, even in leaf-on season. The pink trail to the left of the entrance is an alternate way to start or end a hike or ride.

Red Trail   *Length: 0.5 mile Blaze: red*

Starting on the blue trail, the red trail, one of the three challenging trails in the park, heads very steeply downhill. It passes a large slab rock on the right and ends at an unmarked trail which connects with the blue trail in 0.1 mile.

Vinny's Left Collarbone   *Length: 0.4 mile Blaze: green*

Starting a third of the way around the southern part of the white trail, Vinny's Left

Along the yellow trail.

Collarbone is a direct route downhill to where the blue trail parallels the Saw Mill River Parkway. It is one of the three challenging trails.

White Trail   *Length: 1.0 mile Blaze: white*
Forming a loop off the blue trail, the white trail travels downhill through open woods and joins the yellow trail briefly at 0.2 mile. Gradually descending, it goes through the Rock Garden and then meets the blue/white trail at 0.5 mile. Heading uphill, it passes the Vinny's Left Collarbone at 0.7 mile. Continuing its ascent, it passes the end of the yellow trail just before ending at the blue trail.

Yellow Trail   *Length: 1.3 miles Blaze: yellow*
Beginning on the blue trail, the yellow trail alternately ascends and descends along sweeping turns. At 0.5 mile, it reaches the white trail at a T junction and turns left to join it briefly. The co-aligned trails separate with the yellow trail turning right to continue its uphill journey. The traverses have long uphill and downhill sections as the trail overall ascends. It ends at the white trail.

DRIVING: From the northbound Taconic State Parkway, take the Route 117 Exit and turn right. The park entrance is the first right turn. From southbound Route 9A, take the Route 117 Exit and turn left at the top of the ramp. The park entrance is to the right, past the ramps onto the Taconic State Parkway [41.123342N 73.804893W].

PUBLIC TRANSPORTATION: Metro-North Harlem Line to the Pleasantville Station. Walk south to Bedford Road, cross the road, and follow it to the next intersection where Bedford Road turns left. It is 0.9 mile from the station to the park entrance.

For contact information, see Appendix, Westchester County Parks.

Granite Knolls Park

Shrub Oak • 7.0 miles, 125 acres

A huge granite glacier erratic almost the size of a small house is the centerpiece of Granite Knolls Park, which was once the site of a small scale quarry operation that closed in the 1930s. Dubbed the Giant Boulder, it towers over pieces that had been split off from one end. Some pieces have marks from the quarrymen's drills. Looking at the pieces, you can see where many of them would fit back together and wish you could restore the boulder to its original size.

The park was also once farmland and it is crossed with stone walls built with stones removed from the fields. Trails within Granite Knolls were named to reflect its history and prior use.

With money set aside to purchase open space, the Town of Yorktown purchased 200 acres in 2010 from the heirs of the owner who had bought the property for a development to be called Granite Knolls that was never built. Its proximity to the pedestrian bridge over the Taconic State Parkway, Woodlands Legacy Fields Park, and Sylvan Glen Park Preserve made it possible to have a 20.1 mile trail system, unusual for town parks.

TRAILS

Visitors to Granite Knolls will notice the two kinds of trails: woods roads and narrow, winding trails. The latter with their undulating route were designed for mountain biking, but hikers and trail runners can use those trails to visit small quarries or traverse the top of the knoll.

Within the park, there are four short trails. The 0.3 mile Giant Boulder Trail (blue) leads to the central attraction of Granite Knolls. Take time to walk around

The Giant Boulder.

the boulder. Some workers carved their names into the top. The 0.2-mile Stony Street Trail (orange) provides neighborhood access from Stony Street. Winding 0.2 miles through boulders and small quarry operations, the Stark Hollow Trail (yellow) is named for John Stark, a tenant farmer. The Pond Trail (yellow) is a stub trail which leads 200 feet from the Taconic Bridge Trail to a pond at the edge of the property.

Taconic Bridge Trail   *Length: 1.0 mile Blaze: pink*
The east end of the Taconic Bridge Trail connects Woodlands Legacy Fields Park (0.2 mile) via the Yorktown Trailway to Sylvan Glen Park Preserve (0.7 mile). From the end of the approach to the Bridge over the Taconic, the trail turns right to follow the Yorktown Trailway for 100 feet. It turns left to go into the woods making sweeping turns as it traverses along the side of the hill. At 0.4 mile, it reaches a stone wall and then turns left on a woods road where Dynamite Run (lavender) begins to the right. The Taconic Bridge Trail soon joins the Circolara Trail (white) coming from the right. The two trails are on a narrow treadway and at 0.5 mile, the Taconic Bridge Trail turns left on to a woods road, the Circolara Trail goes straight. Arthur's Ramble is to the right.

Heading downhill, the Taconic Bridge Trail leaves the woods road and then at the bottom of the hill joins another. At 0.7 mile to the left, the large exposed root ball of a fallen tree is at the junction of the Pond Trail (yellow) which goes 200 feet to a pond. Where the Taconic Bridge Trail turns left to go between two pillars, the 0.3 mile Giant Boulder Trail (blue) trail goes straight. The Taconic Bridge Trail parallels a stone wall topped with barbed wire and heads steeply uphill though an area overrun with invasives. The trail crosses a berm, passes a barn slated for demolition, and heads uphill to cross Stony Street where it continues in Sylvan Glen Park Preserve.

Arthur's Ramble   *Length: 0.5 miles Blaze: yellow*
Beginning at a junction with Dynamite Run (lavender), Arthur's Ramble heads north along a woods road. Named for the farmer who owned the property after the

An Unusual Alliance

Hikers and mountain bikers are usually at odds over trail use. But in the Town of Yorktown they have worked together to establish a trail system and did so in record time. With the acquisition of the Granite Knolls property imminent in 2010, the authors of this book, who are residents of the town asked permission on behalf of the Trail Conference to build trails in the parkland that surrounds the Taconic State Parkway. Shortly after permission was granted, members of the Westchester Mountain Biking Association asked to help. These two groups worked together to build trails at Granite Knolls Park, Woodlands Legacy Fields Park, and additional trails at Sylvan Glen Park Preserve. This partnership raised funds, recruited volunteers, and involved youth groups. On average, it takes three years to build 3-4 miles of trail; here 10.7 miles of trails plus board walks, bridges, signs, stone steps, and kiosks were completed in less than two years.

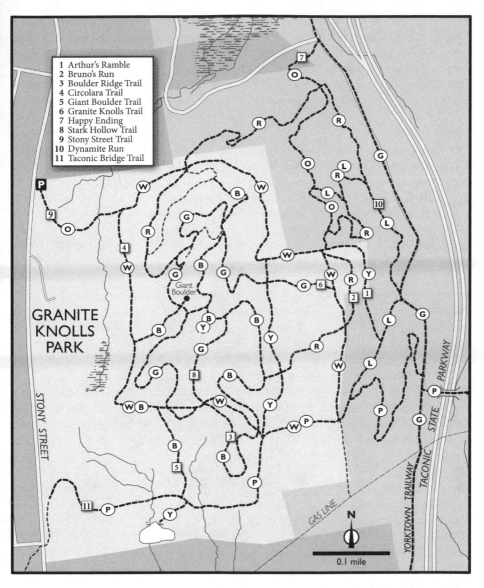

GRANITE
KNOLLS
PARK

1 Arthur's Ramble
2 Bruno's Run
3 Boulder Ridge Trail
4 Circolara Trail
5 Giant Boulder Trail
6 Granite Knolls Trail
7 Happy Ending
8 Stark Hollow Trail
9 Stony Street Trail
10 Dynamite Run
11 Taconic Bridge Trail

Giant
Boulder

STONY STREET

GAS LINE

YORKTOWN TRAILWAY

TACONIC STATE PARKWAY

N

0.1 mile

quarry closed, the trail turns west and passes Bruno's Run to the left and then joins the Circolara Trail (white) coming from the left at 0.2 mile. Continuing west, the co-aligned trails split and Arthur's Ramble turns south to end at the Circolara Trail.

Boulder Ridge Trail

Length: 1.0 mile Blaze: blue

Enjoyed by mountain bikers and hikers alike, the Boulder Ridge Trail meanders through granite boulders of varying sizes. It begins on the Circolara Trail (white) near the junction of the Stark Hollow Trail (yellow) and heads south passing large boulders. It turns to head north and then crosses the Circolara Trail at 0.2 mile and enters a rock field. Squeezing through two boulders, it winds its way uphill. The trail passes Bruno's Run (red) to the right at 0.5 mile and heads downhill. At 0.6 mile, it turns to pass a large boulder with umbilicaria lichen clinging to its side. It joins the Stark Hollow Trail (yellow) briefly and turns to the right at 0.7 mile. Heading downhill it joins the Granite Knolls Trail (green) briefly at 0.8 mile and then leaves to continue its downward trek. It turns to join first Bruno's Run bypass and then Bruno's Run before it ends at the Circolara Trail.

Bruno's Run
Length: 1.3 miles Blaze: red
The longest trail in the park, Bruno's Run was named for Bruno Grenci, one of the owners of the Mohegan Quarry, which was located at what is now Sylvan Glen Park Preserve and Granite Knolls Park. From the Granite Knolls Trail, Bruno's Run heads downhill at a gentle grade along the western flank of the ridge. It passes a paint-blazed (red) 0.2 mile bypass built to offer a challenge to experienced mountain bikers. Just before reaching the Circolara Trail (white), the Boulder Ridge Trail (blue) enters from the left. They reach the Circolara Trail where the Boulder Ridge Trail ends and Bruno's Run continues straight.

Bruno's Run turns to cross a boulder field that is the beginning of the line of granite boulders that are scattered up to and along the ridge. The trail loops uphill, turns, and continue its descent. After crossing a small rock field at 0.4 mile, the trail continues downhill and crosses Happy Ending (orange) at 0.5 mile. It turns right to parallel the Taconic State Parkway, where in leaf-off season, the Yorktown Trailway is visible to the left. Working its way uphill, Bruno's Run turns right to join Dynamite Run (lavender) at 0.7 mile and then separates. Continuing uphill, Bruno's Run turns left to join Happy Ending (orange) at 0.9 mile. Together they reach the Circolara Trail at 1.0 mile and Arthur's Ramble (yellow) where Happy Ending ends and Bruno's Run briefly joins the Circolara Trail. At a Y junction, Bruno's Run heads left, goes through the woods, crosses the Circolara Trail to at Arthur's Ramble at 1.2 miles.

Circolara Trail
Length: 1.2 miles Blaze: white
In Italian, circolara means circular, which describes the Circolara Trail's route around the park. Named to recognize the nationality of many of the quarry workers, the Circolara Trail is almost entirely on woods roads with evidence of quarrying operations along its route.

From the junction with the Taconic Bridge Trail (pink), the co-aligned trails head through the woods on a narrow path paralleling a stone wall. At 0.1 mile, the Circolara Trail goes straight onto a woods road, the Taconic Bridge Trail turns left and Arthur's Ramble (yellow) begins to the right. Almost immediately, the Circolara Trail crosses the Boulder Ridge Trail (blue) to the left and heads downhill. To the right is a cable winch drum just before the start of the Stark Hollow Trail (yellow). At 0.3 mile,

Cable winch drum.

the Giant Boulder Trail (blue) joins from the left. The co-aligned trails make a 90 degree turn to head north and pass a small quarry where cross timbers are visible if the water is low. The Giant Boulder Trail leaves to the right at 0.4 mile. Extensive wetlands are to the left and, as the Circolara Trail heads slightly downhill, the ridge rises above to the right.

At a T junction, the Circolara Trail turns right. To the left, the Stony Street Trail (orange) heads 0.2 mile to Stony Street (no parking). At 0.6 mile, the Circolara Trail goes through stone walls and crosses Bruno's Run (red). Heading uphill, the trail crosses more stone walls and at 0.9 mile, joins Arthur's Ramble (yellow). At the next intersection, they split with Arthur's Ramble going straight. The Circolara Trail turns right as it very briefly joins Bruno's Run which leaves to the left. It passes the Granite Knolls Trail (green) to the right at 1.0 miles. After crossing Bruno's Run, the Circolara Trail passes a series of round pits whose origins or use is unknown. The circle is completed at the Taconic Bridge Trail.

Dynamite Run
Length: 0.4 mile Blaze: lavender
The northern portion of Dynamite Run is a challenging mountain bike trail that connects Happy Ending (orange) to the Yorktown Trailway. From there it heads uphill on an old woods road to the Taconic Bridge Trail (pink).

Granite Knolls Trail
Length: 0.9 mile Blaze: green
On its tour of the top of the ridge, the Granite Knolls Trail winds over and around boulders and slabs of granite. Beginning on the Circolara Trail on the east side of the park, the Granite Knolls Trail heads west. It crosses Arthur's Ramble (yellow) at 0.1 mile. On its climb to the ridge, it briefly joins the Boulder Ridge Trail (blue) and leaves it to go around a long, low rock outcropping and two sloping rock faces at 0.4 mile. After passing Bruno's Run (red) to the left, it winds through a boulder field. It crosses the Giant Boulder Trail (blue) and, at 0.6 mile, passes the end of the Stark Hollow Trail (yellow) to the left. Heading downhill, the trail goes through small quarry operations, passing the last one at 0.8 mile. It crosses the Circolara Trail only to loop back around a large boulder before it ends.

Happy Ending
Length: 0.4 mile Blaze: orange
Mountain bikers built this trail and dubbed it Happy Ending because, for them, it was the happy ending to a good ride. Initially, Happy Ending is briefly co-aligned with Bruno's Run which leaves to the right. It passes Dynamite Run (lavender) to the right at 0.1 mile, crosses Bruno's Run (red) at 0.3 mile and ends where the sewer line joins the Yorktown Trailway.

CONNECTING TRAILS & PARKS: Sylvan Glen Park Preserve, Woodlands Legacy Fields Park, Yorktown Trailway

DRIVING: Access is through either Woodlands Legacy Fields Park when the fields are open (see Woodlands Legacy Fields Park for driving directions) or Buckhorn Street parking for the Yorktown Trailway [41.324734N 73.824787W].

PUBLIC TRANSPORTATION: None available

For contact information, see Appendix, Town of Yorktown.

Irvington Woods
V. Everit Macy Park

Irvington• 5.7 miles, 272 acres

These once sparsely visited parks, Irvington Woods and neighboring V. Everit Macy Park are now popular places for hikers and mountain bikers. Adjacent to the Saw Mill River Parkway, the two parks provide a woodland space and a hill, that blocks much of the traffic noise from either the NYS Thruway or the Saw Mill River Parkway along most of the trails.

Once inside the parks, it is difficult to tell where one park ends and the other begins. The Village of Irvington owns Irvington Woods, while Westchester County owns V. Everit Macy Park, which, however, is managed by the Town of Greenburgh. Some of Irvington Woods is on Irvington Reservoir lands and other parts are on property purchased from a developer as part of a deal to preserve open space. Most of Irvington Woods is property that had once been part of a number of large estates owned by such notables as Cyrus W. Field, the financier who created the company that laid the first transatlantic telegraph cable and Isaac Stern, a founder of the Stern Brothers Department stores. A composting site is located in the northern part of the Irvington Woods and woods roads pass through it.

Macy Park has three sections: ball fields and picnic facilities, Great Hunger Park at Woodland Lakes, and the hills west of the Saw Mill River Parkway, where a trail system connects with Irvington Woods. Great Hunger Memorial Park is adjacent to the South County Trailway and has a picnic tables but no trails.

Originally called Woodlands Park, the park was renamed to honor of V. Everit Macy, a wealthy industrialist and the county's Commissioner of Public Welfare, the first commissioner of any kind in Westchester County. He later served as Commissioner of Parks. It was under his guidance that the Grasslands complex was transformed from a poorhouse to a complex of hospitals and a correctional facility. As a businessman, he assembled a chain of newspapers that ultimately became the *Journal News*.

TRAILS

Visitors enjoy a variety of trails ranging from wide tracks to narrow paths. Most of the wide trails were the result of illegal ATV use. Many Eagle Scout projects improved the trails and as more people began using the trails, the ATV abuse was no longer a problem.

The trail system is named in memory of Peter Oley, a long-time Irvington resident who was a teacher, track coach and local historian. He played an important role in preserving the woods and establishing the trails here.

Irvington Woods has five short trails. The Barney Brook Trail (BB) is a 0.2 mile connection between the Waterline (WL) and Hermit's Grave (HG) trails. The Cross County Trail (XC) is a loop off the Waterline Trail. The Hermit Wetlands Trail (HW) leads 0.1 mile from the North South Trail (NS)to the Hermit Wetlands. The Split Rock Trail (SR) goes 0.1 mile between the North South and Waterline trails to pass a massive glacial erratic, split wide enough to allow hikers to walk easily

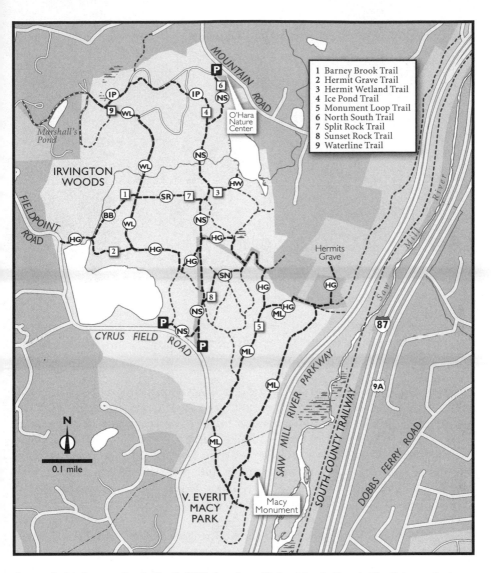

through it. Sunset Rock Trail (SN) heads off the North South Trail to end at an overlook at 0.1 mile.

Ice Pond Trail
Length: 0.9 mile Blaze: IP

Starting from the junction with North South Trail (NS) where it comes into the parking area on Mountain Road, the Ice Pond Trail heads north and crosses the access road to a compost site. The trail reaches a woods road and turns left to head downhill. After briefly leaving the woods road, it joins it again. It passes the Waterline Trail to the left at 0.3 mile and then the ice pond to the right. The Cross Country Trail to the left connects in 0.2 mile to the Waterline Trail. After passing Marshalls Pond with a retaining wall and iron pipe fencing along its edge, it ends at a paved driveway overlooking the ball fields of Irvington High School.

Jenkins Rock along the Hermit's Grave Trail.

Hermit's Grave Trail   *Length: 0.8 mile Blaze: HG*
Beginning at Fieldpoint Road (no parking), the Hermit's Grave Trail is named for Johann Wilhelm Stolting, an eccentric recluse and well educated German immigrant who roamed the area before his death in 1888.

The trail heads downhill through a grove of Norway spruce to Irvington Reservoir and Jenkins Rock. It crosses a bridge and passes the Barney Brook Trail (BB) to the left. After heading uphill, the trail turns away from the reservoir, passing the Waterline Trail (WL) to the right at 0.2 mile. Skirting the edge of another grove of Norway spruce along a woods road, it crosses an open area to head uphill, joins the Sunset Rock Trail (SN) and immediately splits left. The trail wanders through a stream bed and, after crossing the North South Trail (NS), heads uphill. At a T junction, an unmarked trail to the left leads 0.2 mile to the Hermit Wetlands Trail (HW).

At 0.5 mile, the Sunset Rock Trail (SN) to the right leads to Sunset Rock, while Hermit's Grave Trail goes left and turns right heading downhill beside a rock outcropping. At a T junction, an unmarked woods road leads left to a former dump and the trail turns right. The trail reaches a junction where it turns left to join the Monument Loop Trail which comes from the right. The co-aligned trails turn right onto a woods road. At 0.8 mile, the Monument Loop Trail turns right onto a former entrance to the Saw Mill parkway. The Hermits Grave Trail continues for 200 feet, turns left, and climbs uphill to end at the Hermit's Grave, the only marked grave in the village.

North South Trail   *Length: 0.7 mile Blaze: NS*
Beginning at parking lot on Cyrus Field road, the North South Trail Hermits Grave heads uphill. At a former road, it turns left. At 0.2 mile to the right, the Sunset Rock Trail (SN) crosses it and Monument Loop Trail (ML) begins. The North South trail jogs right and then left as it crosses the Hermit's Grave Trail (HG) to ascend steeply.

It passes the Split Rock Trail (SR) to the left, then Hermit Wetlands Trail (HW) to the right at 0.4 mile. It crosses a bridge, left, then reaches a rise and parallels a ravine. After turning tight at the Ice Pond Trail (IP), it heads uphill to end at the O'Hara Nature Center.

Monument Loop Trail   *Length: 0.8 mile Blaze: ML*
Because the Monument Loop Trail is a circle, there are many different places to begin your walk. From the junction where it and the Hermit's Grave Trail (HG) are co-aligned, go counterclockwise. The Monument Loop Trail passes a small split rock on the left. It heads steeply uphill to reach a level section and passes an unmarked woods road to the right which leads downhill to meet the North South Trail (NS) in 0.2 mile.

The Monument Loop Trail passes another unmarked trail to the left as it continues downhill. At 0.3 mile, the trail passes a third unmarked trail leading 80 feet out to Cyrus Field Road. At a rock outcropping far to the right, it crosses a gas line. It reaches a trail junction at 0.4 mile where straight ahead is a tangle of old unmarked ATV tracks. Traffic noise from the Saw Mill River Parkway in the valley below is audible. The trail reaches a junction at 0.5 mile. Bearing left, it is routed on a woods road. To the right, a trail leads to another junction where a side trail heads 100 feet downhill, to the left toward the Macy Monument or straight to pass rock benches and lead into unmarked ATV tracks.

Bearing left along the woods road, the trail immediately passes steps to a stone bench to the left. Crossing the gas line again, the trail passes more benches and, at 0.7 mile, heads uphill along two at-grade sections before reaching still more benches. Ahead on the right is a massive stone retaining wall which supports an abandoned concrete road. The trail turns left, continues uphill, reaches a dirt road 50 feet above the end of concrete paving, and joins the Hermit's Grave Trail (HG). The co-aligned trails continue uphill on a pathway lined with logs. The Monument Loop Trail closes the loop.

Spring Peepers

That intense chirping sound so often heard in the early spring woods is made by one of the smallest native frogs—spring peepers. These harbingers of spring, like wood and tree frogs, survive winter's coldest weather hidden under the damp leaf litter at water's edge, where they do not eat, breath, or even have a heartbeat. As temperatures rise, these creatures come to life, the males singing as they call to mates. By the end of March, the forest abounds with this serenade from the fresh water of vernal pools.

Most animal species avoid freezing and adapt to the cold either by migrating, hibernating, growing dense extra coats of feathers or fur, or burning calories to maintain body warmth. In almost every animal, freezing can cause tissue damage. Spring peepers effectively counteract the cold winter temperatures by creating special antifreeze composed of sugars or sugar alcohols. As ice forms in the frogs' cells, this compound draws water out, leaving behind the anatomical equivalent of thick maple syrup. Once the warmer weather arrives, peepers "spring" back to life and sing.

Waterline Trail   *Length: 0.4 mile Blaze: WL*

Heading south from the Ice Pond Trail (IP), the Waterline Trail follows an underground waterline. It passes the Cross Country Trail (XC), at right, which circles 0.2 mile back to the Ice Pond Trail. It then passes one of several fire hydrants. At the next intersection it turns right, with an unmarked 0.2 mile trail to a composting site. At 0.2 mile, it crosses a stream with a rock-lined course. The Barney Brook Trail (BB) is to the right and the Split Rock Trail (SR) is to the left. Heading downhill, it ends at the Hermit's Grave Trail (HG).

DRIVING: To reach the southern section of the parks, take Route 9 to Irvington, turn east onto Harriman Road heading away from the Hudson River. When Harriman Road reaches the Irvington Reservoir, it makes a sharp right turn and becomes Cyrus Field Road [41.034357N 73.848802W]. Follow Cyrus Field Road to the park entrance to the left. Cyrus Field Road can also be reached from the southbound Saw Mill River Parkway, just south of Great Hunger Memorial at Woodland Lakes Park. There is no access to Cyrus Field Road from the northbound lanes.

To reach the northern section of Irvington Woods, take Route 9 to the Irvington/ Tarrytown line. Turn east onto East Sunnyside Lane and head uphill away from the Hudson River. At 0.6 mile, turn right onto Mountain Road, and head for 0.7 mile to a parking area to the right [41.041874N 73.845965W]. Mountain Road can also be reached from an exit on the southbound Saw Mill River Parkway, just after driving under the Thruway. Take caution as you will cross the traffic entering from the Thruway. There is no access to Mountain Road from the northbound lanes.

PUBLIC TRANSPORTATION: None available

For contact information, see Appendix, Greenburgh, Irvington.

Eugene and Agnes Meyer Preserve

Armonk • 6.7 miles, 247 acres

There are two distinct parts to the Eugene and Agnes Meyer Preserve and they are connected by a long abandoned section of Oregon Road. The preserve offers both gentle and rugged walks. The western portion, located off Sarles Street, has open meadows and woodlands; the eastern portion off Oregon Road has steep ridges and rocky crags. Within the preserve are wildflowers, meadows, vernal pools, rock outcroppings, wetlands, a ravine, and opportunities for birding.

At one time the preserve was Seven Springs, the weekend estate of Eugene and Agnes Meyer. He was, at various times, an investment banker, a public servant under seven presidents, and the owner of a communications network which included the *Washington Post*. His wife Agnes was an activist, journalist, author, lecturer, and

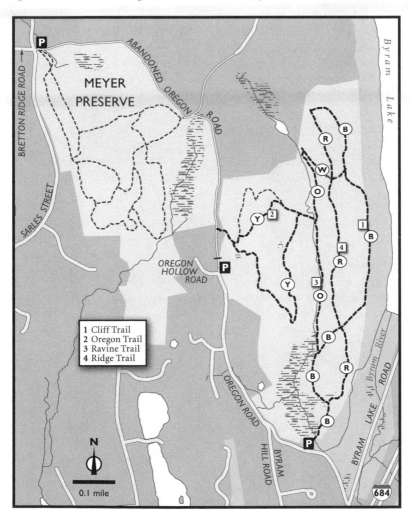

1 Cliff Trail
2 Oregon Trail
3 Ravine Trail
4 Ridge Trail

the first chair of Westchester County's Department of Recreation. Their daughter, Katharine Meyer Graham, eventually owned and ran the *Washington Post*. In 1973, the Meyer Foundation donated the land to The Nature Conservancy.

WESTERN SECTION

The trailhead on Sarles Street is the gateway to the western section of the preserve. The fields are completely mowed every few years, while paths are cut more frequently, although the routing can vary. During hot summer months, the open fields, with butterflies and a cacophony of insect noise, contrast with the woodland trails, where tree cover provides cooler temperatures and where little or no insect noise is heard. None of the trails in the western section are blazed. Although the fields present a challenge to those who prefer their trails marked, hikers should take this opportunity to become comfortable using unmarked tracks.

CONNECTING THE SECTIONS

A woods road and the abandoned section of Oregon Road separate the preserve from private lands and connect the two sections. From parking on Sarles Street, head straight ahead. The trail crosses a brook, continues on a rocky woods road, heads steeply uphill, and passes a glacial erratic. The woods road turns sharply right onto the abandoned section of Oregon Road where a gated road leads into private land. At 0.2 mile, the road skirts a white pine plantation. It passes, at 0.5 mile, the two trails that connect to fields in the western section of the preserve and then the red-blazed trail leading to the western section. Skirting the edge of wetlands to the right, abandoned Oregon Road passes private fields to the left, and at 0.7 mile, continues with preserve property now on both sides. It passes the junction with the Oregon Trail (yellow) at 0.8 mile and, after going through a gate, ends at 0.9 mile.

EASTERN SECTION

Oregon Road, off Byram Lake Road, is the access point to the eastern section of the Meyer Preserve. Hiking through this portion gives an impression of what the whole area might have looked like in its native state. The rocky crags and elevation gains along the trails are a vivid contrast to the trails in the fields of the western section. Mosses and ferns add color to the many gray rocks. In spring, vernal pools are adjacent to, or sometimes on the trails, making wet feet a real possibility. On hot summer days, the towering trees and exposed rock have a cooling effect. All trails are blazed. The Cliff (blue) and the Ridge (red) trails form a figure eight.

Cliff Trail   *Length: 1.0 mile Blaze: blue*
From the first parking area on Oregon Road, the Cliff Trail passes through a mountain bike barrier to enter a wetland and then a hemlock-hardwood forest. At a Y junction at 0.1 mile, the Cliff Trail heads left along the edge of a wetland, while the Ridge Trail (red) goes right through an opening in a large stone wall 50 feet away. The Cliff Trail passes the Ravine Trail (orange) to the left and heads uphill. The Ridge Trail crosses the Cliff Trail at 0.4 mile. Continuing uphill, the Cliff Trail passes a large rock outcropping to the right. Along the ridge, I-684 is both visible

and audible. There are views closer to the top edge of the cliff, but take care. At the bottom of a dip at 0.8 mile, the trail passes a white trail to the left, which leads in 0.1 mile to the Ridge and the Ravine trails. The Cliff Trail turns away from the views of Byram Lake, heads uphill, and leaves the noise from I-684 behind. After turning, the Cliff Trail descends through hemlocks devastated by the woolly adelgid. Dead trees litter the area; their bare dead branches sticking up like spines on a porcupine. The trail reaches the property boundary and turns left to end at the Ridge Trail at 1.0 mile.

Oregon Trail
Length: 0.9 mile Blaze: yellow

Not to be confused with abandoned Oregon Road, the Oregon Trail is a large loop with one stub connecting to the Ravine Trail (orange) and another to abandoned Oregon Road. From the Ravine Trail, the Oregon Trail begins by crossing a bridge and heading steeply uphill. In 250 feet, it reaches a junction where yellow blazes lead in both directions. Head counterclockwise and continue ascending. At the top of the hill, a chimney visible through white pines and Norway spruces is all that remains of the Meyer Estate, destroyed by fire in the 1940s.

The Oregon Trail turns onto a woods road and follows a stone-lined path for a short distance. At 0.3 mile, a short stub bears to the right out to the abandoned Oregon Road, where there is parking and the connection to the preserve's western section. Turning left, the Oregon Trail wiggles its way through the woods, heading downhill. At 0.6 mile, it reaches the southernmost point and turns. It passes around a huge rock to the left, makes a sharp right, and descends. It turns right to descend more steeply, closing the loop at 0.9 mile.

Ravine Trail
Length: 0.5 mile Blaze: orange

Beginning at a Y junction on the Cliff Trail (blue), the Ravine Trail heads north. It passes a large wetland to the left, and a towering ridge to the right. Ascending sometimes steeply, it passes through the narrowest part of the ravine at 0.2 mile,

Hugging the side of the ravine.

WOOLY ADELGID

An aphid-like insect, the woolly adelgid feeds on hemlocks by sucking fluid from the base of the needles. As it feeds, it may also inject toxins into the tree, weakening the tree and accelerating needle drop and branch dieback. Of Asian origin, this insect was first seen in the northeastern United States in the 1950s. It has been devastating hemlocks ever since and is spreading. Many stands of these graceful trees are already gone and few of those remaining are unaffected. Natural selection may eventually replace hemlocks with other species. But they will be missed because they are so often dominant in local woodlands and in moist ravines where they provide year-round shade.

with a stream so close you can touch it. Climbing above the stream, the trail passes, at 0.3 mile, the Oregon Trail (yellow) to the left at a bridge. At 0.5 mile, the Ravine Trail ends at the white trail at the property line. The white trail connects uphill in 0.1 mile to the Ridge (red) and Cliff trails.

Ridge Trail   *Length: 0.8 mile Blaze: red*
From the north end of the preserve, where the Cliff Trail (blue) ends, the Ridge Trail descends into a ravine and a notch, where it crosses the white trail connecting the Cliff Trail with the Ravine Trail (orange). Continuing downhill, it passes a vernal pool at 0.5 mile, then crosses the Cliff Trail. As the trail heads trough a ravine, I-684 can be heard, but not seen. The trail turns right to follow the base of a massive rock outcropping and then enter an open area.

Through the trees to the left is a 0.4 mile aqueduct lined with moss-covered stones. The aqueduct reroutes the stream (which empties the wetlands next to the preserve's entrance) so that the water can enter Bryam Lake, Mt. Kisco's water supply, instead of flowing into the outlet from the lake. It is possible to walk beside the aqueduct down to Route 22 near the dam (parking). The Ridge Trail enters the woods. After it crosses a stone wall capped with flat rocks, it ends at the Cliff Trail at 0.8 mile.

DRIVING: To reach the preserve's western section, take I-684 to N Y 172 and turn west toward Mt. Kisco. Make a left onto Sarles Street and drive 2.7 miles. A small parking area for 2 or 3 cars is located across from the intersection of Sarles Street and Bretton Ridge Road [41.150727N 73.696765W].

To reach the eastern section from southbound I-684, take Exit 3 (Route 22). If northbound, use Exit 3N (Route 22). Take Route 22 north to the traffic light at Cox Avenue and turn left. Follow Cox Avenue to where it bears left, and continue straight on Byram Lake Road. At 1.4 miles, turn left onto Oregon Road, where you will find the parking area in 0.2 mile [41.164993N 73.709158].There is additional parking at the end of the road and access to the Oregon Trail (yellow), beginning just past the fourth telephone pole on the abandoned road, near a boundary sign [41.156981N 73.700844W].

PUBLIC TRANSPORTATION: None available

For contact information, see Appendix, The Nature Conservancy.

Mianus River Gorge Preserve

Bedford Village • 5.0 miles, 719 acres

A sense of tranquility greets you when you enter the Mianus River Gorge Preserve. Photogenic and scenic, it is both relaxing and inspiring. The trail system is laid out to encourage visitors to walk in on one trail, and out on another. With numerous crossover trails, there are hikes of varying distances and one need not walk the full length of the preserve.

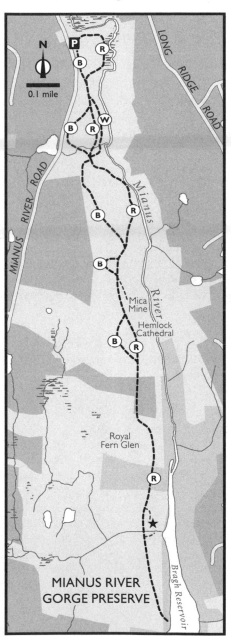

Founded in 1953, the Mianus Gorge Conservation Committee is dedicated to preserving "the virgin forest and abundant wildlife along the Mianus River in Bedford, New Castle, and Pound Ridge." Mianus River Gorge Preserve was the first preserve affiliated with The Nature Conservancy. In 1964, it became the first natural area to be designated a National Natural Historic Landmark. More than 70 transactions have increased the preserve to its present size.

The preserve is open April 1 to November 30 from 8:30 am to 5:00 pm. Entrance is strictly forbidden at all other times. There is no picnicking permitted and eating is permitted only at the entrance area, either in a car or on the grassy rim surrounding the parking area.

TRAILS

The trails are well delineated, with the main trails marked in just one direction. The Brink of Gorge Trail is the outgoing trail to the preserve boundary at the S.J. Bargh Reservoir, and the Fringe of Forest Trail is the return path, a round trip distance of 4.5 miles. At times the trails are co-aligned. The first portion of the Bank of the River Trail is wheelchair accessible until it reaches a bench overlooking the Mianus River.

Brink of Gorge Trail   *Length 2.2 miles Blaze: red*

Beginning at the information kiosk, the Brink of Gorge Trail heads to the left toward a bench on the river at the Streamside Study Area. The trail passes through a series of stone walls, reminders of the area's agricultural heritage (1800-1920), and, at 0.2 mile, reaches the Old Field of Succession. After crossing a stream on a flat stone bridge, the Brink of Gorge Trail joins the Fringe of Forest Trail (blue). To the left, at 0.4 mile, the two trails pass a junction with the 0.2-mile Bank of the River Trail (green), which follows the Mianus River and passes the Safford Cascade, an intermittent tributary.

At 0.5 mile, the trails separate; the Brink of Gorge Trail turns to the left and the Fringe of the Forest Trail heads uphill to the right. After passing a shortcut to the Bank of River Trail at 0.6 mile, the red and the blue trails come together briefly, only to split again. The Brink of Gorge Trail descends to pass the narrowest part of the gorge at the Rockwall Breach. It climbs sharply around a rock outcropping above the river to reach Monte Gloria, so named to honor Gloria Hollister Anable. She, along with four others, worked to protect the gorge, resulting in the establishment of the preserve in 1953. The red and blue trails come together for the third time at 0.9 mile and then split once again. At 1.0 mile, the Hobby Hill Quarry Trail (mica mine) leaves to the left. The red and blue trails join for the fourth time, only to diverge again at 1.1 miles.

With a soft tread underfoot and the gurgle of the river below, the trail passes a hemlock forest with trees 350 years and older. The cathedral-like forest invites hikers to enjoy peace and solitude. Crossing three stone walls in the next 0.3 mile, the two trails join for the final time at 1.3 miles. At 1.8 miles, the co-aligned trails pass a vernal pool. A short side trail leads to a view of the reservoir at 1.9 miles. To the left at 2.0 miles, is a short steep trail leading to Havemeyer Falls. Both trails end at the S.J. Barch Reservoir at 2.2 miles.

Fringe of Forest Trail   *Length 2.1 miles Blaze: blue*

Blazed in a way to be used on the return trip from the reservoir, the Fringe of Forest Trail is initially co-aligned with the Brink of Gorge Trail (red). They pass trails to Havermeyer Falls and views of the reservoir at 0.2 and 0.3 mile respectively.

A LODE OF GLITTER

A 0.1 mile hike off the Brink of Gorge Trail brings you in the remnants of the Hobby Hill Quarry, used in the 1700s and 1800s by local farmers to mine mica, feldspar, and quartz. Mica, a word believed to derive from two Latin words, mica, meaning crumb and micans, for glittering or sparkling, is a translucent and heat resistant mineral that was used in the making of lanterns and ovens as well as some decorative materials, such as wallpaper. Feldspar is an important ingredient in the making of glass and ceramics. Theses minerals are exposed here and flat shining pieces of the mica are visible. Over the years, souvenir seekers have taken some of the mica, a practice that is forbidden. So, please, enjoy the preserve, but don't take a piece of it with you.

Fungus.

After skirting a vernal pool at 0.7 mile, the trails head through the James and Alice de Peyster Todd Woodlands, an area donated by preserve founders. At 0.9 mile the trails split, with the Fringe of Forest Trail going left. They rejoin, having crossed stone walls which like others on the property, date back to the first half of the nineteenth century. In quick succession, the trails pass the Hobby Hill Quarry Trail at 1.2 miles, split, and then join again.

After the third split, the Fringe of Forest Trail passes between fields, some of which were grazed by livestock as recently as the 1920s. At 1.7 miles, the trails join briefly and split. They rejoin, and at 1.9 miles, pass the Bank of River Trail (green) to the right. After the last red/blue trail split, the Fringe of Forest Trail ends at the parking area at 2.1 miles.

DRIVING: Take I-684 to Exit 4 (N Y 172) and head towards Bedford Village. At N Y 22 turn left, and then, at the grassy triangle in Bedford Village, take the right fork onto Pound Ridge Road. At the gas station, turn right onto Long Ridge Road. Take the first right onto Millers Mill Road, make the left turn just past the bridge, and proceed to the preserve parking area [41.185891N 73.621451W].

PUBLIC TRANSPORTATION: None available

For contact information, see Appendix, Mianus River Gorge Preserve.

Muscoot Farm

Somers • 5.7 miles, 777 acres

Asimple sign for Muscoot Farm on Route 100 in Somers doesn't begin to reveal what is in store for visitors. It is a lot more than just a farm: it's a museum, education center and host to miles of old farm roads and blazed trails, as well as a demonstration farm.

The animals at Muscoot Farm are typical of the animals that would have been found at a gentleman's farm in the early twentieth century. There are a variety of domestic animals: fowl, cows, sheep, horses, donkeys, and goats, many of which are unusual or rare breeds. Children may be disappointed by not being able to touch or feed them.

Muscoot meant "something swampy" in the local Native American dialect and the name the Hopkins family used for their estate and dairy farm, owned through three generations. The farm initially served as a summer estate and in 1924, it became their year-round residence. When New York City acquired some of the Hopkins land for expansion of the Croton Reservoir, they moved the Georgian Colonial-style farmhouse to its present location to preserve it. When the water level in the reservoir is low, stone walls and foundations that were once part of the original property are visible. In 1967, the family sold the farm to Westchester County; it opened as a park eight years later.

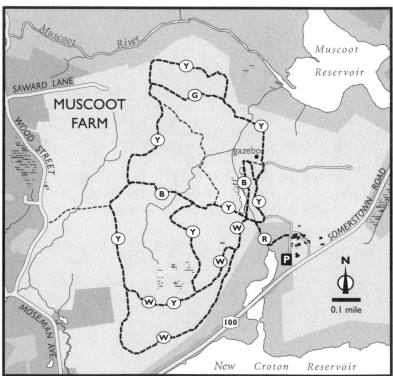

TRAILS

The trails at Muscoot Farm follow rolling hills, sometimes in the woods, at other times across former farm fields. Several unmarked trails head towards the Muscoot River. Although there are no viewpoints along the wooded trails and farm roads, several open fields with expansive vistas of the surrounding forest are a short distance from the farm proper. With sufficient snow cover, the fields are ideal for cross-country skiing.

Beginning at the parking lot and serving as the access trail, the red trail goes 0.2 mile to end at the yellow trail. Both the green and blue trails are 0.3 mile shortcuts on the yellow trail with the former traversing gentle slopes and the latter in a more rugged portion of the farm. The 0.3 mile blue trail connects two pieces of the yellow trail. A blue blazed farm road is an easy stroll that follows along a pond surrounded by an extensive wet area. There is a bench where one can view the pond, bird life, and surrounding vegetation. At the north end, it reaches the edge of a large open field, a biodiversity-protected area,

Yellow Trail
Length: 3.3 miles Blaze: yellow

To reach the yellow trail, go to the far end of the parking lot and follow a service road past a barn. Pass a wooden gate to reach a T junction with a farm road leading from farm buildings to the right. If the gate is closed, start from the middle of the parking lot, pass through farm buildings, and follow around to the farm road beyond the gate. Turn right. From the junction near the wooden gate, the farm road curves to the west with a field to the north. It reaches a junction where yellow blazes head off in both directions. Go counterclockwise to follow the farm road. In front of a sloping field, the yellow trail passes the blue-blazed farm road. Almost immediately there is an intersection with another farm road in an open field. The one to the left descends to merge with the blue farm road, while the one to the right heads east for 0.8 mile, to a section of the park with no blazed trails.

The yellow trail continues straight ahead and ascends a gentle slope past a gazebo to the left. The trail follows the west edge of a long field and stays close to a narrow meadow with seasonal wildflowers. At the end of the grassy traverse, at 0.6 mile, the trail turns left and crosses a narrow strip of trees separating this field from one to the west. It follows the north edge of the second field, crosses a seasonal creek and penetrates another hedgerow. The trail continues along the north edge of a third field and becomes a narrow footpath as it enters the forest.

Passing the east end of the green trail at 0.8 mile, the yellow trail follows along a stone wall. The impressive girth of a white oak tree pushes against a crumbling section of a stone wall at 0.9 mile. The trail turns away from the stone wall and crosses a seasonal stream. Sheltered by a narrow grove of hemlocks, the yellow trail reaches a confluence of stone walls defining the edge of the park and turns south. The yellow trail passes the west end of the green trail at 1.3 miles. Shortly after, it passes a farm road leading down to the center of the park. The trail crosses a stone wall and reaches the west end of the blue trail at 1.8 miles. At the crest of a long broad hill, the forest is noticeably inching forward to reclaim a few fields. The trail follows the east edge of dense shrubs and joins the Big Tree Trail. A farm road leads to the right.

A lunch spot with a view.

The trails merge and then split with the yellow trail going to the left at 2.5 miles, widening as it descends. Once past the junction with the blue trail at 3.0 miles, the yellow trail is on a woods road. At the bottom of the hill, it reaches another woods road bracketed by stone walls. The trail continues with small fields on both sides. In a corner of a field at 3.2 miles, the blue farm road leaves to the left, and soon after, the Big Tree trail is to the right. A short distance further, the red trail begins to the right and the yellow trail closes the loop.

Big Tree Trail   *Length: 1.6 miles Blaze: white*
The Big Tree Trail begins off the yellow-blazed farm road west of the farm buildings and heads southwest. When the trail splits at 0.3 mile, take the left fork to go clockwise around the loop. For 0.5 mile, the trail traverses south-facing steep slopes along a narrow and rough track (suitable for experienced cross-country skiers) with sounds of traffic along Route 100. The steepness moderates as the trail reaches its southernmost point. The trail veers north and heads to the crest of a long broad hill, skirting a field being taken over by scrubby vegetation. The Big Tree trail joins the yellow trail at 1.0 mile and heads east. The trails splits at 1.3 miles and the Big Trail heads downhill to complete the loop.

DRIVING: From I-684 take Exit 6 (NY 35) and head west. At Route 100, turn left and go 1.5 miles to the farm. The gate is locked at 4 pm, so plan accordingly [41.259981N 73.725502W].

PUBLIC TRANSPORTATION: None available

For contact information, see Appendix, Westchester County Parks—Muscoot Farm.

Sprain Ridge Park

Yonkers • 9.1 miles, 278 acres

Known as a mecca for mountain bikers, Sprain Ridge Park is a place of interest to hikers, walkers, and birders as well. Because it is located on a ridge between the Sprain Brook Parkway and the New York State Thruway, road noise is always present. When you cross from the west side of the ridge to the east, the noise shifts from the sounds of heavy trucks to that of fast-moving cars.

Prior to the 1990s, the park had been overrun with ATVs. When access to the power line paralleling the Sprain Brook Parkway was cut off, the abuse ceased. The illegal ATV activity resulted in wider trails, but the rutted banked turns remain as evidence of this destructive activity.

To keep from intruding on the mountain bikers' space, hikers should use the park on weekdays and avoid weekends and evenings, especially during the summer.

There are several theories about the origin of the word "sprain" in the park's name. One claim is that the word is a corruption of "spraint," a Native American word for otter dung; many otters were once found in the area. Another is that it was taken from the Middle English word "sprain," which means "to sow seeds by hand."

TRAILS

The trails in Sprain Ridge Park twist and turn, sometimes snaking down or up the ridge at an angle preferred by bikers but a bit tiresome to hikers. This is particularly true in sections to the south and east of Boyce Thompson Lane. Because there are many informal tracks, it is difficult to determine the exact trail mileage in the park and to figure out exactly where you are. This park is suitable for people who feel comfortable navigating without much direction.

Because trail locations change over time, it is difficult to estimate how many miles of trails there are in the park. The 2.2 miles of trails on the west side of the

FROM PLANT RESEARCH TO PARK

The grounds of Sprain Ridge Park were once part of the Boyce Thompson Institute for Plant Research established in the early 1920s with the idea of improving the world's food supply and promoting conservation.

William Boyce Thompson began his career as a mining engineer and became a leading industrialist, financier, and philanthropist. He was motivated to create the center after seeing the effects of hunger during a trip to Russia in 1917. The center was built across the street from his estate, Alder Mansion, in Yonkers, so that he could take an active part in it. Research continued on that site until 1978 when, because of urban encroachment and pollution, it was relocated to Cornell University in Ithaca, New York, its current home.

Westchester County purchased the property from the institute in 1965. Some of the unusual flora in the park is a legacy from the center.

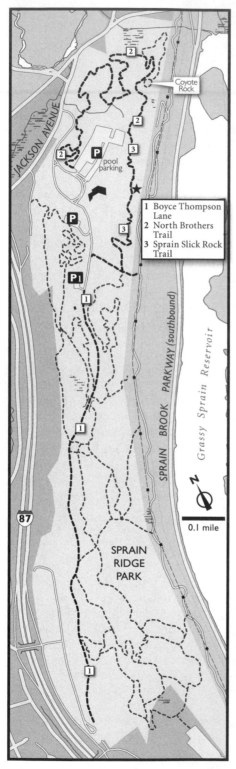

park include Danny Wray Ramble, an easy mountain bike loop. Several woods roads provide access to unmarked trails and the power line pathways. Located east of the picnic parking area, Eric's Over the Log Trail, which traverses steep terrain for 0.9 mile, is suitable for advanced mountain bikers. It is accessible either from Boyce Thompson Lane or the woods road to the power line. The some of the trails in the southeast section of the park are used more than others.

Boyce Thompson Lane

Length: 1.1 miles
Located beside the entrance to Area #1, Boyce Thompson Lane serves as the main route into the network of trails in the southern portion of the park. This route is so prominent that it does not need blazing. Heading downhill, Boyce Thompson Lane passes bike paths on the right and left. Just beyond a bridge at 0.3 mile, it heads gradually uphill; there is access here to a trail to the left and to another trail to the right. As the trail descends, road noise from the Thruway increases. Beginning at 0.7 mile, there is a succession of unmarked trails heading uphill to the left. The trail narrows but still follows the former road. Continuing to gradually descend, it ends at 1.1 miles.

DRIVING: From the Sprain Brook Parkway, take the Jackson Avenue Exit. Turn west and drive 0.5 mile to reach the entrance to the left [40.987538N 73.848412W].

PUBLIC TRANSPORTATION: None available

For contact information, see Appendix, Westchester County Parks—Sprain Ridge Park.

Sylvan Glen Park Preserve

Mohegan Lake • 6.2 miles, 408.2 acres

It is hard to say what impresses visitors to Sylvan Glen Park Preserve the most: the remnants of late 1930s quarry operations or a huge white oak tree with an 18-foot circumference known as the Quarry Oak. There are building foundations, discarded granite columns, polished blocks, old machinery, and cables high in the trees or buried underfoot. In its heyday, Mohegan Granite supplied honey-colored stone to such projects as the Cathedral of St. John the Divine, the approaches to the George Washington and Whitestone bridges in New York City, and the Senate Office Building in Washington, D.C. Because of the historical significance of the site, all artifacts should be left in place

MORRIS LANE ENTRANCE

The main quarry attractions at Sylvan Glen are best reached from the entrance at the end of Morris Lane. Remnants of the quarry operation are more apparent when leaves are off the trees. It is 0.3 mile from the entrance to the 0.3 mile Sylvan Brook Trail (yellow) which has a small quarry. Another quarry is on the Grant

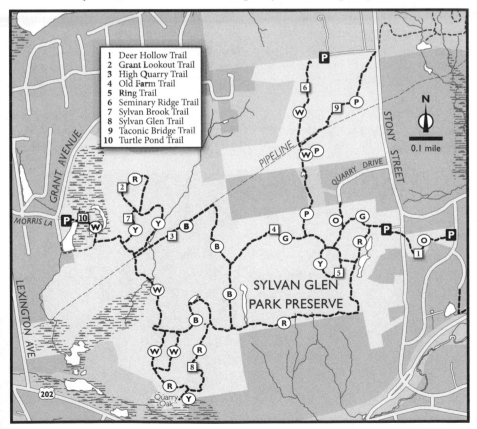

Lookout Trail (red), a 0.2 mile loop on the Sylvan Brook Trail. The foundations of buildings which housed the cutting and polishing operations are 0.6 miles from the entrance. The High Quarry has steep drops so observe caution when looking down into the quarry and stay back from the edge.

The Quarry Oak with its massive girth is at the end of the Quarry Oak Trail (yellow), so named because of the nearby quarry which you can enter.

Turtle Pond Trail   *Length: 0.9 mile Blaze: white*
From the parking lot, the Turtle Pond Trail is on a wide path going through a wetland past a pond. As it leaves the wetlands, it turns left to head uphill on a rocky tread way. Turning right, it passes the Sylvan Brook Trail (yellow) to the left which loops around for 0.3 mile to return to the Turtle Pond Trail. After crossing the gas pipeline right of way where the High Quarry Trail (blue) is to the left, it reenters the woods. After passing through a white pine plantation, the trail turns right onto a woods road and crosses Sylvan Brook on a bridge at 0.4 mile. A stone foundation is visible to the right, the first of remnants of the quarry operation buildings.

At 0.6 mile, more foundations associated with the quarry operations lie in various states of decay; interpretive signs give their history. The trail makes a U turn and heads steeply uphill. The Turtle Pont Trail turns right where the High Quarry Trail begins to the left. After passing a small quarry often filled with water, the Turtle Pond Trail turns left at 0.7 mile and the Sylvan Glen Trail (red) goes straight. Ascending along a woods road, the Turtle Pond Trail turns left again. Near a talus heap, it passes the end of the High Quarry, the main quarry of the site. An opening was left in the excavation to prevent the quarry from filling with water. At 0.9 mile, the Turtle Pond Trail ends at the High Quarry Trail.

High Quarry Trail   *Length: 1.1 miles Blaze: blue*
The High Quarry Trail begins on the Turtle Pond Trail (white) and heads steeply uphill. It passes the end of the Turtle Pond Trail to the right and continues uphill

Abandoned.

to reach the edge of the quarry. Piles of rejected rocks litter the area and pieces of abandoned equipment are scattered along the trail. After leaving the quarry rim, the trail goes under a rock bridge and heads slightly downhill. A water-filled quarry is straight ahead (See cover photo). The trail turns right to pass a stone shed whose roof is a single slab of rock. The shed was used to store explosives. The trail goes through a stone wall and turns to parallel it. At 0.3 mile, the trail reaches an unmarked side trail leading to a view which looks both down into the pit and is only open vista in the preserve with a view to the west.

The High Quarry Trail turns left where the Sylvan Glen Trail (red) joins from straight ahead. The co-aligned trails split at 0.4 mile, with the High Quarry Trail turning left and the Sylvan Glen Trail going straight. After going through stone walls on a relatively level woods road, at 0.6 mile, the High Quarry Trail passes the Old Farm Trail (green) which leads 0.6 mile to the parking at Stony Street. At 0.8 mile, the trail turns sharply left, descending to the gas pipeline right-of-way. To the right, the right-of-way reaches the Seminary Ridge Trail (white) and Taconic BridgeTrail (pink) in 0.3 mile. Turning left, the High Quarry Trail follows the right-of-way downhill. At the base of the descent, the trail crosses a small stream and reaches an orange and white post where it ends at the Turtle Pond Trail.

STONY STREET ENTRANCE

This relatively flat area of Sylvan Glen Park Preserve was farmed. Large ditches were dug in an attempt to drain the wetlands, but to no avail. The staging area for the 1998 Stony Street reconstruction project is now the parking lot and eastern entrance.

The Ring Trail (yellow) is a 0.3 mile former riding ring with its center now overgrown with barberry. The orange-blazed Quarry Drive and Deer Hollow trails provide neighborhood access at 0.1 and 0.3 miles respectively. The latter links to the playground in Deer Hollow which connects to a 0.5 mile walk along sidewalks to the Yorktown Trailway entrance at the end of Deer Track Court.

Old Farm Trail   *Length: 0.6 mile Blaze: green*
Named to acknowledge the agricultural past of this part of Sylvan Glen, the Old Farm Trail goes through former farm fields. From the parking lot on Stony Street, the Old Farm Trail heads west and after crossing puncheon, goes straight at the junction with the Sylvan Glen Trail (red). Heading slightly uphill, the Old Farm Trail passes the Quarry Drive Trail (orange) which goes to 0.1 mile to Quarry Drive (no parking). After going through a stone wall, it turns right onto the Ring Trail (yellow), an old riding ring with railing visible in several places. In about 100 feet, the Old Farm Trail turns right to go through the stone wall a second time. At 0.3 mile, the trail crosses a bridge over a ditch dug in hopes of draining a wet area to the north. It passes the end of the Taconic Bridge Trail (pink) which reaches Woodlands Legacy Fields Park in 2.0 miles. After following a woods road and crossing stone walls, the Old Farm Trail ends at the High Quarry Trail (blue).

Seminary Ridge Trail   *Length: 0.4 mile Blaze: white*
Starting at a small water filled quarry, the Seminary Ridge Trail is co-aligned with

the Taconic Bridge Trail (pink). When they reach the pipeline right-of-way, the Seminary Ridge Trail goes straight and the Taconic Bridge Trail turns right.. Once inside the woods, the Seminary Ridge Trail crosses stone walls, turns left, and enters an area with many invasives. The area becomes more open and the trail turns right heading uphill. At 0.3 mile, it passes hand ball courts that were once part of a Jesuit seminary which became Phoenix Academy, an alternate New York City high school for students with drug and alcohol problems. The trail heads along the telephone line and ends at the entrance to former tennis courts turned into parking for practice ball fields. It is 0.2 mile down the road to the Taconic Bridge Trail which continues across Stony Street to Granite Knolls Park or turns right to loop back 0.5 mile to the small quarry.

The Quarry Oak.

Sylvan Glen Trail *Length: 1.4 miles*
Blaze: red

Crossing and paralleling many stone walls, the Sylvan Glen Trail links the quarries to the parking lot on Stony Street. The trail starts at the Turtle Pond Trail (white), just as it bends sharply left. It heads slightly downhill, crosses a stone wall and heads towards a quarry. After passing a large pile of discarded rocks, the trail enters the quarry. The large stones in the quarry floor offer a great place to stop for lunch or a snack. The trail leaves the quarry, squeezing past a tree and another pile of discarded rocks. At a T junction at 0.2 mile, the Quarry Oak Trail (yellow) leads 200 feet to the right to the huge Quarry Oak.

The Sylvan Glen Trail turns left and goes up stone steps, built by New York-New Jersey Trail Conference volunteers who moved 21 tons of stone. The trail is along the side of the hill, then turns to ascend, sometimes steeply. At 0.3 mile, it crosses the shoulder of the hill, continues along a narrow foot path through laurel, and passes a large pile of rock, the discards from the High Quarry. To the left is a short unmarked trail to a view over the quarry. The Sylvan Glen Trail turns right to join the High Quarry Trail (blue) at 0.5 mile. The trails split at 0.6 mile with the Sylvan Glen Trail going straight. It crosses several wet areas on puncheon and then at 1.0 mile goes up and over a knoll. After going through several stone walls, it passes a large pond to the right at 1.3 miles and then a short trail which leads to the Ring Trail (yellow). The Sylvan Glen Trail ends at the Old Farm Trail. It is 0.1 mile to the right to the parking lot on Stony Street.

Taconic Bridge Trail *Length: 0.7 miles Blaze: pink*

This segment of the Taconic Bridge Trail connects Sylvan Glen Park Preserve to

MOHEGAN GRANITE

About 1895, an outcropping of golden granite was discovered on the hills north of present-day Route 202 near Mohegan Lake. Known as Peekskill Granite, it is part of an igneous complex also found in Blue Mountain Reservation.

Various owners operated the quarry under the name Mohegan Granite. In 1925, Bruno M. Grenci and Thomas H. Ellis acquired the property and the quarrying operations. They modernized the machinery using diesel electric generators instead of steam engines and built a narrow gauge cable railway which eliminated the need for oxen. At the time, the company was the largest employer in Yorktown with 300 workers for quarrying and carving stone. The granite eagles atop Arlington Memorial Bridge on the Potomac River attest to the craftsmanship of their workers.

Although operations continued through the Great Depression, they ended in the early 1940s. The higher cost of manpower in New York coupled with the lower cost of newer construction materials (steel, glass, aluminum) sounded the company's death knell. Various uses were proposed including recreation, which, in 1961, was considered not suitable for most of the property. It lay dormant until 1981 when the Town of Yorktown purchased it from Norman Van Kirk of Red Bank, NJ. When enough adjoining property was acquired, the preserve opened.

Granite Knolls Park. From the Old Farm Trail (green) just west of a small wooden bridge, the Taconic Bridge Trail heads north, crossing, on puncheon, an area that is frequently wet. At 0.2 mile, it reaches a water filled quarry and joins the Seminary Ridge Trail (white). Together they reach the gas line right-of-way where the Seminary Ridge Trail goes straight and the Taconic Bridge Trail turns right to follow the right-of-way marked with plastic posts. At the second pair of plastic posts, at 0.4 mile, the trail turns left, enters the woods, and crosses wet areas on puncheon. At 0.6 mile, it turns left to cross a bridge over a small stream. When it reaches a stone pillar at 0.7 mile, the Taconic Bridge Trail turns right to cross Stony Street to enter Granite Knolls Park. It is 1.0 mile to the bridge over the Taconic Parkway.

DRIVING: Morris Lane entrance: From the Taconic State Parkway, take the Route 202 Exit and turn west. Go 1.8 miles to the traffic light at Lexington Avenue and turn right. Drive 0.6 mile uphill to Morris Lane. Turn right and go 0.2 mile to a parking lot directly ahead at the bottom of the hill [41.299699N 73.856524W].

Stony Street entrance: From the Taconic State Parkway, take the Bear Mountain Parkway exit. Take the first right turn right onto Stony Street and head steeply uphill for 0.5 mile. Just after #2820, turn left onto a dirt entrance road to parking [41.299274N 73.832818W]. If you reach Winding Court to the right, you have gone too far.

PUBLIC TRANSPORTATION: Morris Lane entrance: Take Beeline Bus #15 to the corner of Lexington Avenue and Morris Lane; walk 0.2 mile down Morris Lane to the parking lot directly ahead at the bottom of the hill.

For contact information, see Appendix, Yorktown.

Twin Lakes Park
Nature Study Woods

Eastchester • 7.0 miles, 220 acres

E questrians are heavy users of Twin Lakes Park, but there is plenty of room for walkers as well. There are two stables on the county owned property, one of which includes an indoor riding rink. Nature Study Woods also allows horses, but with no adjacent stables, there are fewer equestrians.

Twin Lakes Park is named for two lakes used as reservoirs to control flooding along the Hutchinson River. The land, which became Twin Lakes Park and Nature Study Woods, was purchased in 1924 and 1927 as part of the Hutchinson River Parkway. From 1917 to 1937, the New York, Westchester and Boston Railway went through Nature Study Woods and a small portion of Twin Lakes Park. For remnants of the line, look for a concrete stub, which shows a center divider where tracks once were, scattered gravel, the straight at-grade path, concrete litter in Reservoir #2, and a large concrete trestle, which supported a viaduct. For additional history of the railroad, see White Plains Greenway (Pocket Parks).

Trestle.

T R A I L S

At Twin Lakes and Nature Study Woods, the trails are primarily along woods roads. Many narrow equestrian trails in Twin Lakes Park connect the woods roads. The Hutchinson River Pathway (Hutch Pathway) and the Colonial Greenway go through both parks and are sometimes co-aligned. Inside the parks, the Hutch Pathway and Colonial Greenway are blazed; for the former, blazes are often faded or missing. There are an additional 2.9 miles of unmarked trails and woods roads.

Colonial Greenway *Length: 2.6 miles Blaze: blue with white star*
Entering Twin Lakes Park from the north (no parking), the Colonial Greenway is co-aligned with the Hutchinson River Pathway for the first 0.3 mile. Together

they pass through a grassy triangle intersection, bearing left. At the next intersection, where the Hutch Pathway goes left, the Colonial Greenway turns right. It crosses trails heading right, which eventually either lead back to the parking lot for the stables or head left towards Reservoir #3. At 0.6 mile, it reaches the reservoir and parallels the shore. The Colonial Greenway turns toward California Road and at 1.0 mile, passes an entrance across from Highland Avenue (limited parking). Turning away from California Road, it continues to follow the shore. A 0.3-mile unmarked path loops up a hill and returns. Noise from the Hutch is audible, and across the reservoir cars are visible.

At 1.2 miles, the Hutch Pathway joins the Colonial Greenway at the Reservoir #3 dam. The co-aligned trails cross a bridge over an entrance ramp to the Hutch, head down a ramp, and cross a bridge below the dam. After passing under the Hutch where the Hutchinson River runs through a concrete channel to the left, at 1.4 miles the pathway enters an area blanketed with invasive plants. It reaches Reservoir #2 and then parallels it. To the right, a short 0.2-mile trail goes through a flood control area to reach a dam. At 1.8 miles, the pathway passes an unmarked trail to the left leading to Bon Air Avenue. Entering Nature Study Woods, the pathway is along the former railbed of the New York, Westchester and Boston Railway. To the right at 2.0 miles, a lone trestle looms overhead. See White Plains Greenway (Pocket Parks) for more information. Just beyond the trestle, at a Y junction, an unmarked trail to the right heads 0.2 mile out into the flood plain of the Hutchinson River.

The co-aligned trails pass a stone outcropping to the left. Numerous unmarked trails join and leave the

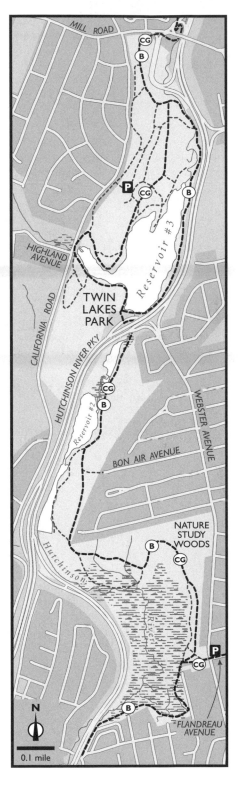

HIGH-TECH HIDE-AND-SEEK

Hidden treasure has always intrigued people and geocaching is a high-tech way to indulge that urge. Instead of a map with sketchy directions, a global positioning system (GPS) receiver is used to locate a hidden object. There are over 2 million registered geocaches worldwide, according to Geocashing.com.

For this adventure to work, someone has to have first hidden a waterproof container with a small object and a log book. They note the latitudinal and longitudinal coordinates of the geocache and then post the coordinates on a website such as www.geocaching.com. To participate, log onto a geocaching website, find a location that interests you, load the posted coordinates into your GPS or smart phone, and find a trinket that you will exchange. Once you have found the geocache, swap your trinket for one in the container, and sign the log book. Upon returning home, log back onto the website to record your trip. Whether placing a geocache or finding one, use existing hiking trails, avoid extensive bushwhacking where possible, and be careful not to trample vegetation when off-trail.

To minimize impact on sensitive areas and protect natural resources, many parks require a permit to leave a geocache. Before establishing a geocache in a park, please obtain permission from the park management. See the appendix for contact information.

co-aligned trails. The Colonial Greenway is a wide path as it goes through a large intersection at 2.6 miles and heads towards Webster and Flandreau avenues.

Hutchinson River Pathway
See Linear Corridors

Length: 2.9 miles

DRIVING: To reach Twin Lakes from the southbound Hutchinson River Parkway, take Exit 18W (Mill Road). Go 0.1 mile and **turn left at California Road. It is 0.5 mile to the entrance of River Ridge Equestrian Center at Twin Lakes Park [40.949267N 73.802089W]. Public parking is to the left. From the northbound Hutchinson River Parkway, take Exit 17 (North Avenue) and go left at the end of the ramp. At the next traffic light, bear left onto Mill Road. Follow the directions from ** above.

To reach Nature Study Woods from northbound Hutchinson River Parkway, take Exit 16 which becomes southbound Webster Avenue. Continue 0.8 mile to the entrance across from 823 Webster Avenue at Flandreau Avenue. Southbound, take Exit 18E (Mill Road East) toward New Rochelle. At 0.3 mile, make a slight right onto North Avenue. Follow North Avenue 1.1 miles to turn right onto Rosehill Avenue. Go 0.2 mile and turn left onto Webster Avenue. It is 0.4 mile to the entrance across from 823 Webster Avenue [40.930598N 73.798211W].

PUBLIC TRANSPORTATION: For Twin Lakes none available; for Nature Study Woods, Beeline Bus #45 on North Avenue and Bus #53 on New Rochelle Road

For contact information, see Appendix, Westchester County Parks.

Westchester Wilderness Walk
Zofnass Family Preserve

Pound Ridge • 5.9 miles, 150 acres

Jurassic Rock, Grand Stone Staircase, Layer Cake Rock, and Lover Trees are a just a few of the places in the Westchester Wilderness Walk that you will find as enticing as their names. But be forewarned, because if there is something interesting to see, the trail designer has routed the trail to go there, even if this means taking a meandering, but intriguing route. The trails travel up and down steps, across stepping stones, along a stream bed, adjacent to a wetland, and even along the top of a stone wall.

Westchester Land Trust board member, Paul Zofnass, assembled 150 acres over the course of more than a decade. He conceived the idea and not only donated the initial properties as part of the Zofnass Family Trust, but also convinced his neighbors to donate land or easements. He then designed and financed the trail system.

TRAILS

All trails are marked with green tags: Westchester Wilderness Walk/Westchester Land Trust. The signs at intersections indicate options and the direction back to

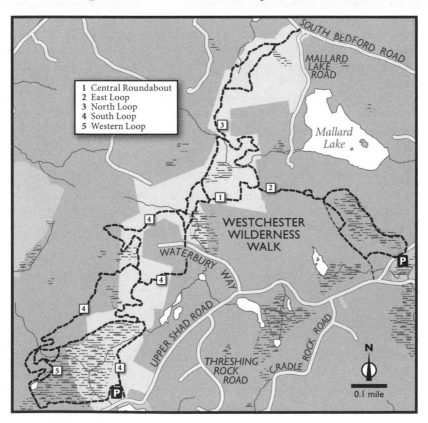

the parking area. Logs of various sizes often delineate the path.

Southern Loop
Length: 2.5 miles Blaze: green

Starting from the parking area on Upper Shad Road, the Southern Loop passes a kiosk and then the Western Loop. It follows a woods road beside wetlands, reaches Buddha Ridge and turns left. After heading along the top of a low stone wall, the trail reaches an intersection at 0.3 mile, where the loop begins. Turn right to go counterclockwise and head towards Becky's Brook. The trail reaches Tom's Cabin at 0.5 mile. After passing the Southern Loop Short Cut at 0.6 mile, the trail descends and crosses a private road at 0.9 mile. On a former road, the Southern Loop next passes a short cut-off trail leading to Fowler Rock and reenters the woods. After heading up hill and passing Tulip Tree Heights, the Southern Loop reaches the Central Roundabout at 1.0 mile and turns left. The trail passes the other end of the Central Roundabout and again turns left, going uphill past Wedge Walk Rock. The trail heads up the aptly named Streambed Steps and reaches Fowler Rock at 1.2 miles.

As the Southern Loop continues along the ridge, there are brief views into the ravine below. After passing Jurassic Rock, the trail descends and reaches, at 1.6 miles, wetlands near the shortcut back to the parking area. The trail passes Layer Cake Rock and continues along the ridge, crossing stone walls. At 2.1 miles, it makes a U turn and heads downhill past a seasonal cascade and the connector for the Western Loop. The Southern Loop skirts the wetlands and closes the loop. It is 0.3 mile to the parking area on Upper Shad Road.

Central Roundabout
Length: 1.0 mile Blaze: green

Forming a hub, the Central Roundabout connects the Southern, Northern and Eastern trails. It starts from the intersection with the Southern Loop, heads uphill, and going counterclockwise at 0.2 mile, meets the East Loop. Turning left at the intersection, the trail crosses a wet area on large flat rocks and reaches Razor Ridge Rock. At 0.5 mile, the trail goes the long way around Little Roundabout Rock. It passes the junction with the Northern Loop and heads south to meet the Southern Loop at 1.0 mile at Wedge Rock.

Eastern Loop
Length: 1.0 mile Blaze: green

From the junction with the Central Roundabout, the Eastern Loop goes through an open area at 0.1 mile and crosses a stone wall. It reaches the top of the Grand Staircase, continues downhill, and reaches a trail junction at 0.2 mile. Turn left to walk along the edge of extensive wetland. The Eastern Loop slowly curves and parallels a stone wall. At 0.3 mile, it passes a rock outcropping looming overhead and the wetland to the right. The trail skirts the wetland and eventually parallels a stone wall. It leaves the wetland at 0.5 mile, reaches a paved road, and turns right to follow the road for 250 feet. Turning right again, it leaves the road at 0.6 mile, follows a stone wall, and reenters the woods. The trail parallels a stone wall, turns away from the wetland, and reaches a T junction with a woods road at 0.7 mile. (To the left, it is 0.1 mile to Upper Shad Road.)

Turn right and follow the woods road. At 0.8 mile, the Eastern Loop leaves the woods road and heads uphill reaching seasonal views over the wetlands below. The trail crosses the rise and heads downhill to close the loop at 1.0 mile. The hike from the Central Roundabout and return is 1.0 miles, omitting the trail out to Upper Shad Road. For those who hike from Upper Shad Road around the loop and return to the road, the hike is 0.9 mile.

Northern Loop
Length: 0.7 mile Blaze: green

From the northwest portion of the Central Roundabout, the Northern Loop heads uphill and, crosses a stone wall. It reaches the loop portion of the Northern Loop at 0.2 mile, where there are a quartz quarry and a 1920s garbage pit. Continuing to the right, the trail is on easy terrain and reaches the other end of the loop at 0.4 mile. The Christmas ferns seem awash as a green sea on the Upper Escarpment.

A solid crossing.

Descending, the Northern Loop reaches the corner of Bedford and Mallard Lake roads at 0.5 mile (no parking). On the return trip, turn right at the trail junction to pass the Awesome Oak and the south end of the Northern Loop to arrive at the trail leading back to the Central Roundabout. This fork of the loop is also 0.2 mile. The trip out to the road and back to the Central Roundabout is a round trip of 1.0 mile.

Western Loop
Length: 0.7 mile Blaze: green

Starting just past the main entrance, the Western Loop heads through wetlands on roots and stepping stones. At one point it is on top of a stone wall. At 0.2 mile it passes logs set on end that look like an honor guard. Continuing through the wetlands, it reaches Cedar Circle at 0.4 mile. Turn right and head on a gentle rise through the woods to a T junction. To the right a trail goes 0.1 mile to the Southern Loop. Turn left and continue to ascend, reaching Fort Mayo at 0.6 mile. The Western Loop descends on switchbacks and closes the loop.

DRIVING: From I-684, take the Route 172 Exit. Follow Route 172 through Bedford and turn right at the gas station at Long Ridge Road. Drive 2.6 miles and turn left onto Upper Shad Road. The parking area is 0.3 mile from the intersection [41.175961N 73.599397W]. Although there are access points at South Bedford and Mallard roads, and Waterbury Way, parking is available only at Upper Shad Road.

PUBLIC TRANSPORTATION: None available

For contact information, see Appendix, Westchester Land Trust.

Westmoreland Sanctuary

Mt. Kisco • 9.2 miles, 625 acres

Visitors are drawn to Westmoreland Sanctuary for several reasons: a variety of habitats, a well laid-out trail system, birding, and nature programs. The portion of the sanctuary between Chestnut Ridge Road and Route 22 is open to the public. But 150 acres on the east side of Route 22 have been set aside for wildlife management activities and group study and is closed to the public.

In 1957, Edwin Bechtel, Helen Clay Frick, John Kieran, Frank E. Mason and Nicholas Shoumatoff established the sanctuary as resource for conservation and natural history education. From the onset, the sanctuary has offered programs with an emphasis on ones for young people. It was named for Westmoreland County, near Pittsburgh, Pennsylvania, where Helen Clay Frick, philanthropist and daughter of Henry Clay Frick, the industrialist, spent her childhood. Additional land donations have increased its size.

The building that houses Westmoreland's museum and headquarters was originally built in 1783 and was, at that time, the Third Church of Bedford. It stood on Guard Hill Road at a spot that is now the Bedford Golf and Tennis Club. In 1973, the church was dismantled and reassembled at its present location.

TRAILS

The trails here range from wide and smooth, to rocky and narrow so there are options to suit a variety of skill levels. The well-marked trails with signs at intersections make Westmoreland Sanctuary a good choice for a novice hiker to hone his skills. Trails pass wetlands, rock outcroppings, seasonal streams, and four ponds. These options offer plenty of exercise; there are ridges to climb and valleys to traverse. But be sure to save some energy as all return trips are uphill.

The Catbird Trail (white) connects the Easy Loop (red) to the Chickadee Trail

Along the Catbird Loop.

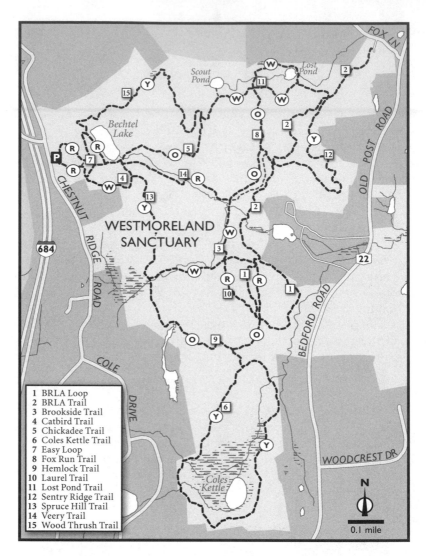

(orange). A Bedford Riding Lanes Association (BRLA) equestrian trail is reached from a private driveway off Fox Lane (no parking). Although not part of the trails maintained by Westmoreland Sanctuary, both BRLA trails are included in total trail mileage.

Easy Loop

Length: 0.6 mile Blaze: red

The entrance to the trail system is through Easy Loop, which starts from the paved drive leading to the sanctuary headquarters. It is actually a figure eight, which makes the easy part of the loop even easier. If the shortcut is used, the hike on Easy Loop is only a quarter-mile. From the entry gate to the right of sanctuary headquarters, Easy Loop passes a trail leading to an outdoor classroom and then heads downhill. At a T junction, there is a short cut to the other side of Easy Loop. To the right, Easy Loop passes through a stone wall and descends steeply, and turns left where the Catbird Trail (white) continues straight ahead. Easy Loop parallels the edge of Bechtel Lake, named for one of the sanctuary's founders and passes a skating shed before turning away from the lake. At 0.3 mile, Easy Loop passes the Wood Thrush Trail (yellow) on the right and heads uphill to overlook the lake. Turning, it continues uphill to pass a shortcut trail to the left. To the right, at 0.5 mile, the trail passes a community cemetery used from 1824-1915. Easy Loop goes over a rock outcropping and heads toward the headquarters to close the loop.

BRLA Loop
Length: 0.6 mile Blaze: BRLA

Intertwined with the Laurel Trail (red) in the heart of Westmoreland Sanctuary, the BRLA Loop is for equestrians as well as for walkers. Start at the intersection of the Hemlock (orange) and Laurel trails go clockwise. The Laurel Trail and BRLA Loop join for 80 feet; the former then heads straight ahead while the latter turns right to go uphill along a wide shelf. The trail curves at the base of a ridge and heads downhill. It enters an open area to cross the Laurel Trail, leaves the open area, and turns right onto a woods road. To the left, it passes the BRLA Trail to Fox Lane. Immediately crossing a stone wall, the trail parallels a fence to the left. At 0.3 mile, it passes below boulders which have tumbled down the hillside. The trail heads along a stream and crosses a seasonal wet area before heading uphill. After passing through another seasonal wet area, the BRLA Loop turns right at 0.5 mile. Ascending, it turns to go through a side ravine and continues its ascent. The BRLA Loop descends to cross a stream and closes the loop at a junction with the Hemlock and Laurel trails.

BRLA Trail to Fox Lane
Length: 1.0 mile Blaze: BRLA

Up, down, and around are the features of the BRLA Trail out to Fox Lane. From the BRLA Loop, the trail parallels a fence to the right as it enters a wetland. A boardwalk here to keep feet dry is not practical because the trail is used by equestrians. Turning away from the fence, the trail reaches slightly higher ground. Massive tulip trees line the trail in an area devoid of rock outcroppings. The trail reaches the top of the rise at 0.3 mile and descends on a narrow path. It crosses a woods road, contours on the side of the hill, and turns left. In the valley to the left, boulders seem perched like oversized hawks searching for prey. The trail turns, continues its ascent, and at 0.4 mile, crosses the Sentry Trail (yellow) for the first time. Continuing uphill, the trail skirts outcroppings to the right. It ascends and descends numerous times, often steeply. There is a sense of isolation in this section with its valleys and ravines. After crossing the Sentry Trail a second time at 0.8 mile, the BRLA Trail is on a well-trod pathway that wiggles its way through the woods and heads uphill. As it passes though a grove of young trees, the trail heads downhill, then turns to parallel a driveway. It ends at a break in a stone wall at the driveway where Fox Lane is in view to the left (no parking).

Brookside Trail
Length: 0.4 mile Blaze: white

From the junction of the Hemlock (orange) and Spruce Hill (yellow) trails, the Brookside Trail meanders downhill on a woods road paralleling a brook to the right. It crosses the brook and continues downhill through a seasonal wet area.

Passing the Laurel Trail (red) at 0.3 mile, the path narrows and crosses the stream Shortly past the lowest point in the sanctuary (390 feet), the Brookside Trail ends at the junction of the Veery (red) and Fox Run (orange) trails.

Chickadee Trail   *Length: 0.4 mile Blaze: orange*
From the junction of Easy Loop (red), near Bechtel Lake, the Chickadee Trail heads downhill and passes the Catbird Trail (white), the outlet from Bechtel Lake, and then a glacial erratic. After going over a rock ledge, it bears left to ascend a short rise at 0.3 mile. the trail descends to a more level path at the base of rock outcroppings, where the noise from I-684 is no longer audible. The Chickadee Trail ends at a trail junction with the Lost Pond (white) and Wood Thrush (yellow) trails

Coles Kettle Trail   *Length: 1.4 miles Blaze: yellow*
From the Hemlock Trail (orange), the Coles Kettle Trail crosses a stone wall and reaches a T junction. Going counterclockwise, the trail passes wetlands which are part of Coles Kettle on the left and boulders on the right. A kettle is a geologic feature created by a receding glacier leaving behind blocks of ice, which after melting, leaves a hollow.

After crossing a seasonal stream, the trail heads uphill, passes rock outcroppings to the right, and turns downhill to cross seasonal wet areas, streams, and stone walls. It veers left at 0.4 mile, passing more outcroppings. At 0.6 mile, the trail goes along a 400-foot boardwalk and turns left at a T junction. Heading uphill, it travels between wetlands to the left and a hill that rises to the right. The pathway narrows at 0.8 mile and it is necessary to walk carefully along the steep slope.

The Coles Kettle Trail heads uphill steeply, reaches the top of the rise, and then descends on a woods road. The trail is at the edge of the wetlands, just far enough away for feet to stay dry, but close enough to see and feel the more open space.

Cinnamon Ferns in Coles Kettle.

At 1.0 mile, the trail turns and heads up through rocks along a woods road. Now heading downhill, it passes by an unmarked trail into private property. It crosses a seasonal wet area and, at 1.2 miles on a woods road above a stone wall, leaves the kettle behind. It turns left to cross a bridge over a stream and head uphill to an area of stately trees. At 1.4 miles, it closes the loop. Turn right to return to the Hemlock Trail on the opposite side of the stone wall.

Fox Run Trail
Length: 0.4 mile Blaze: orange

From the junction with the Lost Pond Trail (white), the Fox Run Trail heads south along a wood road with rock outcroppings to the left. It gradually ascends and, at 0.2 mile, intersects the Sentry Ridge Trail (yellow). The Fox Run Trail enters a steep-sided, but wide valley with rock outcroppings towering overhead. After crossing the shoulder of the hill to leave the valley, the trail heads downhill steeply on a loose gravel pathway to end at the Brookside Trail (white).

Hemlock Trail
Length: 0.5 mile Blaze: orange

Starting from the junction with the Brookside (white) and Spruce Hill (yellow) trails, the Hemlock Trail crosses a bridge over a creek and heads uphill on a woods road. Passing a broad ravine to the right, it crosses a seasonal wet area at 0.2 mile and again heads uphill. It continues through a valley with small rocky ridges sticking up to appear like the backs of sleeping dinosaurs. At 0.4 mile, it passes the Coles Kettle Trail (yellow) and gradually descends. Shortly after crossing a stone wall, the Hemlock Trail ends at the Laurel (red) and BRLA trails.

Laurel Trail
Length: 0.5 mile Blaze: red

Forming a loop in the heart of the sanctuary, the Laurel Trail is a connection to the Brookside (white), Hemlock (orange), and BRLA Loop trails. Going clockwise from the eastern end of the Hemlock Trail, the Laurel Trail heads uphill through a small ravine and the BRLA Loop Trail leaves to the right. It ascends steeply into a valley where it levels out and then resumes its steep ascent. At 0.1 mile, the trail descends and passes, to the right, large stone slabs that appear as if glued to the hill. It turns right at 0.3 mile at a junction with the Brookside Trail which enters from the left and continues straight. Continuing downhill into an open area with bluebird boxes, it crosses the BRLA Loop Trail. At the far side of the open area, the Laurel Trail heads uphill passing a rock outcropping on the right. It closes the loop when it meets the Hemlock Trail straight ahead and the BRLA Loop Trail to the left.

Lost Pond Trail
Length: 0.6 mile Blaze: white

From the junction with the Wood Thrush (yellow) and Chickadee (orange) trails, the Lost Pond Trail descends to cross a stone wall. It passes a short, unmarked side trail out to Scout Pond, a vernal pool. At 0.2 mile, it reaches a junction with the Fox Run Trail (orange) to the right. The Lost Pond Trail makes a loop around the pond and leaves it to turn left at the junction with the Sentry Ridge Trail (yellow). On a bridge, the trail crosses the outlet of Lost Pond then parallels its shore. The trail reaches a bench with a view of the pond at 0.4 mile, and veers away from the pond to follow a woods road. After crossing a stone wall, the trail passes along a vernal pool on a woods road, and then turns left off the woods road. The trail crosses the inlet of Lost Pond and heads uphill to close the loop.

Sentry Ridge Trail
Length: 1.0 mile Blaze: yellow

Going clockwise from the junction with the Lost Pond Trail (white), the Sentry Ridge Trail heads gradually downhill through a valley. It turns right onto the BRLA Trail, joins it for 10 feet, and leaves to the left. The trail wiggles its way through the woods, sometimes steeply. Over the next 0.4 mile, the Sentry Ridge Trail goes up and down along the ridge. At 0.5 mile, it parallels the edge along the top of a steep drop to the left, and then heads uphill. The trail continues its undulating path and at 0.7 mile, heads steeply downhill, passing below rock outcroppings. At 0.9 mile, it crosses the BRLA Trail. Heading gradually uphill, the Sentry Ridge Trail ends at the Fox Run Trail (orange).

Spruce Hill Trail
Length: 0.4 mile Blaze: yellow

From the Catbird Trail (white), the Spruce Hill Trail heads south along a woods road. After crossing a stone wall, it goes uphill into a forest, then downhill to end at the Hemlock (orange) and Brookside (white) trails.

Veery Trail
Length: 0.4 mile Blaze: red

From the Fox Run (orange) and Brookside (white) trails, the Veery Trail parallels a stream and a stone wall as it heads uphill. It crosses a series of stone walls, enters a small valley with more stone walls, and turns right onto a woods road at 0.2 mile. Continuing its ascent, the Veery Trail enters a hemlock grove and ends at the Catbird Trail (white).

Wood Thrush Trail
Length: 0.7 mile Blaze: yellow

From the junction with Easy Loop (red), the Wood Thrush Trail goes through a stone wall and heads slightly uphill. After crossing a stone wall, it turns and then begins heads steeply uphill along a narrow path overlooking Bechtel Lake. It reaches rock outcroppings on both sides of the pathway. Leveling off, the trail passes vernal pools and heads uphill. At 0.4 mile, it reaches a sign noting the park's high point (730 feet), crosses stone walls, and then descends, After reaching a flat area at 0.6 mile, the trail makes a sharp right turn and descends steeply. A brief ascent leads to a junction with the Lost Pond (white) and Chickadee (orange) trails.

NEARBY PARK: Butler Memorial Sanctuary

DRIVING: From I-684, take Exit 4 (Mt. Kisco/Bedford Hills) and turn west onto Route 172 towards Mt. Kisco. Take the first left onto Chestnut Ridge Road. Westmoreland Sanctuary is 1.3 miles to the left [41.180292N 73.684269W].

PUBLIC TRANSPORTATION: None available

For contact information, see Appendix, Westmoreland Sanctuary.

Keeping your feet dry at Teatown Lake Reservation.

SECTION VI

LARGE PARKS

- ◆ Have ten plus miles of trails
- ◆ Encompass extensive ecologically diverse areas
- ◆ Provide enough trails for multiple visits
- ◆ Offer longer and more complex hiking opportunities

Angle Fly Preserve

Somers • 10.1miles, 654 acres

Protecting the fresh, pure water of the last brown-trout spawning stream and one of the largest remaining undeveloped tracts in Westchester County were at the heart of efforts to create Angle Fly Preserve, named for the stream running through the property. (Fly is from the old Dutch "vlaie" or "vly" meaning swamp but can also apply to creek or wetlands in the vicinity.) A coalition of the Town of Somers, Westchester County, New York State, New York City, and the Westchester and Somers land trusts came together to acquire the property from a developer. He had planned to build 108 homes on the site, which is in the heart of the drainage basin of the Muscoot Reservoir in the Croton watershed.

The preserve was officially opened to the public on October 2009 with the trails built by the summer of 2012. The Town of Somers has given the Somers Land Trust responsibility to develop and maintain Angle Fly Preserve. Most of property is owned jointly by New York State, Westchester County and the Town of Somers, while 269 acres is owned by the NYC Department of Environmental Protection and 15 acres was deeded to the Town of Somers as part of the final transaction.

It is safe to say that Angle Fly will be remembered as a preserve that the community built: the trail system and the work to preserve historical features have been done with volunteers, pro bono services, grants, and membership dues from the Somers Land Trust. The preserve is unique in that volunteers not only designed the trail system, but also planned the whole preserve. With acres of wetlands, woodlands, hillside, and slopes there are opportunities for hours of great hiking.

TRAILS

A large entrance sign on Route 139 welcomes you to Angle Fly Preserve, setting the tone that this park is user friendly. Maps with an arrow indicating your location are at trail junctions. The preserve is divided into three sections, based in part on ownership and by Route 139, which runs through it. Trails have unique colors and the blue trail connects the three sections. Many of the trails are loops which mean a novice hiker can follow the same color blazes for an entire hike. Aside from the blue trail from parking at Reis Park, secondary access trails have a blaze with a white cross.

At first glance, the three sections seem the same, as they all have stone walls, lots of barberry, and wetlands. But differences exist. The central section has a 0.1 mile handicapped accessible trail around Reynolds Pond and composting toilets. The Somers Land Trust plans to make use of the buildings in this section, one of which dates from the early

1800s. In the eastern section, there are elevation gains and losses, meadows, and puncheon board walks which allow hikers to cross the extensive wetlands. The western section is more remote. It only has road noise near Route 35. Several rock outcroppings are visible from the blue trail.

CENTRAL SECTION

Forming the core of Angle Fly Preserve, the central section has many visitors as evidenced by the well-trod trails. A popular destination is the 40-foot bridge across Angle Fly Brook, constructed by volunteers.

Blue Trail   *Length: 1.2 miles Blaze: blue*
After crossing Route 139, the blue trail parallels the road, goes through the entrance gate to cross the access road and goes behind Reynolds Pond. After crossing the entrance road, the blue trail reaches a T junction and turns right as the yellow trail joins from the left. At 0.3 mile, the two trails cross the entrance road. The white trail joins briefly from the right at 0.4 mile and then leaves to the right.

After heading downhill, the blue and yellow trails cross several wet areas on puncheon. At 0.8 mile, the trails split with the yellow trail going straight and the blue trail turning right. The blue trail goes over the bridge and crosses a stone wall and parallels wetlands. After passing the end of the white trail at 1.0 mile, the

A LONG DEVELOPMENT

Long before the first colonist set foot on this land, the Kitchawanks of the Mohegan tribe lived in the area and called the land Amapaugh, meaning "fresh water fish." Several of their sites have been identified along Angle Fly Brook.

The property became a part of Cortlandt Manor grant of 1697. Several homesteads were established on the property. During the American Revolution, Westchester County was considered neutral ground. It was contested by cowboys (loyalist renegades) and skinners, (their Patriot counterparts) and residents frequently found themselves preyed upon by either or both groups.

The Reynolds homestead near the entrance to the preserve dates back to that era. Although the house has been traced back to 1803, it is likely a replacement for an earlier dwelling. In 1905, Edwin Tatham purchased the property for an estate and built a large house with formal gardens. After his death in 1933, his wife sold the estate to Warner D. Orvis, a broker, who held the property until his death in 1967.

In 1970 the property was sold to a development group which combined it with adjacent properties and planned an extensive development. Eight model condominiums were built, but the venture failed before the project went further. The empty condo buildings remain on the property, a visual reminder of what might have been.

A subsequent plan to develop the site into 108 homes with 4.5 miles of new road was thwarted when a coalition of government and private groups arranged the funding to purchase the property. The sale was announced in 2005 and the property opened to the public in 2009.

Angle Fly Brook.

blue trails begins to ascend through open woodlands. It passes a rock outcropping which pokes above the forest floor. At 1.2 miles, it enters the western section as the red trail joins from the right. Together they are along the AT&T line. For the next section of the blue trail, see the Western Section.

Yellow Trail   *Length: 1.6 miles Blaze: yellow*
Circling the core of Angle Fly Preserve, the yellow trail is co-aligned for half of its length with the blue trail. Head towards the composting toilet at the southeast corner of the parking lot near the deer exclosure fence and turn left. The yellow trail turns again to parallel a large wetland. The blue trail comes in at a stone wall and at 0.4 mile the co-aligned trails cross the entrance road. The white trail joins briefly from the right at 0.5 mile and then leaves to the right. After heading downhill, the blue and yellow trails cross wet areas on puncheon. At 0.9 mile, the trails split with the blue trail turning right and the yellow trail going straight.

The yellow trail crosses several stone walls and parallels Angle Fly Brook. It turns at 1.1 miles to parallel a tributary and is above the flood plain. The trail enters an area infested with barberry at 1.2 miles and then heads uphill. Building the trail required creating a wide path to prevent this non-native shrub from encroaching on the trail. The trail goes through a stone wall at 1.4 miles and then turns right to parallel it. The yellow trail turns left to leave stone wall and ends by the composting toilet.

White Trail   *Length: 1.2 miles Blaze: white*
Providing access to the north portion of the central section of Angle Fly Preserve, the white trail goes by the former mansion. It starts at Reynolds Pond at the main

entrance and heads uphill along the former road to the mansion. It turns right at 0.1 mile and passes what seems like a massive copper beech which is really a cluster of four trees. After crossing the AT&T line, the trail skirts the hill. After going through a thicket, it is briefly in an overgrown field which is an example of ecological succession. This is the process of change brought about by the replacement of one ecological system by another; in this case, invasive species taking over the former cultivated field.

At 0.7 mile, the white trail turns right to join the co-aligned blue and yellow trails and then at 0.8 mile turns right to leave them. After turning left onto a woods road, the white trail crosses a stream on well placed rocks. A small dam is to the right at 1.0 mile. The white trail goes straight to leave the woods road and heads uphill. It passes the pink and white trail which leads 0.3 mile uphill to the red trail. Heading downhill, the white trail crosses several stone walls. It then heads uphill to end at the blue trail.

WESTERN SECTION

Hikers wishing to take longer hikes will need to make a foray into the Western Section. The red trail circles the northwest portion of this section and the many connecting trails allow variations for longer or shorter hikes.

There are four points of access to the Western Section with the entrance on Hilltop Road for short hikes. The 0.1 mile access trail (red with white cross) connects Hilltop Road to the red trail. The pink and white trail is a 0.3 mile connection between the Central and Western sections. It is along the AT&T line for a short distance. Both the 0.2 mile blue access trail (blue with white cross) and the blue trail (0.9 miles provide access to Route 35. Eventually there will be a connection to the Lasdon Estate.

Blue Trail   *Length 0.9 mile Blaze: blue*
Shortly after joining the red trail on the AT&T line, the blue trail goes straight the blue trail goes through a series of rock fields. At 0.4 mile it enters an area following a woods road when the red trail turns right. After heading downhill, overgrown with barberry. It turns right at the junction with the blue and white

---

THE PRICKLY INVADER

The invasive Japanese Barberry found throughout Angle Fly was first introduced in the United States as an ornamental shrub in 1875 and used for hedgerows, dye, and jam. Described by one popular website as "landscaping with barbed wire," it has proved to be a tough plant to deal with as it has few natural enemies - even deer avoid it. Birds and rabbits eat the berries which pass through their system and are dispersed. Existing bushes send out runners which sprout and spread and branches touching the ground will take root. Forming dense stands in natural habitats including canopy forests, open woodlands, wetlands, pastures, and meadows, it has been placed on the "Least Wanted" list of alien plant invaders by the Plant Conservation Alliance.

Streamside.

trail. At 0.5 miles it crosses a series of streams, some of which are small enough to step over, while others require a stone or two. The blue trail crosses a large stream on a bridge, turns right and heads towards Route 35.

Red Trail   *Length: 1.6 miles Blaze: red*
Circling the northwest section of the property, the red trail is the core of the Western Section, but it is necessary to hike another trail to reach it. The many low stone walls indicate that this area was once cultivated farmland. At the end of the red access trail to Hilltop Road, the red trail heads into the woods on a woods road. After crossing a stone wall at 0.2 mile the trail goes through a heavy barberry infestation and passes the red and white trail (red dot on white) to the right. Over the next 0.5 mile, the red trail is on and off wood roads and crosses stone walls. It reaches a junction with the pink trail at 0.8 mile and then crosses many stone walls. At a T junction at 1.0 mile, the red trail turns right. The pink and white trail (pink dot on white) is to the left and connects to the pink trail.

In 1.2 mile, at another T junction, the red trail again goes right, passing the end of the red and white trail (red dot on white) to the left. After going over a hill, the red trail turns right onto the AT&T line where the dark red trail (dark red) is to the left. At 1.4 miles in quick succession, the blue trail joins the red trail from the left and then leaves when the red trail turns right. Now on a woods road, the red trail heads uphill and then goes downhill where it meets the red access trail to Hilltop Road at 1.6 miles.

Red and White Trail   *Length 0.6 miles Blaze: red dot on white*
The red and white trail crosses numerous stone walls as it slices across the center of the Western Section. Heading south from the red trail, it is along a woods

road. At 0.2 mile, it crosses a small expanse of exposed rock slabs. The trail passes the junction with the pink trail which leads to the red trail and heads downhill. Leaving the woods road, red and white trail makes a sweeping turn and levels out at 0.4 mile as it enters an infestation of barberry. After crossing stone walls only to parallel them, the trail goes through another massive barberry infestation and ends at the red trail.

EASTERN SECTION

The trails in the Eastern Section go through meadows, woodlands, wetlands, and past a small pond. They connect the main entrance on Route 139 to Reis Park.

Blue Trail   *Length 1.0 mile Blaze: blue*
In the eastern section, the blue trail connects Reis Park to Route 139. The blue trail starts from behind the southwest corner of tennis courts in Reis Park and heads south. It turns to pass a foundation before reaching Plum Brook Road and in 0.2 mile, turns left to follow the shoulder of the road. Upon reaching the AT&T right of way, it turns right and enters a small parking lot. It soon bears right off a woods road, returns to the road, enters a meadow at 0.6 mile and turns right at the junction with the green trail. The blue trail parallels a stone wall and passes foundations to the right. It heads downhill between two parallel stone walls and crosses two other stone walls. It reaches a junction with the orange trail to the left and then crosses a bridge at 0.9 mile. After leaving the woods, the blue trail crosses Route 139 and turns left at the entrance road to Angle Fly Preserve.

Green Trail   *Length: 1.2 miles Blaze: green*
Traversing the southeast section of Angle Fly Preserve, the green trail is a lollypop trail, with a loop at the southern end. Starting at a junction with the blue trail 0.1 mile south of Plum Brook Road, the green trail goes south along the edge of a meadow. After re-entering the woods, the trail passes the orange trail which heads downhill 0.4 mile to the blue trail.

At 0.4 mile, the green trail begins its loop. Seasonally there are black walnuts scattered on the ground. Stay to the right. After crossing a stone wall, the trail goes through wet areas, crosses more stone walls, streams and a farmer's drainage ditch. The trail is alternately on puncheon or only slightly drier ground until 0.9 mile when it reaches the green-white trail (green cross on white background). It is 100 feet out to Route 100. Turning north the green trail passes a large cedar tree, briefly crosses the edge of a meadow and then passes a pond to the right. The trail begins to ascend gradually and then more steeply to close the loop at 1.2 miles.

Orange Trail   *Length 0.4 mile Blazes: orange*
From the green trail, the orange trail heads steadily downhill. After crossing a stone wall at 0.1 mile, it reaches a large tree and turns right. Now mostly on level ground, the trail winds through former farmland. At 0.3 mile, the trail goes along a berm of a drainage ditch and then leaves it. It ends at the blue trail.

ADJACENT PARKS: Lasdon Estate, Arboretum, and Veterans Memorial Park, Reis Park

DRIVING: Central section: Take I-684 to Exit 6 (Route 35) and go west to Route 100. Turn right and go 0.6 mile and turn left onto Route 139 (Primrose Street). Go 1.0 mile to the main entrance to the left [41.291211N 73.719194W]. Parking is at the end of the entrance road.

Eastern Section: Follow the above directions, but continue on Route 100 for another 0.4mile to Reis Park and turn right. Park near the southwest corner of the tennis courts [41.302429N 73.713728W].

Western Section: Take I-684 to Exit 6 (Route 35), go west for 3.5 miles and turn right on Orchard Hill Road. Go 0.6 mile to Hilltop Road. Parking is 0.4 mile alongside the road [41.289048N 73.734915W].

PUBLIC TRANSPORTATION: None available

For contact information, see Appendix, Somers Land Trust.

Reis Park

Somers • 1.8 miles, 80 acres

The Somers Library, playground, and tennis courts are what visitors first see on arriving at Reis Park. Further into the park, trails skirt the perimeters of ball fields. The park was a bequest to the Town of Somers from Carolyn Wright-Reis who died in 1967. It was her wish that the land be used for a recreation and education. As a result, the park was established, the farmhouse was converted to a museum, and the Somers Library moved to the property.

T R A I L S

The simple trail system at Reis Park effectively uses a small area to provide three trails with portions of a fitness course along each one. The gravel surface makes for easy jogging and walking. All three trails can be reached from the top of the wooden steps at the near end of the parking lot just past the ball field to the left. At the top of the steps, the first trail to the right is the yellow trail, the red trail is 30 feet further, and the 0.3 mile blue trail is 40 feet beyond the red. Many short trails connect the parallel marked trails. All three trails have stations for an advanced timber challenge fitness course. To visit every station, it is necessary to walk all three trails.

A 0.3-mile trail connects the ball fields adjacent to the Somers Library to the soccer field at Van Tassel Park and Primrose School. Over most of its length, its surface is crushed stone; it is handicapped accessible only from the soccer field to the edge of the field at Primrose School.

Yellow Trail   *Length: 0.7 mile Blaze: yellow*
The largest of the three loops, the yellow trail begins to the right from a grassy strip at the top of the wooden steps. Going counterclockwise, the trail gradually turns left through a forest with little understory. At 0.3 mile, the yellow trail heads downhill into an area with more shrubs and small trees. The red trail enters from the left at 0.6 mile and together they cross the mowed lawn around the end of the

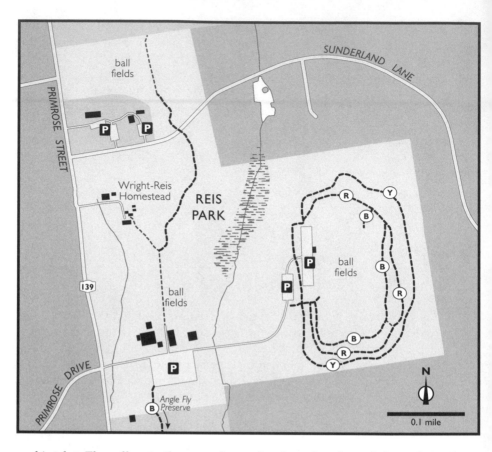

parking lot. The yellow trail crosses the road and reaches the path from the parking lot to close the loop.

Red Trail

Length: 0.5 mile Blaze: red

The red trail parallels a stone wall on a woods road. When the woods road becomes gravel, the trail turns and crosses the stone wall. It crosses exposed bedrock and heads downhill on dirt, only to change back to gravel. At 0.3 mile, the blue trail joins from the left and then leaves. The red trail joins the yellow trail at 0.5 mile.

DRIVING: From I-684, take Exit 6 (Route 35) west to Route 100. Turn right and head north for 0.6 mile. Turn left at Route 139 and go 1.4 miles to the park entrance to the right. Drive past the library, playground, and tennis courts, to the end of the road. Park and head up the steps [41.304629N 73.710228W].

PUBLIC TRANSPORTATION: None available.

For contact information, see Appendix, Somers.

Blue Mountain Reservation
Depew Park

Peekskill • 22.6 miles, 1,538 acres

Rolling woodlands with large granite boulders, glacial erratics, and rock outcroppings make Blue Mountain Reservation a great place to hike. Massive rock formations tower above trails while stately trees, tiny lichens, and abundant ferns make a picturesque setting. A favorite destination for mountain bikes, the reservation is large enough so that hikers will meet few bikers except when races are held. To minimize encounters, they should visit on weekdays, when there are no or few bikers around.

As with many places near the Hudson River, the land that is now Blue Mountain Reservation was originally part of Van Cortlandt Manor, purchased from local Native Americans in 1677. Much later, the Loundsbury family owned and operated a sand, gravel, cement, brick, and general contracting business; the gravel pit was located at the present-day beach parking lot. New Pond and Loundsbury Pond were constructed for making ice; once cut, the ice was stored to be sold in summer. The county purchased the property in 1926. During Franklin D. Roosevelt's administration, a Civilian Conservation Corps (CCC) camp was established there. They built the woods roads as well as the Trail Lodge and two comfort stations, now designated as historically significant.

TRAILS

The trails in Blue Mountain meander up hills and down through valleys. Aside from the single-track trails created by mountain bikers, the trails are on woods roads. Blazes and numbered posts change all too frequently because groups decide on their own to mark a trail. The blazes might or might not agree with this book. Single-track trails are mentioned, but not described.

Unpaved Montrose Station Road goes 1.4 miles across the park; gated at both ends to prevent vehicular access, it is an alternate access to trails. From the white trail, a 0.3 mile purple trail goes uphill along the north shore of a pond and turns where an unmarked trail leads 0.1 mile to the co-aligned blue trail and the Briarcliff Peekskill Trailway (green). The purple trail descends and ends at the white trail at 0.3 mile. The blue disk trail is a continuation of the Blue Mountain Access Trail (green) from Depew Park. After passing a 0.1-mile yellow trail and a 0.4 mile unmarked trail to the overflow parking area at the entrance to the park, it ends at the entrance road across from Loundsbury Pond.

The 10.1 miles of marked and unmarked single-track mountain bike trails snake in and out of areas circled by woods roads. These trails often change and might not be exactly where they are shown on the map. They travel through narrow valleys, past rock outcroppings, and through hemlock groves. Because they have a short line of sight, hikers are encouraged to avoid them.

Blue Trail *Length: 2.4 miles Blaze: blue*
Of course, there is a blue trail in Blue Mountain Reservation—it branches out and

nearly circles the park's higher sections. From the main parking lot, the blue trail and the Briarcliff Peekskill Trailway (green) head uphill. After passing the yellow trail to the left and the yellow/orange trail to the right, the co-aligned trails go through a hemlock grove. At 0.3 mile, they turn left and the white trail heads 1.1 miles to connect to the Briarcliff Peekskill Trailway (green).

The blue trail and the Briarcliff Peekskill Trailway continue uphill, passing a trail to the left at 0.5 mile. The woods road makes a turn to the right. It passes to the right a 0.1-mile unmarked trail to the purple trail around the lake and then a single-track trail to the left as it continues to ascend. At 0.8 mile, it reaches a terminus of the red trail to the left. After passing a massive wetland and heading downhill, the trails turn left at 1.1 miles to follow a pipeline right-of way.

After the Briarcliff Peekskill Trailway turns right to cross former Montrose Station Road, the blue trail follows the pipeline right-of-way and then leaves it to

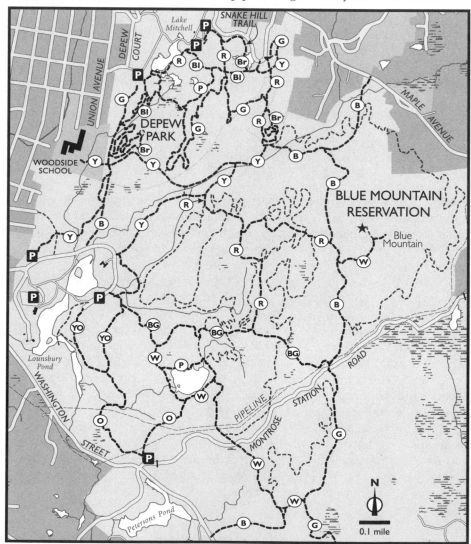

RELIEF ON TWO FRONTS

In the depths of the Great Depression, the country was suffering from massive unemployment. The newly elected president, Franklin D. Roosevelt, and his administration raced to push through relief legislation. Less than a month after his inauguration, a bill was quickly passed by Congress and signed into law on March 31, 1933 establishing the Civilian Conservation Corps (CCC). It was one of the first acts of the New Deal, a vast program of relief and reform. The first men were inducted 37 days later.

The program provided employment to young men to work on conservation projects across the country. Applicants had to be single males, between 18 and 25, unemployed, from a needy family, not in school, healthy, and capable of doing physical labor. Later, veterans and women were admitted to the program. Sent out into healthful surroundings, this army of the unemployed renewed decimated forests, fought soil erosion, and rebuilt infrastructure.

Camps were set up for work projects and closed when the work was done. Initially, there were 32 camps in New York and at one time there were 102 camps in operation, the largest number in any state. Camps in Westchester County were at Blue Mountain and Ward Pound Ridge Reservations, Crugers Park, now FDR Veterans Hospital, and Mohansic County Park, now FDR State Park. More that 220,000 New Yorkers were among the 2 million across the country who served.

Although the program is cited as restoring depleted natural resources, it also provided economic support to the families of enrollees and stimulated the local economy of CCC host communities. But there were other benefits as well. The health and physical development of corps members improved, they received technical training and, for some 40,000 corps members, they learned to read and write. The program ended in 1942 with the onset of World War II.

enter the woods where, to the right, a tree is nearly consuming a blaze. Passing a rock outcropping, the blue trail heads uphill and, at 1.3 miles, passes a 2.8-mile unmarked bike trail to the right which reconnects to the blue trail. The cobbled surface of the woods road has just enough incline to provide a workout, but not enough to exhaust you. The forest has predominantly deciduous trees. At 1.5 miles, the blue trail passes a white trail leading a quarter-mile steeply up to a viewpoint near the top of Blue Mountain and then to the top without a view. Continuing straight as it descends to cross a seasonal stream, the blue trail passes an arm of the red trail at 1.6 miles. The heavily cobbled section ends and the trail passes broken-off boulders, scattered and looking like the pieces of a puzzle. Under massive trees, the blue trail is on a bumpy treadway and then heads down a sweeping turn. At the bottom, maple trees and extensive barberry bushes line the trail.

At a T junction at 2.0 miles, the blue trail goes left, while a different blue trail goes 0.3 mile through wetlands to the Maple Avenue entrance (no parking). The blue trail passes the other end of the 2.8-mile unmarked bike trail and veers left. At 2.2 miles the blue trail passes the Blue Mt. Summit Trail (red) leading 0.4 mile into Depew Park and acquires an additional blaze—a yellow disc. They end at the junction with the yellow trail.

The road less traveled.

Briarcliff Peekskill Trailway   *Length: 2.9 miles Blaze: green*
The northern terminus of the Briarcliff Peekskill Trailway is in the main parking lot. It is co-aligned with the blue trail north of Montrose Station Road. (See Briarcliff Peekskill Trailway in Linear Corridors)

Orange Trail   *Length: 0.8 mile Blaze: orange*
From the yellow/orange trail, the orange trail parallels a stone wall and wetlands. At 0.2 mile, it crosses the pond outlet stream and goes through a stone wall. After reaching a gas pipeline, it crosses a stream on rocks and heads along on a rock causeway to cross wetlands. Turning left and heading uphill along another pipeline, the orange trail then leaves the pipeline and turns right to pass through a gap in a massive stone wall. It reaches a T junction with an unmarked road heading 100 feet to Montrose Station Road with parking at Washington Street. After turning left at the junction, the orange trail crosses pipeline rights-of-way at 0.6 and 0.7 mile. The orange trail ascends, then descends, to reach a pond where it ends on the white trail.

Red Trail   *Length: 1.0 mile Blaze: red*
On the map, the red trail is shown as a path shaped like a Y with the jitters. It begins at the intersection of the yellow trail in the northern part of the park and heads uphill. It passes the first of four unmarked mountain bike trails and, at 0.4 mile, reaches a large rock outcropping and splits. To the right, the red trail heads 0.4 mile to the co-aligned blue trail and Briarcliff Peekskill Trailway. Turn left and go steeply uphill. The red trail passes a single-track trail to the left and then curves past a sloping face of bedrock. The red trail passes a vernal pool and then more single-track trails. It works its way uphill and ends at 0.6 mile at the blue trail. At the trail junction where the red trail splits, this section of the red trail heads downhill

and crosses the first of several low areas on a raised treadway. It makes a sharp left and then a sharp right. It passes a green and white trail so convoluted that only mountain bikers could love it. After crossing a stream on a raised treadway, the red trail passes another vernal pool at 0.2 mile and heads uphill. It ends at a junction with the blue trail and Briarcliff Peekskill Trailway.

White Trail
Length: 1.1 miles Blaze: white

From the blue trail 0.3 mile from the main parking lot, the white trail goes right at a Y junction where the blue trail and Briarcliff Peekskill Trailway turn left. The white trail passes the purple trail to the left, heads through an open area, and crosses the outlet of a pond. After going downhill, it turns and passes to the right the orange trail, which leads to Montrose Station Road in 0.3 mile. The white trail follows the shore of the pond with a short side trail out to a view and then heads uphill. At a T intersection at 0.4 mile, it turns right where the purple trail is to the left. The white trail ascends more steeply, crosses two gas pipelines, reaches a rock barrier, and crosses Montrose Station Road at 0.7 mile. Continuing past an expanse of skunk cabbage, the white trail goes uphill and at 0.9 mile passes a mountain bike trail to the left. At a wide intersection it turns left; straight ahead is a blue trail (not connected to the 2.4 mile main blue trail) leading 0.3 mile to Washington Street (no parking). The white trail heads uphill to end at the Briarcliff Peekskill Trailway.

Yellow Trail (north from parking lot)
Length: 0.8 mile Blaze: yellow

From the co-aligned blue trail and Briarcliff Peekskill Trailway, the yellow trail crosses a seasonal stream and heads uphill. At 0.1 mile, it passes a mountain bike trail connecting to other bike trails which are fine for hiking. The yellow trail heads downhill and passes a trail to the left leading to the Trail Lodge. It goes through hemlock groves and passes rocks that have tumbled down the hillside. After the trail heads more steeply uphill, it parallels a rushing stream in a ravine to the left. The yellow trail heads steeply uphill. At 0.5 mile, an unmarked trail to the left leads to the yellow disk trail. After passing several vernal pools, the yellow trail reaches a T junction where the red trail begins to the right. Turning left, the yellow trail passes through an area littered with debris from hemlocks destroyed by woolly adelgid infestation. The trail crosses a stream on a bridge and ends at a T junction with the yellow disk and blue trails.

Yellow Disk Trail
Length: 0.6 mile Blaze: yellow disk

Connecting Blue Mountain Reservation to Depew Park, the yellow disk trail begins at the terminus of the blue and yellow trails. It heads west along a woods road that parallels a stream. The trail passes to the left, a bridge over a stream and enters Depew Park, but there are no signs. Vernal pools are to the left at 0.3 mile. At a cross junction at 0.5 mile, the yellow disk trail continues and ends at the Woodside School at 0.1 mile. To the left is a blue disk trail with occasional yellow blazes. To the right, a green trail leads to Depew Park.

Yellow/Orange Trail
Length: 0.5 mile Blaze: yellow/orange

On terrain gentler than other sections of the park, the yellow/orange trail is a

Meet the neighbors.

short loop connecting both ends of the main parking lot. Starting from the co-aligned blue trail and the Briarcliff Peekskill Trailway (green), the yellow/orange trail passes tall trees with sparse understory. It goes steeply uphill and then down. At a Y junction at a quarter-mile, the orange trail leads left 0.5 mile to Montrose Station Road. The yellow/orange trail turns right and heads downhill. It parallels the outlet stream from Loundsbury Pond and at a Y junction, turns right. It heads uphill and ends at the parking lot.

DRIVING: From Route 9, take the Welcher Avenue Exit and turn east away from the river. Follow Welcher Avenue to the park entrance [41.271410N 73.926610W]. Alternately turn right at Washington Street and drive 0.9 mile to the parking at Montrose Station Road [41.261933N 73.919105W].

PUBLIC TRANSPORTATION: From the Metro-North Hudson Line Peekskill Station, head east on Hudson Avenue for 0.7-mile to Walnut Street, where there is a sign: To Depew Park. Follow Walnut Street 0.1 mile into the park and then take the Lake Mitchell Trail (to the swimming pool parking lot into Blue Mountain Reservation.

For contact information, see Appendix, Westchester County Parks—Blue Mountain.

Depew Park

Peekskill • 5.5 miles, 192 acres

Named after Chauncey Mitchell Depew, whose ancestors were among the original settlers of Peekskill, Depew Park provides many different recreational opportunities. This urban park is where neighbors make good use of the opportunities to walk and teens to congregate. The park's origins are traced to 1901, when this witty and skilled, orator, lawyer, businessman, and politician donated 40 acres of what was long-known as Depew's Woods to the Village of Peekskill. Two years later the land became a public park. Through gifts and purchases, the park has grown to its current size. Depew, a Republican, served in the United States Senate (1899-1911). After his defeat in a bid for a third term, he served as counsel and, later, president of New York Central Railroad.

TRAILS

Once away from the frenzied activity of organized sports, the atmosphere within the park is relaxed. In spite of a 1973 City of Peekskill ordinance which states "No person shall ride a bicycle, tricycle, velocipede or motorcycle upon any walk or footpath, but persons may push such machines in single file along the same", mountain bikers use the trails. Trails change frequently; they might not be as described.

Abraham Depew Promenade, an unmarked 0.4-mile paved road closed to vehicles, connects the vehicular exit at Hudson Avenue to the pedestrian entrances at Montross Avenue and at Ferris Street (no parking). The 0.3 mile Snake Hill Trail (brown) begins near the park maintenance building and connects to the Hudson Trail (red) and the Rosie Trail (blue). The Hudson Trail (red) heads south for 0.1 mile to join the Abraham Depew Promenade with the Rosie Trail. Making a loop with the Abraham Depew Promenade, the Rosie Trail (blue) goes 0.3 mile from the parking lot by Lake Mitchell to the red trail.

The Lake Mitchell Trail (orange) heads west from the parking lot in front of the horseshoe pits and ends in 0.2 mile at the parking lot by the swimming pool. The Nature Center Trail (blue) heads south 0.2 mile to end at the Blue Mountain Access Trail (green). On the eastern side of the park, the Hawley Green Trail (yellow) is a narrow 0.1 mile trail that connects the Rosie Trail to the 0.2 mile Ruth Rusch Interpretive Trail (green). For mountain bikers and trail runners, the 0.3 mile Rock Ledge Loop is a less steep but a longer route to Depew Park.

Blue Mountain Access Trail
Length: 0.5 mile Blaze: green

Beginning at a low wooden bridge at the south side of a swimming pool parking lot on the west side of the park, the Blue Mountain Access Trail goes south into Blue Mountain Reservation. The trail crosses a stone wall and a massive upended root ball of a downed tree. It goes downhill, passing at 0.1 mile the Nature Center Trail coming from the left and, at 0.3 mile, it passes the Singleton Trail (brown). Continuing south, the trail crosses a yellow trail and, at 0.5 mile, enters Blue Mountain Reservation. The Blue Mountain Assess Trail, now with additional and occasional yellow paint blazes, continues south into Blue Mountain Reservation to end on the entrance road near Loundsbury Pond.

Blue Mountain Summit Trail
Length: 0.4 mile Blaze: red

Beginning at the Abraham Depew Promenade, the Blue Mountain Summit Trail goes steeply downhill. After crossing a stream, the trail enters a more open area and turns to parallel the stream while heading slightly downhill. It ends at junction 35 at a yellow trail in Blue Mountain Reservation.

Beecher Trail
Length: 0.4 mile Blaze: purple

Starting just past a kiosk on the Lake Mitchell Trail, the Beecher Trail heads uphill and descends into a small valley. It passes the Singleton Trail at 0.2 mile. The trail crosses a seasonal wet area on a bridge and passes the Dr. Jekyll Trail (green) to the right at 0.3 mile and heads uphill to end at the Rosie Trail (blue).

Lake Mitchell.

Dr. Jekyll Trail
Length: 1.3 miles Blaze: green

If you want a meandering tour of Depew Park, take a hike on the Dr. Jekyll Trail. Starting from the Beecher Trail, it heads downhill, passes a rock outcropping to the right at 0.2 miles, and turns. At a Y junction, an unmarked trail to the right goes 150 feet to the yellow trail that runs along the border between Depew Park and Blue Mountain Reservation. The Dr. Jekyll Trail turns left making the first of three sweeping turns as it heads uphill primarily in a valley. At 0.6 mile, it goes through a stone wall and continues with short descents as it continues its uphill trek. The trail passes a rock outcropping to the right and turns to pass another one. It turns right at a trail junction. The Beecher Trail (purple) is 100 feet to the left. At 1.2 miles, the trail goes up and then down a rock face and turns to avoid entering a gully. It ends at the Blue Mountain Summit Trail (red).

Singleton Trail
Length: 1.0 mile Blaze: brown

The rolling terrain of the Singleton Trail will please both mountain bikers and trail runners. Beginning on the Blue Mountain Access Trail (green), the Singleton Trail goes into a valley. At 0.2 mile, the trail turns left at a T junction. After going downhill, the trail turns 180 degrees and heads uphill. At 0.6 mile, the trail heads downhill and parallels a stone wall briefly. When it reaches the Nature Center Trail at 0.9 mile, it turns first right, then left. It ends at the Beecher Trail.

DRIVING: From Route 9, take the South Street/Hudson Avenue Exit and head uphill on Hudson Avenue away from the river and train station. At 0.5 mile, turn right onto Walnut Street at a sign, Depew Park Entrance. The entrance is 0.1 mile straight ahead [41.283803N 73.918056W]. Alternate entrances are via two trails from Blue Mountain Reservation and off either Montross Avenue or Ferris Street (no parking). Parking is at the entrance at the end of Bay Street [41.280595N 73.919094W].

PUBLIC TRANSPORTATION: From the Metro-North Hudson Line Peekskill Station, head east on Hudson Avenue, away from the river. It is a 0.7-mile walk to Walnut Street, where there is the sign for the park. Follow Walnut Street 0.1 mile into the park.

For contact information, see Appendix, Peekskill.

Mountain Lakes Park

North Salem • 13.0 miles, 1,083 acres

The highest point in Westchester County (982 feet) is located in the northernmost park of the county's park system, Mountain Lakes Park. Up until 1731, it wasn't even in New York: it was part of Connecticut. A redrawing of the state line that year ceded it to the Town of North Salem. Although it is still commonly referred to by that name, the park's formal name was changed in 2009 to the Sal J. Prezioso Mountain Lakes Park, to honor the man who helped shape public policy in Westchester and was instrumental in acquiring the property in 1961.

There are many reasons to visit: a rugged landscape in a hardwood forest, streams, trails that pass four lakes, and that high point, reached by a 0.3 mile hike up Mount Bailey, where, alas, there is no view. Serenity prevails though, as little road noise is audible throughout the park.

TRAILS

No matter what the season, Mountain Lakes Park is a favorite walking place for local residents. The yellow and blue trails circle the eastern portion of the park. The orange trail along the road has a gentle grade that makes elevation changes almost imperceptible. Because the first 0.7 mile of trail is paved and well-graded, the orange trail is handicapped accessible. The 0.2 mile North Salem Trail (NS) connects the orange trail to the Hearst-Mead Preserve, open space that has been protected by the North Salem Open Space Foundation.

The AT&T right-of-way and a power line cross the northern part of the park. The former is 1.6 miles long, but is closed to hiking. The latter cuts through and then parallels the northern edge of the park. Ostensibly, the 1.1 miles should be clear enough to walk, but the right of way is often overgrown with multiflora rose and barberry bushes. When trails cross these utility lines, there are birding opportunities along the edges.

Orange Trail   *Length: 3.7 miles Blaze: orange*
Beginning from the entrance into Mountain Lakes Park, a road with orange blazes makes a loop through the park. Although walking along a road might seem not challenging enough for a hiker, it is easy to follow and allows several people to walk abreast. Aside from some buildings and trail junctions, there are few landmarks. The grades make for easy cross-country skiing when snow cover is sufficient and not too many people have walked on the road.

From the parking area near the entrance gate, the orange trail heads uphill through an open forest. It passes to the left, at 0.1 mile, a paved road leading into Camp Morty. Continuing uphill, at 0.3 mile, the trail reaches the white trail to the right. At 0.5 mile, it passes the paved road leading into Hemlock Camp. At 0.6 mile, a gate blocks vehicles and the blue and white trail to the left connects to the blue trail in 0.2 mile. An unmarked road leads into Tamarack Camp to the right. The pavement ends at 0.7 mile and until the trail leaves the road at 3.0 miles, its surface

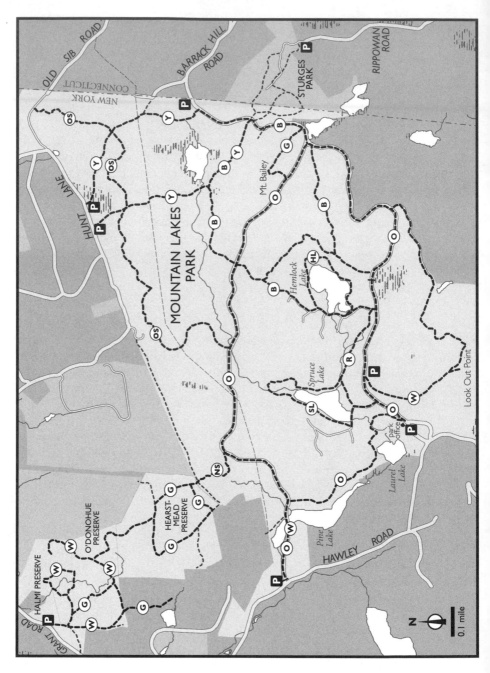

is crushed stone. After crossing a long stone causeway, the orange trail passes the other end of the white trail. The orange trail gently curves first left, then right, and, at 1.0 mile, passes the Larch lean-to, one of several that were left over from the camp and are still being used. Following the edge of the property, the trail passes the blue trail to the left at 1.4 miles. This latter trail is easily missed because it is just shy of a major triangle intersection.

From the triangle intersection, the blue trail leads to the right and the orange trail heads left and slightly downhill. It passes the Balsam lean-to at 1.5 miles and then the two Cedar lean-tos. Continuing downhill, at 1.9 miles the orange trail crosses the blue trail. At 2.2 miles, it crosses a small stonework bridge over a stream and then the Old Sib Trail (OS) to the right. The AT&T right-of-way crosses the orange trail for the first time at 2.4 miles. After passing the Roaring Tent campsite to the left, the trail heads downhill. At 2.7 miles, it passes the North Salem Trail (NS) which goes 0.2 mile to the Hearst-Mead Tract and then crosses the AT&T line a second time. At 3.0 miles, the orange trail turns left onto a woods road. Straight ahead the orange and white trail continues on the road for 0.2 mile to end at parking at Hawley Road.

The orange trail passes the three Big Pine lean-tos and heads uphill. To the right the trail overlooks Pine Lake, where, in the summer, lily pads cover much of the surface. At 3.2 miles, just shy of the crest of the hill, the orange trail turns right onto a narrow path. To the left and uphill, yurts are visible. These tent-like structures of the style used by nomads in Central Asia are the living quarters for the campers at Camp Morty. The trail heads downhill on a rock outcropping with ledges and steps. It turns away from the lake and wetlands and makes a sharp left to parallel a stream. It crosses the stream on a bridge at 3.5 miles and begins its ascent to the park office. It closes the loop at the kiosk outside of the park office.

Blue Trail   *Length: 1.9 miles Blaze: blue*

A variety of habitats and terrain are characteristics of the blue trail as it circles the eastern portion of the park. It is accessible from the blue and white trail 0.7 mile from the beginning of the orange trail just past a gate and at two intersections with the orange trail. At the end of the blue-white trail, turn right to go counterclockwise. The trail goes very steeply uphill and, at 0.1 mile, passes stones set in a row (for reasons unknown). It reaches a trail junction and turns left. The unmarked trail to the right leads to the Larch lean-to. The blue trail heads downhill, passes a stone pile and then heads uphill. It turns left at 0.4 mile to join the orange trail. Almost immediately the orange trail turns left at a large triangle intersection and the blue continues straight along an unpaved road. At 0.5 mile, the blue trail passes the green trail which goes to the top of Mt. Bailey. Unmarked trails to the right at 0.6 mile lead to Sturges Park, a park in Ridgefield, CT with a 0.9-mile network of trails.

The blue trail turns left to join the yellow trail along a narrow path which then widens out. The trail becomes more and more gullied as it gradually heads downhill. At 1.0 mile, the trails split with the yellow trail going straight and the blue trail turning left. It crosses two stone walls and then parallels another. It crosses a stream at 1.2 miles, goes along a berm and heads uphill to cross the orange trail. At 1.5 miles, the trail turns left. Straight ahead is an unmarked trail into Hemlock Camp. The blue trail goes below a rock outcropping. It turns left as it continues uphill with ragged rocks encrusted with lichen on both sides of the trail. Heading downhill through open woods, the trail crosses a stream at 1.7 miles and turns left. At 0.9 miles, the blue trail reaches a T-junction with blue and white trail and closes the loop.

Hemlock Lake Trail   *Length: 0.7 mile Blaze: red with white HL*
From the second gate to the left, 0.5 mile along the orange trail, a paved road leads into Hemlock Camp. It passes the red trail which leads 0.2 miles downhill to the Spruce Lake Trail. At the lake, the Hemlock Lake trail enters the woods to begin a counterclockwise loop. The Hemlock Lake Trail enters the wood and turns right to pass through the parking lot behind the dining hall. Following the shore, at times closer than at others, the trail reaches the far end of Hemlock Lake and turns at 0.3 mile. It crosses the end of a stone wall and passes a lean-to at 0.5 mile as it reenters the camp. The trail reaches a paved road and turns left. After crossing the lake's outlet at 0.6 mile, the trail completes the loop at the former dining hall.

Old Sib Trail   *Length: 1.9 miles Blaze: OS*
Traversing the northern part of the park, the Old Sib Trail opens up additional hiking opportunities. Starting at Hunt Lane, the Old Sib Trail heads along Old Sib Road. At 0.2 mile it turns right to leave the road, heads uphill and turns left. Just past the end of a rock outcropping, the trail turns right again and heads uphill at 0.3 mile. It crosses the yellow trail for at 0.5 mile and then enters a flat area. After traversing across the top of a rocky ridge, the trail crosses the yellow trail a second time at 0.9 miles.

On second portion of the Old Sib Trail, the rolling cadence along former mountain biking trails makes for pleasant walking. The trail, for the most part, heads downhill going through many stone walls. At 1.1 miles, it goes through barberry bushes. After crossing the last stone wall at 1.4 miles, it heads up a slight rise to cross the AT&T right-of-way at 1.6 miles. It turns to head briefly uphill and, at 1.8 miles, begins its descent to end at the orange trail.

Spruce Lake Trail   *Length: 0.8 mile Blaze: red with white SL*
From the first gate to the left on the orange trail, a paved road leads into Camp Morty and crosses the spillway of the dam. Just past the bridge, opposite the camp director's cabin, the Spruce Lake Trail begins. The trail follows the shore,

sometimes closely and other times either farther away or just above it. At 0.3 mile, it turns left crossing water lines, parallels an inlet stream to Spruce Lake and heads uphill. Descending, it turns to cross a stream on an arched bridge at 0.4 mile and heads uphill again. The trail follows the lakeshore and, at one point, is just inches from the edge. It traverses the top of a rock outcropping at 0.6 mile and crosses a stone wall. At 0.7 mile, it reaches a bridge over a second inlet stream and a T junction. To the left, the red trail heads uphill following the edge of the stream and ends at 0.2 mile at the entrance road to Hemlock Camp. To the right, the trail heads towards Camp Morty and ends at 0.8 mile at the swimming area. It is 0.1 mile through the camp to the other end of the trail.

White Trail
Length: 1.2 miles Blaze: white

Primarily on woods roads, the white trail also offers the only long distance views in the park. From parking 0.3 mile from the park office, the white trail is on a wide woods road which heads uphill at a gentle grade. At 0.3 mile, it reaches an unmarked side trail to a sweeping view over Lake Waccabuc and Lake Oscaleta. The white trail goes down through a ravine and then turns to gracefully ascend long forgotten steps which are next to a rock outcropping At 0.4 mile, it reaches a seasonal view, goes through rock outcroppings, and continues to ascend sometimes more steeply than others. It goes downhill and passes a vernal pool at 0.7 mile. The white trail, at 0.9 mile, turns onto a woods road along the edge of the property that was carved into the side of the hill to maintain a reasonable grade. Stone walls line the woods road and the trail descends to meet the orange trail at 1.2 miles.

Yellow Trail
Length: 2.0 miles Blaze: yellow

Beginning at Hunt Lane, across from #222, the yellow trail enters the woods on a woods road. Heading uphill at an even grade, it crosses the Old Sib Trail (OS) at 0.3 mile and the AT&T right-of-way at 0.4 mile. Straight ahead is an unmarked trail to

Sharp edges.

Barrack Hill Road, which if followed leads to a triangle intersection. Turning right, the yellow trail leaves the woods road to wiggle through woods, in sharp contrast to the woods roads it connects. After crossing a stream on a bridge at 0.6 mile, the trail heads gradually uphill to reach the grade of a woods road. Turning right, the yellow trail continues on the woods road through the open woods. It turns right to join the blue trail at 0.9 mile, almost directly opposite two unmarked trails to the left which lead into Sturges Park.

The co-aligned yellow and blue trails run along a narrow path which then widens. The trail becomes more gullied as it gradually heads downhill. At 1.2 miles, the trails split with the blue trail turning left and yellow continuing straight. After crossing a stream, the yellow trail heads uphill along a stone wall to the left. It passes a pit 20-foot in diameter and reaches the AT&T line at 1.7 miles. It turns left and then right to leave it. It crosses the Old Sib Trail at 1.8 miles and reaches Hunt Lane in 1.9 miles. Turn right and go 0.1 mile to close the loop.

DRIVING: Take I-684 to Exit 6 (Route 35) and drive east on Route 35 for 4.4 miles from the northbound exit. Turn left where Route 121 leaves Route 35, and head north for 4.5 miles. At Hawley Road, turn right and continue 0.7 miles to parking adjacent to Hawley Road [41.312564N 73.580700W] or 0.8 more miles to the park entrance to the left [41.305296N 73.571531W]. To reach the yellow trail on Hunt Lane, continue on Route 121 for 1.5 more miles. Turn right on Keeler Lane, drive 1.4 miles to where it becomes Hunt Lane. Parking is 0.1 mile to the right [41.322195N 73.556269W] and another parking spot is just down the road [41.322111N 73.556824W].

PUBLIC TRANSPORTATION: None available

For contact information, see Appendix, Westchester County Parks—Mountain Lakes Park.

Halmi, Hearst-Mead, and O'Donohue Preserves

North Salem • 3.1 miles, 134 acres

A series of donations to the North Salem Open Land Foundation between 1977 and 2006 made possible a trail system for walking and riding. Entrance to the three properties is through a narrow right-of-way along a woods road off Grant Road (Route 121) and the Halmi Tract. The North Salem Trail (NS) in Mountain Lakes provides access to the 70 acre Hearst Mead property.

Robert Halmi, Jr. donated the 53 acre Halmi Tract in 2002. Two white trails wind miles through the property. Green trails connect to private property and to the Hearst-Mead Preserve. A stone outcropping on the highest point provides a view of the Titicus Reservoir.

The 11-acre O'Donohue Tract is adjacent to the Halmi Tract and is named to honor the leadership contribution made by Kevin and Laura O'Donohue.

In 1977, Eugenie Mead donated the steeply sloped and wooded 70-acres which became the Hearst-Mead Preserve. The 1.1 miles of green-blazed trails are along woods roads and cross many stone walls. Hikers will find North Salem Bridle Trail

Contrasts in nature.

Association blazes as well as green diamond tags. The trails connect to Mountain Lakes Park via the 0.2 mile North Salem Trail (NS).

DRIVING: Take I-684 to Exit 6 (Route 35) and drive east on Route 35 for 4.4 miles from the northbound exit. Turn left where Route 121 leaves Route 35, and head north for 5.0 miles. To right, there is parking along the road edge for one or two cars [N41.324574 W73.583424].

PUBLIC TRANSPORTATION: None available

For contact information, see Appendix, North Salem Open Land Foundation Park.

Rockefeller State Park Preserve
Greenrock Corporation

Sleepy Hollow • 40.4 miles, 1,385 acres

In the seemingly tranquil landscape at Rockefeller State Park Preserve, there is plenty of activity regardless of the season or time of day. There are few benches and picnicking is not permitted, but the well-graded carriageways are ideal for jogging, walking, or riding. Dogs are required to be leashed and, unlike in many other parks, the rule is enforced. Horses and carriages are welcome at the park, but riders and drivers must secure a non-transferable permit from the office. Licensed anglers can fish in Swan Lake and the Pocantico River. Birders should note that 180 species of birds have been recorded here.

The Greenrock Corporation manages the adjacent Rockefeller family-owned property and the public is permitted to walk or ride through the farm and adjacent woodlands. Signs are posted where the roads enter the Greenrock managed property, however, unlike most trails in the park, these trails have no identifying signs. Visitors are asked to be aware of farm vehicles and give them the right-of-way. For walkers wishing more solitude, these unmarked roads are less crowded than the named trails in more developed parts of the state preserve.

TRAILS

At these properties, most of the trails are wide gravel carriageways. The 15.7 miles of named trails are on state-owned property; there are 24.7 additional miles of trails that are unmarked and unnamed. Some of the unmarked trails are part of the park, and others are on Greenrock lands. Trail names are posted at intersections along with arrows pointing toward a return route to the visitor' center. However, names on some signs are visible only from one direction.

The trails go through or by a variety of habitats: stream, river, lake, wetland, woodland, and meadow. There are relatively few unobstructed views and most of those are along farm roads. Trails are clustered into four areas, two of which contain unnamed farm and carriage roads. With several roads crossing the park, there are multiple access points to trails. The park-issued map has more detail than the ones included in this book. However, the park-issued map does not show any of the unmarked trails through Greenrock Corporation property or the land east of Route 448.

Because the trails were originally designed as carriageways, the intersections are often triangles to allow for the wide turning radius of carriages. Sometimes these intersections are large enough so that a trail branches off to end at two separate places on the same trail. Witch's Spring trail ends at two places on the Pocantico River Trail. Spook Rock Trail, which starts at the Big Tree Trail then comes downhill to pass Spook Rock on the inside of a switchback, continues on to the triangle intersection where it forks to meet the Witch's Spring Trail.

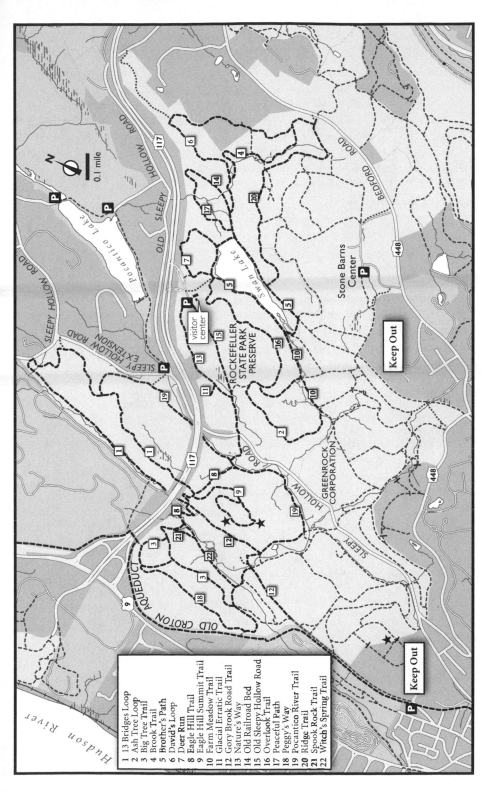

1 13 Bridges Loop
2 Ash Tree Loop
3 Big Tree Trail
4 Brook Trail
5 Brother's Path
6 David's Loop
7 Deer Run
8 Eagle Hill Trail
9 Eagle Hill Summit Trail
10 Farm Meadow Trail
11 Glacial Erratic Trail
12 Gory Brook Road Trail
13 Nature's Way
14 Old Railroad Bed
15 Old Sleepy Hollow Road
16 Overlook Trail
17 Peaceful Path
18 Peggy's Way
19 Pocantico River Trail
20 Ridge Trail
21 Spook Rock Trail
22 Witch's Spring Trail

Pocantico Lake

Swan Lake

visitor center

ROCKEFELLER STATE PARK PRESERVE

Stone Barns Center

GREENROCK CORPORATION

Keep Out

Keep Out

Hudson River

OLD CROTON AQUEDUCT

SLEEPY HOLLOW ROAD

SLEEPY HOLLOW ROAD EXTENSION

OLD SLEEPY HOLLOW ROAD

BEDFORD ROAD

N

0.1 mile

SWAN LAKE AREA

A short access trail from the visitor center leads to Brother's Path, which circles Swan Lake and serves as the hub for trails in the Swan Lake Area, a popular spot any time of the year. Expect to see hikers, joggers, dog walkers, and birders there. In winter, gentle grades and wide roads attract cross-country skiers.

The 0.3 mile Old Railroad Bed is what remains of the section of the Putnam Division Line which passed through the estate until 1931, when John D. Rockefeller, Jr. financed the moving of a section of the line away from his estate. When Route 117 was built between 1969 and 1971, the railbed was cut off.

From David's Loop, an equestrian trail provides a 0.9-mile access route for two local stables on the north side of Route 117. At 0.2 mile along the trail, a loop goes off to the left. Rows of linden trees planted in a level area grace what might have been a landscaped overlook, but now they obstruct the view.

Ash Tree Loop   *Length: 0.8 mile*

From the south end of the Farm Meadow Trail, across from where two roads enter the Greenrock property, the Ash Tree Loop begins to the right. As it heads uphill, the size of trees decreases. Many of the ash trees along the trail have succumbed to ash yellows disease. The trail is somewhat level as it circles the top. To the left at 0.5 mile, a shortcut leads 0.1 mile steeply down to the Old Sleepy Hollow Road Trail. The Ash Tree Loop turns right at the junction with the Overlook Trail. A small quarry is to the left at 0.7 mile, just before the junction with the Farm Meadow Trail.

Brook Trail   *Length: 0.8 mile*

Starting on the Old Railroad Bed, the Brook Trail for most of its length meanders along a brook, crossing it frequently. It passes the junction with David's Loop to the left and a breached dam. At 0.2 mile, the Brook Trail curves away from the brook and levels off, only to ascend more steeply. To the right at 0.4 mile, a side trail crosses two bridges and then rejoins the main trail. To the left, an unmarked trail connects with David's Loop. At 0.5 mile, a short, steep uphill path to the right connects to the Ridge Trail. After crossing another bridge, the Brook Trail passes a drained cistern with a large rock inside it that was never removed. To the left, the trail heads upstream along the cascading brook that includes spillways of small dams. At 0.6 mile it turns away from the brook and passes the other end of David's Loop. Heading slightly downhill, the Brook Trail ends at a T junction with the Ridge Trail. To the left is an unmarked carriageway which leads under Route 448 to

---

ASH YELLOWS

In the northeast, ash yellows disease is causing severe growth reduction, decline, and dieback of white ash trees; green ashes appear to be more tolerant. It is unclear how this mycoplasma-like organism (MLO) enters the trees; insect vectors are one possibility. The MLO inhabits the living vascular tissue just inside the tree's bark. The problem has greatly worsened and many standing dead ash trees can be seen on the Ash Tree Loop.

Ducks on Swan Lake.

unmarked farm roads on Greenrock property. Narrow unmarked paths lead up to Route 448 (limited parking).

Brother's Path   *Length: 1.1 miles*

Extremely popular, Brother's Path circles Swan Lake and could be called crowded on midsummer weekends, since there seems to be visitors every 100 feet or so. However, the trail's width offers plenty of space with little noise. From the access trail at the visitor center, head counterclockwise around the lake. At 0.4 mile, the Farm Meadow Trail goes right. Brother's Path crosses two inlet streams as it rounds the end of the lake. It reaches an intersection with two carriageways into Greenrock property. Brother's Path passes two access roads to the Greenrock property to the right at 0.5 mile and enters a rock cut to overlook the lake. Set on top of the retaining wall, large rocks serve as balustrade and guardrail. At 0.7 mile, the trail drifts downhill to lake level with the Ridge Trail to the right.

The Brother's Path reaches a triangle junction at 0.9 mile. The Old Railroad Bed is straight ahead. Brother's Path turns left to cross the outlet from Swan Lake on stepping stones to reach the other side of the triangle. It passes one end of Deer Run to the right and then, to the left, two stone benches, most likely the only benches in the park. Brother's Path passes the other end of Deer Run and then closes the loop at the trail to the visitor center.

David's Loop   *Length: 0.9 mile*

Beginning at a junction with the Brook Trail close to Route 448, David's Loop passes through tall trees. At 0.2 mile, it passes an unmarked trail to the left leading 0.1 mile down to the Brook Trail and then to the first of three trails into private property. To the right at 0.6 mile, an equestrian trail leads 0.4 mile downhill to Old Sleepy Hollow Road. Just past the equestrian trail, David's Loop heads downhill. The wet areas have a thick, lush understory, mostly invasive plants. Sometimes there doesn't seem to be a transition between areas with dense and sparse understory. At 0.8 mile, the Brook Trail is visible across the brook. David's Loop closes the loop at the Brook Trail.

Deer Run   *Length: 0.4 mile*

Beginning on Brother's Path and heading clockwise 130 feet past the access trail to the visitor' center, Deer Run immediately heads uphill. At 0.1 mile, an access trail goes steeply down to the equestrian parking lot to the left. The trail gently wiggles its way downhill and ends at Brother's Path. It is 0.1 mile back to the access trail to the visitor' center.

Farm Meadow Trail   *Length: 0.4 mile*

Turn right from a Y junction with the Brother's Path at the southwest end of Swan Lake where the Farm Meadow Trail heads slightly downhill. It passes one end of the Ash Tree Loop at 0.2 mile. Dense understory and wetlands are to the right. The trail passes a farm road into Greenrock property to the left. At 0.4 mile the Farm Meadow Trail ends. Straight ahead and to the left, the roads lead into Greenrock property. To the right is the beginning of the Ash Tree Loop.

Nature's Way   *Length: 0.4 mile*

Beginning on the north side of the parking lot, Nature's Way is along a narrow path. It heads southwest, passing a maintenance area almost immediately. At a quarter-mile, the Glacial Erratic Trail leaves to the right and ends in 300 feet at a glacial erratic more than 20 feet high. Nature's Way ends at Old Sleepy Hollow Road Trail.

Old Sleepy Hollow Road Trail   *Length: 0.6 mile*

Beginning from the far end of parking lot, Old Sleepy Hollow Road Trail goes through a gate. Heading gradually downhill, at 0.3 mile it passes a 0.1-mile unnamed trail to the Ash Tree Loop to the left and a little further, passes Nature's Way to the right. Old Sleepy Hollow Road Trail crosses Sleepy Hollow Road (limited parking) and continues as an access road to the Eagle Hill Area.

Overlook Trail
Length: 0.7 mile

At the end of the access trail to the visitor' center, just before reaching the Brother's Path is the Overlook Trail. It immediately heads uphill on one of the steeper grades in the park. It circles a grassy area to the left. The grade lessens, but the trail continues uphill. At 0.3 mile, it passes a sugar maple whose trunk is covered with poison ivy. It leaves the meadow and passes a low flat building which is a water tank. Heading downhill through the woods, the Overlook Trail ends at 0.7 mile at the Ash Tree Loop.

Peaceful Path
Length: 0.4 mile

With all the road noise from adjacent Route 117, it is ironic this trail was named Peaceful Path. From the north end of the Old Railroad Bed, the trail heads downhill. It crosses a bridge at 0.1 mile and turns; here the road noise is barely heard. The trail leaves the woods to join Brother's Path near the dam of Swan Lake.

Ridge Trail
Length: 0.9 mile

Beginning at the junction of the Brook Trail and a farm road that leads under Route 448, the Ridge Trail is one of the few trails in the park with a view. It goes along fields and passes two unmarked roads into Greenrock property. It enters the woods at 0.2 mile and heads gently downhill. At 0.4 mile, an unmarked path leads steeply downhill to the Brook Trail, which is visible through the trees. To the left is a small retaining wall, showing the cut and fill necessary to build the carriageways in the park. The Ridge Trail passes two entrances to Greenrock maintenance areas at 0.5 and 0.6 mile. Making a sweeping curve to the right, it heads downhill to end on Brother's Path at Swan Lake.

EAGLE HILL AREA

More trees and fewer meadows are characteristic of the terrain surrounding the trails in the Eagle Hill Area. There are elevation gains and losses, but most often the trails maintain an even grade. There are two access points to this section of the park. One is off Sleepy Hollow Road where a 0.1-mile section of the Old Sleepy Hollow Road Trail provides access to the Pocantico River Trail. The second access point is at the end of Gory Brook Road in Sleepy Hollow. Parking is limited at both places.

The 0.3 mile Eagle Hill Trail connects the 13 Bridges and Gory Brook trails to the Eagle Hill Summit Trail and Pocantico River Trail. The 0.2 mile Spook Rock Trail has two legs that lead from the Witch's Spring Trail; the short one is steep and the other is a gentle climb, but twice as long. Spook Rock is an easily missed boulder on the inside of the turn in the switchback.

13 Bridges Loop
Length: 1.9 miles

Beginning at the intersection of the Eagle Hill and Eagle Hill Summit trails, 13 Bridges Loop heads north crossing Route 117 on a bridge. Along each side of the bridge, there is a separate pedestrian walkway; the vegetation growing there indicates that this walkway portion of the bridge is not used. The open terrain has little or no understory and by 0.3 mile, the noise from Route 117 is no longer

13 Bridges Loop.

audible. The trail passes the north terminus of the Pocantico River Trail at 0.6 mile and then heads slightly uphill. After passing a rock outcropping to the left, it stays at-grade on a retaining wall. At 0.8 mile, Sleepy Hollow Road is both seen and heard. An unmarked trail to the right leads 400 feet out to gate P6 near the intersection of Sleepy Hollow Road and Sleepy Hollow Road Extension (limited parking). At 0.9 mile, the trail turns left with wetlands visible below to the right. An unmarked trail at 1.0 mile goes out 200 feet to the Sleepy Hollow Road Extension (parking for one car).

As the 13 Bridges Loop enters a hemlock grove, Gory Brook below is audible. The trail goes down a switchback and begins to live up to its name as it crosses a bridge, the first of thirteen, over a feeder stream into Gory Brook. The brook and the trail are intertwined in a valley with trees towering overhead. At 1.2 miles, the trail passes an unmarked carriageway leading to a gate into private property. It is not until 1.4 miles that the trail crosses the second bridge. With an unobstructed view of the trail ahead, it is easy to spot the upcoming bridges. At about 1.6 miles, bridge nine, ten, and eleven cross Gory Brook within 100 yards of each other. In this area Route 117 can again be heard. An unmarked carriageway leads to the Old Croton Aqueduct at 1.7 miles and the 13 Bridges Loop crosses the last bridge. The trail then passes under Route 117 to end at the intersection of Eagle Hill and Gory Brook Road trails at 1.9 miles.

Big Tree Trail   *Length: 0.9 mile*
Beginning at the intersection of Peggy's Way and the access trail from the Old Croton Aqueduct, the Big Tree Trail heads downhill to meet the Witch's Spring Trail at 0.1 mile. It bears left to go uphill along a retaining wall with large rocks looking like a jagged balustrade. It is easy to see how the trail got its name: there are many towering trees lining the trail. The trail gently curves, straightens, and continues uphill. At 0.5 mile, it reaches the beginning of a loop with the Big Tree Trail going in both directions. To the right, the trail ascends to meet the

Spook Rock Trail at 0.6 mile and continues uphill to the crest of the ridge. It heads downhill to meet a side trail to the right which connects to the Old Croton Aqueduct. Continuing downhill, the Big Tree Trail passes the north terminus of Peggy's Way at 0.8 mile. After passing a rock outcropping to the left, the Big Tree Trail closes the loop at 0.9 mile.

Eagle Hill Summit Trail   *Length: 0.6 mile*

From the junction of Eagle Hill Trail and 13 Bridges Loop, the Eagle Hill Summit Trail heads uphill. At 0.2 mile, it reaches a junction with the loop that circles the top of the hill. The left branch reaches the viewless top at 0.3 mile. The trail curves right and descends to close the loop at 0.6 mile.

Gory Brook Road Trail   *Length: 0.7 mile*

Portions of Gory Brook Road were abandoned in 1979 and the Gory Brook Road Trail utilized some of them. At the end of Gory Brook Road in Sleepy Hollow, an abandoned 0.4 mile portion parallels the Old Croton Aqueduct and is outside of the park. It has several crossovers to the Aqueduct and three junctions with farm roads into Greenrock property.

Inside the park, the Gory Brook Road Trail begins at a Y junction where the gravel carriageway goes left and the trail is a small path continuing straight. It joins the Pocantico River Trail at 0.2 mile and turns right. The co-aligned trails follow the Pocantico River upstream and turn left at the next junction to cross it. At the intersection across the river, the Pocantico River Trail turns right. The Gory Brook Road Trail leaves the abandoned road and goes straight. It enters woods where there is a meadow to the left and cliffs to the right. Between the junction of the Witch's Spring Trail at 0.6 mile and the Eagle Hill Trail, the abandoned roadbed is visible to the left. Gory Brook Road Trail ends at the junction of 13 Bridges Loop and the Eagle Hill Trail.

Peggy's Way   *Length: 0.5 mile*

At the south end of Peggy's Way, a large rock carved with the words Peggy's Way 1994 greets hikers. Named for Peggy Rockefeller, wife of David Rockefeller, the trail is about three feet narrower than, and not as straight as other trails in the park. It traverses a long ridge (no views). Peggy's Way descends to end at the Big Tree Trail.

Pocantico River Trail   *Length: 1.9 miles*

As the Pocantico River meanders through the park, the Pocantico River Trail tags along. The trail begins at the junction of the Big Tree and Witch's Spring trails and crosses the Pocantico River on a stone bridge with triple arches. It turns left at a T junction with an unmarked trail heading to the abandoned Gory Brook Road and immediately passes a fire hydrant. Continuing upstream, the trail turns right at a T junction at 0.4 mile. The Witch's Spring Trail is to the left over a stone bridge. The Pocantico River Trail curves away from the river, but returns to it upon reaching abandoned Gory Brook Road at 0.5 mile.

Co-aligned with Gory Brook Road Trail, the Pocantico River Trail heads upstream sometimes close to the river. It turns left to cross the Pocantico River and then

Triple Arch Bridge.

turns right. To the left, an unnamed road enters a meadow where a road leads into Greenrock property; Gory Brook Road Trail is to the left. The Pocantico River Trail circles the base of Eagle Hill and passes a meadow to the left. At 0.7 mile, it reaches an intersection with a fire hydrant to the left and a barrel arch stone bridge to the right. Unnamed roads lead into Greenrock property. The trail turns left with the river below to the right.

The Pocantico River Trail heads uphill at 1.0 mile, turns away from the river, and returns 0.1 mile later above a series of cascades. At 1.2 miles, it passes Eagle Hill Trail to the left and then Old Sleepy Hollow Road Trail to the right. After going under Route 117 at 1.4 miles, the trail passes an unmarked access trail to the right. It is 400 feet to gate P6 near the junction of Sleepy Hollow Road Extension and Sleepy Hollow Road (limited parking). Continuing at grade, the Pocantico River Trail ends at the 13 Bridges Loop.

Witch's Spring Trail   *Length: 0.5 mile*
From Gory Brook Road Trail, Witch's Spring Trail heads downhill and crosses abandoned Gory Brook Road. It passes one end of Spook Rock Trail at 0.2 mile and then the other. After following Gory Brook for a short distance, it reaches and heads along the Pocantico River. At 0.4 mile, the trail splits. The segment to the right soon reaches the end of the Pocantico River Trail while the segment to the left crosses a bridge and also ends at the Pocantico River Trail.

EAST OF ROUTE 448

If you want to be alone and far from crowds, walk the roads in the area east of Route 448. Aside from trail runners, expect to see far fewer people than in any of the other sections of the park. The open farm fields with vistas beg to be explored. Along the ridge, crags provide habitat for raptors who hunt along the Saw Mill River Parkway and the power line. The viewpoint atop of Buttermilk Hill has been used since Revolutionary War times.

Access to this area is from Route 448 (0.7 mile north of Stone Barns), across from the entrance to Stone Barns (no parking), about 0.4 mile north on Route 448 or from a large parking lot adjacent to the parking lot for the North County Trailway on Route 117. A footpath leads from the southwest corner of the woods.

Unlike trails in the Eagle Hill or Swan Lake areas, these 16.5 miles of trail are unnamed and without signs. The North County Trailway, Route 9A/100, and the

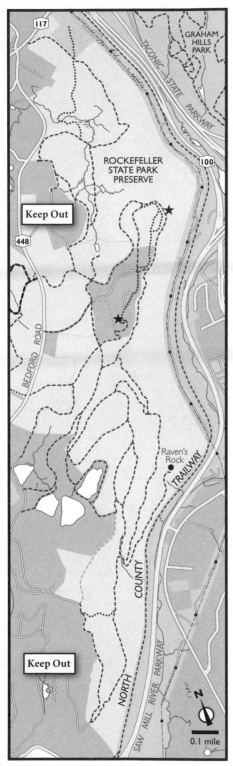

Saw Mill River Parkway are below the ridge and form a barrier to the east.

CONNECTING TRAILS & NEARBY PARKS: Old Croton Aqueduct, North County Trailway, Douglas Park, Pocantico Lake Park, Rockwood Hall, Sleepy Hollow Cemetery

DRIVING: There are numerous access points. To reach parking at the visitor center from Route 9, north of Phelps Memorial Hospital in Sleepy Hollow, take Route 117 east. The park entrance is to the right on the road's south side [41.113396N 73.834835W]. Alternately, take Route 9A to Route 117 and head west for 1.6 miles to the park entrance to the left [41.113396N 73.834835W].

To reach parking along Route 448, take Route 9A to Route 117 and head west. Turn left at the traffic light to follow Route 448 for 1.0 mile (limited parking). Continue 0.7 more miles to reach the Stone Barns Center. No parking is permitted near the entrance road to Stone Barns Center. There is a seasonal parking fee at Stone Barns [41.103474N 73.829615W].

For parking on Sleepy Hollow Road, take Route 9A to Route 117 and head west. Turn left at the traffic light to follow Route 448 to the first right turn, Sleepy Hollow Road, which crosses under Route 117. Cross under Route 117 a second time for parking just beyond the overpass [41.106043N 73.844412W].

For parking at Gory Brook Road in Sleepy Hollow, follow Route 9 north to a complex intersection with Route 448. Do not turn onto Route 448; instead, continue straight on New Broadway. At 0.2 mile, turn right onto Gory Brook Road, which dead ends at parking near the Old Croton Aqueduct [41.092378N 73.857374W].

To reach parking for the trails east of Route 448, take Route 9A to Route 117 and head west. Turn left into the second parking lot which is the larger of the two [41.122203N 73.811369W].

PUBLIC TRANSPORTATION: Although there is no direct public transportation available, it is possible to walk from the Metro-North Hudson Line Tarrytown Station to the preserve. Walk north on Depot Place to Main Street, turn right and head uphill to Route 9 (Broadway). Turn left, walk north toward Route 448, and follow the Gory Brook Road driving directions given above.

Beeline Bus #13 stops near Rockwood Hall. A walk through Rockwood Hall to the Old Croton Aqueduct provides access to the Eagle Hill area in the park.

For contact information, see Appendix, Rockefeller State Park Preserve.

Pocantico Lake Park

Sleepy Hollow • 1.0 mile, 164 acres

An undeveloped county park, Pocantico Lake Park has year-round views out over a former reservoir. Much of the access road follows the Pocantico River. Roads closed to traffic lead north and south from parking at barriers on Pocantico Lake Road. To the southwest, the road ends in 0.3 mile at a dilapidated building, once part of county waterworks. Just before the building, a trail leads out 370 feet to the dam with an open view of the entire lake. A footpath leads around the side of the building. It reaches an access road from Sleepy Hollow Road to the buildings at the base of the dam. It is not safe to enter these buildings, which are becoming more and more decrepit. Going northwest, the road is a bit farther from the lake. It turns to cross a causeway and ends at a barrier at Old Sleepy Hollow Road.

NEARBY PARK: Rockefeller State Park Preserve

DRIVING: From Route 9A, take Route 117 and turn west toward Tarrytown. Turn left at the traffic light at Route 448 (Bedford Road). Take the first right onto Sleepy Hollow Road. Go 0.9 mile to Pocantico Lake Road and turn right. The road dead ends at a barrier where there is parking [41.117051N 73.832445W].

PUBLIC TRANSPORTATION: None available

For contact information, see Appendix, Westchester County Parks.

Saxon Woods Park

Scarsdale • 12.9 miles, 711 acres

If you live in southern Westchester County and want a half-day hike with as little driving as possible, look no further than Saxon Woods Park. Its topography is best described as typical Westchester woodland with tall trees, wetlands, rock outcroppings, and little understory. For the most part, the trails have gentle grades with only small elevation changes and are along woods roads.

The trails in Saxon Woods were designed to be connected and were developed

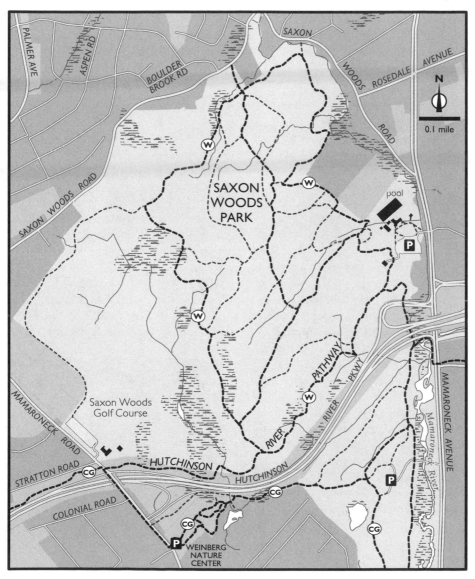

at about 1929 when the Hutchinson River Parkway was built. The parkway cuts the park into two sections which are linked by the Hutchinson River Pathway near Mamaroneck Avenue and the Colonial Greenway along Mamaroneck Road.

Traffic noise is audible in most of the southern section, but not in many parts of the northern section. The latter has a swimming pool and ball field off Mamaroneck Avenue and a golf course off Mamaroneck Road. The southern section has a picnic area. Even with signs posted "No Bikes," mountain bikers use the park, especially the southern part. They have not damaged the woods roads, but in the southern section have created bike trails which connect Loop #1.

The area was known as Saxton Forest in Colonial times, named for William Saxton, owner of a saw mill on the West Branch of the Mamaroneck River. Eventually, local usage changed the name to Saxon, which was the name adopted for the park. Westchester County purchased what is now Saxon Woods Park in 1925. It was first managed as woodlands, but later, in 1931, the county opened an 18-hole golf course on the site.

NORTHERN SECTION

Except for the white trail, the trails in the northern section are not blazed. Two trails have signs, but only in one direction. There are 2.2 miles of unmarked trails and woods roads in the woods. An unmarked 0.8-mile trail skirts the golf course on the northwest side of the park and there is 0.8 mile of narrow bike trails (not on the map). After a snow fall, this section is good for cross-country skiing.

White Trail   *Length: 3.0 miles Blaze: white*
On woods roads for its entire length, the white trail circles the wooded area of the park. There are multiple access points to the trail and the easiest place to park is the swimming pool parking lot. Most trails and woods roads that the white trail passes are to the left and cross the interior of the park. To reach the white trail from the swimming pool parking lot, go to the driveway on the side opposite the entrance. Take the white trail as it crosses the driveway and go counterclockwise. There are short steep ascents and descents as the trail heads north. It enters the woods and heads uphill through a small ravine. Road noise from the Hutch decreases as the trail passes unmarked woods roads which loop back. At a T junction at 0.2 mile, the white trail turns right to cross a stone bridge. To the left is a 0.6-mile woods road which, when walked from the other direction, is marked at intersections with signs To Mamaroneck Avenue. The trail continues on a stone retaining wall. It crosses a stream at 0.3 mile at a T junction and turns onto a road built by the Civilian Conservation Corps. To the left, a

Large fungus.

woods road loops back to join the trails mentioned above. The white trail narrows down at 0.5 mile and descends along an eroded treadway.

The trail turns right at the bottom of the descent and parallels a stone wall. Houses are visible through the trees. At 0.7 mile there is a noticeable change in the understory. Invasive species crowd the trail in a section that at one time was cobbled. Several bike paths go off to the left. The trail reaches a Y junction and turns left. To the right an unmarked trail leads 175 feet to Saxon Woods Road. After passing the other end of the triangle intersection at 1.0 mile, the white trail heads gradually uphill at a steady grade. It crosses the Saxon Woods Trail at 1.1 miles. To the right is an entrance from Saxon Woods Road (no parking).

The trail passes two unmarked trails to the left: the first leading back to the Saxon Woods Trail and the other to a trail winding through the woods. The trail is at-grade as it passes through a seasonal wetland and goes uphill. At 1.3 miles, it climbs more steeply, then levels off. It turns left at 1.5 miles, where a trail to the right continues west and south along the edge of the golf course, to reach the clubhouse in 0.8 mile. After passing restrooms, the trail briefly skirts the golf course only to leave it at 1.6 miles. The trail goes uphill and passes an unmarked trail to the left at 1.7 miles and two others in quick succession at 2.0 miles. The whine of high-speed traffic is audible and gradually becomes more pronounced. At 2.2 miles, the golf course is once again visible through trees to the right. After passing the Mamaroneck Avenue Trail to the left, the white trail reaches a T junction with the Hutchinson River Pathway at 2.3 miles and turns left to join it. As it heads downhill, the white trail is on an eroded woods road, often 12 to 18 inches lower than the surrounding woodland. At 2.7 miles, there are trestles and an unmarked trail goes straight while the trail heads uphill on a switchback. At 2.9 miles, the white trail goes straight when the Hutchinson River Pathway turns right toward the parkway. Heading downhill on a gravel path to the parking lot, the white trail closes the loop at the driveway of a park residence.

Hutchinson River Pathway   *Length: 1.2 miles*
Use the Hutchinson River Pathway to connect the two sections of Saxon Woods Park. It is 0.2 mile from a trail leading into Saxon Woods Park South to where the pathway joins the white trail. The pathway is co-aligned with the white trail for 0.6 mile and then parallels the Hutch before leaving the park at Mamaroneck Road. For a full description, see Hutchinson River Pathway in Linear Corridors.

Mamaroneck Avenue Trail   *Length: 0.6 mile*
Signs along unmarked Mamaroneck Avenue Trail point to Mamaroneck Avenue. This alternative to the white trail provides a shorter route with less road noise. At the junction with the white trail, the Mamaroneck Avenue Trail heads northeast, passing an unmarked 0.3 mile bike trail, which leads to the white trail. It passes one end of the Saxon Woods Trail at 0.3 mile. At a Y junction at 0.5 mile, the trail bears left and immediately turns right where an unmarked trail merges from the right. Just before a bridge, it ends on the white trail.

Saxon Woods Trail   *Length: 0.7 mile*
Consider the Saxon Woods Trail to be a belt across the middle of the north section

with many side trails connecting to the white trail. Beginning at an entrance off Saxon Woods Road, the trail crosses the white trail and almost immediately passes

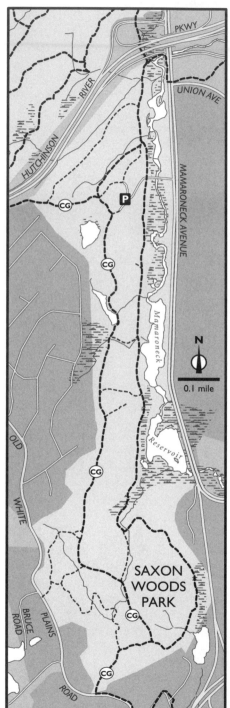

a trail going to the left. Heading straight ahead, the Saxon Woods Trail crosses this trail two more times. At 0.6 mile, the Saxon Woods Trail crosses yet another unmarked trail which connects to the white trail. The Saxon Woods Trail ends at the Mamaroneck Avenue Trail.

SOUTHERN SECTION

Massive rock outcroppings and towering trees line woods roads and three ponds, roads, and the western branch of the Mamaroneck River provide natural barriers. In summer months, picnickers flock to this section of Saxon Woods Park. Only the Colonial Greenway is blazed. In spite of signs saying no mountain bikes, they are common in this section where the terrain is more challenging. There is a mile of short connecting trails. The many bike tracks connecting the long sides of Loop #1 are not included in the mileage for the connecting trails.

Loop #1   *Length: 3.0 miles*
The main trail in the southern section is Loop #1 which has cross and side trails. Go clockwise from the entrance road. On a wide gravel road, Loop #1 passes large rocks and a rock outcropping. An unmarked trail enters from the right. At 0.4 mile, the trail reaches a Y junction with an unmarked woods road leading uphill past a utilities building to the other side of Loop #1. The trail goes left on a stone bridge over a stream. The gravel ends and the western branch of the Mamaroneck River is visible through trees. Following the river, the trail passes wetlands to the left at 0.8 mile and then goes through a massive split rock. Road noise from from Mamaroneck Avenue has diminished. At a trail junction at 0.9 mile, go left. Straight ahead, the trail

Passing through.

continues for 0.1 mile to connect with Loop #1 on the other side of the circuit.

The trail heads uphill, gradually turns and passes backyards. The path narrows. Descending, it is in woodland with dense understory. It passes a pond to the left at 1.3 miles. An impressive rock outcropping to the left has scratches where mountain bikes have come down its face. Just past the rock face, the Colonial Greenway joins Loop #1 for the next 1.2 miles. When Colonial Greenway leaves to the left, Loop #1 continues slightly right on a narrow path, while a road in the picnic area turns right. After crossing a stone bridge at 1.6 miles, Loop #1 passes, to the right, a woods road, the shortcut mentioned above. Loop #1 passes an unmarked trail and a stone building, once restrooms. The side trail leads 0.2 mile out to Old White Plains Road with parking.

At 2.0 mile, the treadway is at grade on a slightly raised bed. Houses are visible to the left and the whine of vehicles on I-95 is audible. At 2.2 miles, the trail goes down slab rock. It reaches an unmarked woods road to the right heading downhill to the stream mentioned earlier. Heading uphill, Loop #1 follows the edge of a pond, then turns away at 2.4 miles. It again goes along slab rock. It reaches the picnic area at 2.7 miles and turns away from it. At a Y junction, where the Colonial Greenway leaves to the left, the Loop #1 continues slightly right, while a road in the picnic area turns right. At a triangle intersection at 2.9 miles, Loop #1 turns right again. To the left, it is 0.2 mile to the Hutchinson River Pathway. Loop #1 closes the loop at the entrance road.

Colonial Greenway   *Length: 2.1 miles*
Signs at the trailheads for the Colonial Greenway have maps noting "You are here." From Old White Plains Road between #1015 and #1011, the Colonial Greenway heads into the woods on a footpath sometimes lined with logs. At 0.2 mile it turns left to join Loop #1. The two trails are co-aligned for 1.2 miles and split, just past the restrooms, with the Colonial Greenway turning left at a Y junction.

At the triangle intersection at 1.6 miles, a trail to the right goes 0.4 mile to the Hutchinson River Pathway. On a gravel path paralleling the Hutch, the Colonial Greenway Trail fords a stream and crosses a bridge at 1.8 miles. It turns left onto a narrow path leading to Weinberg Nature Center, reaches the parking lot and turns right. It crosses an equestrian trail and then the northbound ramps for the Hutchinson River Parkway. After crossing over the Hutch, it turns left to join the Hutchinson River Pathway at 2.3 miles, just beyond the parkway's southbound entrance ramp. For the next section, see Hutchinson River Pathway (Mamaroneck Road) in Linear Corridors.

DRIVING: All entrances to Saxon Woods Park are accessible from the Hutchinson River Parkway. For Saxon Woods (pool area), if north bound, take Exit 23S (Mamaroneck Avenue) and turn left. The pool area is the first left after the southbound entrance ramp [40.985407N 73.745554W]. South bound, take Exit 23N and turn right and the pool area is the first left.

Access to the northern section of Saxon Woods Park for cross-country skiing is through Saxon Woods Golf Course. Take Exit 22 (Mamaroneck Road) and turn right. The golf course is to the right, at the first right turn after the southbound exit ramp [40.978041N 73.759642W].

For the southern section of Saxon Wood Park (picnic area), if northbound, take Exit 23S and turn right at the end of the exit ramp. If southbound, take Exit 23N and turn left. The entrance road is the first right [40.977722N 73.745493W].

PUBLIC TRANSPORTATION: Beeline Bus #60 along Mamaroneck Avenue

For contact information, see Appendix, Westchester County Parks—Saxon Woods Park.

Weinberg Nature Center

Scarsdale • 0.6 mile, 11 acres

The Village of Scarsdale's nature center is a memorial to Wilhem Weinberg (1886-1957), financier, art collector, and philanthropist. Located on 11 acres at the site of his estate, the nature center opened in 1958. The 0.6-mile of unmarked trails wander through young forest, meadow, wetlands, former gardens, and along streams. These habitats provide the basis for nature programs. One trail is part of the Colonial Greenway.

DRIVING: From the Hutchinson River Parkway, take Exit 22 (Mamaroneck Road) and turn left. Weinberg Nature Center is to the left, just east of northbound entrance and exit ramps of the parkway [40.974885N 73.755980W].

PUBLIC TRANSPORTATION: Beeline Bus #60 along Mamaroneck Avenue

For contact information, see Appendix, Weinberg Nature Center.

Teatown Lake Reservation

Teatown • 14.4 miles, 1,000 acres

There is something interesting year-round at Teatown Lake Reservation: buckets hanging on sugar maple trees heralding the start of spring; wildflowers bursting in bloom from April through September; shaded woods shielding walkers from summer's heat and lakes reflecting back a blaze of autumnal color. In the grip of winter, with Teatown Lake frozen and the grounds blanketed in snow, cross-country skiers and snowshoers see the reservation from a totally different perspective.

Teatown's grounds include lakes, a scenic ravine, streams, hardwood swamps, mixed forests, vernal pools, meadows, and hemlock and laurel groves. Its trails spread in every direction from Teatown's Nature Center and make it possible to have long or short hikes. The shortcut trails can shorten a hike as well as connect trails to create longer hikes.

A GIFT OF OPEN SPACE

Teatown Lake Reservation has its genesis in 1963 with the donation of property that had been acquired by Gerard Swope, Sr, a leading industrialist and president of General Electric. In creating his country estate, he assembled pieces of property that were once part of the old Van Cortlandt Manor. He took over a residence called The Croft and dammed Bailey Brook to create Teatown Lake. After his death in 1957, his heirs donated 194 acres of this land to create Teatown Lake Reservation under the stewardship of the Brooklyn Botanic Gardens. The reservation was incorporated in 1971 and became an independent nonprofit in 1987, with the mission of providing environmental and educational opportunities for both children and adults.

Over the years, additional gifts, including the 160-acre Cliffdale Farm and purchases have enlarged the reservation to its present size. These purchases included The Croft and 59 acres from the estate of Phil E. Gilbert, Jr.

NATURE CENTER

The hub of Teatown Lake Reservation is the Nature Center with a a sugar house and a small collection of animals. Hawks, eagles, owls, and turkey vultures, none of which could survive in the wild on their own, are housed outdoors. Reptiles and amphibians are on display inside the Nature Center.

The Cliffdale-Teatown Trail connects the trails at Cliffdale Farm to the trails around Teatown Lake. The Teatown Kitchawan Trail (purple) connects Teatown Lake Reservation to Hand Park and Kitchawan Preserve. See Teatown-Kitchawan Trail in Linear Corridors for a full description of the trail. In Teatown, its first mile is co-aligned with the Lakeside Trail and the Briarcliff Peekskill Trailway.

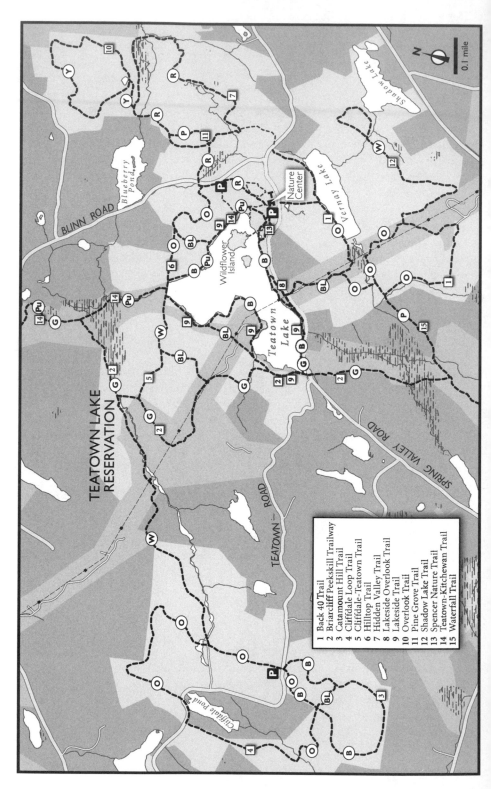

TEATOWN LAKE RESERVATION

Teatown Lake.

Lakeside Trail

Length: 1.6 miles Blaze: blue

Why is the Lakeside Trail is the most popular trail at Teatown? It goes around Teatown Lake, offering hikers a pleasant walk in all seasons and leading to an array of other trails. Directions are given counterclockwise, but for variety, you can walk the trail in the opposite direction. Reach the Lakeside Trail either from the front of or through a gate behind the Nature Center. Head toward a kiosk and then go downhill. At the bottom of the hill is a gate into Wildflower Woods, Erica's Way is inside the fencing and leads to a bird blind.

Continue straight along the shore of the lake, passing, in quick succession, the trail to the Lakeside parking lot, a boathouse, and the Hilltop Shortcut Trail (black). The latter goes 0.1 mile up steps to the Hilltop Trail (orange). The Lakeside Trail reaches a Y junction and heads left to follow the lakeshore. The unmarked trail to the right is a wet weather route and, at 0.3 mile, joins from the right. At a T junction, where the Lakeside Trail turns left, the Hilltop Trail is to the right. Descending to below the dam, the TK trail leaves to the right and the Lakeside Trail continues straight. Heading uphill, the Lakeside Trail reaches the end of the dam and turns left. Straight ahead, the Cliffdale-Teatown Trail (white) goes 1.1 miles to Cliffdale Farm. The Lakeside Trail crosses a wet area on two sections of puncheon. It turns left at 0.5 mile, where the Lakeside Shortcut Trail (black) heads straight, going 0.2 mile across a peninsula.

If you avoid the shortcut, the Lakeside Trail crosses a long section of puncheon and heads out onto a peninsula with open views across Teatown Lake. It passes under power lines at 0.7 mile, goes through a stand of fir trees, then moves away from the edge of the lake. At 0.9 mile, the other end of the Lakeside Shortcut Trail is to the right. After crossing a bridge and passing through a stone wall, the Lakeside Trail reaches a junction with the Briarcliff Peekskill Trailway (green), which come in from the right. Together, they head downhill.

At 1.1 miles, the Briarcliff Peekskill Trail goes straight to cross Spring Valley Road, while the Lakeside Trail turns left onto a 0.1-mile floating boardwalk on

Teatown Lake. At the end of the boardwalk, the trail crosses a bridge and then a short access road. It heads uphill over and close to large rocks. At 1.4 miles, the 0.2-mile Lakeside Overlook Trail (pink) leaves to the right. It provides views over the lake and connects with a 0.2-mile black-blazed trail which leads to the Back 40 Trail (orange). The Lakeside Trail descends to lake level, passes the other end of the Lakeside Overlook Trail and enters Wildflower Woods. At 1.5 miles, the gated entrance to Wildflower Island is to the left. The Lakeside Trail goes onto a boardwalk, leaves Wildflower Woods, and closes the loop at the access trail which leads back to the Nature Center.

Back 40 Trail *Length: 1.1 miles Blaze: orange*
Beginning at the Croft Trail (yellow) at Vernay Lake, the Back 40 Trail is the access trail to Shadow Lake and Waterfall trails. Paralleling the shore of Vernay Lake, the Back 40 reaches a dam at 0.1 mile. It heads steeply uphill on a road built to repair the dam and goes under high tension power lines. At a trail junction, a black-blazed side trail to the right goes 0.2 mile to the Lakeside Overlook Trail (pink).

The Back 40 Trail turns left to head downhill into the woods. After passing through a stone wall, the Back 40 Trail reaches a boardwalk at 0.4 mile. At the end of the boardwalk at a T junction, turn right. At the next junction, turn left. To the right, the Waterfall Trail (pink) connects in 0.3 mile to the Briarcliff Peekskill Trailway. The Back 40 Trail ascends with a short steep section and then more gradually, going on and off woods roads. It passes a stream in a gully to the right and then wiggles steadily uphill. Before reaching the top, the trail turns right just as it passes two large concrete and rock pillars to the left.

At a T junction with the Con Edison access road at 0.7 mile, the trail turns left and passes a third stone pillar. After reaching the top of the hill, the Back 40 Trail briefly descends and then goes back up to cross under the power lines with a view to the north. It reenters the woods and turns left to descend steeply, passing the end of the Shadow Lake Trail to the right at 0.8 miles. Turning right, the Back 40 Trail leaves the wide treadway and continues to descend. It crosses under the power lines several times, heads into the woods, and closes the loop at 1.1 miles. Turn right to return retrace your steps to Vernay Lake and the Croft Trail.

Not shaped by nature.

Briarcliff Peekskill Trailway   *Length 1.4 miles Blaze: green*

A lakeside view, board walks across wetlands, and rock outcroppings are along the Briarcliff Peekskill Trailway. It is co-aligned with the Lakeside Trail (blue) for 0.1 mile as it enters Teatown at the southern end and with the Teatown-Kitchawan Trail (purple) for 0.3 mile when it leaves. For a full description, see Briarcliff Peekskill Trailway in Linear Corridors.

Croft Trail   *Length 0.4 mile Blaze: yellow*

From the gate across the street from the Nature Center, the Croft Trail passes a small triangular pond and goes along a woods road. At the bottom of the steps, it turns left and the Back 40 Trail (orange) begins to the right. The Croft Trail passes a platform next to Vernay Lake and follows along the shore of the lake. It turns left at 0.2 mile and heads uphill. After going through a field, it ends at Spring Valley Road. Across the road a black trail goes uphill to connect to the Hidden Valley Trail (red) in 0.1 mile.

Hidden Valley Trail   *Length 1.5 miles Blaze: red*

Starting from behind the Nature Center, the Hidden Valley Trail passes the sugar house and outdoor exhibits. It heads towards Blinn Road, then parallels it. To the right, the flat fence wire has been fastened to trees for so long that the trees have grown around it. After crossing the Lakeside parking lot, the trail passes the Hilltop Trail (orange) to the left. The Hidden Valley Trail turns right, crosses Blinn Road at 0.2 mile, and enters the woods. It crosses a wetland on a boardwalk with sensitive ferns along its edge and enters a field. At 0.3 mile, the trail reaches a junction which is the start of a loop. Straight ahead, the Pine Grove Trail (pink) connects in 0.1 mile with the Hidden Valley Trail to the left.

Turn right. The trail reenters the woods on a woods road and passes a sugar maple grove. After turning left off the woods road, the trail goes uphill, passing

Harbingers of spring.

through rock outcroppings. After leveling off, the trail passes a vernal pool at 0.7 mile. It goes through a laurel grove and descends into Hidden Valley, first gradually, then more steeply. At the base of the descent, it begins to parallel a stream. The trail reaches a boardwalk and crosses wetlands at 1.0 mile. At the end of the boardwalk, the trail turns left along a woods road. Although sections are built slightly above the wetlands, the trail is often muddy in wet weather. New York, Christmas, and cinnamon ferns line the path to the left, with rocks rising steeply to the right.

At 1.2 miles, the Overlook Trail (yellow) begins to the right. The Hidden Valley Trail soon bears left to cross a stream on a bridge. After ascending quite steeply, the trail passes through a gap in a stone wall. It levels off and passes the Pine Grove Trail to the left. After turning right to cross another stone wall, the Hidden Valley Trail enters a meadow and then closes the loop at 1.5 miles. From here, it is a 0.3 mile walk back to the Nature Center.

Hilltop Trail   *Length: 0.4 mile Blaze: orange*
The Hilltop Trail provides access from the Lakeside parking area to the dam at Teatown Lake. From the Hidden Valley Trail (red) just beyond the Lakeside parking lot, the Hilltop Trail climbs through an open forest of mixed deciduous trees. At 0.2 mile, the trail parallels a stone wall and passes the Hilltop Shortcut (black) which leads 0.1 mile back to the boathouse. After descending, the Hilltop Trail ends at the Lakeside Trail (blue), just before the dam.

Overlook Trail   *Length: 1.0 mile Blaze: yellow*
Like the Hidden Valley Trail, the Overlook Trail is one of the more strenuous trails at Teatown. From the Nature Center, it can be reached via the Hidden Valley Trail (red) at 1.2 miles if going counterclockwise, or at 0.6 mile if going clockwise. Immediately after leaving the Hidden Valley Trail, the Overlook Trail begins a steep ascent up a rock strewn slope. It reaches the start of a loop at the edge of a

pond across from an old house, which dates from Revolutionary War times. Turn right to go counterclockwise around the loop. The trail crosses a short bridge, climbs steeply, and passes to the right a side trail leading to a seasonal view over Hidden Valley. The trail continues to climb steeply with occasional dips.

Ascending on rock steps, the Overlook Trail reaches the viewless high point at 0.4 mile. After descending through evergreens, it goes down steps and then turns left onto a woods road that parallels a stone wall. Gently ascending the shoulder of a knob, the trail reaches an open meadow with blueberry bushes at 0.6 mile. The trail continues to descend and then levels out as it passes behind several homes. It turns left onto a private paved drive at 0.8 mile, then turns right, leaves the road at the end of a stone wall, and winds its way downhill. After passing the pond, mentioned above, it closes the loop at 1.0 mile.

Shadow Lake Trail *Length: 0.9 mile Blaze: white*

To reach the Shadow Lake Trail, it is necessary to walk 0.8 mile before reaching the trail. From the Back 40 Trail (orange), turn left at the end of the boardwalk, and head uphill. After going steeply uphill on switchbacks, the Shadow Lake Trail follows the edge of the power lines, but is in the woods. It goes through a stone wall and crosses a mat of tree roots which indicate just how shallow the soil is. At 0.2 mile, after passing through a stone wall, it turns left and is among tall trees with no understory. It goes through a stone wall at 0.5 mile and crosses a bridge over a creek. When the trail splits, turn right to follow the loop counterclockwise. At 0.7 mile, the Shadow Lake Trail reaches the dam of Shadow Lake with wildlife viewing opportunities. It turns left along a woods road and then shortly leaves the woods road to loop back to the bridge at 0.9 mile.

CLIFFDALE FARM

Marion Rosenwald Ascoli, a former trustee bequeathed Cliffdale Farm and its surrounding property to Teatown in 1990. A portion of the property is one of the sites of Teatown's summer day camp, which focuses on nature and the outdoors.

Cliffdale-Teatown Trail *Length: 1.1 miles Blaze: white*

From the gate at the Cliffdale Farm parking on Teatown Road, follow the Cliffdale Loop Trail (orange) towards the building at the far end of the field. Just past it, a red post marks the beginning of the Cliffdale-Teatown Trail, which goes right, while the Cliffdale Loop Trail continues straight. Almost immediately, the Cliffdale-Teatown Trail leaves the woods road and descends on a path flanked by a stone wall to the right. After crossing a small bridge over a stream, the trail passes through

Along a boardwalk.

extensive wetlands and heads uphill. At 0.5 mile, it passes under a power line and crosses two bridges. At a T junction with an obscure woods road, the trail turns left shortly after reaching another wetland and passes rock cliffs. Numerous bridges cross over streams and wet areas in Griffin Swamp. At 0.8 mile, Briarcliff Peekskill Trailway (green) is straight ahead. The trails turn right and cross a boardwalk. At a Y junction, split: The Cliffdale-Teatown Trail turns left and the Briarcliff Peekskill Trailway goes right.

At 0.9 mile, the Cliffdale-Teatown Trail passes the Briarcliff Peekskill Shortcut Trail (black) and follows a stone wall. Turning left and heading uphill, the trail crosses several stone walls before descending. As the trail reaches the crest of the rise, Teatown Lake is visible to the right. The Cliffdale-Teatown Trail ends at the dam. It is 0.5 mile back to the Nature Center along the Lakeside Trail.

Catamount Hill Trail
Length: 1.0 mile Blaze: blue

From the Cliffdale Farm parking area on Teatown Road, cross the road. Go past a gate and turn right. The Catamount Hill Trail and the Cliffdale Loop Trail (orange) are co-aligned as they cross the field and enter the woods on a woods road. At 0.1 mile, the 0.1-mile Catamount Hill Shortcut (black) is to the left. As the trails enter the next field, they split; the Cliffdale Loop Trail heads diagonally across the field, while the Catamount Hill Trail follows the edge of the field. After diagonally crossing the next field, it enters the woods, goes uphill, and passes a rock outcropping. The trail descends at 0.7 mile to reach the Catamount Hill Shortcut. It enters a field and at 1.0 mile closes the loop at the gate.

Cliffdale Loop Trail
Length: 1.6 miles Blaze: orange

From the Cliffdale Farm parking lot on Teatown Road, the Cliffdale Loop Trail heads towards the building at the far end of the field, passing it to the left to reach a woods road. It goes past a red post at the end of a stone wall, where the Cliffdale-Teatown Trail (white) turns right. The Cliffdale Loop Trail follows a woods road through a mixed forest, reaches a grassy area, and then exits along a barberry-lined path. At 0.3 mile, the trail reaches another grassy area, continues across it, and then turns left to follow a stone wall lined with maple trees. It goes through a stone wall into another field at 0.4 mile and follows the right edge.

Near the far end of the field, the Cliffdale Loop Trail passes through another stone wall and reenters the woods. It reaches a T junction with a woods road and turns left just beyond a vernal pool. Going downhill, the trail reaches a gate at Teatown Road at 0.7 mile. The trail turns right to follow the road and then turns left at a gate onto a woods road. Turning left again onto another woods road, it climbs and passes a low rock outcropping. The treadway narrows and continues uphill with a view of a pond to the left. After reaching the top, the trail descends steeply with wide steps and a handrail to aid the descent.

At 1.2 miles, the Cliffdale Loop crosses a bridge over a wetland and joins a woods road. It crosses a stream on two bridges. At an intersection of two woods roads, it turns left and goes steeply uphill. Leveling off at 1.4 miles, the trail reaches an open field. Going diagonally across, it joins the Catamount Hill Trail (blue) at the far end of the field. The two trails reenter the woods along a woods road. As the trails curve to the right, Teatown Road is visible The trails enter a field, curve to the left, and end at Teatown Road.

CONNECTING TRAILS & NEARBY PARK: Briarcliff Peekskill Trailway, John E. Hand Park, Teatown-Kitchawan Trail.

DRIVING: From the Taconic State Parkway, take the Route 134 Exit and turn west towards Ossining. Just past the southbound entrance ramp, turn right onto Grant Street, immediately passing a small house to the left. (Do NOT make the hard right turn onto Illington Road.) At a stop sign, turn right onto Spring Valley Road. Continue 0.6 mile to a large wide intersection and continue on Spring Valley Road. The Nature Center parking is 0.1 mile past the intersection and just after the buildings [41.211228N 73.827243W]. The Lakeside parking lot is on Blinn Road; take the right-hand turn at the previously mentioned large intersection [41.213528N 73.826613W].

To reach Cliffdale Farm from the Nature Center parking lot, return to Blinn Road and turn left passing Lakeside parking. Continue 1.4 miles to Quaker Ridge Road. Turn left and, in 1.1 miles, turn left again onto Teatown Road. Cliffdale Farm parking is 0.9 mile to the left [41.206270N 73.850623W].

PUBLIC TRANSPORTATION: None available

For contact information, see Appendix, Teatown Lake Reservation.

Ward Pound Ridge Reservation

Cross River • 41.2 miles, 4,315 acres

D warfing by far all the other parks in Westchester County, one visit to Ward
Pound Ridge Reservation does not even begin to reveal all that the reservation
has to offer. Visitors can picnic, camp, explore a stream, visit the Trailside Nature
Museum and wildflower garden, and depending on the season, walk, hike,
snowshoe, or cross-country ski along the 41.2 miles of trails and woods roads. The
Trailside Nature Museum features exhibits of birds, reptiles, mammals, insects,
minerals, and Native American artifacts, as well as weekly nature programs
throughout the year. Adjacent to the Trailside Nature Museum is the half-acre
Luquer-Marble Memorial Garden, home to over 100 species of wildflowers. Art
in the Park in the administration building is a changing exhibition of work by
Westchester artists.

The reservation is more than five times the size of Manhattan's Central Park and
serves as the core of a 22,000-acre biodiversity area that extends beyond all sides
of the reservation. In 2001, it was designated a biodiversity reserve which assures
that environmental considerations within the reservation will take precedence
over recreational ones.

TRAILS

The named blazed trails are loops, making it easy for hikers to follow one color
blaze for an entire hike. Aside from the Deer Hollow and Fox Hill trails, other trails
do not cross Reservation Road, which bisects the park. The trail descriptions are
divided to reflect that segmentation. A sign at Michigan Road directing visitors to
"hiking" is slightly misleading because trails are accessible from all parking lots.
Except for the Rocks Trail and the Blue Trail, the trails do not gain or lose much

---

AN APPETITE FOR ITS SURROUNDINGS

Deer over-population is a serious problem for anywhere green. They have a
voracious appetite, with each adult consuming on average more than five
pounds of food a day or about a ton of food per year. That food is likely to
be native flora. Ground-nesting birds lose the protection of cover as do some
species of pollinating insects. Studies have also
found a correlation between deer over-density
and the spread of invasive plant species.

To study the threat and promote natural
growth a deer-proof fence, called a deer
exclosure allow park management to compare
the species growing inside and outside the
enclosed area. It is hoped that tree seedlings
and native flora will flourish and eventually lead
to a more native and diverse habitat.

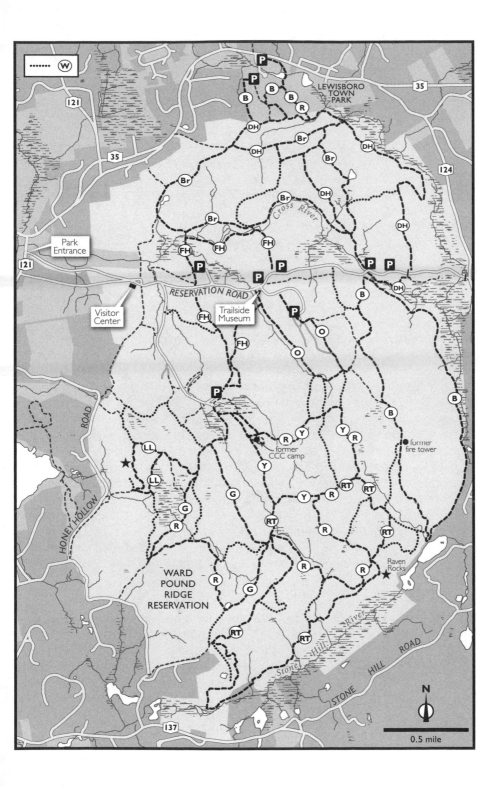

LEWISBORO
TOWN
PARK

35

121

35

124

Park
Entrance

121

Cross River

Visitor
Center

RESERVATION ROAD

Trailside
Museum

former
CCC camp

former
fire tower

Raven
Rocks

HONEY HOLLOW ROAD

WARD
POUND
RIDGE
RESERVATION

Stone Hill River

STONE HILL ROAD

137

N

0.5 mile

Putting the Pieces Together

In 1925, the county purchased a 796-acre tract of land, eventually combining it with fields and wood lots of more than 32 farms to create Pound Ridge Reservation. Over the years, additional land purchases increased the park's area to 4,700 acres. In 1926, there were more than 40 dwellings within park boundaries, mostly modest two-story frame buildings. Through neglect, fire, and the ravages of nature, they fell into disrepair. Because preservation of older buildings was not a common practice at that time, the county demolished rather than do the needed repairs. The eight remaining buildings have become the park office and residences for park employees.

Pound Ridge Reservation, as it was known before 1938, was the base for a unit of the Civilian Conservation Corps (CCC). Remains of their camp, called Camp Merkel, are along a white trail which is off the unmarked trail east of junction 23. Their work is evident throughout the park: the Trailside Museum, stone bridges, graded treadways, lean-tos, and stonework to direct water off woods roads. They also planted thousands of young trees, including Norway spruce, red pine, and white pine. These plantings are found throughout the park, easily recognized by the rows of similarly sized trees.

elevation, but the changes are noticeable. Lower elevations were once farmed and have more stone walls and wetland; slab rock, laurel, and rock outcroppings are indicative of slightly higher elevations.

Trail descriptions reference the county-issued map available at the reservation entrance and kiosks. This color map is more detailed than the map in this book and has trail junction numbers. However, that map does not include the trails in adjacent Lewisboro Town Park, which are included in the maps with this book.

The 8.6 miles of white-blazed trails connect the major trails and make it easy to shorten or lengthen hikes. These connections are mentioned in the trail descriptions and often provide more solitude. To aid navigation, the numbered junctions also have signs indicating where the trail goes.

Almost all trails are suitable for cross-country skiing. But trails are not groomed and hikers are asked to stay out of the ski tracks.

The roads bordering the reservation are narrow, twisty, and without shoulders. No parking is allowed along any of them and local police actively ticket offenders.

NORTH OF RESERVATION ROAD

All picnic area parking lots along Reservation Road provide access to trails in the northern section of the reservation. Trails are suitable for cross-country skiing with short, steep sections as well as longer hills. White trails connect the Brown Trail and the Fox Hill Trail (described with trails south of Reservation Road) and make it possible to have interesting loops. Open meadows parallel Reservation Road east of the reservation entrance, providing an opportunity to walk in a field environment. The park mows 0.5 mile of paths which connect the Meadow Picnic Area past a stream and interconnecting ponds to the maintenance barns.

The eastern most portion of Reservation Road is closed to vehicular traffic, but is open for hikers, cyclists, and equestrians. Features along the 0.6-mile road include a large oak tree, known as the Boutonville Oak (accessible from a short side trail), and a scenic spot by the bridge over the Waccabuc River. Reservation Road is accessible to the handicapped.

Brown Trail
Length: 3.8 miles Blaze: brown on white

Making a large loop, the Brown Trail is accessible from all picnic area parking lots along Reservation Road. To reach it from the Meadow parking lot, follow the Fox Hill Trail (FH) north for 0.1 mile. Continue straight where the Fox Hill Trail turns right. The Brown Trail is just over the bridge at junction 1. Turn right to follow the Brown Trail counterclockwise.

After entering a white pine "plantation" with needles cushioning the path, the Brown Trail parallels the Cross River. The trail crosses feeder streams as it goes gently up and down. At 0.3 mile, it crosses the corner of a stone wall and parallels it to the left. At 0.4 mile, the Brown Trail reaches junction 2, where, to the left, a white trail heads 0.6 mile uphill to connect to the Deer Hollow Trail at junction 4. To the right, a bridge leads to the Fox Hill Trail, which runs along the opposite side of the Cross River.

The Brown Trail goes uphill, follows the river, and turns away at 0.5 mile. Multiple short trails provide access to the water. At 0.7 mile, the trail has several routes through seasonal wet areas. To the right it passes a ford of the river used by equestrians, too deep and wide to cross on foot because of the lack of stepping stones. The trail passes rock outcroppings uphill and to the left. At 0.9 mile, the treadway widens as it goes through a seasonal wet area. It reaches a 165-foot boardwalk and then two other sections of boardwalk at 1.1 miles. The Deer Hollow Trail enters from the left at 1.2 miles to briefly join the Brown Trail. At junction 3, the Brown Trail turns left to head uphill, while the Deer Hollow Trail turns right to reach the Kimberly Bridge Picnic Area in 0.2 mile.

Heading uphill steeply, the Brown Trail crosses a stone wall and reaches the top of a rise near a small rock outcropping. At 1.4 miles at junction 7, a white trail to

THE CHANGING LANDSCAPE

The park landscape is always changing. Pioneer vegetation had been allowed to reclaim farmland in some places. But in other areas, efforts are made to keep the former farm fields open. They are mowed annually to prevent forest from encroaching and at the same time, provide meadow habitat and edge environment for wildlife. Frequently mowed paths lead visitors through the grass. Farm fields left on their own often become overrun with invasive plants. However, when compared with other parks, Ward Pound Ridge Reservation has relatively few invasives. But it has had its share of trauma to the trees. A big storm in 1950 felled a quarter of the white pines in a section north of Reservation Road; a tornado touched down near the Cross River in 1992; a micro-burst in May 2007 felled white pines along the south side of the entrance road (that area is being reforested and protected from deer by a high fence), and Hurricane Sandy in 2013 caused extensive damage to the pine trees planted by the CCC.

the right leads 0.3 mile to junction 8 and the Deer Hollow Trail. The Brown Trail contours uphill, then curves left to ascend more steeply. At the top, the Brown Trail crosses a stone wall at 1.7 miles. Heading downhill, it crosses additional stone walls. At junction 41, a 0.1-mile white trail to the left leads to the Deer Hollow Trail at junction 42. The Brown Trail turns right, continues downhill, and at 2.0 miles reaches junction 6 where it turns left. To the right, a 0.1-mile white trail leads to the Deer Hollow Trail at junction 40.

At 2.3 miles at junction 43, the Deer Hollow Trail comes in from the left, joining the Brown Trail. After heading downhill, the co-aligned trails follow a causeway through wetlands and then climb steadily past acres of barberry. At 2.5 miles, the Brown Trail turns left at junction 5, while the Deer Hollow Trail turns right. The Brown Trail descends and, at junction 44, passes a broad woods road leading 0.3 mile to Route 35 (no parking).

On a slightly raised level treadway, the Brown Trail passes extensive barberry bushes to the left and at 3.2 miles heads uphill. At 3.4 miles, at junction 45, an unmarked woods road to the right goes 0.2 mile to the edge of the property; adjacent landowners use the trail for equestrian access. The Brown Trail reaches junction 46 at 3.6 miles and turns left. To the right, a woods road heads into meadows with mowed paths leading 0.5 mile to maintenance barns and the reservation entrance. The trail descends on a woods road and crosses a stone wall. It enters a mixed evergreen grove and an area with dense undergrowth. It crosses another stone wall and closes the loop at junction 1.

Deer Hollow Trail   *Length: 4.0 miles Blaze: DH*
Beginning in the northwest corner of the parking lot for the Kimberly Bridge Picnic Area, the Deer Hollow Trail follows a woods road paralleling the Cross River. It enters the woods on a narrow path which soon becomes a woods road. At 0.2 mile, it reaches a Y intersection with the Brown Trail at junction 3. The Deer Hollow Trail turns left, joins the Brown Trail, goes uphill, and almost immediately turns right to leave it.

The Deer Hollow Trail continues uphill, with the treadway becoming somewhat more rugged as it proceeds through a forest with low understory. At 0.5 mile, the trail levels off. The forest opens up at 0.8 mile and the trail reaches junction 42 where it turns left. To the right, a white trail leads 0.1 mile to the Brown Trail. At junction 4, the Deer Hollow Trail turns right. To the left, a white trail leads

0.6 mile downhill to the Brown Trail at junction 3. At 1.1 miles at junction 43 at 1.1 miles, the Deer Hollow Trail turns left to join the Brown Trail. After heading downhill, the two trails follow a causeway through wetlands and climb steadily, passing huge stands of barberry. At 1.3 miles at junction 5, the Brown Trail turns left, while the Deer Hollow Trail turns right to head into Deer Hollow. At 1.6 miles, the Deer Hollow Trail passes a blue trail to the left leading into the Lewisboro Nature Preserve. Under the power line, the trail ascends, then descends, and passes a second blue trail into the preserve.

From the high point along the trail at 1.8 miles, the Deer Hollow Trail descends steeply. Before crossing an intermittent stream near a horse fence, a third blue trail leaves to the left to a bridge and private property. Heading uphill, The Deer Hollow Trail reaches junction 40 at 2.1 miles. A trail to the right leads 0.1 mile to the Brown Trail at junction 6. To the left a short trail leads to private property. From Junction 40, the Deer Hollow Trail descends on a woods road through sensitive, cinnamon, and New York ferns. It turns away from a stream, passes the first of many outcroppings, and traverses several seasonal wet areas. At 2.5 miles, it crosses a stone wall and reaches the top of a rise. After descending steeply, it levels out and passes a rock outcropping with the stream and a marshy area visible on the left. Going uphill at 2.7 miles, it passes several more rock outcroppings. It heads left onto a narrow path to avoid an eroded section of the woods road and crosses that road to ascend steeply, avoiding another eroded section. The trail returns to the road and levels out.

The Deer Hollow Trail reaches junction 8 at 3.0 miles, where a 0.3-mile white trail to the right heads to the Brown Trail at junction 7. Passing through dense understory of scrub oak and blueberry, the Deer Hollow Trail goes downhill. It heads uphill at 3.4 miles and then descends steeply. It reaches Reservation Road at 3.6 miles and crosses the road diagonally to the right to reenter the woods at a

Along the Deer Hollow Trail.

maple tree. Now on a narrow path, the Deer Hollow Trail turns to parallel the road, just in sight of it. It crosses stone walls and reaches the Cross River at 3.8 miles. Turning right, the trail follows the stream, then leaves it to head steeply uphill. It descends and, at 4.0 miles, crosses Reservation Road to return to parking at the Kimberly Bridge Picnic Area.

SOUTH OF RESERVATION ROAD

Trailheads for trails south of Reservation Road are off Michigan Road, on Pell Hill, at Kimberly Bridge, and near the Trailside Nature Museum. North of the Michigan Road parking area, the Mill Pond Trail leads 0.3 miles through an area where a saw mill operated. A sign explains why the stream was dammed a distance away from the mill: more power was created, allowing more powerful saws as well as better control.

Red Trail   *Length: 5.6 miles Blaze: red*
The main trail in the southwest portion of the reservation is the Red Trail, accessible from the Michigan Road parking area. Many trails lead off it, making it possible to have other loop hikes and explore the reservation in more depth. The Red Trail is also a cross-country ski trail and has a recommended direction of travel (counterclockwise). It is co-aligned with the Green Trail for the first 2.4 miles and with the Yellow Trail for the last 1.6 miles.

The Red Trail begins at the kiosk near the circle at the Michigan Road parking area and is co-aligned with the Green and Yellow trails. At junction 70, the Yellow Trail heads left, while the Red and Green trails go right. The two trails are on a built-up gravel road which, at 0.2 mile, crosses a stream. There are wet areas on both sides of the trail. The Red-Green Trail heads uphill to junction 53, where to the left the Green Trail closes its loop. At 0.3 mile at junction 54, the Red-Green Trail passes to the right, a white trail heading toward lean-to 8. To the right at junction 31, the Leatherman's Loop (LL) leads to Leatherman's Cave. At junction 25, the Red-Green Trail passes a white trail leading 0.4 mile south to junction 32. The Red-Green Trail is on a raised bed as it passes wetlands in Honey Hollow and, at 0.8 mile, crosses a stream flowing through a large culvert into Honey Hollow. Going gradually uphill, it reaches junction 30 at 1.1 miles and makes a sharp left turn. Ahead is a woods road leading downhill a short distance to a 0.4-mile woods road around Honey Hollow to junction 28 and the Leatherman's Loop (LL), and continuing 0.3 mile to Honey Hollow Road (no parking).

On a raised treadway created by cut-and-fill, the Red-Green Trail goes gradually uphill. It curves left, levels off, and reaches junction 32, where a white trail on the left goes 0.4 mile back to junction 25. It approaches a stream and then veers away from it at 1.4 miles. After crossing the stream, the Red-Green Trail begins to climb significantly. At 1.6 miles, at junction 34, it passes a white trail to the left leading 0.4 mile to junction 35. The Red-Green Trail passes a rock outcropping to the right and maintains a steady grade on a cut-and-fill treadway. It passes through laurel to reach, at 1.8 miles, a hollow with a very large seasonal puddle, at times 80 feet long, which is possible to skirt.

The Red-Green Trail continues to climb and reaches junction 38 at 1.9 miles.

CCC BY THE NUMBERS

Most Civilian Conservation Corps work was done without the aid of power tools. Nationwide, they:

- Stocked more than one billion fish
- Planted more than three billion trees
- Established 8,192 parks
- Treated more than 21 million acres for tree disease and pest control
- Built 9,805 small reservoirs
- Constructed 3,400 fire towers
- Established 4,622 fish-rearing ponds
- Built 651,087 miles of roadway
- Constructed 28,087 miles of trails
- Spent 6.5 million work days fighting forest fires

The woods road to the right leads 0.2 mile to the Rocks Trail at junction 39 and continues another 04 mile along the power line to Honey Hollow Road (no parking). The Red-Green Trail bears left at junction 38 and climbs to the top of a rise, with a rock field on both sides of the trail at 2.0 miles. It goes through laurel as it heads gradually downhill and crosses a stream at 2.2 miles. It reaches junction 35 at 2.4 miles, where the Red and Green trails separate; the Green Trail heads left to return to Michigan Road, while the Red Trail continues straight ahead.

In a short distance the Red Trail reaches junction 36, where the Rocks Trail joins from the right and leaves to the left almost immediately. Bearing right, the Red Trail goes uphill along a woods road through hay scented, royal, New York, and Christmas ferns. At junction 47 at 2.9 miles, a white trail goes 0.4 mile downhill through a scenic valley to the Rocks Trail at junction 59. Turning uphill, the Red Trail passes through laurel. At 3.3 miles it reaches junction 48 where the Rocks Trail (RT) goes right to Raven Rocks and straight ahead to descend into a valley. After descending, the Red Trail continues through more laurel before again heading uphill. At 3.5 miles it reaches junction 21, where a 0.3-mile white trail to the right leads to the Indian Rock Shelter. The Red Trail goes downhill on a rocky tread only to flatten out and then to descend again. At 4.0 miles, it reaches junction 33, where the Yellow Trail joins from the left. The Red Trail turns right and joins the Rock and Yellow trails until the former leaves at junction 19 and the latter for the remaining 1.6 miles to Michigan Road.

After passing lean-to 6 with an inviting grassy front lawn, the co-aligned trails reach junction 20. The white trail to the left leads 0.5 mile to junction 50 and provides an alternate route to the Red-Yellow Trail. At 4.2 miles, they reach junction 19, where the Rocks Trail turns right. The Red-Yellow Trail continues through laurel and passes a rock outcropping to the left at 4.4 miles. Heading downhill on an eroded section of woods road and crossing wetlands, the trail turns, continues downhill to junction 12 and turns left. Straight ahead is a white trail leading 0.2 mile to the Orange Trail at junction 13.

At 4.8 miles, the Red-Yellow Trail crosses a white trail at junction 50. To the left, it is 0.5 mile to junction 20, and to the right it is 0.2 mile to junction 51 on the

Orange Trail. The Red-Yellow Trail reaches junction 11 at 4.9 miles where another white trail heads 0.2 mile to the Orange Trail at junction 10. After passing through a grassy area and then heading uphill, the Red-Yellow Trail turns right where an unmarked woods road continues ahead through the site of the former CCC camp toward junction 23. The Red-Yellow Trail goes gradually uphill. At 5.4 miles, it heads into a meadow, where an unmarked trail to the right leads through wetlands to the open area near lean-to 5. The Red-Yellow Trail leaves the meadow and at junction 70 closes the loop.

Blue Trail   *Length: 3.8 miles Blaze: blue*
The trailhead for the Blue Trail, a loop in the southeast section of the park, is in a tiny picnic area southwest of Kimberly Bridge. Going clockwise around the loop, the first half of the Blue Trail is along a Civilian Conservation Corps built woods road. Its gentle ups and downs make it ideal for a leisurely stroll or cross-country skiing. In sharp contrast, the middle section, which reaches the high point in the reservation, is steep with some rock scrambles. The last part of the loop is a woods road coming down off the ridge.

Banks of ferns line the woods road, which at 0.1 mile, crosses the first of many small dips designed to channel run-off from the steep slopes to prevent its flowing onto the trail. At 0.7 mile, rock outcroppings loom high on the hillside. The woods road passes a balanced rock on the right that is directly next to the trail at 0.9 mile and then parallels a stream and wetlands to the left beginning at 1.0 mile. To the right is a large talus field and the Blue Trail continues uphill leaving the wetlands behind. The built-up roadway is another example of the quality of CCC work, which has lasted for over 70 years. The trail passes a rock field and a stream in wetlands to the left, and a talus field to the right. At 1.9 miles, the Blue Trail leaves the woods road and turns right. To the left is a woods road into private property at Gilmore Pond; straight ahead, the woods road ends at a gate.

Here, the character of the Blue Trail changes. Heading uphill steadily, it passes through a laurel grove and reaches junction 17 at 2.0 miles where a white trail leads uphill to join the Rocks Trail (RT) at junction 58 in 0.4 mile. Curving gently around rock outcroppings, the trail passes a seasonal stream and goes through a root-filled seasonal wet area. After following a rocky creek bed, it ascends quite steeply. At 2.1 miles, it heads downhill and curves slightly to the left. Ferns carpet the forest floor and large rock outcroppings tower above. The trail resumes its steep ascent and enters a laurel grove at 2.3 miles. It goes through a seasonal wet area and crosses another wet area littered with uprooted trees and dead or dying hemlocks, in sharp contrast to the area just 0.2 mile back.

The Blue Trail continues through a rock field with a high rock outcropping and climbs a steep rock face almost straight up the fall line. Scrub oak and blueberry bushes are on the level top. To the left at junction 16, the Blue Trail passes a white trail leading 0.5 mile downhill to the Rocks Trail just south of the Indian Rock Shelter at junction 49. Now on a woods road, it reaches, site of a former fire tower at 2.6 miles, the highest point in the reservation (elevation 860 feet). The open area has a bench, a pump (usually dry in the summer), and the ruins of a stone cabin formerly used by the forest fire observer. The trail heads downhill.

Hiking when laurel is in bloom.

At junction 15 at 2.9 miles, the Blue Trail heads right. To the left, a white trail leads 0.3 mile downhill to junctions 52 and 13 and the lean-tos and picnic area on Pell Hill. The Blue Trail passes a vernal pool and goes downhill to reach junction 14 at 3.3 miles. At this four-way intersection, a white trail heads straight and descends along a woods road to reach the Pell Hill Road in 0.4 mile. The white trail to the left goes 0.2 mile downhill to junctions 52 and 13. The Blue Trail turns right onto a narrow treadway. At 3.4 miles, it goes through a wash gully, a dense laurel grove, and then another gully. It levels out and passes junction 56 where a white trail leads 0.7 mile back to the Trailside Nature Museum. After descending it goes onto a woods road and closes the loop at the picnic area.

Fox Hill Trail
Length: 2.2 miles Blaze: FH

To reach the Fox Hill Trail, take the Orange Trail from the Trailside Nature Museum to junction 9 where the Fox Hill Trail crosses a stream. It immediately heads uphill to cross another stone wall at 0.1 mile and turn left. It briefly skirts an overgrown field, follows a stone wall, and turns left to reenter the forest. The trail ascends and crosses several stone walls and turns right. It heads downhill, descends the Magic Steps at 0.4 mile and crosses another stone wall. After crossing two more stone walls at 0.6 mile, it reaches an intersection and turns right. At the next intersection, a white trail connects to the upper parking area at the end of Michigan Road. The trail now bears right and, at 0.9 mile, descends. At 1.0 mile, it passes a white blazed trail which leads 0.2 mile downhill to Michigan Road. Continuing downhill, the trail passes two pine plantations, many of which were devastated by Hurricane Sandy in 2012. It enters an open field and crosses Reservation Road at 1.3 miles.

On a mowed path, the trail follows the edge of the Meadow Picnic Area parking lot and passes a kiosk. The trail crosses boardwalk and enters the woods on a bridge over a stream. Just before reaching the Cross River, it turns right to follow the shore on a woods road. On a high bank, the trail follows the river and then bypasses the picnic area. The trail passes a ford to the left at 1.9 miles where, a bridge leads to junction 2 and the Brown Trail. Turning right, the trail heads uphill, passing a restroom built by the CCC. The road to the right leads to lean-to 7. The Fox Hill Trail ends at the Bergfield Picnic Area. To return to the parking at the Trailside Nature Museum, turn right and walk along the road.

Green Trail
Length: 3.1 miles Blaze: green

For the first 2.4 miles, the Green Trail is co-aligned with the Red Trail (for a description, see the entry for the Red Trail). The Green Trail is also a cross-country ski trail, but with a caveat: after it diverges from the Red Trail at junction 35, there is a portion which is, in skier's terms, "most difficult." The Green Trail is described counterclockwise although hikers can walk the trail in either direction. At junction 35, the Green Trail splits from the Red Trail and turns left. The trail goes through laurel and then a wooded section with no understory. At 2.7 miles, it reaches a height of land and heads downhill. It drops more steeply at 3.0 miles and closes the loop with the Red Trail at 3.1 miles.

Leatherman's Loop
Length: 1.3 miles Blaze: LL

A popular hiking destination, Leatherman's Cave, is on a side trail off Leatherman's Loop, which begins from junction 31 on the Red-Green Trail at a sign for Leatherman's Cave. After crossing a raised treadway, the Leatherman's Loop heads uphill. At 0.2 mile, it passes to the left a 0.3-mile woods road which leads past a glacial erratic to end at the Red-Green Trail.

The loop begins at junction 26. To reach Leatherman's Cave via the shorter route, turn left. After descending steeply on a narrow footpath, the trail levels off and widens. It passes Honey Hollow Swamp to the left, goes up a rise, and descends to a convergence of stone walls. At 0.5 mile, it reaches junction 28 and turns right. To the left, a white trail goes 0.4 mile through Honey Hollow to intersect with a woods road just south of junction 30. Passing a foundation to the right, the trail parallels a stone wall and heads downhill. At junction 29, a 0.2-mile unmarked trail goes straight to Honey Hollow Road and a BRLA trail, which if taken leads to the Richards Preserve.

Turn right. Leatherman's Cave is up a short steep trail to the left. The trail, ascends a narrow treadway to an overlook and passes a large overhang at 0.7 mile. It turns left away from a stone wall and climbs steeply. The trail reaches an overlook to the left and then a second overlook with a view over the Cross River Reservoir. The trail makes a sharp right and at the bottom of a steep section curves left. At 1.0 mile, Leatherman's Loop levels out and at junction 27, turns right. A white trail heads left to reach junction 55 in 0.9 mile. It follows a built-to-grade woods road, another example of CCC work. It closes the loop at 1.2 miles at junction 26. Straight ahead, it is 0.2 mile back to the Red-Green Trail.

Orange Trail
Length: 1.6 miles Blaze: orange

Beginning at Reservation Road, west of the Trailside Nature Museum, the Orange Trail is a loop that goes up to the Pell Hill parking area and returns to Reservation Road. Heading uphill on a woods road, the Orange Trail passes the trail to the

A Leather Clad Mystery

Any history of Ward Pound Ridge Reservation would be incomplete if it did not mention the Leatherman. This mysterious traveler first appeared in the area in 1850's. Because he rarely spoke, little was known about him, adding to his mystique. Clad in a suit made entirely of leather and weighing 60 pounds, he walked a 365-mile circuit through parts of Westchester, Putnam and Fairfield counties from 1883 until his death in 1889. The Leatherman completed this circuit every 34 days on a route which did not vary, sometimes on roads, at other times bushwhacking cross-country.

He regularly visited certain families, many of whom kept dishes for his use. He begged for food, but would not stop at a household which had once made him feel unwelcome. No reports exist of his doing work of any kind, although he did establish small shelters which he kept supplied with firewood, boughs for a bed, and cooking utensils. If he found that anyone disturbed his things, he would abandon that place and never return to it. Leatherman's Cave is one of his many stopping places.

After Leatherman's death from cancer in his cave near Ossining, the mystery continued. He was identified as Jules Bourglay, the son of a French woodcarver, the name put on his headstone. But reports varied about him. Some say he worked for a leather merchant and fell in love with his employer's daughter with conflicting reports having him ruining the business in an attempt to win her hand or being refused as a potential suitor. Other reports identified him as the wealthy son of a wool merchant from Lyon.

After more than 120 years of wondering, the Ossining Historical Society tried to find an answer and oversaw the exhumation of his body for DNA testing to try to trace his origins. But no genetic material was found. So the soil, nails, and coffin were interred in a new coffin with a new brass plaque identifying him as "The Leatherman."

Wildflower Garden, fenced to keep out deer. A path from the Trailside Museum merges from the left just before a boardwalk. At 0.1 mile, the Orange Trail passes an outdoor classroom to the right and the Fox Hill Trail (FH) at junction 9. The Orange Trail continues uphill at a constant grade and parallels a stream to the left. It enters a broad valley and heads onto a causeway over a wet area. At 0.6 mile, the trail passes a stream water level gauge to the right and crosses a bridge to reach junction 10. Straight ahead, a white trail goes 0.2 mile to junction 11 on the Red-Yellow Trail.

The Orange Trail turns left and heads uphill. At junction 51, the white trail to the right leads 0.2 mile to junction 50, also on the Red-Yellow Trail. The Orange Trail goes left, crosses a bridge, and passes stone walls of a former lean-to. Continuing uphill, it reaches lean-to 29 to the right and then junction 13, where a white trail leads to junction 12 and then junction 52 in 0.2 mile. The Orange Trail bears left along the access road to the lean-tos; at 1.0 mile, when the road splits, it continues straight. At the next intersection, the trail turns left and to the right, a white trail leads 0.4 mile uphill to junction 14 on the Blue Trail. The Orange Trail reaches a major junction of gravel roads and a kiosk at 1.2 miles.

From the kiosk, the trail heads towards the parking lot near the playground. It bears left toward lean-to 15 and goes between lean-tos 15 and 16. At the front of the lean-to, it crosses an open rock surface and then heads steeply downhill. At the bottom of the steep pitch, the trail goes left and enters a pine forest. Take care, because the other paths in this area can be confusing. The Orange Trail turns onto a woods road, turns right at a T junction with another woods road, and goes through a stone wall. At 1.5 mile, the trail passes through white pines, crosses a field, and ends at the paved road to Pell Hill at 1.6 miles. To return to the trailhead, walk downhill and turn left onto Reservation Road.

Rocks Trail
Length 4.9 miles Blaze RT

A loop through the southern portion of the park, the Rocks Trail visits six rock features along its route: Indian Rock Shelter, Raven Rocks, Castle Rock, Spy Rock, Bear Rock, and Dancing Rock. Beginning at junction 19, the Rocks Trail leaves the co-aligned Red-Yellow trail and descends steeply, turning right to cross several bridges before leveling off. It passes first the Indian Rock Shelter to the left and then junction 18 to the right where a white trail to the right heads 0.3 mile uphill to junction 21 at the Red Trail. The Rocks Trail makes a right turn at 0.4 mile to head uphill through laurel. At junction 58 at 0.6 mile, a white trail heads left to join the Blue Trail at junction 17. Continuing uphill through laurel, the Rocks Trail touches the Red Trail at 0.7 mile at junction 48. It immediately turns left to Raven Rocks and then follows the ridge. It turns right and leaves the ridge at 1.1 miles. Descending, steeply at times, it crosses first a stream and then a seasonally wet area. At junction 59, it turns left where, to the right, a white trail ends in 0.4 mile at junction 47 at the Red Trail. There is a feeling of remoteness as the trail continues downhill through the valley with rock outcroppings high overhead.

At 1.4 miles, the Rocks Trail passes below Castle Rock, looming up to the right. It crosses under a power line and reenters the woods. The trail descends next to a stream along the side of a hill, crosses the stream and briefly ascends to a view of the Stone Hill River below. After a steep ascent, the trail enters a flat area at 1.8 miles. Rock outcroppings punctuate the uphill side of the trail. The trail again descends steeply and then turns right crossing a stone wall and stream and joins a BRLA trail at 2.5 miles. The trail turns left and heads downhill leveling off before entering a hemlock grove. The Stone Hill River can be seen to the left.

ROADS WITH A HISTORY

Property deeds for large tracts of land in the early part of the eighteenth century often included an allowance for roads. This meant that five acres were to be set aside for roads for every 100 acres of land. Old maps show a network of woods roads; some of these were originally designed as paths for oxen to transport logs by wagon or cart from wood lots. County and CCC attempts at improving them for use as fire roads were limited. In many places, these roads continue to be rugged and inhospitable to vehicles, particularly at higher elevations. In addition, steep slopes and rocky terrain discourage east-west travel. This network of woods roads has become the basis for the trail system in Ward Pound Ridge Reservation.

A soft shoe on Dancing Rock.

The Rocks Trail turns right to go through a hemlock grove at 2.3 miles and begins a steep climb made easier with 80 stone steps which gracefully ascend the hill. When the volunteer trail builders learned about the old steps, they change the route to use them. After the trail becomes less steep, it briefly descends to a view to the left of a rock formation and downhill to a large flat rock and the BRLA/Rocks Trail at the foot of the stone stairway. The trail ascends to a view and the start of a ridge at 2.6 miles. Before leaving the ridge, The Rocks Trail reaches Spy Rock. Views from Spy Rock and the ridge are partially obscured when leaves are on the trees.

Leaving Spy Rock, the trail turns left, descends briefly and follows a stone wall. A BRLA trail joins just before the Rocks Trail turns right, and then immediately leaves to the left. The trail crosses several bridges, turns sharply left, and ascends to go through a stone wall. Another BRLA trail is to the left. At 3.0 miles, the Rocks Trail reaches a woods road and turns right, running briefly next to power lines. It curves to the right and reaches Bear Rock which has an outline resembling bear's head on its surface. After heading up a short section of slab rock, the trail again parallels the power line and then crosses under it. At junction 60 at 3.5 miles, a white trail heads to Dancing Rock, a large open flat rock with no view. Dancing Rock was so named because farm workers danced on it to celebrate the end of the harvest. The 0.4 mile loop rejoins the Rocks Trail at junction 37. Turning right, the Rocks Trail passes through laurel, and then descends to join the Red Trail. The two trails are co-aligned briefly, splitting at junction 36 at 4.2 miles. The Rocks Trail continues on a woods road crossing a bridge over a stream before turning right at 4.4 miles to join the Yellow Trail at junction 22. The co-aligned trails reached the Red Trail at 4.7 miles at junction 33. The three trails continue to junction 19, closing the loop for the Rocks Trail where the Red and Yellow trails turn left.

Trailside Museum (Wheeler Trail) *Length: 0.7 mile Blaze: white*

From the parking lot for the Trailside Nature Museum, the Wheeler Trail heads

A tree grows through a discarded CCC bedstead.

across a field on a mowed path. It enters the woods at 0.1 mile and crosses two bridges. After a third bridge, it turns right at 0.4 mile and heads uphill to end at junction 56 on the Blue Trail.

Yellow Trail

Length: 2.6 miles Blaze: yellow

Like the Green Trail, the Yellow Trail is co-aligned with the Red Trail for most of its length and can be used to make a shorter loop. It is co-aligned with the Red Trail for the last 1.6 miles. The Red-Yellow Trail begins at the kiosk near the circle at the Michigan Road parking area. At first, it is co-aligned with the Red-Green Trail. At junction 70, the Red-Yellow Trail heads left, while the Red- Green Trail goes right. At 0.1 mile, at junction 24, the Yellow Trail turns right and the Red Trail proceeds straight. Then, at junction 23, a 0.1 mile unmarked trail to the left leads to a white trail which goes 0.2 mile through the ruins of Camp Merkel, the former CCC camp. A short distance past junction 23, there is a flight of stone stairs leading to a concrete walkway into the camp. Continuing uphill, the Yellow Trail passes a sugar maple perched on a rock to the left. At 0.5 mile, it goes through a section of the forest where the trees are smaller and closer together. Passing a vernal pool to the left, the trail parallels a broken-down stone wall and reaches junction 22 at 0.7 mile and turns left joining the Rocks Trail. Straight ahead, the Rocks Trail leads 0.2 mile to the Red Trail at junction 36. The co-aligned trails go slightly downhill and cross several stone walls before heading uphill again. They pass an unmarked woods road and reach junction 33 at 1.0 mile where the Red Trail joins from the right. For the next 0.2 mile, the Yellow Trail is co-aligned with both the Rocks and Red trails. When the co-aligned trails reach junction 19, the Rocks Trail turns right. (For a description of the return route to the Michigan Road parking area, see the entry for the Red Trail).

The many unmarked trails at the reservation are indicated by dotted lines on the county issued map. They offer interesting alternatives to the marked trails and open up other areas to explore. Some trails lead out to Honey Hollow Road (no parking) while others are along the meadows parallel to Reservation Road, providing birding opportunities along the edges of the meadows. A short hike from the Red-Yellow Trail leads through a wetlands to the open area in front of lean-to 5 and is an easy walk back to parking at Michigan Road. Two unmarked trails, the 0.4 mile trail from Junction 39 to Honey Hollow Road and the 0.7 mile trail from Old Schoolhouse Road to Honey Hollow Road are of interest to hikers. The former is lined with dogwood trees, a habitat attractive to birds adapted to living in edge environments; the latter passes an old cemetery and passes by a Christmas tree plantation and horse field.

CONNECTING PARK & TRAILS: Lewisboro Nature Preserve, Lewisboro Horsemen's Association trails, Bedford Riding Lanes Association trails, Richards Preserve

DRIVING: From I-684, take Exit 6 (Route 35) and turn east. Go 3.8 miles and turn right onto Route 121. It is 0.1 mile to the reservation entrance [41.261161N 73.614716W]. An entrance fee is charged during the week in season and on weekends year-round. Westchester County residents can register for a card which reduces the fee.
   Bergfield Picnic Area [41.259173N 73.586585W]
   Kimberly Bridge [41.259319N 73.577008W]
   Meadow Parking Area [41.259648N 73.595700W]
   Michigan Road parking [41.248105N 73.594858W]
   Pell Hill Picnic Area [41.254986N 73.584263W]
   Trailside Museum [41.257972N 73.588382W]

PUBLIC TRANSPORTATION: None available

For contact information, see Appendix, Westchester County Parks—Ward Pound Ridge Reservation.

Lewisboro Town Park & Lewisboro Nature Preserve

Cross River • 0.9 mile, 68 acres

Asmall white sign along Route 35 is at the entrance to Lewisboro Town Park, and the entrance to Lewisboro Nature Preserve. Wedged between the town park and Ward Pound Ridge Reservation, there is no visible boundary between the two town entities. The 0.3 mile blue trail connects to Ward Pound Ridge Reservation. Another blue trail has an occasional red blaze of the Lewisboro Horsemen's Association (LHA) trails.

Blue-Red Trail   *Length: 0.6 mile Blaze: blue-red*
From Deer Hollow Trail in Ward Pound Ridge Reservation, the blue-red trail heads under power lines. It reenters the woods, goes uphill and then enters an area

overgrown with honeysuckle and barberry. After going steeply downhill it levels off near a horse farm. The trail goes behind tennis courts and circles around to the service road. It turns right at 0.4 mile and crosses a bridge by a pond where an unmarked trail heads around the pond The trail passes an outdoor craft center housed in a lean-to and turns left to parallel Route 35. It turns toward the road and then turns left to parallel it once more, finally ending at the road at 0.6 mile. The LHA trail into Old Field Preserve is across the road from the entrance to town facilities.

CONNECTING PARKS: Ward Pound Ridge Reservation, Old Field Preserve

DRIVING: From I-684, take Exit 6 (Route 35) and turn east onto Route 35. Drive 5.7 miles to the park entrance [41.277371N 73.588786W].

PUBLIC TRANSPORTATION: None available

For contact information, see Appendix, Lewisboro.

Low tide at Hummocks Conservation Area.

SECTION VII

LINEAR CORRIDORS

- Offer one-way walks with return via public transportation
- Provide a wide range of distances to walk
- Are corridors for wildlife
- Highlight the ecological, economic, and social diversity of the county

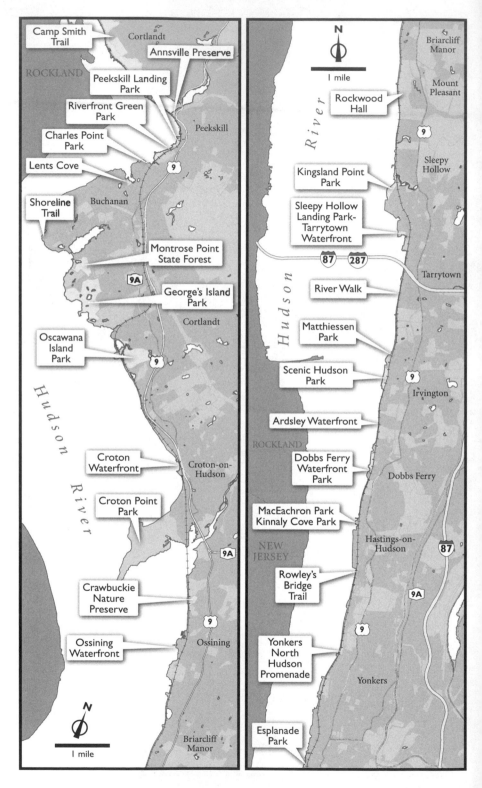

Camp Smith
Trail

Cortlandt

Annsville Preserve

ROCKLAND

Peekskill Landing
Park

Riverfront Green
Park

Peekskill

Charles Point
Park

Lents Cove

Shoreline
Trail

Buchanan

Montrose Point
State Forest

9A

George's Island
Park

Cortlandt

Oscawana
Island
Park

9

H u d s o n

R i v e r

Croton
Waterfront

Croton-on-
Hudson

Croton Point
Park

9A

Crawbuckie
Nature
Preserve

9

Ossining
Waterfront

Ossining

N

1 mile

Briarcliff
Manor

N

1 mile

River

Briarcliff
Manor

Rockwood
Hall

Mount
Pleasant

9

Kingsland Point
Park

Sleepy
Hollow

Sleepy Hollow
Landing Park-
Tarrytown
Waterfront

87   287

Tarrytown

H u d s o n

River Walk

Matthiessen
Park

Scenic Hudson
Park

9

Irvington

Ardsley Waterfront

ROCKLAND

Dobbs Ferry
Waterfront
Park

Dobbs Ferry

MacEachron Park
Kinnaly Cove Park

Hastings-on-
Hudson

NEW
JERSEY

87

Rowley's
Bridge
Trail

9A

Yonkers
North
Hudson
Promenade

9

Yonkers

Esplanade
Park

Along the River

Cortlandt to Yonkers • 15.9 miles

Dotting the shoreline like small pearls on a string, the tiny parks and preserves along the Hudson River provide access to the water and stunning river scenery. Parks with more than one mile of trail are cross-referenced. When several small parks are adjacent and it is not obvious where jurisdictions start and end, they are described as a unit.

The Hudson's waterfront has not always been a jewel: it had few parks and many industrial sites. In 1989 the Hudson River Access Forum surveyed sites along its shoreline and made recommendations for increased public access. In the 1990s, a state initiative, the Hudson River Valley Greenway, established the idea of a route that stretched along both sides of the river. In 2003 to fulfill their part of the Greenway trail, the county published Hudson RiverWalk, a description of the route and some of its challenges. To see the plan online, go to www. westchestergov.com/planning and search for RiverWalk under "Initiatives."

Beginning at the north end, Charles Point Park in Peekskill has a 0.2 mile path to Fleichmann's Pier with views of Peekskill Bay and beyond. Lents Cove in Buchanan has a trail honoring Joseph Tropiano, a village trustee. It begins on the north side of the ballfield and leads to a view toward Dunderburg Mountain [41.271923N 73.942388W]. Matthiessen, Waterfront, MacEachron, and Esplanade parks have under 0.3 mile of paths and are within walking distance of their respective Metro North stations: Irvington, Dobbs Ferry, Hastings, and Yonkers. All have expansive views across the river. Matthiessen Park is for Irvington residents only. Esplanade Park includes the Yonkers Sculpture Garden.

Metro-North Hudson Line for most of its length is close to the river and is a convenient way to shuttle between parks. Parking at train stations is free on weekends, except at Croton-Harmon.

Camp Smith Trail *See Day Trippers*

Annsville Creek Paddle Sport Center and Annsville Creek Preserve

Peekskill • 0.9 mile, 2.7 and 9.7 acres

Cooperation between two municipalities and two state agencies has resulted in a trail that connects two parks: Annsville Creek Paddlesport Center and Annsville Creek Preserve. Now a part of Hudson Highlands State Park, the Paddlesport Center was a New York State Department of Transportation equipment yard. A 0.2 mile gravel path circles part of the property preserve. After heading out onto busy Route 6/202, walkers reach a cantilevered pedestrian walkway along Annsville Bridge at 0.4 mile. At the end of the bridge, a sidewalk heads uphill to the right leading to a path, which at 0.6 mile, heads downhill into Annsville

Creek Preserve, a City of Peekskill park. There is an overlook called the Annsville Pavilion, a paved path at the preserve and a dirt path along the creek. Continue south along the road parallel to the tracks, protected by a chain-link fence, to reach a gate at 0.9 mile and several parking spots. The gate is locked at night and unlocked at about 7:30 am. The Peekskill Station and Riverfront Green are a 0.6-mile walk along Pemart Avenue, whose name changes first to Water Street and then to South Water Street.

DRIVING: To reach the Paddlesport Center from Route 9, go to the Annsville Circle and take the Route 6/202 Exit for Bear Mountain Bridge and Camp Smith. The entrance to the Paddlesport Center is almost immediately to the left [41.297405N 73.937616W].

To reach Annsville Creek Preserve from Route 9, take the Route 6/202 Exit and turn right onto Main Street heading downhill toward the river. Turn right onto Pemart Avenue, which goes through a commercial area. Parking is at the end of the road [41.293205N 73.935826W].

PUBLIC TRANSPORTATION: Metro-North Hudson Line Peekskill Station. Walk along South Water Street, which becomes Water Street, and then Pemart Avenue. Continue through the commercial area to end at a gate. The distance from train station to trailhead is 0.6 mile.

For contact information, see Appendix, Peekskill.

Peekskill Landing Park and Riverfront Green Park

Peekskill • 1.3 mile, 4.4 acres and 23.9 acres

Looking out over Peekskill Bay, Peekskill Landing Park and Riverfront Green Park are testaments to urban waterfront revitalization. The space was once crowded with commercial shipping but now offers a pleasant stretch with inspiring views along the Hudson River. Riverfront Green is often busy with events, but at other times visitors are there simply for a walk. During weekends in the summer or even on cool misty days, the park is a popular spot to picnic, fish, or just relax. Peekskill Landing Park provides a space to walk but, as of 2013, was still a work in progress by Scenic Hudson and the City of Peekskill.

For most of the nineteenth century, Peekskill's waterfront was a port for shipping and receiving raw materials. Its docks bustled with industrial and commercial activities which were an economic engine for the city and region. American Stove Works, Seymour Coal Yard, and Ombony and Dain's Son's Lumber Yards occupied the property through the first quarter of the twentieth century. By the mid 1960s, however, the majority of land north of the docks was vacant. In 1998, Scenic Hudson Land Trust and the City of Peekskill purchased the property to create a passive use public park and extension of Riverfront Green. The project languished for several years until the New York's Department of State required the city to begin a new public participation process for the project. Site remediation was finally completed at the end of 2011. Although there are no paths, following the shoreline is easy. Walk north from the parking area to enter Peekskill Landing

Family time.

Park at a bridge over McGregory Brook. Follow the railroad tracks as far as you can, turn left, and follow the shore back to the bridge. This round trip is 0.6 mile.

The route through Riverfront Green is along a sidewalk leading from a cement pad at the edge of the river. When the sidewalk meets another sidewalk, turn right and head toward a kiosk with information about the Hudson River Estuary. Continue toward the boat launch at 0.3 mile. Go through the boat launch access road toward the station, turn right, and head south on the road paralleling the tracks. Passing the high chain-link fence of Peekskill Yacht Club, the road continues, curving right at 0.5 mile, and then bearing left onto Bushey Way. Just beyond a stop sign, turn left onto a gravel road, a parking area for boat mooring permit holders. At a turnaround, a path leads through a rock barrier to end at 0.7 mile. Unfortunately, the cove and the railroad tracks cut off access to Louisa Street.

DRIVING: From Route 9, take the Hudson Street Exit and head downhill to the river following signs to the railroad station. Cross the railroad tracks to enter the park [41.287832N 73.930536W]. There is free four hour parking at the north end.

PUBLIC TRANSPORTATION: Metro-North Hudson Line Peekskill Station

For contact information, see Appendix, Peekskill.

Shoreline Trail to Montrose Point State Forest

Verplanck • 2.6 miles

Beginning at the Buchanan/Verplanck line, the green-blazed Shoreline Trail heads south on Broadway in Verplanck. The first 0.2 mile has a sidewalk on the east side. It reaches Hardie Street at 1.7 miles. Steamboat Dock (3.6 acres) is 0.1 mile to the right. It is 0.5 mile from the dock along Hardie Street/Riverview Avenue to the sidewalk on Kings Ferry Road across from the marina. Montrose

Point State Forest is 0.4 mile further along Kings Ferry Road, which in some places has no sidewalk.

DRIVING: From Route 9, take the Louisa Street Exit and head toward the river. At John Welch Boulevard, turn left and continue 1.6 miles to where Broadway begins in Verplanck [41.271923N 73.942388W].

PUBLIC TRANSPORTATION: None available

For contact information, see Appendix, Cortlandt.

Montrose Point State Forest *See Afternoon Jaunts*

George's Island Park *See Afternoon Jaunts*

Oscawana Park *See Morning Strolls*

Croton Waterfront to Ossining

Croton-on-Hudson • 3.8 miles, 25.1 acres

A recipe for success: take two small linear parks along the Hudson River, then add public access behind condominiums, a road walk with access to a train station, and a safe bike/pedestrian route along a busy road which connects to another linear park. The end result is a convenient, accessible place to exercise and spend time outdoors.

Thanks to the developers of the Half Moon Bay and Echo Bay condominiums, the Village of Croton, and Metro-North, the portion through the condominiums is now a pedestrian commuter route. It also provides public access to two parks through private property. To the walker, it is a continuous path with views over the Hudson River and access to its shoreline, but boundaries between the four parcels exist in terms of ownership and maintenance.

As part of repairs to Route 9 near the Croton River, the New York State Department of Transportation built pedestrian and cyclist access along the road. CrOssining, as it is called, is a combination of the names of the two communities it joins. A barrier separates the high-speed traffic from pedestrians and cyclists.

From Croton Landing Park, a paved path heads north and wiggles along the edge of the river just back from the riprap at the shoreline. Because it reaches a dead end at 0.7 mile, the route must be retraced. At the south end of the parking lot, the pathway parallels a road with the railroad on the opposite side. To the left at 0.8 mile, a handicapped pedestrian overpass crosses the tracks and Route 9. The pathway then passes the entrance to the Croton Yacht Club and at 0.9 mile, passes Senesqua Park (Croton residents only). At 0.1.1 miles, the trail passes a low tunnel (dated 1912) under the road and then heads uphill on a ramp. It crosses the entrance road and parallels the tracks. After passing under a bridge at 1.4 miles, the trail parallels the Metro-North Croton-Harmon Yards.

At the water's edge.

Between the rail yards and a fence, the trail passes through a gate behind the Echo Bay condominiums. Gates in the fence allow condominium residents access to the bikeway and pedestrian commuter route to the Croton-Harmon Station. The trail crosses the emergency entrance gate to Echo Bay at 1.9 miles. The trail heads up along the back of a landfill, passing riprap drainage on both sides. At 2.3 miles, it reaches Croton Point Avenue. To the right is Croton Point Park. (See Day Trippers). From the end of the access road, turn left and walk facing traffic along Croton Point Avenue. Cross the road to the sidewalk and at 2.5 miles, reach the bridge over the railroad tracks. Pass the entrance road to the Croton-Harmon Station at 2.7 miles and continue to the entrance ramp to southbound Route 9. Turn right onto the path alongside the entrance ramp where a bike path begins at 2.8 miles. Benches, interpretive signs, and a viewing platform are along the route. Once across the Croton River, the path passes, to the right, a rock cut with interesting shaped inclusions. The bike path ends at 3.8 miles. It is 0.5 mile along the sidewalk to the Old Croton Aqueduct.

DRIVING: From Route 9, take the Route 9A/129 Exit. Turn west toward the river and then turn left toward Half Moon Bay. At a stop sign, turn right and take the ramp down to the parks. There is parking at the end of the road in Croton Landing Park [41.183355N 73.869746W].

PUBLIC TRANSPORTATION: Metro-North Hudson Line Croton-Harmon Station

For contact information, see Appendix, Croton.

Edward M. Wheeler
Crawbuckie Nature Preserve

Ossining • 0.8 mile, 26 acres

Major improvements in 2012 to the Crawbuckie Nature Preserve have changed a little used park on the upland side of the Metro-North tracks. Now the park has a 0.1 mile handicapped accessible loop to a view over the Hudson River and a 0.7 mile trail with views over tidal marshes and the Hudson River.

The Village of Ossining purchased the property in 1967 from the federal government under an open space program. The land had been intended as an interchange of the proposed Hudson River Expressway (I-487), but in 1961 the plan was scrapped and I-684 in the eastern part of the county was built instead. (See http://www.nycroads.com/roads/croton.) The park was renamed to honor Edward M. Wheeler who was mayor when the property was protected.

Just past the entrance, the trail splits and to the left is the handicapped accessible trail. To the right, the trail heads downhill, passes a view and crosses streams, where from a boardwalk, an old dam is visible to the left. At 0.3 miles, the trail reaches a flight of stone steps which curve gracefully around to ascend the hill. The trail reaches the top of the bluff, where, at a trail junction, a loop goes to two viewing platforms with the second one on dead spur. To the left the trail continues and at 0.7 mile ends at a driveway. Following the driveway, head toward Beach Road where the entrance is downhill 0.2 mile to the left and the Old Croton Aqueduct is uphill 0.3 mile to the right.

DRIVING: From Route 9 north of Ossining, turn west onto Beach Road. Northbound, the left turn is a block past Cedar Lane. Southbound, the turn is 0.5 mile south of Eagle Bay Condominiums and there is gas station on the corner.. Follow Beach Road to parking in the cul-de-sac [41.172273N 73.870182W].

PUBLIC TRANSPORTATION: Metro-North Hudson Line Ossining Station; Beeline Bus #14 on Route 9. A 0.6 mile walk along Beach Road leads to the preserve.

For contact information, see Appendix, Ossining.

Ossining Waterfront

Ossining • 0.4 mile, 5.3 acres

Short walks are possible along Ossining's waterfront. Harbor Square is just beyond the Ossining Metro-North Station and is connected via a sidewalk to Engel Park, north of Sing Sing Correctional Facility. Engel Park has a short walking trail. For those interested in the prison's history, visit the Joseph G. Caputo Community Center near the intersection of Broadway and North Highland Avenue which houses the Ossining Heritage Area Visitor Center. This small museum has exhibits about the Old Croton Aqueduct and Sing Sing including a furnished cell and another cell that visitors may enter.

DRIVING: From Route 9, take Main Street and head downhill toward the river, following signs for the Ossining Station. Cross the bridge at the station and head south to the end of the parking lot [41.155062N 73.869535W].

PUBLIC TRANSPORTATION: Metro-North Hudson Line Ossining Station; Beeline Bus #13 and #14.

For contact information, see Appendix, Ossining.

Rockwood Hall *See Afternoon Jaunts*

Kingsland Point Park

Sleepy Hollow • 0.5 mile, 18.7 acres

One of the first county parks, Kingsland Point Park was once home to Ambrose C. Kingsland (1804-1878), a little known New York City mayor (1851-1853). His summer estate became Philipse Manor Country Club and was to include an amusement park, which was never built. The county purchased the property in 1924 which is now managed by the Village of Sleepy Hollow.

In 1976, the beach closed because of pollution in the Hudson River, and the Spanish Renaissance-style bathhouse, no longer in use, deteriorated. The building has been restored and repurposed as an environmental education and water-related recreational activities center. In 2011, the bathhouse was named the Kathryn R. Davis RiverWalk Center after the Tarrytown resident who funded the project.

There are no trails at Kingsland Point Park, but the open areas along the shore lead to views of the Tappan Zee and the bridge. South of the park is the site of the former General Motors plant, which closed in 1996. From the parking lot, it is a 0.5-mile round trip walk along the retaining wall to the gate blocking the path to Tarrytown Lighthouse, built in 1883. The lighthouse was originally further from shore, but in 1923 General Motors expanded its automobile plant along the river. Slowly, the east shore of the river expanded until only 50 feet separated the lighthouse from the shoreline. Taken out of service in 1961, the lighthouse was decommissioned in 1965. Fourteen years later it was listed on the National Register of Historic Places. Group tours are available by appointment.

DRIVING: From northbound Route 9 from Tarrytown into Sleepy Hollow, just north of the entrance to Philipsburg Manor, turn left onto Pierson Street which becomes Bellwood. Turn left onto Palmer Avenue following signs to the park. Cross over the railroad tracks and turn left. Southbound on Route 9, 1.3 miles from the westbound junction with Route 117, turn right onto Palmer Avenue. Follow signs to the park [41.081066N 73.868098W].

PUBLIC TRANSPORTATION: Metro-North Hudson Line Philipse Manor Station; Beeline Bus #13 along Route 9 near Sleepy Hollow Cemetery. It is about a 0.3-mile walk to the park entrance from either the train station or the bus stop.

For contact information, see Appendix, Westchester County Parks.

Tarrytown Waterfront
Sleepy Hollow Landing Park

Tarrytown • 0.8 mile, 6.1 acres

Enjoy the sweeping views across the Hudson River along Westchester County's RiverWalk as it connects Pierson Park to the site of the former General Motors plant, which closed in 1996. This section of RiverWalk, completed in 2011, has interpretive signs, benches, and, aside from a short gravel section in Pierson Park, is handicapped accessible.

DRIVING: From Route 9, take Main Street toward the river. At the traffic light at the bottom of the street drive up the ramp. Once at the top turn left, cross the bridge over the tracks, and turn left down the ramp on the other side. Follow signs to Pierson Park [41.081066N 73.868098W].

PUBLIC TRANSPORTATION: Metro-North Hudson Line Tarrytown Station

For contact information, see Appendix, Tarrytown.

RiverWalk - South of Tarrytown

Tarrytown • 0.8 mile

More than river views await walkers along the segment of RiverWalk south of Tarrytown which links a neighborhood to Lyndhurst and the Old Croton Aqueduct. The paved path has interpretive signs, overlooks, and an 80 foot bridge over a gorge. In Lyndhurst, reproductions of antique street lamps line the path as they did once years ago. The project was a joint effort of the county, Metro North, Lyndhurst, Kraft Foods, and Village of Tarrytown, who manages the site.

From the end of Van Wert Avenue, the paved path heads downhill only to go uphill onto the bluff. The path parallels the river high above the Metro North railroad tracks. At 0.3 mile, it crosses a gorge over a stream on a bridge and enters Lyndhurst, where it passes the bowling alley. It reaches parking at 0.8 miles and heads uphill along the road where it ends at the Old Croton Aqueduct.

DRIVING: From Route 9, just south of the bridge over I-287, turn west onto Paulding Avenue. Almost immediately turn left onto Van Wert Avenue and drive to the end [41.064316N 73.867474W]. About 0.7 miles further south on Route 9, turn left at Lyndhurst Museum Lane to parking near the carriage house at Lyndhurst [41.052773N 73.867126W].

PUBLIC TRANSPORTATION: Beeline Bus #1W on Route 9 to Main Street and follow the driving directions above.

For contact information, see Appendix, Village of Tarrytown.

Lyndhurst.

Scenic Hudson Park

Irvington • 0.6 mile, 17.5 acres

S ituated directly on the Hudson River, Scenic Hudson Park is the result of a larger waterfront revitalization project in Irvington. The site was originally part of the Dearman Farm. In 1849 with the arrival of railroads along the Hudson River, small industries flourished. Lumberyards occupied the property beginning in 1853. From 1890 to 1940, parts of the river were filled to accommodate the need for additional land. Scenic Hudson Land Trust saved this land from proposed residential development. Through a partnership of Scenic Hudson Land Trust, the Village of Irvington, Westchester County, and New York State, 12 acres of contaminated land were restored and the park was created. The trail is handicapped accessible with benches for enjoying views of the Palisades, Hudson River, Manhattan skyline, and Tappan Zee Bridge.

DRIVING: From Route 9, take Main Street downhill to the river. Turn right onto North Astor Street and then left to cross the tracks. Turn left to reach the park [41.037956N 73.874045W].

PUBLIC TRANSPORTATION: Metro-North Hudson Line Irvington Station; Beeline Bus #1W on Route 9 to Main Street and follow the driving directions above.

For contact information, see Appendix, Irvington.

Ardsley Waterfront

Ardsley-on-Hudson • 0.6 mile, 8.6 acres

A n unmarked route leads from Metro-North Hudson Line's Ardsley-on-Hudson Station to riverfront access at the end of Landing Drive at The Landing condominiums. From the station, head south and uphill. A paved path to the right leads to Mercy College. Cross the basketball courts and parking lot and walk toward and through the athletic field. Take the stairs near the southeast corner and turn right.and turn right at the emergency access gate at 0.3 mile and head downhill, bearing right at all intersections. At the end of Club House Drive, turn right onto the bridge over the tracks. At the bottom of the steps on the river side is access to the river where a seawall extends along a phragmite marsh. There are views to the Tappan Zee Bridge, the George Washington Bridge, and the Palisades.

DRIVING: From Route 9, follow signs to the Ardsley-on-Hudson Station and take West Ardsley Avenue toward the river. On weekends and holidays, parking is permitted without a permit. Parking for six hours or less is possible uphill from the station, in a lot near tennis courts [41.026740N 73.876318W].

PUBLIC TRANSPORTATION: Metro-North Hudson Line Ardsley Station

For contact information, see Appendix, Dobbs Ferry.

Rowley's Bridge Trail

Hastings-on-Hudson • 0.5 mile

T ucked between railroad tracks and a busy road in Hastings, Rowley's Bridge Trail and the Hubbard Trail Extension use an area heavily overgrown with invasives. The 100-foot stone arch masonry bridge designed in 1892 was named for gentlemen farmers who, in 1846, settled in the Pinecrest area of Hastings.

Beginning at the parking area, the Rowley's Bridge Trail heads south, passing a garden and two views of the Palisades. The wood chip trail reaches a bench at a second viewpoint. At a Y junction, go left to cross Rowley's Brook and continue uphill, reaching Rowley's Bridge at 0.3 mile. To the right is the Hubbard Trail Extension, at 0.1 mile going uphill steeply on steps, and then becoming considerably steeper. The deep side cuts accommodate the trail. At 0.2 mile, the trail reaches Warburton Avenue (no parking). To reach the Old Croton Aqueduct, head up the stone steps or take the Graham School service road.

DRIVING: From Route 9, follow signs to the Hastings Station. Head south for 0.8 mile along Southside Avenue. A parking area for four cars is just beyond the closed Zinsser Bridge [40.985832N 73.884816W].

PUBLIC TRANSPORTATION: Metro-North Hudson Line Hastings Station; Beeline Bus #1 along Warburton Avenue

For contact information, see Appendix, Hastings.

View of the Palisades.

Yonkers North Hudson Promenade

Yonkers • 0.4 mile

Beginning at Hudson Fulton Park with a statue dedicated to both Henry Hudson and Robert Fulton, the Yonkers North Hudson Promenade heads south along Warburton Avenue to Otis Park. There are sweeping views across to the Palisades and two places to sit and enjoy them. Steps lead from Hudson Fulton Park down to the Metro-North Hudson Line Greystone Station.

DRIVING: From Route 9, just north of Untermyer Park, take Odell Avenue down to Warburton Avenue. Turn left. Hudson Fulton Park is directly across the street [40.971413N 73.888568W].

PUBLIC TRANSPORTATION: Metro-North Hudson Line Graystone Station; Beeline Bus #1 along Warburton Avenue

For contact information, see Appendix, Yonkers.

Along the Sound

New Rochelle to Rye • 7.9 miles

The numerous parks that dot the ragged shoreline of Long Island Sound are a lure to walkers seeking the solitude of a walk along the beach, perhaps to watch the ebb and flow of the tide or listen to the waves lap upon the shore. This is especially tempting in the cooler weather, when the crowds that fill the beaches in summer have vanished. Where there are restrictions on who can use the parks, it is so noted as well when those restrictions apply.

Hudson Park in New Rochelle has commanding views over the harbor from the grassy areas above the beach. It was established in 1886 at the site where Huguenot settlers first landed in 1688. Bronze tablets on a large granite boulder commemorate the event and list the names of the original settlers. A New Rochelle OMNICARD is required year round [40.908154N 73.768011W]. Away from the sands, the 13-acre Premium Marsh Conservation Area in Larchmont is squeezed in among houses, but has a 0.1 mile trail to the edge of the salt marsh [40.919926N 73.761015W]. Marshlands Conservancy and Edith G. Read Sanctuary are covered in chapters in Morning Strolls.

Pelham Manor Shore Park

Pelham Manor 0.4 mile, 11 acres

Very close to and almost in the Bronx, Pelham Manor Shore Park overlooks Long Island Sound. Its vast expanse of grass has a 0.4-mile path around its edge. Shore Road southbound has a bike lane, which becomes a bike path to Pelham Bay Park in the Bronx. The park is for Pelham Manor residents and a pass is required. DRIVING: From I-95, take Exit 15 and head south on Route 1. Turn left onto Pelhamdale Avenue (the first major crossroad) and follow it to Shore Road. Turn right onto Shore Road and then left into the park, just past the entrance to the New York Athletic Club [40.885165N 73.791778W].

PUBLIC TRANSPORTATION: Beeline Bus #45 along Shore Road

For contact information, see Appendix, Pelham Manor.

Glen Island Park

New Rochelle • 1.7 miles, 105 acres

Highly developed and county-owned, Glen Island Park attracts multitudes of visitors to its beach and picnic areas in summer, but during off-season months, walkers, cyclists, and in-line skaters come for the fresh air and sunshine. A walk around the perimeter of the park, primarily on the seawall, is 1.7 miles long. Part of the route is handicapped accessible. In season, a Westchester County Parks Pass is required. There is an extra charge for beach use.

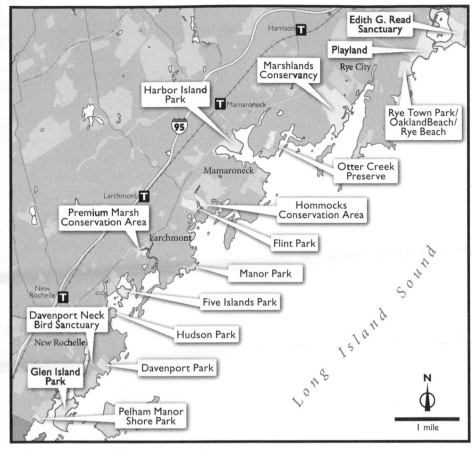

The park is on the site of a former amusement park operated by John H. Starin from 1881-1906. It was located on a cluster of five islands, each of which had a cultural theme. Castles, reminiscent of Germany's Rhineland, were constructed for the park's beer garden. The castles remain, but the five islands have become one with the addition of fill. A drawbridge to the park was built in 1929 after the park had been open for two years.

DRIVING: From I-95, take Exit 15 and turn north onto Route 1 (Boston Post Road). Turn right onto Weyman Avenue and follow it to the park [40.888643N 73.782104W].

PUBLIC TRANSPORTATION: Beeline Bus #45 along Pelham Road

For contact information, see Appendix, Westchester County Parks—Glen Island Park.

Davenport Park and Davenport Neck Sanctuary

New Rochelle • 0.5 mile and 0.2 mile, 20 acres and 2.4 acres

The sweeping view of Long Island Sound from Davenport Park is a good incentive to walk out to the shore. However, the sea wall protecting the grassy area from erosion prevents easy access to the water.

Located across the street from and south of the entrance to Davenport Park, Davenport Neck Bird Sanctuary offers a different view. A short trail through the woods loops around the property with a view out over New Rochelle Creek. Bring binoculars for better viewing of the more than 50 bird species observed there.

DRIVING: Take I-95 to Exit 15 and turn north onto Route 1 (Boston Post Road). Go 0.2 mile, turn right onto Weyman Avenue, and continue 0.7 mile. Turn left onto Pelham Road. Continue for 1.0 mile and turn right at Church Street, which becomes Davenport Avenue. Follow Davenport Avenue, turning right at a traffic light. It is 0.2 mile to the park on the left. A New Rochelle OMNICARD is required year round [40.896459N 73.773026W].

PUBLIC TRANSPORTATION: Beeline Bus #45 along Pelham Road

For contact information, see Appendix, New Rochelle.

Five Islands Park

New Rochelle • 0.6 mile, 18 acres

Connected by fill to the mainland, Oakwood Island is the largest island of Five Islands Park. Bridges connect Oakwood Island to Big and Little Harrison islands. The park has many amenities, but the paths along the shore are of the most interest with several short paths leading right to the water.

DRIVING: Take I-95 to Exit 15 and turn north onto Route 1 (Boston Post Road). It is 1.8 miles to the corner of Lefevres Lane. Look for Salesian High School on the northeast corner, a better landmark than the small park sign. Follow Lefevres Lane past the sewage treatment plant where the road ends in the park. A New Rochelle OMNICARD is required year-round [40.912570N 73.766111W].

PUBLIC TRANSPORTATION: Beeline Bus #60 along Boston Post Road

For contact information, see Appendix, New Rochelle.

GROUNDS FOR A PARK

Flint Park was a little slow in taking shape. It began in 1915 with Helena Flint's donation of 27 acres of mostly marshland to the Village of Larchmont. Garbage was dumped there as fill and the park grew as the landfill advanced. A report from 1928 reveals a call to speed up the process because the marsh was a "breeding spot for malaria."

During the Depression, WPA projects added tennis courts, clubhouse, a baseball field, and playground. A garbage incinerator had been installed and its ash was used as fill. With complaints about its smokestack marring the view of Long Island Sound, a faux windmill was build around it. But the smokestack was too tall and the façade too short. A false roof was added, described as being in the shape of a German trench helmet, but that, unfortunately, gave the whole assembly a phallic appearance, fostering even greater complaints. Eventually, the incinerator was razed and the entire site converted to parkland.

Sunday in Manor Park.

Larchmont Manor Park

Larchmont • 0.5 mile, 16 acres

Surrounded by stately Victorian houses originally built as summer homes and estates for the wealthy of New York City, Larchmont Manor Park has views over Long Island Sound. In 1892, residents established Larchmont Manor Park Society to maintain and protect the park, which is open to the public. A narrow paved path meanders along the shoreline. Portions of the path are handicapped accessible.

DRIVING: From Route 1 (Boston Post Road) in Larchmont, head towards Long Island Sound on either Beach or Larchmont avenues; both roads dead end at the park. Parking is available on some streets, but not on weekends or legal holidays [40.918109N 73.747089W].

PUBLIC TRANSPORTATION: None available

For contact information, see Appendix, Larchmont Manor Park Society.

Flint Park
Hommocks Conservation Area

Larchmont • 0.2 mile, 27 acres,
Mamaroneck 0.3 mile, 10.6 acres

Of special interest at Flint Park is the Waterfront Nature Trail which runs along the shore. There are several benches set along the way and a platform offers scenic views over a marsh and Little Harbor Sound, where the remnants of old docks can be seen at low tide. The park, a former landfill and incinerator site, has paved paths around the ball fields which are handicapped accessible.

Hommocks Conservation Area is adjacent to Flint Park with a small trail system through meadows, woodlands, and salt marsh. The area was named by sailors of an earlier age who would sight the hillocks along the marshy shore. Salt grasses here were once harvested to thatch roofs, feed livestock, and fill mattresses. Ralph Burger donated 3.5 acres of his property adjacent to existing municipal land to shape the Hommocks Conservation Area to its present dimensions because his wife's ardent interest in conservation. He had been president of A&P in the 1950's and 60s, when the company was the largest food chain in the country.

The trail at the preserve starts at a fence at Hommocks Middle School's ball field. From the parking lot, a side trail leads to a bird observation deck with a view over the marsh and to adjacent Flint Park. One can also walk out to the shore.

DRIVING: *Flint Park*: From the junction of Route 1 (Boston Post Road) and Bronson Avenue, turn east towards the sound. Go two blocks, turn left onto Locust Avenue, and continue into Flint Park [40.932744N 73.745570W].

Hommocks Conservation Area: From the junction of Route 1 (Boston Post Road) and Route 125 (Weaver Street) in Mamaroneck, head towards Hommocks Middle School on Hommocks Road. The parking lot is on the right side of Hommocks Road across from #510 [40.933390N 73.742233W].

PUBLIC TRANSPORTATION: None available

For contact information, see Appendix, Larchmont Mamaroneck (Town).

Harbor Island Park

Mamaroneck • 1.1 miles, 44.5 acres

Jutting out into Mamaroneck Harbor, Harbor Island Park offers a choice to walk either on an expanse of grass or on a seawall. A paved path goes along one section of the harbor and a well-trod path with swinging benches is along another. There is no access through the beach during the summer. Dogs are permitted only between December 1 and April 1.

DRIVING: From northbound I-95, take Exit 18A and turn right onto Fennimore Road. Go 0.6 mile to Route 1 (Boston Post Road) and turn left. The park entrance is on the right. There is a parking fee when the beach is open.

From southbound I-95, take Exit 18A (Mamaroneck Avenue) and turn right onto Mamaroneck Avenue heading toward Long Island Sound and Route 1 (Boston Post Road). Harbor Island Park is at the intersection of Mamaroneck Avenue and Boston Post Road [40.947188N 73.733084W].

PUBLIC TRANSPORTATION: Metro-North New Haven Line Mamaroneck Station. Walk along Mamaroneck Avenue through the business district. Beeline Bus #60 on Palmer Avenue.

For contact information, see Appendix, Mamaroneck (Town).

Out for a stroll, Harbor Island Park.

Otter Creek Preserve

Mamaroneck • 0.6 mile, 27 acres

Bring your binoculars to Otter Creek Preserve for this jewel is teeming with wildlife along its short loop trail through a tidal creek, marsh, and upland woodlands. In addition to providing habitat for migratory birds, this tidal marsh stabilizes the shoreline and filters pollutants from water entering Long Island Sound. More than 100 species of birds, as well as abundant land and marine life, make this region their home. The preserve is owned and managed by The Nature Conservancy. Like many places in the area, it suffered significant damage from Hurricane Sandy in 2012.

DRIVING: From northbound I-95, take Exit 18A (Fenimore Road). Turn right and head 0.6 mile to Route 1 (Boston Post Road). Turn left, go 1.1 miles, and turn right onto Taylors Lane. *Follow the road for 0.4 mile until the Private Entrance sign. Park on the right hand side of the road and walk approximately 300 feet to the preserve entrance. From southbound I-95, take Exit 18A (Mamaroneck Avenue) and head toward the Mamaroneck Station. Continue past the station to Route 1(Boston Post Road). Turn left to head north on Route 1 for 0.8 mile and turn right onto Taylor Lane. Follow the directions from * above [40.943893N 73.719330W].

PUBLIC TRANSPORTATION: None available

For contact information, see Appendix, The Nature Conservancy.

Marshlands Conservancy *See Morning Strolls.*

Playland, Rye Town Park, Oakland Beach/Rye Beach

Rye • 0.7 and 0.3 mile, 121 and 36 acres

When the crowds leave Playland at the end of the season, the boardwalk is nearly empty and beckons to those who love to walk close to the shore or along the boardwalk. Water lapping the beach helps reinforce a sense of serenity in the area. With the change of seasons, walkers reclaim the grounds to enjoy the outdoors amid the art deco architecture. Playland is one of the few government-owned and operated amusement parks in the country. It became a National Historic Landmark in 1987. The walk on the boardwalk is short but combined with the stretches in Rye Beach, Rye Town Park, and Oakland Beach, offers some good exercise. Again, walks here are best done in the off-season or early in the morning during summer months. Binoculars are a must during bird migrations.

DRIVING: From I-95 take Exit 19 (Playland Parkway). Follow the parkway directly into the park and around the traffic circle. A parking fee is charged from May through October [40.965218N 73.675715W]. For Rye Town Park, [40.965218N 73.675715W].

PUBLIC TRANSPORTATION: Three seasonal Beeline Buses stop at the bus terminal: #75-Rye Railroad Station; #76-Portchester, Rye runs on a commuter schedule; #91-New Rochelle, Mt. Vernon, Yonkers; #92-White Plains Express.

For contact information, see Appendix, Westchester County Parks—Playland.

Edith G. Read Sanctuary *See Morning Strolls.*

Along the boardwalk at Playland.

Briarcliff Peekskill Trailway

Ossining to Peekskill • 13.5 miles, 206 acres

The Briarcliff Peekskill Trailway wends through forest and wetland, under power lines, and past backyards on a route that was purchased in 1929 as part of a plan to become a parkway connecting Briarcliff Manor with Peekskill. Only the section of the proposed parkway between Briarcliff and the Armory on Route 9A in Ossining was ever built. The rest of the route became a footpath officially designated a trailway in 1977. County publications indicate that the trailway ends at Watch Hill Road, but on the ground the green blazes continue to the main parking lot in Blue Mountain Reservation.

THE TRAILWAY

Hikers are encouraged to stay on the trail at all times because Briarcliff Peekskill Trailway is always close to private property. Even as it goes through deep woods, the trail borders homes when it crosses paved roads. Because the trailway is a linear footpath, hikers must retrace their steps, leave a car where they will end their hike, or rely on public transportation. Because the trailway either connects to or is near five parks, circuit hikes are possible. Trail descriptions are arranged in segments dictated primarily by major road crossings or access to parking.

Ryder Road to Spring Valley Road　　　　　　*Length: 2.8 miles Blaze: green*
The section starts from Ryder Road on the east side of the overpass over Route 9A where there is limited parking. This trail section is lightly used and was heavily damaged by Hurricane Sandy in 2012. It proceeds north on the edge of a grassy strip at the edge of the woods until it enters the woods and turns away from the noise of Route 9A in the first half-mile.

A stream runs to the west of the trail between the trailway and Route 9A. At 0.5 mile, the trail crosses the stream, goes through a stone wall, and heads away from Route 9A. At 1.1 miles, the trail crosses Grace Lane and passes a kennel with a chorus of barking dogs. After heading slightly uphill, the trail runs parallel to a stone wall to reach Route 134 at 1.8 miles. It now crosses a succession of streams and, at 2.0 miles, goes by a massive moss-covered rock face to the left. The trail follows a woods road. At 2.4 miles to the right is the Waterfall Trail (pink) which leads 0.3 mile to the Back Forty Trail at Teatown Lake Reservation. The trailway passes wetlands and reenters the woods. It reaches Spring Valley Road at 2.8 miles and turns left to cross the road.

Spring Valley Road to Croton Dam　　　　　　*Length: 3.2 miles Blaze: green*
Beginning at Spring Valley Road, the Briarcliff Peekskill Trailway enters Teatown Lake Reservation and joins the Lakeside Trail (blue). A boardwalk to the right heads along Teatown Lake and back to parking at the Nature Center. At 0.3 mile, the trail leaves the Lakeside Trail and begins a short climb toward the power line. The

trail crosses under power lines twice and at 0.7 mile, heads steeply downhill.

The trail runs north along a generally straight woods road through laurel and hemlock. The Cliffdale-Teatown Trail (white) joins from the right and leaves to the left. The Briarcliff Peekskill Trailway now follows the west edge of Griffin Swamp sometimes on boardwalks. At the north end of the swamp, the the Teatown Kitchawan Trail (purple) joins from the right. At 1.0 mile, the co-aligned trails jog left along a stone wall to leave Teatown Reservation.

The co-aligned trails cross Blinn Road at 1.4 miles. The Teatown-Kitchawan Trail turns right and the Briarcliff Peekskill Trail goes left, goes through a stone wall, and follows a brook. It reaches a Y junction at 1.6 miles and turns right. At the next trail junction, it turns left and at 2.0 miles, enters a wetland. When it reaches the intersection of Croton Lake and Croton Dam roads, the trailway heads straight across and follows Croton Dam Road to the Croton Dam. (open only to pedestrians and bicycles

New Croton Dam to Watch Hill Road

Length: 4.7miles Blaze: green

The trail crosses the New Croton Dam which has sweeping views. Below the dam is the picnic area of Croton Gorge Park. Just past the lip of the dam, water tumbles over the steps of the spillway and flows through an impressive gorge leading to the Hudson River.

In winter, when the reservoir freezes, bald eagles have been seen out on the ice, sometimes feasting on a kill. From the dam, the Briarcliff Peekskill Trailway heads along the access road. At 0.4 mile it turns right into the woods to head steeply uphill. The trail rounds the end of the knob

Spillway.

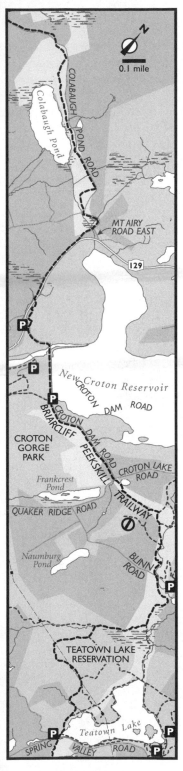

and parallels Route 129. It exits the woods to cross Route 129 at 0.6 mile and turns right. Use caution walking along this busy road.

At 0.9 mile, the trailway reaches Mt. Airy Road East, follows it to a junction with Colabaugh Pond Road at 1.0 mile, and reenters the woods. The trailway parallels the road and, at 1.3 miles, enters wetlands adjacent to Colabaugh Pond. The trailway crosses the inlet of the pond at 1.9 miles and is once again on a woods road. It turns left at 2.1 miles and follows Colabaugh Pond Road. It turns right at 2.3 miles and enters the woods on a woods road between stone walls (parking for one car).

After crossing a stream, the trail heads uphill where at the top, on days when the Sportsman Center is open, you may hear the sound of gun fire. At this point, the shooting range is more than 2 miles away. At 2.7 miles, the park buildings of Charles Cook Park can be seen to the left and, in summer, the laughter of children enjoying a swim can be heard. The trailway crosses Furnace Dock Road at 3.1 miles and heads along a woods road. It reaches a 0.1-mile footbridge over wetland at 3.4 miles. The trail turns right at 3.7 miles and works its way uphill to end at a large parking area on Watch Hill Road.

Watch Hill Road through Blue Mountain Reservation   *Length: 2.9 miles Blaze: green*

From the parking area on Watch Hill Road, the trailway crosses the road and heads along the entrance road to the Sportsman Center. It crosses the parking lot to the northwest corner where, at 0.4 mile, the trail enters the woods and ascends steeply along a wide woods road. It passes to the left, at 0.8 mile, the trail to Mt. Spitzenberg, with a short steep climb to the top and views of the Hudson Valley. After crossing wetlands on a built-up treadway, it passes the end of the white trail at 1.3 miles and turns right. At 1.8 miles the trail crosses former Montrose Station Road, reaches the gas pipeline, and turns left heading uphill. It reenters the woods and heads gradually downhill on a woods road. At the junction with the blue and red trails at 2.1 miles, the trail turns left. At 2.4

miles, it turns right, continues to follow the blue trail, and turns right again co-aligned with the white trail as together they head downhill. After going through a grove of hemlocks devastated by the wooly adelgid infestation, the Briarcliff Peekskill Trailway passes an orange/yellow trail at 2.8 miles and then the yellow trail as it ends at Blue Mountain Reservation's parking lot #3 (main parking lot).

CONNECTING PARKS AND TRAILS: Teatown Lake Reservation, Teatown-Kitchawan Trail, John E. Hand Park, Old Croton Aqueduct, Blue Mountain Reservation

DRIVING: There are many access points to the trailway, but not all road crossings have parking. Parking is available at the following locations:

Ryder Road [41.171930N 73.839594W];
Spring Valley Road [41.208014N 73.835422W];
Teatown Lake Reservation (use the Lakeside, Northwest, or Cliffdale-Teatown trails)
John E. Hand Park [41.220597N 73.835926W];
Croton Dam - south end [41.225109N 73.854215W];
Croton Dam - north end [41.228145N 73.860308W];
Colobaugh Pond Road [41.243045N 73.879261W];
Watch Hill Road [41.254911N 73.897429W];
Sportsman's Center (gated at times) [41.257073N 73.900724W];
Blue Mountain Reservation (seasonal fee) [41.270035N 73.921681W].

PUBLIC TRANSPORTATION: Metro-North Hudson Line Ossining Station (taxi to Rider Road); Croton-Harmon Station (taxi to Croton Gorge Park); Peekskill (taxi to entrance of Blue Mountain Reservation)

For contact information see Appendix, Westchester County Parks.

Bronx River Reservation

Valhalla to Mount Vernon • 12.3 miles, 807 acres

In a green swath that entwines a high-speed roadway, a rail line, and a river the Bronx River Pathway is never far from any of the three. While the parkway may conjure up images of cars hurtling by, the pathway draws its own traffic in walkers, joggers, and cyclists or people simply enjoying the outdoors seated on a bench in a somewhat urban area. Except for a 1.1- mile piece north of Hartsdale, the pathway is paved for its entire length and many sections are handicapped accessible. Completed in 1925, the Bronx River Reservation is one of the first of Westchester County's parks, helping to lay the groundwork for an impressive park system that continues to grow. The Friends of Westchester Parks has prepared an audio tour of the pathway, which provides information on history, flora, and fauna. It may be accessed at www.friendsofwestchesterparks.org or by dialing (914) 517-5575. Signs along the route indicate the number indexed to the audio available.

THE PATHWAY

There are three distinct paved segments of the Bronx River Pathway. They can be savored in small or large bites, given the proximity of the Metro-North Harlem Line stations every few miles. Safety improvements to the parkway in Scarsdale in 1967 resulted in the removal of a two-mile section. Adjacent local streets now serve as access to the portions along the parkway and are included in the total mileage. Metro North between Hartsdale and Scarsdale can be used to bypass this section. Except at Kensico Dam Plaza, little parking is available and using public transportation is recommended.

At the start, the pathway is a wide asphalt path, but later narrows to four or five feet in places. After White Plains, there are short, steep bluffs, sudden turns, and unpaved sections unsuitable for cyclists who prefer riding on paved surfaces. Inexperienced cyclists may find significant challenges because of poor surface conditions, a twisting route, and sharp climbs and descents.

Valhalla to Scarsdale (Greenacres Avenue) *Length: 5.3 miles*

The north end of the Bronx River Pathway is at the 97-acre Kensico Dam Plaza. Wide stretches of lawn, shaded walkways and expansive parking areas sit at the base of this massive dam, whose stone was quarried in what is now Cranberry Lake Preserve.

The trail begins on the east side of the near the steps leading to the top of the dam and by The Rising, a memorial to Westchester County residents who were killed in the terrorist attacks on the World Trade Center on September 11, 2001.

At the entrance to the plaza, it crosses the access road to Route 22 and turns left to parallel it. After going beneath an overpass, the pathway turns right, passes ball fields, and crosses Washington Avenue North. The pathway goes over the Metro-North railroad tracks on a viaduct which was designed to look like a suspension

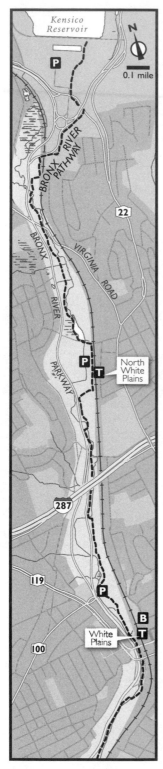

The Bronx River Parkway, the roadway portion of the Bronx River Reservation, is the first limited access motor parkway to be built in the country: it introduced the concept of entrance and exit ramps, extensive landscaping, green medians, and limits on commercial traffic.

The idea of the parkway grew from pollution and flood control project along the Bronx River conceived in the 1890s. The river had served as a dumping ground and periodic flooding exacerbated the unsanitary conditions. Over the years, the original winding route has been straightened in some places to accommodate heavier commuter traffic.

Westchester County owns and operates the Bronx River Reservation, the only parkway in Westchester not owned and managed by the East Hudson Parkway Authority. For more history, see www.westchestergov.com/wcarchives/

bridge. The plaques in the brickwork give details of the construction of the parkway and its dedication at this site in 1925.

The pathway turns left and enters a wooded section between the river and the railroad. It crosses Virginia Road at 1.0 mile and then Parkway Homes Road, which leads to the Metro-North rail yards. Paralleling the Bronx River, the path crosses Fisher Lane at 1.6 mile. Turn left and head toward the railroad underpass, passing the parking lot entrance to Metro-North Harlem Line North White Plains Station. Just past the parking lot entrance, turn right and follow the pavement between the guardrail and the railroad embankment. Pass the two accesses to the platforms and turn right to cross the road leading to additional parking at 2.0 miles.

After leaving the parking area, the paved path goes through park-like meadows while paralleling the parkway and then heads into the woods. It crosses the Bronx River, more like a stream at this point and then crosses Old Tarrytown Road at 2.3 miles. The pathway goes under the I-287 bridges, passes a gas pipeline transmission station and crosses another foot bridge over the river. After crossing an exit road from the parking lot of the Westchester County Center, it reaches the parking lot and crosses its access road.

It follows a meandering paved path along the perimeter of the parking lot. After passing a brick building to the left, the pathway turns right at 3.2 miles. A 1913 pedestrian tunnel which leads to the Metro North White Plains Station and Transportation Center is visible to the left.

The pathway crosses a footbridge over a tributary of the Bronx River and closely parallels the river, passing under three bridges. After the third bridge, another path enters from the left. At 3.6 miles, the pathway crosses a bridge over the river. From here to Greenacres Avenue in Scarsdale, the pathway, river, railroad tracks, and parkway twist like the strands of a rope crossing each other sometimes closely and at other times out of sight of each other.

Looming overhead at 4.1 miles are the massive arches of the Woodlands Viaduct which carry the parkway across the valley, the river, the pathway, and the railroad. About 100 feet beyond the viaduct, the pathway makes a sharp left to cross the river on a footbridge. It immediately goes under the railroad and turns right to wedge between the parkway and the river. At 4.6 miles, the pathway passes through an extremely low arch of a bridge under the parkway, then heads uphill through the woods onto a bluff above the river.

The path ascends and descends frequently as it traverses the most natural setting in all the sections. It is often narrow and gravel, although there are some paved sections. After passing a small dam at 5.1 miles, the river curves back under the highway as the pathway turns away from it. Following a narrow path along a fence behind the private County Tennis Club of Westchester, the pathway passes a small pond constructed for the Haubold Gunpowder Mill in the 1840s.

When the pathway reaches Greenacres Avenue at 5.3 miles, walkers who wish to follow the road should cross Greenacres Avenue onto Fountain Terrace. Cyclists may prefer to turn right onto Greenacres Avenue, go past the Hartsdale Station, and then up a short hill to connect with Fenimore Avenue (no parking). To reach the Hartsdale Station, turn right onto Greenacres Avenue and cross the bridge over the parkway. Metered parking is for permit holders, but free on Sundays.

BICYCLE SUNDAY

Every Sunday from 10am to 2pm in May, June, and September, the Bronx River Parkway is closed to motorized traffic. Although motorist groups originally were critical of this event when it began in 1974, it has become a popular tradition. Originally limited to cyclists and skaters, the program was expanded to include walkers and joggers in 2008. Rain cancels the event.

Scarsdale (Greenacres Avenue to Scarsdale Station)

Length: 1.8 miles

A walk through residential areas along quiet streets connects the two off-road sections. With

The bridge is just ahead.

numerous shops near the train station, there are plenty of places to stop. Directly across the street from the end of the pathway at Greenacres Avenue is Fountain Terrace (a private road). Walk up the road passing the remains of a formal garden, once part of the Bronx River Reservation. Take the steps up to Fenimore Road and turn left. Use the pedestrian crosswalks to cross over and then go south on Fox Meadow Road. While walking along this residential street, notice the variety of architecture. At 0.8 mile, pass Butler Woods with a 0.2 mile loop trail. It was once part of a 500-acre tract known as Fox Meadow Estate. Emily Butler donated 25 acres to the Parkway Commission in 1913 and later added 7.5 acres. Continue south on Fox Meadow Road to reach Crane Road at 1.6 miles; cross it and turn right heading towards the parkway. Watch for turning cars because this intersection is next to an exit/entrance ramp. Turn left onto East Parkway, go through the parking area, and head towards the Scarsdale Station.

Scarsdale Station to Bronxville   *Length: 4.5 miles*
The paved pathway from the Scarsdale Station into Bronxville is mostly flat, wide, and anything but straight. From Harney Road, the path crosses the Bronx River numerous times and is frequently sandwiched between the railroad and the parkway. Residents of the many adjacent apartment buildings use this section to walk or just sit on benches reading and enjoying fresh air. Many road crossings are exit and entrance ramps

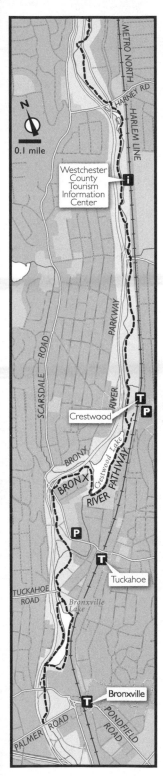

of the parkway. Use caution and do not assume that traffic will stop if you are in a crosswalk.

At the Scarsdale Station, cross to the southbound tracks. The pathway resumes just west and across the parking area of the building. The pathway gracefully curves down to a bridge over the Bronx River just below Scarsdale Falls. It runs along the river, paralleling the northbound parkway, and enters Garth Woods, named for David Garth whose estate donated the land to the Parkway Commission in 1915. At 0.4 mile, the pathway turns left to cross the river on a rustic bentwood bridge. Wiggling its way through large trees, the pathway heads under the parkway, just inches from the water in the Bronx River. It is necessary to duck because the girders are slightly more than five feet above the path. The pathway crosses a truss bridge onto an island in the river and then leaves the island on another bridge. This wide wooded section is between the north and southbound lanes of the parkway. At 0.9 mile, the pathway turns left to cross the northbound parkway and then turns right to cross Harney Road. It heads across a large open area, passes a pond to the right, and then re-crosses the river. At 1.2 miles, a former gas station, now a Westchester County Tourist Information Center, is open on weekends in July and August.

The pathway crosses the river again and, at 1.5 miles, crosses Leewood Drive. Staying within view of the parkway, the pathway turns right at 2.1 miles onto a service road leading to the central facilities of Westchester County Department of Parks, Recreation and Conservation. Following the service road, the pathway crosses Thompson Avenue, the access road to the Crestwood Station. Continuing to meander along the river, the pathway reaches Crestwood Lake. Passing ball fields at Malcolm Wilson Park at 2.7 miles, it reaches the dam at the south end of the lake. Here it turns around the end of the lake to head towards the parkway. The pathway crosses Exit 16 and reaches a cul-de-sac. At 3.1 miles, it crosses Scarsdale Road. Use caution during the next 0.5 mile because the pathway crosses three roads including Tuckahoe Road, a main thoroughfare. The pathway splits at 3.7 miles with paths along both sides of Bronxville Lake, with the left-side further from traffic noise. The two trails meet at a T intersection at the south end of the lake. Turn left to continue south. After a short distance, the trail splits again. Follow the left fork, which passes the foundation of the Swian's Mill (on the opposite bank of the river) continue to crossing at Pondfield Road. The pathway ends at 4.5 miles at Palmer Avenue behind Lawrence Hospital. To reach the Metro-North Station Harlem Line Bronxville Station, turn left. There are places to eat near the train station.

Mount Vernon (Oak Street Path)   *Length: 0.6 mile*

Separated from the longer off-road sections, the Oak Street Path is tucked between the parkway, the Bronx River, and Metro-North tracks. The pathway heads north for 0.1 mile, turns away from the parkway, and crosses the river. It immediately turns again to head north between the river and the railroad. At 0.4 mile it splits, then, reconnects in an open area just before a Cross County Parkway exit ramp and near the access road to Metro-North tracks.

CONNECTING PARK: Kenisco Dam Plaza

DRIVING: For the Valhalla to Hartsdale section, take the Bronx River Parkway to Kenisco Dam Plaza. There is parking at

Kenisco Dam Plaza [41.071911N 73.768732W];

Metro-North Harlem Line North White Plains Station (free on weekends) [41.053234N 73.772428W];

County Center [41.037062N 73.776959W],

Crestwood Station [40.959305N 73.821418W],

Tuckahoe Station [40.952021N 73.830546W].

No parking is available in Hartsdale and in Scarsdale only on Sundays.

For the section in Mount Vernon, from the northbound Bronx River Parkway, take Exit 10A and turn left on Yonkers Avenue. Cross over the parkway, turn right on Bronx River Road, and then turn right on Oak Street.** The easily missed entrance to the pathway is by the guardrail at the northbound entrance ramp. From the south parkway, take Exit 10B and turn on right on Bronx River Road. Go 0.2 mile, turn left onto Oak Street and follow the directions from the **.

PUBLIC TRANSPORTATION: Metro-North Harlem Line stations at Valhalla, North White Plains, White Plains, Hartsdale, Scarsdale, Bronxville, and Mount Vernon West. To reach the Kensico Dam Plaza from the Valhalla Station walk to the old station (currently a restaurant). Cross the Taconic State Parkway at the traffic light, turn right onto Broadway, and continue until you reach a church. Just beyond the church parking lot, take the faint path heading off to the left through the woods to the plaza.

For contact information, see Appendix, Westchester County Parks.

Hutchinson River Pathway

White Plains to Mount Vernon • 12.9 miles, 717 acres

Commuters speeding south toward the Bronx on the Hutchinson River Parkway might not realize a trail parallels the parkway. In 1924, the Westchester County Parks Commission recommended construction of a parkway in southern Westchester, which would also be a park while acting as a buffer to protect water sources. Construction began the same year and in December 1927, a two-mile section in Pelham was complete. By October 1928, the 11-miles between Route 1 in Pelham and Westchester Avenue in White Plains serving mostly local traffic was finished. Complying with design standards of the era, the parkway's four 9-foot-wide travel lanes were designed for speeds up to 40 mph; it did not have shoulders, median separators, or acceleration-deceleration lanes. The $12 million cost of the 11 miles of parkway included establishing a bridle path along the right-of-way and a riding academy where the public could hire horses.

Over the years, sections of the Hutch, as it is nicknamed, have been upgraded, but not without local opposition. The parkway has been made safer, but, in the process, some trails and pathways were moved or eliminated.

THE PATHWAY

Most of the Hutchinson River Pathway is never far from the steady whine of traffic. But there are short buffered sections where the trail is a pleasant place to walk and houses are not visible. Overall, it's best to bring either an MP3 player or earplugs on this trail, originally designed for equestrians. The description of the pathway is divided into sections based on where parking is available. Nearby residents have access to the trail at numerous road crossings or directly from their property.

The pathway is only occasionally blazed. When co-aligned with the Colonial Greenway on county property, it has a painted blue blaze with a star. The last 3.2 miles of the pathway are along streets; in some publications, this last section is part of the pathway, in others, it is not. The section north of Route 127 (North Street) parallels the Hutch within sight and sound and dead ends in 0.6 mile.

Route 127 (North Street) through Saxon Woods Golf Course

Length: 3.0 miles

From the parking lot at Maple Moor Golf Course, head east on Route 127 (North Street) and pass all entrance and exit ramps. Cross Route 127 and look for an opening in the woods near a manhole cover. The trail turns onto a woods road and then turns left to parallel the Hutch. Wooden guardrails separate the trail from the parkway and keep horses, who are allowed on the pathway, from straying into traffic or going down steep banks.

Heading downhill, the trail passes several houses to the left at 0.6 mile. It alternates between being within sight of the parkway and separated from it by a buffer. At 1.0 mile, it turns to cross the East Branch of the Mamaroneck River and then passes along the base of a retaining wall supporting the parkway. It passes a

breached dam and later turns to parallel the northbound entrance ramp. The pathway crosses the river at 1.4 miles and turns away from the entrance ramp. Once across the entrance to the Kentucky Riding Stable at 1.6 miles, it heads across Mamaroneck Avenue (no parking).

On the south side of Mamaroneck Avenue, the trail turns and heads northwest, now protected from traffic by a guardrail. Turning left away from Mamaroneck Avenue at 1.8 miles, it crosses two bridges over the West Branch of the Mamaroneck River. It reaches a junction with an unmarked trail to the left, which leads 0.2 mile into Saxon Woods Park South. Bearing right, the trail goes under the Hutch and heads upstream. After passing through a tunnel under the southbound entrance ramp, it goes toward a soccer field, but turns left before reaching it. The trail then heads uphill away from the field and enters the woods at 2.0 miles at an easily missed trail junction. Both trails end up in the same spot, but the right one is shorter.

Turning away from the parkway, the Hutchinson River Pathway reaches a Y junction with a white trail at 2.0 miles and turns left to join it. Although noise from the parkway is present, it decreases in the next half-mile. The trail passes two unmarked trails to the right in quick succession. After passing another unmarked trail to the left, it goes downhill on switchbacks, passes stone trestles to the right, then heads uphill. The tread is often eroded and in places is 12-18 inches lower than the forest floor. At 2.6 miles, the white trail turns right and the pathway continues straight. Once again the noise level rises and parkway traffic is visible through trees. The trail crosses a bridge heading towards the golf course. Turning left, it comes close to the parkway at 2.8 miles. It parallels the southbound exit ramp and reaches Mamaroneck Road at 3.0 miles. To continue on the next section, cross Mamaroneck Road at the break in the stone wall.

Saxon Woods Golf Course to Webster Avenue

Length: 5.6 miles

From the parking lot at Saxon Woods Golf Course head toward the entrance and walk along the stone wall at the east side of the entrance road. After going through the break in a stone wall east of the golf course entrance, cross Mamaroneck Road. The pathway entrance is between Stratton Road and the southbound entrance ramp to the Hutch. Here the Colonial Greenway joins

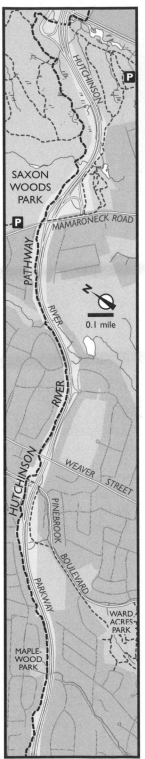

SAXON
WOODS
PARK

MAMARONECK ROAD

PATHWAY

RIVER

0.1 mile

RIVER

HUTCHINSON

WEAVER STREET

PINEBROOK BOULEVARD

PARKWAY

WARD
ACRES
PARK

MAPLE-
WOOD
PARK

Dam at Lake Innisfree.

the Hutchinson River Pathway and they are co-aligned for the next 3.2 miles.

The trail is on a grassy strip with traffic so close it can be disconcerting. Over the next half-mile, the trail alternates between having buffers and being right next to the traffic. The trail crosses a stream, parallels the southbound exit ramp, and crosses Weaver Street at 1.0 mile. It heads downhill to reach Pinebrook Boulevard. To the left, a section of the Colonial Greenway goes 0.6 mile along Pinebrook Boulevard to Ward Acres Park.

The pathway crosses Pinebrook Boulevard and then parallels the southbound entrance to the Hutch. Over the next mile, it again alternates between being close to the Hutch and having a buffer. At 1.9 miles there is access from Maplewood Park off Gaby Lane. The trail parallels the southbound exit ramp, turns left at 2.5 miles to cross Wilmot Road and follow the sidewalk. It reenters the woods near a fire hydrant.

The path heads downhill to the base of the dam of Lake Innisfree to cross the spillway. (The lake was created by damming the Hutchinson River.) The pathway crosses the bridge over exit and entrance ramps and then goes steeply down to follow the Hutchinson River under Mill Road. Emerging on the south side of Mill Road, the pathway crosses ramps. The trail enters Twin Lakes Park on a grassy strip at 3.0 miles, where the trees are heavily draped with invasive vines. Equestrians are the primary users of Twin Lakes Park and hikers are asked to yield to them on trails. In the park, trails are constrained by the parkway, reservoirs, and California Road. Unmarked

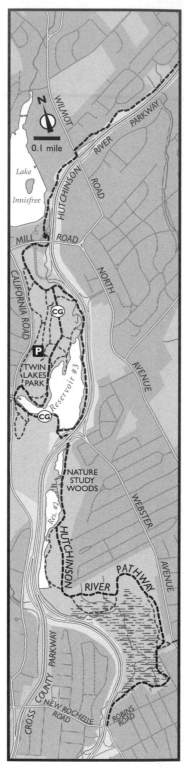

paths to the right lead to the River Ridge Equestrian Center.

At a grassy intersection, the pathway turns left and heads toward the parkway. At the next intersection, at 3.2 miles, the Colonial Greenway leaves to the right. The pathway turns left at a T junction at 3.4 miles to cross a bridge, and then turns again, wedged between the river and the parkway. It passes a breached dam at 3.6 miles, enters a heavily overgrown area, and turns onto a woods road. Leaving the woods at 3.9 miles, the pathway is between the shore of Reservoir #3 and the Hutch. At the end of the reservoir, it turns right to cross the dam.

At a T junction, the trail turns left to rejoin the Colonial Greenway; they are co-aligned for the next 1.3 miles. After crossing a bridge over an entrance ramp, the path heads down a ramp to cross a bridge below the dam. Having passed under the Hutch at 4.1 miles, with the Hutchinson River in a concrete channel to the left, it enters an area blanketed with invasives. It reaches Reservoir #2 and then parallels it. To the right at 4.5 miles, a 0.2- mile trail goes through a flood control area to reach a dam. The pathway passes, to the left, an unmarked trail to Bon Air Avenue. Entering Nature Study Woods, it is along a railbed and passes to the right at 2.0 miles, a lone trestle of the former New York, Westchester and Boston Railway. Just beyond it at a Y junction, an unmarked trail to the right heads 0.2 mile into the flood plain of the Hutchinson River. The pathway passes a large stone outcropping to the left at 5.0 miles and turns left where the path coming from the dam joins. A narrow unmarked path enters from the right. The pathway crosses a bridge at 5.2 miles and, at a wide intersection, turns right. The Colonial Greenway goes through the intersection and heads toward Webster Avenue. The pathway is on a narrow path and turns right when it meets another trail coming from Webster Avenue opposite Flandreau Avenue.

Webster Avenue to New Rochelle Road

Length: 0.5 mile

To reach this section, follow the wide unmarked entrance trail at the corner of Webster and

Flandreau Avenues. Head across the intersection, go slightly downhill, and then turn left at the next trail junction. At 0.3 mile, the trail passes a massive beech tree. It leaves the woods and heads onto a grassy strip behind apartment buildings to end at Robins and New Rochelle roads (no parking).

New Rochelle Road to St. Paul's Episcopal Church   Length: 3.2 miles
Radically different from sections north of New Rochelle Road, the Hutchinson River Pathway follows city streets through residential, small retail, urban sprawl, and industrial areas.

At the end of Robins Road, turn right onto New Rochelle Road following the sidewalk under The Hutch. Cross New Rochelle Road at 0.1 mile and follow Hutchinson Boulevard past houses with small landscaped lawns. Initially there are no sidewalks. The Hutchinson River is between the parkway and the street. Cross East Lincoln Avenue at 1.0 mile to Bradford Park Road. Take care to stay to the right side of the street to avoid crossing the parkway's exit and entrance ramps. Willson's Woods Park with about 0.5 mile of paved paths is to the right.

Follow Bradford Park Avenue and go under the stone viaduct of the Metro-North New Haven Line. At 1.5 miles turn left onto Beechwood Avenue. At the end of Beechwood Avenue, the path crosses a pedestrian bridge over the parkway to Sparks Avenue. Walk along Sparks Avenue and turn right at Wolf's Lane at 1.9 miles. Wolf's Lane is along the retail section of Pelham and is, for a short distance, across the street from a strip of green space. At 2.1 miles, when Wolf's Lane ends at Colonial Avenue, turn right and pass under the parkway to enter Mount Vernon. The route becomes more commercial with box stores on both sides of the wide street. Just after passing Memorial Field to the right at 2.4 miles, turn left onto Columbus Avenue (Route 22). Continue through an area which gradually becomes more heavily industrialized, to end at St. Paul's Episcopal Church (a National Historic Site).

CONNECTING PARKS: Saxon Woods Park, Weinberg Nature Center, Twin Lakes/ Nature Study Woods, Willson's Woods Park

DRIVING: All sections of the pathway are accessible from the Hutchinson River Parkway.

Maple Moor Golf Course: The entrance to the Hutchinson River Pathway is on North Street, east of the northbound exit/entrance ramps [41.001531N 73.727120W]. Saxon Woods (pool area): For driving directions, see Saxon Woods Park in Large Parks [40.985407N 73.745554W].

Weinberg Nature Center: For driving directions, see Weinberg Nature Center in Large Parks [40.974885N 73.755980W].

Twin Lakes/Nature Study Woods: For driving directions, see Twin Lakes/ Nature Study Woods in Day Trippers [40.949267N 73.802089W] and [40.930598N 73.798211W].

PUBLIC TRANSPORTATION: Saxon Woods Park: Beeline Bus #60; Nature Study Woods: Beeline Bus #45 along Webster Avenue; Beeline Bus #53 on New Rochelle Road

For contact information, see Appendix, Westchester County Parks.

Leatherstocking Trail

New Rochelle to Mamaroneck • 2.6 miles, 67.5 acres

To the north and west of I-95, a short strip of green known as the Leatherstocking Trail cuts across the Town of Mamaroneck. Abutting it is Sheldrake River Trails. At one time, these two pieces were a county bridle trail and in 1926, were slated to become a parkway from Port Chester to the Bronx. Once the New England Thruway was built in the 1950s, this land was no longer needed. Thinking ahead, local and county groups worked together to preserve the land for passive recreation.

The Leatherstocking Trail is part of the outer loop of the Colonial Greenway and eventually connects to Saxon Woods Park. The cross piece of the Colonial Greenway goes from the Leatherstocking Trail to the Hutchinson River Pathway north of Ward Acres Park.

LEATHERSTOCKING TRAIL

Blazed white, the Leatherstocking Trail follows a narrow strip from Pinebrook Boulevard in New Rochelle to Old White Plains Road in Mamaroneck. As part of the Colonial Greenway, it has many access points, most without parking. The distinguishing features along the Leatherstocking Trail are road crossings and side trails. This pleasant meandering path has houses on one side or the other. In spring before leaves appear, abundant wildflowers are found along the path. Yellow marsh marigolds carpet moist areas in mid-April.

From Pinebrook Boulevard (no parking), the Leatherstocking Trail goes uphill on a wide path, passing houses, sometimes closer than at others, along its 200-foot wide corridor. At 0.4 mile, it goes by a side trail to the right, which heads 0.1 mile to end at a driveway off Devonshire Road. After crossing a stone bridge at 0.5 mile, the Leatherstocking Trail passes a large vernal pool. It next goes by a trail to the right that continues 0.1 mile to end across from 87 Beechtree Drive.

At 0.7 mile, there is a huge burl near the base of a tree to the left, where the Colonial Greenway heads to a wooden bridge and boardwalk ending at Bonnie Way. It is 0.3 mile along Bonnie Way to Weaver Street and the parking area at Sheldrake Environmental Center. Just beyond the trail to Bonnie Way, the Leatherstocking Trail heads uphill and splits. An unmarked trail leads to Knollwood Drive. The pieces join, and at 1.0 mile, cross a side trail leading right to South Drive and leading left to a shared driveway off Sacket Circle.

Marsh marigold.

OLD WHITE PLAINS ROAD

95

CG

LEATHERSTOCKING

N

0.1 mile

FENIMORE ROAD

SHELDRAKE RIVER TRAILS CONSERVATION AREA

P

P

TRAIL

CG

STREET

WEAVER

Y

B

CG

PINEBROOK

BOULEVARD

Just after crossing Weaver Street at 1.1 miles, the Leatherstocking Trail heads onto a 300-foot long boardwalk and then onto another shorter one. After crossing Highland Road at 1.3 miles, the trail parallels Stratford Road. A short side trail to the right provides access to Woody Lane. At 1.6 miles, the first of the unmarked trails at Sheldrake River Trails leaves to the right. Access and limited parking are on Rockland Avenue on the far side of the Sheldrake River Trails. At Post D, the Leatherstocking Trail turns left, goes over a bridge, and onto a 400-foot long boardwalk. It passes Post J just before the boardwalk ends. At 1.7 miles, the trail crosses Winged Foot Drive (parking).

After passing a large vernal pool, the Leatherstocking Trail crosses Avon and Fenimore roads in quick succession. It reaches the top of a rise at 2.2 miles and crosses Country Road at 2.3 miles. The trail passes by the Town of Mamaroneck's tree nursery, established in 1976, and turns right. It heads downhill and at 2.5 miles, reaches a boardwalk. The Leatherstocking Trail ends on Old White Plains Road at 2.6 miles, but the Colonial Greenway continues across the street.

DRIVING: The many entrances to the Leatherstocking Trail include eight road crossings, side trails out to nearby streets, and many others established by adjacent private homeowners. Use a map of Westchester County to reach the various road crossings. Parking is limited, which is to be expected, considering that the Leatherstocking Trail passes through residential areas for most of its length. Parking areas are located at Sheldrake Reservoir [40.950383N 73.768758W] and Winged Foot Drive [40.951128N 73.754904W]. There are many places to park a car or two on streets near the trail, but if specifically mentioned, the influx of cars and people might overwhelm an area.

PUBLIC TRANSPORTATION: None available

For contact information, see Appendix, Mamaroneck (Town).

Sheldrake River Trails Conservation Area

Larchmont • 1.0 mile, 23 acres

As depicted on a map, the Sheldrake River Trails Conservation Area seems like a bulge along the Leatherstocking Trail. Instead, consider it a jewel on a necklace. Its one- mile trail system of six short trails winds through woodlands, along a stream, and through a wetland. Lettered posts are located at intersections. The Town of Mamaroneck manages the area for conservation of native plants and animals.

DRIVING: From the southbound Hutchinson River Parkway, take Exit 20 (Weaver Street/Route 125) and turn left onto Route 125. **Go 1.8 miles and turn left onto Rockland Avenue. It is 0.3 mile to the park entrance, two blocks past Highland Avenue. If northbound, take Exit 21 and turn right onto Hutchinson Avenue. At Route 125, turn left and follow the directions from**. Parking on Rockland Avenue is limited to two or three cars [40.949566N 73.758086W].

PUBLIC TRANSPORTATION: None available

For contact information, see Appendix, Mamaroneck (Town).

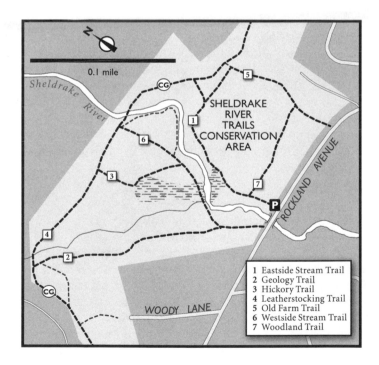

1 Eastside Stream Trail
2 Geology Trail
3 Hickory Trail
4 Leatherstocking Trail
5 Old Farm Trail
6 Westside Stream Trail
7 Woodland Trail

North County Trailway

Baldwin Place to Eastview • 21 miles, 88 acres

Agreen pathway stretching from the Putnam border to Eastview, the North County Trailway sits on the right-of-way of the old Putnam Division of the New York Central Railroad. On a walk along sections of the trailway, you will see a cross-section of the county as it passes backyards, parks, and businesses. Sometimes the trailway runs parallel and close to high-speed roads while at others it seems far removed from any development at all.

Along its course, the trailway wends through a variety of habitat: wetland, rock cuts, woodlands, and edge environments. Near road crossings and at the sites of former stations, the county has placed interpretive signs with information about the history of the railroad and the surrounding habitats. South of Millwood and north of Chappaqua Road, there are houses right on the trailway. To get a good look at them, however, bring field glasses, for these houses are in the trees and their occupants are likely to take flight at any moment.

All along the 21-mile route, remnants of the old railroad, mostly mileage markers and telephone poles, can be found. Two former stations, in Yorktown Heights and Briarcliff, remain, with the Briarcliff Station now housing the Briarcliff Manor Public Library. Two concrete pads are all that is left of the Kitchawan Station. The Millwood station was demolished in 2013. The railroad's roundtable was located in Yorktown Heights, just south of Underhill Avenue in an area that is now Patriot Park. Just north of Eastview at the trail leading to the park-and-ride is a section of track with switches. The Yorktown Museum has a display of the section of the Old Putnam Railroad between Kitchawan and Amawalk. For more information, see www.yorktownmuseum.org.

The trailway is handicapped accessible for its entire length. Recommended destinations along the trail are the wetlands south of Yorktown and the bridge over the Croton Reservoir.

THE TRAILWAY

This converted railbed is a popular place for walkers, joggers, cyclists, and in-line skaters. Even in winter, the trails get a good workout. Each time of the day seems to attract different users with joggers dominating in the early morning and evenings and in-line skaters in the afternoons. Cyclists seem to be the exception, gliding by almost all day long. Weekends seem to bring out people of all ages sharing pathways shaded by arching branches and buffered by hedges and bushes. For the naturalist, the nearby wetlands are teeming with wildlife.

Because the North County Trailway is a linear footpath, unless hikers plan to retrace their steps, they will have to either leave a car where they will end their hike or rely on public transportation. The trail descriptions are in sections dictated primarily by major road crossings or amenities.

From the northern end of the North County Trailway at Baldwin Place, the paved path continues as the Putnam Trailway, 12 miles into Putnam County and

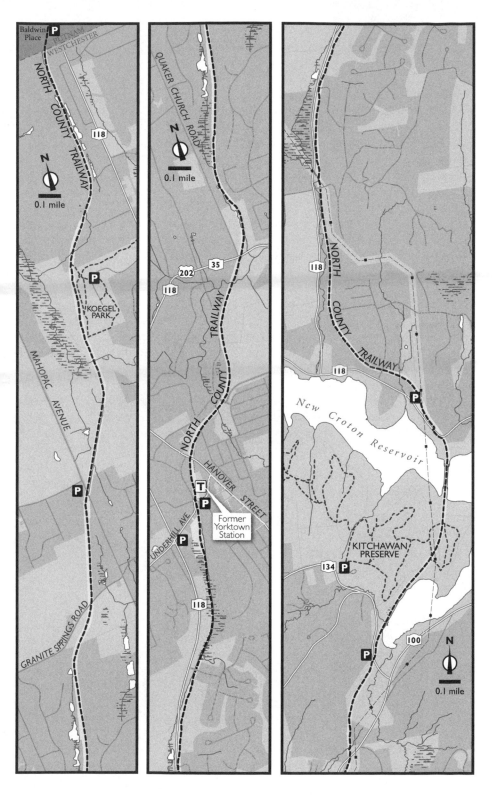

Baldwin
Place

PUTNAM
WESTCHESTER

NORTH COUNTY TRAILWAY

118

N

0.1 mile

P

KOEGEL
PARK

MAHOPAC AVENUE

P

GRANITE SPRINGS ROAD

QUAKER CHURCH ROAD

N

0.1 mile

202 35

118

NORTH COUNTY TRAILWAY

NORTH COUNTY TRAILWAY

HANOVER STREET

T

P

Former
Yorktown
Station

UNDERHILL AVE

P

118

118

NORTH COUNTY TRAILWAY

118

P

New Croton Reservoir

KITCHAWAN
PRESERVE

134 P

100

N

0.1 mile

P

ends in Brewster. While from the southern end at Eastview, the North County Trailway changes its name to the South County Trailway as it heads south 13.9 miles to the New York City line in the Bronx.

Baldwin Place to Yorktown Heights: *Length: 5.6 miles*
From Route 118 in Baldwin Place, the trail heads south, passing homes and then the entrance to Koegel Park at 1.0 mile. Running parallel to a power line, the trail is on an embankment at times lined with a split rail fence. It crosses Mahopac Avenue at 2.4 miles and then the entrance and parking lot at Jilco (a window company). The trail crosses Granite Springs Road at 2.9 miles. It leaves the power line when it crosses Route 202 at 4.5 miles and then passes back yards again.

In Yorktown Heights, at 5.5 miles to the right of the trailway's intersection with Hanover Street, are numerous restaurants and services. There is a bike shop on Commerce Street a minute from the trailway. Railroad Park has the original Yorktown Station, with benches and old-style lighting. Shopping centers are across Commerce Street. At 5.6 miles, the trailway crosses Underhill Avenue (parking).

Yorktown Heights to Millwood *Length: 6.7 miles*
The 4.5 mile-section between Underhill Avenue and Route 134, with its stretch of wetlands and a former railroad bridge, is probably the most scenic part of the trailway. In Yorktown, 0.2 mile south of the crossing at Underhill Avenue, the trail passes through an extensive wetland often bustling with wildlife activity. Rabbits scurry into the underbrush and red-winged blackbirds perch on phragmite reeds. Depending on the season, turtles bask atop partly submerged logs and plop into the water when startled. South of the wetlands, the trailway passes through huge culverts under roads at 0.9, 1.4, and 1.9 miles. While traveling south, the slight but steady downgrade beginning at the second culvert means cyclists can coast for a

Walkway over the reservoir in fall.

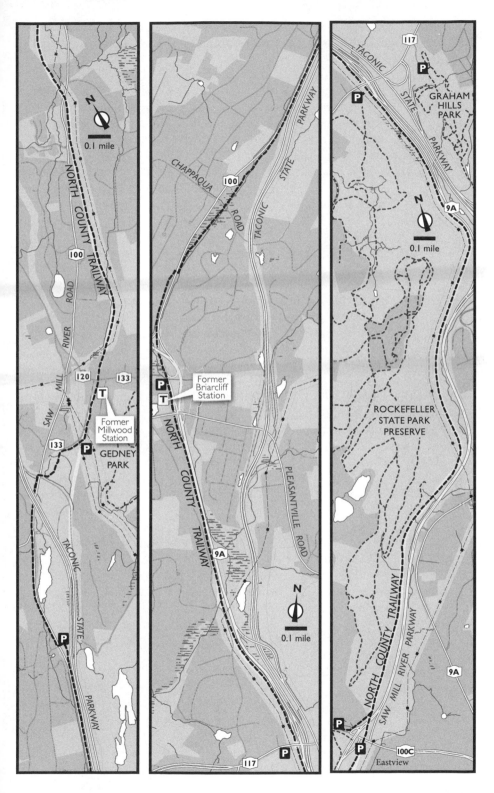

NORTH COUNTY TRAILWAY

100

MILL RIVER ROAD

SAW

120   133

T

Former
Millwood
Station

133   P

GEDNEY
PARK

TACONIC

STATE

PARKWAY

P

N

0.1 mile

CHAPPAQUA

100

TACONIC STATE PARKWAY

P
T

Former
Briarcliff
Station

NORTH

COUNTY

PLEASANTVILLE ROAD

TRAILWAY

9A

N

0.1 mile

117   P

117

P

TACONIC

STATE

117

PARKWAY

P

GRAHAM
HILLS
PARK

9A

N

0.1 mile

ROCKEFELLER
STATE PARK
PRESERVE

NORTH COUNTY TRAILWAY

SAW MILL RIVER PARKWAY

9A

P

P   100C

Eastview

long distance. The trailway parallels Route 118, but well out of sight and sound of it. It turns to parallel the reservoir and crosses Birdsall Drive at-grade, at 2.9 miles.

After passing a parking lot next to the trailway, the trailway crosses Route 118 at 3.3 miles. Take care because there is a poor line of sight to the left. The trailway passes over the Croton Reservoir on a restored railroad bridge, a popular destination with sweeping views out over the water. After going through a densely wooded section, the trailway passes under power lines. At 3.9 miles, there are trails into Kitchawan Preserve, where bicycles are not permitted. Passing the site of the former Kitchawan Station, the trail goes through a massive culvert under Route 134 at 4.5 miles, where there is roadside parking uphill to the right. Continuing through woodlands, it crosses Route 100 on a former railroad bridge. Beyond the back yards of houses, the trailway crosses Route 120 at 6.4 miles. Across Route 133 is a small shopping center near the junction with Route 100.

Millwood to Route 117 *Length: 5.5 miles*

Being alert is the best way to travel along this section of the North County Trailway. From where it crosses Route 100 to Route 9A, the trailway alternates between being along the road, behind a guardrail, or along a path through wetlands and woods. Whenever it leaves the road, there is the inherent danger of crossing a busy highway, which makes this part of the section more suitable as a bicycle commuter route than for weekend family outings.

From the parking lot in Millwood the trail curves as it parallels Route 133 and enters wetlands. It reaches Route 100 at the traffic light by the northbound entrance to the Taconic State Parkway at 0.3 mile. Trailway users heading south are on the shoulder of the southbound lanes of Route 100 and when heading north are next to the northbound lanes. The trailway is on the shoulder until North State Street when it enters a parking area. From this point, it is behind a barrier along the east side of Route 100. At 1.9 miles, the trailway leaves Route 100 to head through the woods. Passing wetlands, the trailway crosses Chappaqua Road at 2.4 miles. Take care when crossing Route 100 and the exit ramp for Route 9A at 3.1 miles, because drivers in merging lanes are not always aware of pedestrians and cyclists.

Leaving Route 100, the trailway returns to the off-road portion at 3.3 miles and reaches the former Briarcliff Station. Built in 1909, it was a gift from Walter Law, a Village founder. Since 1959, the station has been the Briarcliff Manor Public Library. A significant expansion to the library is a two-story building reflecting the station's English gable design. At 3.5 miles, the trailway is behind a barrier as it goes under Pleasantville Road. It continues to parallel routes 9A and 100, never far from ambient roadway noise. At 5.5 miles, an access path heads up to Route 117 and the trailway goes through a large culvert under Route 117. It passes another access path to a parking lot.

Route 117 to Eastview *Length: 3.2 miles*

Unlike the other sections, this section has no road crossings. From the parking area on Route 117, the trailway initially parallels a power line and routes 9A and 100. At 0.9 mile, it passes behind a police facility. Sometimes in the woods, it parallels the Saw Mill River Parkway, the power line and routes 9A and 100. At 0.9 mile,

Approaching Eastview, the trailway reaches a Y junction. Immediately to the right are remains of railroad track. The South County Trailway is to the left across the bridge over the Saw Mill River Parkway. The right fork heads to Saw Mill River Road/Neperan Road and a commuter parking lot just to the west.

All that remains.

CONNECTING TRAILS & NEARBY PARKS: Putnam Trailway, South County Trailway, Tarrytown Lakes Park, Koegel Park, Turkey Mountain Nature Preserve, Kitchawan Preserve, Gedney Park, Law Memorial Park, Rockefeller State Park Preserve

DRIVING: The many access points to the trailway include some established by adjacent residents. Use a Westchester County map to reach parking areas. Parking is available at:

Baldwin Place [41.344693N 73.755276W];
Jilco (weekends only) [41.314337N 73.762422W];
Route 202 [41.286200N 73.770193W];
Underhill Avenue (Yorktown) [41.270610N 73.779987W];
Route 118 [41.231427N 73.779102W];
Route 134 [41.214760N 73.783767W];
Route 133 [41.186829N 73.800700W];
Route 100 [41.175239N 73.811615W];
Chappaqua Road [41.159939N 73.820661W];
Law Park in Briarcliff Manor [41.146241N 73.824293W];
Route 117 [41.123386N 73.811138W];
Eastview commuter lot [41.082434N 73.830832W]; and
Route 100 C northbound off ramp [41.080484N 73.829329W].

PUBLIC TRANSPORTATION: Beeline Bus #16 to the Somers Town (shopping) Center in Baldwin Place and Beeline Bus #15 to Millwood

For contact information, see Appendix, Westchester County Parks.

Old Croton Aqueduct State Historic Park

Cortlandt to the Bronx • 26.2 miles, 207.8 acres

Water has been called the driving force of nature. The pure and bountiful supply that flowed inside the 26-mile portion of an aqueduct that is now the Old Croton Aqueduct State Historic Park nourished the growth and powered the expansion of New York City. The park's 60-foot wide corridor is the right-of-way for an underground brick conduit that brought much needed water from the Croton Reservoir to Manhattan. Completed in 1842 after five years of work, the aqueduct system was an engineering and architectural marvel of its time.

As the city grew, the aqueduct as a water source was supplemented and, by 1955, replaced by other systems coming from different and more distant water sources. At the urging of the New York-New Jersey Trail Conference and other groups, the state purchased the 26-mile long section in Westchester in 1968 which became the Old Croton Aqueduct State Historic Park. The Aqueduct (when capitalized, it refers to the historic structure and when in lower case, it refers to the path on top of that structure) was designated a National Historic Landmark in 1992.

THE AQUEDUCT

Although water may no longer flow through its physical structure, the aqueduct is heavily used by its neighbors. Joggers, cyclists, dog walkers, nannies, and visitors of all ages use it, some for a "green" route to work or to the train stations and for children to school

About every mile along its course, the aqueduct passes cylindrical stone towers or ventilators which allowed air to circulate over the water. Less frequently on the route are larger rectangular stone structures known as waste weirs. Each contains a metal gate, which could be lowered to either regulate the flow of water or divert the excess water into a nearby stream, permitting maintenance downstream inside the tunnel. The brick conduit itself is only a few feet beneath the trail.

Wending its way through and between towns, villages, and cities, the aqueduct traverses woodlands, meadows, and estates. The gravity-fed aqueduct drops only 13 inches per mile along its course and employs some engineering principles used since Roman times. To maintain that gradient as it crossed stream beds and other lowlands, it had to be carried across on earthen embankments. However, hikers will encounter some significant elevation changes near the John F. Welch Development Center of the General Electric Corporation, at Piping Rock Road and in Rockefeller State Park Preserve.

Each section has its own appeal and flavor, which makes the Aqueduct a popular place for so many people. In some places its presence is quite obvious, with a raised bed and a level surface. The walking route diverges from the historic structure at several points for various reasons: a sale of property, a road crossing considered unsafe, or a section actually being removed. Although the description that follows provides a detailed guide to the walking route, it is recommended that walkers also

consult the map published by the Friends of the Old Croton Aqueduct. The walking route seldom has signs, although some road crossings do have signposts.

The aqueduct generally has a dirt or grass surface with occasional obstacles such as tree roots, street curbs, stairways, and puddles. In most sections, the path is at least four feet wide and sometimes has a narrow well-worn path down the center. There are areas as wide as 12 feet, while others pass through a back yard because its present or previous owner had encroached on the 60-foot right-of-way.

For convenience, the description of the route of the Aqueduct is divided into sections with public transportation available either nearby or at one end. The Metro-North Hudson Line directly parallels the Aqueduct for most of the way and is a practical way to access it. Suggested places to park are listed with the driving directions. Parking may also be available at some road crossings or on adjacent streets.

New Croton Dam to Ossining *Length: 4.9 miles*

The first 2.8 miles of the aqueduct pass through the most natural setting of its entire length. Trees tower overhead and few houses are visible. There are two access points at the New Croton Dam. Croton Gorge Park off Route 129 has ample parking, great views, and restrooms. To reach the aqueduct, walk uphill on a wide path and turn right at the top of a hill onto a wide flat path. Alternately, access to the aqueduct is at a parking area at the southeast end of the dam on Croton Dam Road. Regardless of which access point is used, follow the aqueduct downhill along a wide path. At 0.2 mile, bear left at the sign for the Old Croton Aqueduct where it begins an almost imperceptible descent towards New York City. At 0.4 mile, it passes the first of 21 ventilators; this one is not numbered. The aqueduct continues through woods with the Croton River far below. It passes through a rock cut, and at 1.0 mile, crosses Quaker Bridge Road East. Another unnumbered ventilator is at 1.4 miles. After crossing Quaker Bridge Road, the aqueduct goes through the DEC Croton Gorge Unique Area at 1.8 miles, where a 0.2-mile side trail leads down into the gorge. At 2.4 miles, it passes a third unnumbered ventilator and crosses Quaker Bridge Road again.

The walking route turns right off the Aqueduct

and crosses Fowler Avenue at 2.8 miles. It enters Ossining, ascends to follows the perimeter of a fence at GE's John F. Welch Development Center, and then descends. At 3.1 miles, turn right onto the GE entrance road, turn left onto Old Albany Post Road, and cross under Route 9A. Make the next left onto Ogden Road, proceed steeply uphill, and turn right to rejoin the Aqueduct at 3.4 miles.

An unnumbered ventilator stands at 3.5 miles. Just past this ventilator, the Aqueduct tunnels through a hill and the trail goes up a very steep climb, not easy for bicyclists. After crossing Piping Rock Road, the aqueduct heads down a steep bank. It crosses Route 9 (Highland Avenue) at 3.8 miles, turns left and crosses a lawn and paved driveway at 4.0 miles. At 4.3 miles, the aqueduct crosses Beach Road, where to the right is Crawbuckie Nature Preserve at the end of the road.

Double Arch.

At 4.5 miles, the aqueduct passes a stone structure (not a weir), crosses Snowden Avenue diagonally, and then Van Wyck and North Malcolm streets. The paved pathway turns right to descend two sets of steps. After crossing Ann Street, the aqueduct reaches a weir and an imposing stone structure which carries the Aqueduct over the Sing Sing Kill valley, a formidable natural obstacle. At the center is a great arch with an 88-foot span. Started in 1837, this construction project was a significant engineering achievement. Passing under this arch is another arched bridge, built at a later date, carrying Broadway over the stream and giving rise to the name "double arch" for this crossing.

South of the bridge, a trail to the left leads to the Joseph G. Caputo Community Center, housing the Ossining Heritage Area Visitor Center, a museum providing information about the Old Croton Aqueduct and Sing Sing Correctional Facility. The trail to the right leads to a platform with a partial view of the double arch.

For further information about tours inside the weir and Aqueduct tunnel, call Friends of the Old Croton Aqueduct, 914-693-4117, or Old Croton Aqueduct State Historic Park, 914-693-5259.

Ossining to Sleepy Hollow (Gory Brook Road) *Length: 6.8 miles*
There are several sections of road walking in this segment from Ossining to Gory Brook Road, as well as connections to parks and long stretches of wooded areas. From the Joseph G. Caputo Community Center on Broadway, head up to the Aqueduct and turn left. Cross to the south side of Main Street where

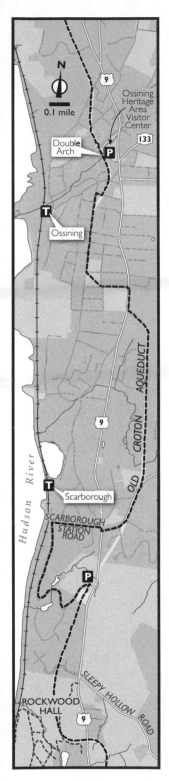

WATER FOR A GROWING CITY

If water were rated like wine, then New York City's would be the Bordeux of municipal water systems. But a clean and plentiful supply of water was not the case until one of the most ambitious engineering feats of its time was completed in 1842. Originally, the city took most of its water supply from wells and from the Collect, a pond in Lower Manhattan. But with a growing population and no sewers, those water sources became foul. Poor quality, the threat of fire, and periodic epidemics of cholera and yellow fever led city planners to adopt a plan to build a dam and reservoir on the Croton River, an ample and clean source to meet their demands. It would be linked to the city via a 42-mile gravity-fed aqueduct that led to holding reservoirs in what would be Central Park and in Midtown, where the New York Public Library now sits.

Work started in 1837 and the cost including land acquisition was $12.5 million, which did not reflect the toll on families displaced when homes were seized for the reservoir or for the Aqueduct's corridor. Like many early major construction projects, it was built primarily by immigrant labor, in this case Irish workers, who were paid between 75 cents and a dollar for a 10-hour workday.

The Aqueduct was capable of delivering over 60 million gallons per day. But the city's exponential growth and changing habits, including indoor plumbing and sewers, rendered the system inadequate. A second aqueduct and new dam three miles downstream from the original one were completed in 1890. This New Croton Aqueduct had three times the capacity of Old Croton Aqueduct, which continued to supply the city until 1955 and some suburban communities until 1968. In later years, the city's water system grew to reach into the Catskill and Delaware watersheds.

the trail continues between buildings. The Metro-North Ossining Station is downhill to the right. At Maple Place at 0.1 mile, the walking route turns right to leave the park. Turn left onto Spring Street and cross four streets. At 0.5 mile, ventilator #8 sits in the schoolyard to the left. The aqueduct crosses Everett Avenue and follows a paved path cutting

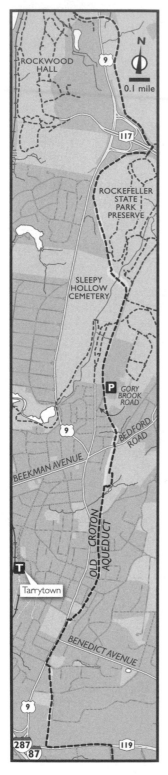

diagonally across Nelson Park to reach the corner of Edward Street and Washington Avenue Turn left onto Washington Avenue and follow it to Route 9 (South Highland Avenue). At 0.9 mile, cross Route 9 and turn right onto the sidewalk. Just beyond the entrance to the parking lot of the apartments, turn left onto a narrow path into trees leading to another parking lot. At the far side of the lot, return to the Aqueduct route.

The aqueduct enters the woods, curving to the right. It continues past more apartments, sometimes along a high embankment. After passing ventilator #9 at 1.6 miles, the aqueduct crosses Sparta Brook on an embankment. Leaving this wooded section, it diagonally crosses Scarborough Road at 1.8 miles. At Long Hill Road West, the walking route leaves the Aqueduct. Turn right onto Long Hill Road West, continue 50 feet, and at 2.2 miles turn left onto Scarborough Road. Cross Route 9 (Albany Post Road), turn right, then immediately left, to follow Scarborough Station Road. For safety reasons do not walk along Route 9, which has no shoulders, very short sight distances, and a lot of truck and high-speed traffic. Instead, take the safer and more scenic route. At the T junction with River Road at 2.5 miles, go left. To the right is the Metro-North Hudson Line's Scarborough Station. Take River Road uphill to the junction with Creighton Lane and turn left. When Creighton Lane ends at River Road, continue uphill to the left.

Weir which functioned to control water flow.

At 3.3 miles, just before River Road reaches Route 9, turn right into a parking lot and then immediately jog right to return to the Aqueduct. Now on a grassy path at 3.4 miles, the aqueduct passes ventilator #10. It turns right and follows a driveway for 50 feet and then turns left and rejoins the Aqueduct path. Going up an embankment, it crosses Country Club Drive at 3.7 miles and reenters the woods. From here to Gory Brook Road, horses are permitted. To the right at a wide intersection is the trail to Rockwood Hall with a "No Bikes" sign. The aqueduct continues left and reaches, at 4.1 miles, the Archville Bridge, built in 1998 to create a safe crossing over Route 9. The original bridge was removed in the 1920s to accommodate increased traffic on Route 9. Plaques commemorate construction of the bridge, the Aqueduct, and the original stone arch bridge, which gave rise to the name "Archville".

The aqueduct continues slightly uphill and turns right onto a wide gravel road to pass ventilator #11 at 4.3 miles. It turns left, leaving the Aqueduct route and bypassing the exit and entrance ramps of Route 117. After heading uphill along a chainlink fence, it turns right to cross Route 117. Straight ahead is a trail leading to the 13 Bridges Trail in Rockefeller State Park Preserve. At 5.0 miles on the south side of the bridge over Route 117, the trail turns right. A short connecting trail leads straight ahead to the Big Tree Trail also in Rockefeller State Park Preserve.

Turning right, the path parallels a fence, passes through a rock formation at 5.3 miles, and then returns to the Aqueduct. It reaches an intersection with a "No Bikes" sign and a gate to the right. Continuing straight, the aqueduct passes Sleepy Hollow Cemetery to the right and then a weir at 6.1 miles. Curving left, the Aqueduct crosses a valley on a 90-foot high embankment with the Pocantico River far below. On the east side of the trail before crossing the Aqueduct embankment, is a path which descends to the Pocantico River and affords a view of the river as it passes through the base of the embankment. The aqueduct curves right to pass more of Sleepy Hollow Cemetery and parallels the closed portion of Gory Brook Road to the left. At 6.5 miles, unmarked trails to the right lead to the cemetery and Douglas Park. The aqueduct reaches a metal gate marked with "OCA" at 6.8 miles. Limited parking is available at Gory Brook Road to the left.

Sleepy Hollow (Gory Brook Road) to Dobbs Ferry (Walnut Street)

Length: 6.0 miles

Stately homes with well-kept lawns and gardens are adjacent to the Aqueduct in this segment. There are also historic sites in several Hudson River villages, but, unfortunately, also two road walks, one of which is along busy roads.

From the gate at Gory Brook Road, the trail diagonally crosses that road and Ridge Road to pass houses and ventilator #12. It passes more houses and continues up onto an embankment. At 0.3 mile, it crosses Bedford Road and enters the parking lot of Sleepy Hollow High School. At the far end of the parking lot, head left around the school building. At 0.6 mile, go back up onto the Aqueduct as the trail continues south on a high embankment and crosses over Andre Brook. The aqueduct squeezes past back yards as it heads in quick succession between Cobb Lane, McKeel Avenue, and Hamilton Place. These streets provide easy access to Route 9 in Tarrytown where there is on-street metered and non-metered parking.

The aqueduct passes ventilator #13 and crosses Neperan Road at 1.1 miles. Follow Neperan Road and Main Street downhill to the Metro-North Hudson Line Tarrytown Station. Passing through an opening in a hedge, it then literally travels through back yards (which have made use of the right-of-way) and reaches East Elizabeth Street. It continues between buildings until reaching East Franklin Street, where it is necessary to leave the Aqueduct at 1.3 miles. Turn right, and upon reaching Route 9 (South Broadway), turn left. Follow Route 9 to Leroy Avenue and turn left at 1.5 miles. Turn right into a parking lot behind a medical arts center and rejoin the Aqueduct as it continues on a high embankment behind the building.

Leaving the woods, the aqueduct crosses Prospect Avenue at 1.7 miles and a parking lot at Martling Avenue. Passing behind a number of buildings, it reaches ventilator #14 at 2.0 miles just before Route 119. The walking route once again diverges from the Aqueduct and there are two ways to return to it. The first one is more direct, but is along busy Route 9. The second is longer, but more scenic.

For the first route, turn right and follow Route 119. When you reach Route 9, cross it, turn left, and head south. After crossing over the NYS Thruway, go past entrances to a hotel and to Kraft Foods and continue ahead until reaching an opening in a wall.

For the scenic route, turn left onto Route 119 (White Plains Road), continue to the second traffic light, and turn right onto Meadow Street. Bear left at the fork and continue under the New York Thruway. Turn right onto Sheldon Street (the first street after the NYS Thruway) and continue to just beyond Chestnut Street, where the Aqueduct crosses. Turn left and rejoin the Aqueduct, which follows an embankment. After crossing Gracemere Street, turn right onto a gravel path, departing from the Aqueduct. Follow the gravel path through a small parking area to Route 9, where you cross at the traffic light and turn left.

At 2.6 miles, turn right to return to the Aqueduct and enter the Lyndhurst property, home of Jay Gould, a nineteenth-century railroad magnate and speculator. A fee is required to explore any part of the grounds other than the aqueduct. Trees and shrubs accenting the sweeping lawn are part of an outstanding example of nineteenth-century landscape design.

The aqueduct passes ventilator #15 at 3.0 miles. The high stone walls to the left are part of Belvedere, a private estate once known as Zeeview, the residence of Sun Myung Moon, the South Korean religious leader and founder of the Unification Church. In 2004, a conservation easement on land west of the Aqueduct was created as part of a deal with New York State, Westchester County, and the Town of Greenburgh. The aqueduct crosses Sunnyside Lane at 3.4 miles, entering the Village of Irvington. Down the hill to the right is Washington Irving's home, Sunnyside, an historic site.

The aqueduct then passes some large and elaborate houses. On the south side of Fargo Road to the left is an elaborate Italianate garden, part of Villa Lewaro, the former home of Madame C.J. Walker, a self-made African-American entrepreneur and philanthropist of the early 1900s. The aqueduct parallels Aqueduct Lane at 3.9 miles, enters the parking lot of Main Street School, and crosses Main Street. Downhill to the right is the Metro-North Hudson Line Irvington Station.

Across Main Street, the aqueduct enters a permit parking lot. After passing ventilator #16 at 4.0 miles, the aqueduct crosses Barney Brook (formerly Jewells Brook) on a very high embankment. Cyclists should walk their bikes because traction on the gravel is poor. Ball fields of Memorial Park are to the left at 4.3 miles. Approaching Dows Lane, houses are once again adjacent to the trail. At 4.5 miles, the Aqueduct crosses Clinton Avenue and passes, to the right, the Octagon House, built in 1860. It enters the grounds of Nevis, the stately columned mansion built in 1835 by Alexander Hamilton's son James. Nevis is the name of the West Indian Island where his father was born. The mansion once housed Columbia University's primary center for experimental physics and, in 2014, the property is for sale.

The aqueduct crosses Ardsley Road, which leads to the Metro-North Hudson Line Ardsley Station. It passes stately houses with well-groomed yards and gardens. Reaching ventilator #17 at 5.0 miles, on a narrow dirt track through grass, the aqueduct then crosses Hudson Road and enters the grounds of Mercy College and the Village of Dobbs Ferry. After cutting across the back of Our Lady of Victory Academy, it crosses an access road to condominiums and the Sisters of Mercy Convent. For a short while, it is easy to forget that the aqueduct is in a busy village. No houses are nearby and it is so quiet crossing over Wicker's Creek on the high embankment that flowing water can be heard. Passing a side trail up to Dobbs Ferry High School, the aqueduct curves right to cross over South Wicker's Creek. To the left at 5.6 miles, a trail descends to the creek. Ahead the aqueduct goes under Cedar Street in Dobbs Ferry. Walkers climb steps to Cedar Street and cross the street. A handicapped-accessible ramp leading to Cedar Street is to the right.

The aqueduct passes through a permit parking lot, crosses Oak Street, and heads through the municipal parking lot for Dobbs Ferry Village Hall. The dirt path crosses Elm Street and Chestnut Street. Apartment buildings to the left are in view just before the aqueduct reaches the state park headquarters on Walnut Street, at 6.0 miles. A kiosk with an interpretive exhibit is outside the office. The Metro-North Hudson Line Dobbs Ferry Station is to the right, down Walnut Street, which crosses Main Street and becomes Palisades Street. The station is to the left at Station Plaza.

Dobbs Ferry (Walnut Street) to Yonkers (Lamartine Avenue)

Length: 5.1 miles

Views of the Palisades across the Hudson River, access to other parks, and long expanses with no road crossings are features of this section. The aqueduct passes the Keeper's House on the south side of Walnut Street. This brick structure was built in 1857 and was occupied until 1955. It is the only structure built for Aqueduct caretakers that is still extant. Restoration of the house is ongoing and eventually it will become a visitor and education center.

Crossing Broadway (Route 9) at Hatch Terrace, the Aqueduct passes back yards of adjacent homes. It crosses Colonial Street and diagonally crosses Hillside Road at 0.3 mile on an embankment above Route 9. After paralleling Parkway Drive to the left, the aqueduct crosses Flower Avenue at 0.6 mile and enters the Village of Hastings-on-Hudson. Soon after crossing Minturn Street, the aqueduct passes stone cottages to the left, which were originally Dutch farm buildings and later became a stagecoach stop on the Albany Post Road. To the right is Zinsser Park with ball fields and community gardens.

After crossing Edgars Lane, Villard Avenue, and Baker Lane, the aqueduct reaches Five Corners, a busy convergence of Chauncey Lane, Farragut Avenue, Main Street, Old Broadway, and Route 9. Hillside Woods is to the left up Chauncey Lane. To reach the Metro-North Hudson Line Hastings Station from Five Corners, walk down Main Street, cross Warburton Avenue, and continue straight on a driveway into a parking lot. Descend a flight of stairs and the station is almost in front of you.

Diagonally across Five Corners, the aqueduct reenters the woods next to Grace Episcopal Church. It is on a high embankment until reaching Washington Avenue. Beyond Washington Avenue, the aqueduct passes Draper Park, the home of nineteenth century scientist-photographer John William Draper and five generations of his family. It is a National Historic Landmark.

After paralleling Aqueduct Lane at 1.6 miles, the aqueduct passes, to the left, a former quarry, which in the nineteenth century supplied dolomitic marble to the east coast. It served as a park in the early twentieth century and much later as the village dump for yard waste, a use halted partially at the urging of the Friends of the Old Croton Aqueduct. It is hoped that the quarry will once again be a park. The aqueduct reaches a view of the Hudson River and the Palisades, one of many views of the river and the Palisades in the next 2.4 miles. After passing ventilator #18 at 1.9 miles, the aqueduct briefly follows Pinecrest Drive and reenters the woods. Passing views across the river, it crosses a stream on an embankment. At 2.3 miles, it crosses a narrow road leading uphill to the Graham School and downhill to Warburton Avenue, where there are stops for Beeline Bus #6.

There is an unobstructed view of the river at 2.6 miles. At the end of a row of townhouses, the aqueduct enters Yonkers. A path leads up to the Lenoir Preserve. Before reaching Odell Avenue at 2.9 miles, the trail passes a stone building, which once served as a stable for one of the mansions lining the heights. It is a quarter-mile walk downhill along Odell Avenue to reach steps down to the Metro-North Hudson Line Greystone Station.

After passing ventilator #19, the Aqueduct reaches stone pillars to the left. A carved lion and headless unicorn guard the overgrown gates, where a former carriage road leads uphill to Untermyer Park. Reaching a rock cut and then a weir at 3.5 miles, the aqueduct is again on a high embankment. After paralleling Aqueduct Place, it crosses Arthur Place and passes ventilator #20 at 3.9 miles. Here again are views of the Hudson River and the Palisades.

The character of the adjacent area begins to change; houses are closer and there are more apartment buildings. When the aqueduct reaches Shonnard Terrace, it goes through front yards. At 4.5 miles, the aqueduct crosses Philipse Road which leads downhill to Trevor Park and the Hudson River Museum. At 4.7 miles, the aqueduct crosses Glenwood Avenue. It is a quarter-mile walk downhill to the Metro-North Hudson Line Glenwood Station. The aqueduct crosses Wicker Street near an empty lot, reaches ventilator #21 and an interpretive sign just before reaching Lamartine Avenue at 5.1 miles. To reach the Metro-North Hudson Line Yonkers Station, head west on Lamartine Avenue, turn left (south) onto Warburton Avenue, and turn right (west) onto Main Street.

Yonkers (Lamartine Avenue) to the Bronx   *Length: 3.9 miles*
The fifth segment of the aqueduct is along bustling city streets, wedged behind buildings, or through Tibbetts Brook Park. In Yonkers, large granite posts inscribed with OCA mark where the walking route is actually atop the Aqueduct. The aqueduct turns east and ceases to parallel the Hudson River. It crosses Lamartine Avenue goes through the parking lot behind the Yonkers Christian Assembly. Continuing through a grassy field and an unpaved surface behind building, it emerges at the corner of Bishop William J. Walls Place and North Broadway. Walk to Ashburton Avenue and then turn right onto Palisade Avenue at 0.5 mile and immediately make a left onto the Aqueduct with its granite post. Beeline Bus #2 stops here.

Leaving behind the bustle of Yonkers, the path heads downhill. It levels out on a high embankment, passes close to apartment buildings, and, at 0.8 mile, crosses Summit Street where there is an interpretive sign. The aqueduct crosses Nepperhan Avenue on a stone arch bridge dating from 1842, with views from both sides. The Saw Mill River is the river flowing in the concrete channel through the double arches. It crosses Walnut Street and continues behind buildings. After crossing Seymour Street, the walking route follows a macadam path that leads up to Yonkers Avenue and passes ventilator #22. It reaches Yonkers Avenue at 1.0 mile, and at Prescott Street, the walking route diverges once again from the Aqueduct. Cross Yonkers Avenue and walk along the sidewalk on the south side. Rather than following Yonkers Avenue and having to cross the entrance and exit ramps of parkways, walk along Yonkers Avenue to the former railroad bridge and ascend the

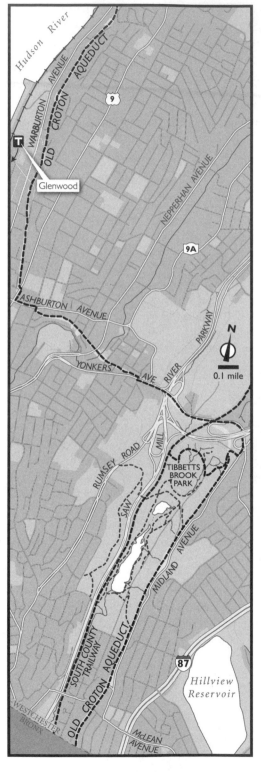

stairs to the South County Trailway. Head south, pass the back wall of a motel, cross the Cross County Parkway on a bridge, and turn left down a paved path into Tibbetts Brook Park. Using paths and park roads, cross the park and head uphill to the Aqueduct. Because the route across the park is not well-defined, it is likely that you will rejoin the Aqueduct south of the weir and ventilator #23.

The aqueduct joins a paved path. At 2.4 miles it goes under the park entrance road and the surface once again becomes dirt. The entrance road leads to many amenities in Tibbetts Brook Park including a pool, restrooms, playground, and sports fields. An unmarked trail to the right leads down to ball fields in the park. After leaving the south end of the park, the aqueduct passes back yards, most with gates in their fences and a stairway leading up to the Aqueduct. At 3.3 miles, the aqueduct passes another ventilator and then crosses McLean Avenue. Beeline Bus #4 stops to the left. After crossing Lawton Street, the state park segment of the aqueduct ends at a divider at 3.9 miles. The aqueduct continues into the Bronx, entering Van Cortlandt Park, a New York City park.

CONNECTING TRAILS & PARKS: Briarcliff Peekskill Trailway, Rockwood Hall, Rockefeller State Park Preserve, Sleepy Hollow Cemetery, Hillside Woods, Lenoir Preserve, Untermyer Park, South County Trailway, Tibbetts Brook Park, Van Cortlandt Park

To learn more about the Aqueduct:

Visit: Ossining Heritage Area Visitor Center on Broadway in Ossining.

Read: *Water for Gotham: A History;* Koeppel, Gerard T.; Princeton University Press, 2001.

Water-Works: The Architecture and Engineering of the New York City Water Supply; Bone, Kevin; Monancelli Press, 2006.

The Old Croton Aqueduct: Rural Resources Meet Urban Needs; Hudson River Museum of Westchester, 1992.

Request: a full-color trail map and guide from Friends of the Old Croton Aqueduct, 95 Broadway, Dobbs Ferry, N Y 10522. Include a check for $5.75 and a SASE.

Ventilator #23.

DRIVING: The Old Croton Aqueduct has multiple access points including 90 road crossings. Use the Aqueduct map or a Westchester County map to reach various road crossings. Where the Aqueduct runs through residential areas, parking is limited, but there are places along streets. Parking areas are listed below, but not municipal lots as they require a permit on weekdays.

Southeast end of Croton Dam [41.225109N 73.854215W]
Quaker Bridge Road east [41.212950N 73.865080W]
Quaker Bridge Road [41.203297N 73.870720W]
Hillcrest Road at GE Management Center [41.190287N 73.867848W]
Old Albany Post Road and Route 9 [41.183477N 73.869535W]
Caputo Community Center (Ossining) [41.163337N 73.862847W]
River Road south of Clear View School [41.130413N 73.861443W]
Gory Brook Road [41.090878N 73.857374W]
Shopping center at routes 9 and 119 [41.064113N 73.861323W]
Lyndhurst [41.052778N 73.867161W]
Walnut Street in Dobbs Ferry [41.011719 N73.877413W]
Draper Park [40.991489N 73.879244W]
Tibbetts Brook Park [40.926636 N73.874899W]

PUBLIC TRANSPORTATION: Metro-North Hudson Line Croton-Harmon, Ossining, Scarborough, Tarrytown, Irvington, Ardsley-on-Hudson, Dobbs Ferry, Hastings, Greystone, Glenwood, and Yonkers stations are within walking distance of the Aqueduct. Although Beeline Buses run along Route 9, they often have limited service. The 1C, 1T and 1W buses along Warburton Avenue terminate at the 242nd Street/Broadway subway station (MTA #1) at Van Cortlandt Park in the Bronx.

For contact information, see Appendix, Old Croton Aqueduct.

South County Trailway

Eastview to the Bronx • 13.9 miles, 48.2 acres

Along much of its length, the South County Trailway is wedged between the Saw Mill River Parkway and the New York State Thruway, both with the expected sounds and sights. In addition, the trailway crosses the Saw Mill River many times. One can look at distribution centers, check out the backs of restaurants and shops, see school buses crammed into storage lots, and view the undersides of overpasses and parkway interchanges. In spite of these trappings of civilization, there are many places to find birds along power line corridors, wetlands, woodlands, and even neighbors' gardens. Frequently, the transition from industrial to woodland and visa versa is abrupt.

Like its northern partner, the North County Trailway, the trailway uses the right-of-way of the Putnam Division of the New York Central which ran for 54 miles between the Bronx and Brewster in Putnam County from 1881 to 1958, when passenger service ceased. The line continued to be used for occasional freight until 1982. Westchester County acquired the 36.2 miles of right-of-way in 1992.

One of the stations on the Putnam Division was Woodlands Lake, which is also the name of a pond on the Saw Mill River. The name is also shared by this section of V. Everit Macy Park, a county park fragmented by the Saw Mill River Parkway. This section includes the Great Hunger Memorial Park, a memorial to those who died or who were forced to emigrate to American as a result of the Irish potato famine of the mid 1800's.

THE TRAILWAY

Occasional remnants of the rail line, such as track, ties, whistle signs, foundations, and old telephone poles, are found along the South County Trailway. At former station sites, interpretive signs provide the history of the railroad and details about that station and its community. The trailway passes through residential, highly industrial, commercial, as well as wooded areas. Unfortunately, industry has intruded on the right-of-way in Elmsford, resulting in a break in the route.

Because the South County Trailway is a linear corridor, hikers have the option to walk out and back on the same route, leave a car where they will end their hike, or rely on public transportation. The trail descriptions are in sections, dictated either by major road crossings or the availability of parking.

Eastview to Warehouse Lane   *Length: 1.8 miles*
The North County and South County trailways connect at Eastview, forming a continuous path. Access to the two trailways is near the intersection of the Saw Mill River Parkway and Saw Mill River Road/Neperan Road. From the northbound exit of the exit ramp of the Saw Mill River Parkway, turn into the parking lot providing access to the trailway. The exit ramp is two-way only as far as the parking

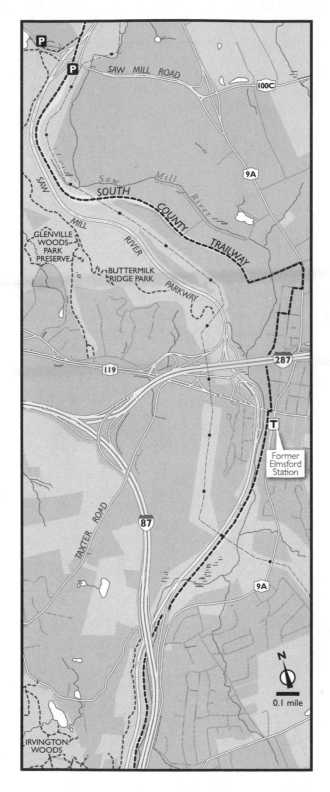

lot entrance. Parking is also available at the commuter lot on Neperan Road just west of the parkway. From the commuter lot, turn left to follow the road and then left again to go up the path along the southbound parkway exit/entrance ramp.

From the North County Trailway, the South County Trailway heads south and crosses over the Saw Mill River Parkway on a bridge. It passes the parking lot off the northbound exit ramp of the parkway. To the right, the noise of the parkway is audible, while to the left the songs of birds living along the power line can be heard. The sounds of the parkway gradually diminish, and after the trailway crosses under the power line at 0.9 mile, parkway noise is gone. Continuing downhill, the trail crosses Fairview Park Drive and then suddenly is at the back of a Coca Cola distribution center. It passes numerous warehouses and reaches Warehouse Lane. There is a gap between here and NY 119 in Elmsford. The detour along Warehouse Lane to NY 9A as it heads south to NY 119 is along heavily traveled roads with few sidewalks. It is not a safe route, especially for families with children and cyclists who are not comfortable riding in heavy truck traffic.

Elmsford (NY 119) to Woodlands Lake
Length: 2.6 miles

Just south of NY 119 and immediately west of Route 9A, the South County squeezes along its narrow right-of-way and passes shops, restaurants, distribution centers, and light industry. The only remaining station along the South County Trailway now functions as a restaurant; it is located off NY 9A in Elmsford, adjacent to the trailway.

At 0.2 mile, the South County Trailway suddenly leaves commercial and industrial areas and enters the woods. Aside from a short stretch in the open near

INVASIVE INTRUDERS

Except for a few highly manicured parks, most of the parks described in this book typically have problems with opportunistic invasive plants. Commonly referred to as "invasives," these plants have aggressive growing habits and few natural competitors. They tend to dominate the flora of an area and may crowd out native, rare, or beneficial plants. Usually, an invasive is from a foreign country, but popular use of the term includes fast-growing, adaptive native plants such as poison ivy and greenbriar. Some invasives, such as Japanese barberry, were imported because they were useful, familiar, or attractive. Others arrived by piggybacking on other commerce. In both cases, their natural control mechanisms were left behind.

Common invasives in Westchester parks include Japanese barberry, Asian bittersweet, multiflora rose, and native grape vine. These aggressive plants can create problems along trails by encroaching on footpaths, to the point of making them impassable. Oriental bittersweet and native grape vines can completely encompass a tree and either strangle it or cause it to fall. Other invasives, such as garlic mustard, Japanese stiltgrass, and mile-a-minute vine, can quickly overrun an area and threaten native plants. Wetlands are threatened by invasives which are at home in that particular ecosystem. Such plants include phragmite reeds, purple loosestrife, and a variety of pond weeds. The Invasive Plant Council of New York State has a more complete list. See http://www.ipcnys.org/.

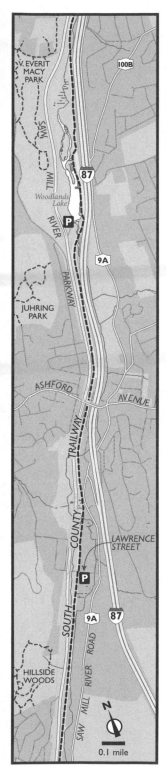

Woodlands Lake.

the thruway exit ramp leading to the Saw Mill River Parkway, the trail is almost always in woods or near wetland. It parallels the parkway, staying just inside the woods, out of sight of cars zooming along. It passes under power lines at 0.6 mile and the parkway and thruway interchanges at 1.1 miles. Entering wetlands on the right, the trailway reaches Woodlands Lake at 2.6 miles where parking and picnic tables are available across the dam that forms Woodlands Lake.

Woodlands Lake to Barney Street

Length: 3.6 miles

Because trains still ran on the Putnam Division when the Saw Mill Parkway was built, this narrow corridor between river and parkway was protected from development. From Woodlands Lake south, the noise from two high-speed roads is never far away; however, the trailway has thick vegetation on both sides, which helps to screen out some traffic noise in leaf-on season. Just beyond where the trail passes under the Ashford Avenue bridge at 0.9 mile, the surroundings suddenly become industrial. To reach the commercial area in Ardsley, turn left at the entrance at Elm Street, just past the Ardsley Bus Company yards. At this point, the thruway diverges and the road noise decreases. The trailway passes a factory and reaches Lawrence Street at 1.6 miles.

Here, the South County Trailway leaves the industrial area. The vegetation is indicative of heavily

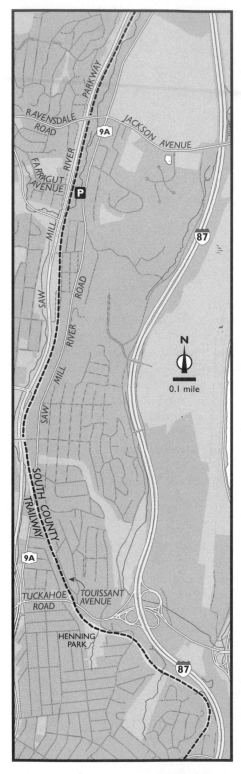

N

0.1 mile

disturbed soil and trees are so densely covered with invasive vines that it is difficult to discern exactly how many trees are underneath. The trailway parallels the Saw Mill River to the left and the parkway to the right. At 2.6 miles, at the site of Mt. Hope Station, a few railroad ties are to the left and a steel girder stands naked and forlorn in the midst of heavy undergrowth. At 3.1 miles, the trailway crosses Farragut Avenue with a parking lot to the left, and then passes many back yards. It crosses Tompkins Avenue at 3.4 miles, parallels Railroad Avenue, and reaches Barney Street.

Barney Street to Redmond Park
Length:3.5 miles
The South County Trailway heads along the edge of a parking lot. Through the chain-link fences lining the trail, there are glimpses of a wide variety of light industry. The trailway goes under the Odell Viaduct at 0.7 mile and passes the former site of the Grey Oaks Station. After crossing a massive bridge over Route 9A, the trailway enters a more residential section with access for residents at the ends of dead end streets. A building immediately adjacent to the trail has evidence of an old freight siding. At 1.4 miles, the trailway passes a pedestrian entrance at Touissant Avenue and the site of the former Nepperhan Station with an interpretive sign. After going under Tuckahoe Road, the South County Trailway passes a pedestrian entrance in a shopping plaza. It heads uphill and goes onto a built up causeway which has split rail fence along the side. At 1.8 miles, it goes under Mile Square Road. A woods road that was cut off when the thruway was built is visible in leaf off season at 2.0 miles. Sounds of the thruway fill the air as the trail passes

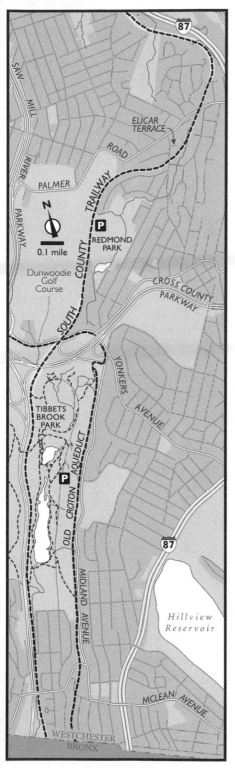

below houses, rounds a stone retaining wall, and then enters a rock cut. Just after it goes under Palmer Road at 2.6 miles, there is a pedestrian entrance with stairs up to Palmer Road (no parking). The former Byrn Mawr station and an interpretive sign are adjacent to the trail. Now heading slightly downhill, the trailway crosses Mile Square Road at 2.9 miles. The back yards of houses, some with paths leading onto the trailway are up against the right of way. To the right at 3.1 miles, Dunwoodie Golf Course is steeply uphill. At 3.5 miles, the trailway reaches the junction with a trail heading steeply downhill to a parking lot in Redmond Park.

Redmond Park to Van Cortlandt Park
Length: 2.4 miles
For two-thirds of its length, this southernmost section of the South County Trailway is wedged between Tibbetts Brook Park and the Saw Mill River Parkway. From the parking lot farthest from Redmond Park's entrance, an access trail to the trailway heads uphill. Once on the trailway, almost immediately the Catskill Aqueduct is visible downhill to the left and the Dunwoodie Golf Course is uphill to the right. The trailway goes alongside a fence where a gate and an adjacent parking area indicate that before the trailway was paved, there were encroachments on the right-of-way. The trailway passes the site of the former Dunwoodie Station with steps down to Yonkers Avenue at 0.3 mile. The back wall of a motel is most likely on the railroad's right-of-way.

After passing over the Cross County Parkway at 0.6 mile, the trailway enters Tibbetts Brook Park. At 0.8 mile a 0.1-mile paved path to the left enters the park. Paralleling the Saw Mill River Parkway, the trailway is never far from the sight and sound of cars. At 1.0 mile, it passes under a pedestrian bridge over the Saw Mill River Parkway; the bridge leads to 1.2 miles of unmarked paths in open space on the west side of the parkway.

At 1.6 miles, a paved path to the left leads into Tibbetts Brook Park. The trailway crosses a bridge over Tibbetts Brook and then at 2.0 miles passes a paved path to Harrison Avenue. The site of the former Lincoln Station is at 2.1 miles, adjacent to the McLean Avenue viaduct. It reaches the county line at 2.4 miles where the pavement ends as the right of way enters Van Cortlandt Park, a New York City park.

CONNECTING TRAIL & PARK: North County Trailway, Buttermilk Ridge, V. Everit Macy Park, Redmond Park, and Tibbetts Brook Park

DRIVING: Because of proximity to the Saw Mill Parkway, the NYS Thruway, and the Saw Mill River, there are far fewer access points to the South County Trailway than along a comparable length of the North County Trailway. Parking is available at
Eastview commuter lot [41.082434N 73.830832W];
Route 100 C at the northbound off ramp [41.080484N 73.829329W];
Great Hunger Memorial Park (Woodlands) [41.025132N 73.845710W];
Lawrence Street at Route 9A [41.001507N 73.853894W];
Farragut Avenue [40.983005N 73.865981W];
Barney Street [40.976195N 73.867681W];
Redmond Park [40.938349N 73.869254W]; and
Tibbetts Brook Park [40.926636N 73.874899W].
Access to Woodland Lakes/Great Hunger Memorial Park is only from the northbound lane of the Saw Mill River Parkway. To reach the park if southbound on the Saw Mill River Parkway, exit at Ashford Avenue, cross over the parkway, and reenter it to head north. One can exit the park only to go north on the parkway. To go south, head north and exit the parkway for westbound Route 119; go under the parkway and take the southbound entrance ramp.

PUBLIC TRANSPORTATION: Beeline Buses: #1C, #11, #14, #17, near Elmsford; #5 along Route 9A; #91 on Yonkers Avenue

For contact information, see Appendix, Westchester County Parks.

Teatown-Kitchawan Trail

Teatown to Kitchawan • 6.5 miles

*O*h, the Places You'll Go! says Dr. Seuss in his book by the same name, for there's "Fun to be done," he tells You. He could have had the Teatown Kitchawan Trail in mind for here's a trail that will take you further than you thought, with links to other trails that can take you almost anywhere. The "TK Trail," as it is known, heads east from Teatown Lake Reservation, to connect to John E. Hand Park and Kitchawan Preserve. It is the county's only primarily east-west linear corridor.

The trail is a direct link to the Briarcliff Peekskill Trailway and indirectly to the Old Croton Aqueduct and North County Trailway. The former will take you south to New York City and latter will take you north almost to Brewster in Putnam County or south to the South County Trailway and then to New York City. Teatown Lake Reservation and the NYC Department of Environmental Protection (DEP) partnered to build this trail with the New York-New Jersey Trail Conference providing expertise and volunteers to build and maintain it.

TEATOWN-KITCHAWAN TRAIL

Sporting a purple blaze, the Teatown Kitchawan Trail piggybacks on existing trails as it travels through a varied terrain of wetlands, hills, valleys, meadows, and forest. It crosses streams and provides an occasional view down to Croton Reservoir. Passing through an isolated portion of pristine DEP property, it provides a peaceful setting for hikers.

Starting from the Nature Center in Teatown Lake Reservation, this trail is co-aligned with the Lakeside Trail (blue) going counterclockwise around the lake. Just before the dam, it turns right, leaves the Lakeside Trail and then at 0.6 mile, upon meeting the Briarcliff-Peekskill Trailway (green), turns right again. It reaches Blinn Road, turns right to cross the road as the Briarcliff-Peekskill Trailway turns left. At 1.0 mile, the trail turns left to the parking area for John E. Hand Park.

The Teatown-Kitchawan Trail then heads uphill on a barberry lined path, passing unmarked mountain bike trails almost immediately and at 1.3 and 1.5 miles. It turns left off the main trail at 1.6 miles and winds through the woods with many elevation gains and losses. It enters DEP property and at 1.8 miles turns onto a woods road as it descends. At 2.0 miles, the trail heads uphill, enters a field, and passes stands of white pines, a lone laurel bush, and cedar trees. Unfortunately, there are no views.

Heading steadily downhill, hikers can catch their first glimpse of the Croton Reservoir at 2.4 miles. At the bottom of the hill, the trail turns right onto Croton Dam Road which has limited views of the reservoir through trees. The trail goes under the southbound Taconic State Parkway bridge at 3.1 miles and under the northbound bridge. At 3.8 miles, it turns right onto Aqueduct Road.

Now paralleling the northbound Taconic State Parkway, the trail heads uphill and to the right passes a road bridge over the parkway. Almost at the top of the rise, the trail turns left and enters DEP property for a second time. It enters a field

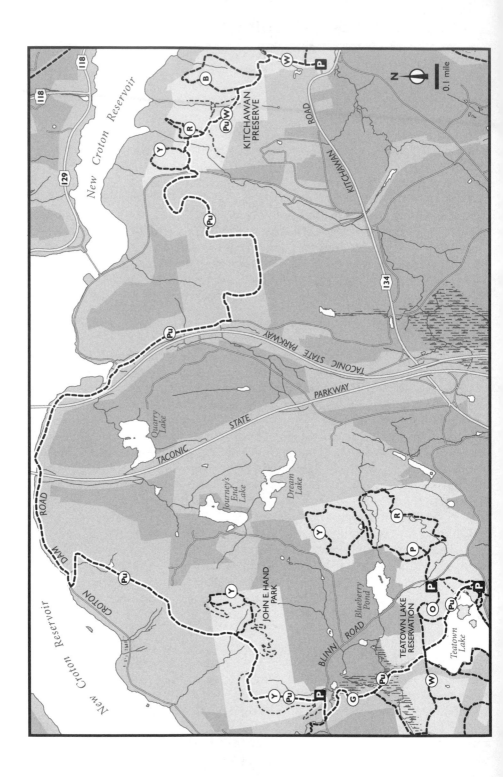

Under the southbound Taconic State Parkway bridge.

on a mowed path at 4.4 miles and then enters the woods to begin a long, slow climb uphill. Going left through a stone wall at 4.8 miles, the trail is once more on a mowed path and begins to descend. Twice it is on a raised area supported by a stone wall, which keeps the path on an even grade. At 5.1 miles the trail heads downhill at a steady grade on a woods road, makes a series of left turns, and crosses Arcady Road at 5.6 miles. To the left is the entrance to Kitchawan Preserve.

In Kitchawan Preserve, the trail is co-aligned with the Kitchawan Trail (white), which is the main route through the preserve. The co-aligned trails pass first one end of the Chestnut Hill Trail (yellow) and the other just before descending to Big Brook. It crosses Big Brook on large stepping stones and then heads uphill. At 5.8 miles, they pass one end of the Hemlock Ravine Trail (red) to the left and then turn right as they pass the other end. They go through a series of four fields separated by hedgerows, where, in an old orchard, the Old Barn Trail (blue) is to the left. Just after passing the Old Barn Trail for a second time at 6.2 miles, they turn left to enter the woods. They descend to Little Brook, cross it on a bridge and turn right. To the left is the Little Brook Nature Trail (yellow). In spring, a vast array of skunk cabbage lines both sides of Little Brook. At a broad intersection, the Teatown-Kitchawan Trail heads to the parking area at Kitchawan Preserve. The Kitchawan Trail continues to the left to end at the North County Trailway, which it is possible to follow north to Brewster in Putnam County or south to New York City.

CONNECTING TRAILS & PARKS: Kitchawan Preserve, John E. Hand Park, and Teatown Lake Reservation

DRIVING: Only three road access points have adequate parking. Use the driving directions for the Nature Center at Teatown Lake Reservation [41.211228N 73.827243W], John E. Hand Park [41.050511N 73.849653W], and Kitchawan Preserve [41.220635N 73.786393W] to access parking.

PUBLIC TRANSPORTATION: none available

For contact information, see Appendix, Teatown Lake Reservation.

John E. Hand Park

Teatown • 2.8 miles, 112 acres

No demon lives on this Bald Mountain, located in John E. Hand Park. Unlike the frightful images conjured up for Mussorsky's *A Night on Bald Mountain* in the 1940 Disney film *Fantasia*, all is serene here. A woods road winds gracefully to the base of this Bald Mountain where a trail circles to the top, with limited views. Westchester acquired the lands in 1992 to preserve the open space which is part of the watershed of the Croton Reservoir. In 1995, the park was renamed to honor the late John E. Hand, a county legislator from Yorktown.

TRAILS

Although Hand Park is riddled with mountain bike trails, it is easy walking along the yellow-blazed woods road. There are 1.6 miles of bike trails. The tracks on the northwest flank of Bald Mountain are not pleasant hiking and are not included in the total trail miles.

Yellow Trail   *Length: 1.2 miles Blaze: yellow*
From the parking area on Blinn Road, the yellow trail and the Teatown-Kitchawan Trail (purple) head uphill through multiflora rose and barberry bushes. The co-aligned trails pass, to the left, the first of many unmarked mountain bike trails. The trails continue their gradual ascent. After the yellow trail crosses a stone wall, an unmarked 0.8 mile bike track from Blinn Road enters from the left which is easily missed as one heads uphill. After a sharp right turn, the trails split at 0.7 mile, with the Teatown-Kitchawan Trail turning left. A second unmarked bike path leaves to the right and snakes its way 0.8 mile uphill to rejoin the yellow trail.

The yellow trail ascends and, at 1.0 mile, passes the other end of the second bike path mentioned above. At a stone wall, the yellow trail turns left, where an unmarked path heads into New York City Department of Environmental Protection property (hiking permit required). The yellow trail ascends 0.2 mile to the top of Bald Mountain with its seasonal views.

NEABY TRAIL & PARK: Briarcliff Peekskill Trailway, Teatown Lake Reservation

DRIVING: From the Taconic State Parkway, take the Route 134 Exit and turn west towards Ossining. Just past the southbound entrance ramp, turn right onto Grant Street, immediately passing a small house to the left. Do not make the hard right turn onto Illington Road. At the stop sign, turn right onto Spring Valley Road and continue 0.6 mile. Turn right onto Blinn Road and at 1.6 miles, turn right into the small parking area [41.050511N 73.849653W].

PUBLIC TRANSPORTATION: none available

For contact information, see Appendix, Westchester County Parks.

Yorktown Trailway

Shrub Oak to Crompond • 3.4 miles

Paralleling the Taconic State Parkway near the Westchester-Putnam county line, the Yorktown Trailway utilizes a former equestrian trail and a sewer right-of-way. During public hearings held about widening the Taconic Parkway, comments were made about having a pedestrian bridge to connect the parkland on both sides of the roadway. In return for the town's approval of the changes to the parkway, an agreement was made to build the bridge. The Yorktown Trailway Taconic Bridge Overpass completed in 2007 connects Woodlands Legacy Fields Parks with the Yorktown Trailway and Granite Knolls Park.

The Yorktown Trailway is along a former equestrian trail that was built as part of the Taconic State Parkway in 1927. The Bridle Trail, as it was then known, connected what is now Mohansic Golf Course with Fahnestock State Park. Over the years, various road improvements in the area destroyed the Bridle Trail and the Yorktown Trailway has restored much of that route in Westchester.

THE TRAILWAY

At a stone wall at the Putnam-Westchester county line, the Yorktown Trailway heads south into the woods, but never far from the Taconic State Parkway. At 0.5 mile, it crosses Route 6 and follows the southbound entrance ramp, at times inches from high-speed traffic. It crosses Route 132 at 0.9 mile, again follows an entrance ramp, and at one point is high above the parkway. A chain-link fence separates back yards from the trailway and ends near the cul-de-sac on Buckhorn Street. A wood bridge connects to a path at the entrance to Buckhorn Street. At 1.3 miles, the trailway crosses wetlands on an extensive boardwalk, and then onto a second board walk at 1.6 miles.

At 2.1 miles, the Yorktown Trailway turns away from the Taconic. It reaches a wide intersection with a raised manhole, where on the west side, Dynamite Run (lavender) skirts the intersection and heads uphill on a woods road into Granite Knolls Park. At 2.3 miles, the Taconic Bridge Trail (pink) enters from the right from Granite Knolls Park. The two trails head south and reach the pedestrian bridge

Yorktown Trailway Taconic Bridge Overpass.

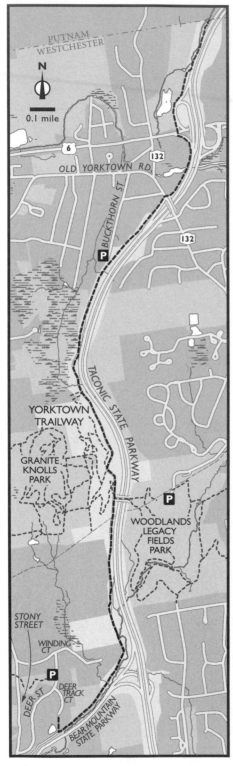

over the Taconic.

Built as a result of citizen input when the Taconic State Parkway was widened, the Yorktown Trailway Taconic Parkway Overpass connected undeveloped parkland to the Yorktown Trailway. Completed in 2007, the bridge was referred to, with unfortunate regularity, as the Bridge to Nowhere. In 2010, with the Town of Yorktown's purchase of what is now Granite Knolls Park, plans for an extensive trail system took root. Hikers and mountain bikers joined to construct more than 10 miles of new trails in the two parks making the bridge a popular destination.

An interpretive kiosk displaying historic photos of the parkway is at each end of the bridge. The Taconic Bridge Trail turns left and continues into Woodlands Legacy Fields Park. The Yorktown Trailway continues south, still on the west side of the Taconic. It goes through many wet areas before paralleling Hunter Brook and the Bear Mountain Extension. At 1.1 miles from the bridge, the trailway leaves the woods and reaches the right-of-way to Deer Track Court (no parking). The sewer line continues on to reach Stony Street and Route 202.

ADJACENT & NEARBY PARKS: Granite Knolls Park, Woodlands Legacy Fields Park

DRIVING: From the Taconic State Parkway, take the Route 6 Exit and head west to Shrub Oak. Turn left on to Buckhorn Street and drive to the end where there is parking [41.324634N 73.824787W].

PUBLIC TRANSPORTATION: At the north end, Beeline Bus #16 on Old Main Street in Shrub Oak; at the south end, Beeline Bus #15 on Route 202 at the Staples Shopping Center.

For contact information, see Appendix, Yorktown.

Along a stream in Durand Preserve.

SECTION VIII

TRAIL SYSTEMS

- Link communities, parks, and open space
- Offer a wide range of distances to walk or hike
- Are corridors for wildlife

TRAIL SYSTEMS

Entire County • 273 miles

There are trails in Westchester County which extend beyond park boundaries, connect parks, and form networks. These trail systems allow for extended hikes and, like the linear corridors, allow wildlife to move safely between open spaces. Each trail system is unique and provides recreational opportunities for different user groups: hikers, mountain bikers, and equestrians. For example, the equestrian trail systems do more than just provide trails: they also bring together citizens who wish to sustain the rural character of areas and protect open spaces through purchases and conservation easements.

Bedford Riding Lanes Association

Bedford • Over 100 miles

Formerly known as the Private Lanes Association (PLA), the Bedford Riding Lanes Association (BRLA) today preserves and maintains over 100 miles of

TRAIL PIONEERS, BUT ON HORSEBACK

The concept of a trail system is not a new one in Westchester County and some of the pioneers were equestrians. As early as the 1920s and 1930s, owners of large properties who were horse lovers joined to develop networks of trails that would allow equestrians and fox hunters to travel across the county to events or visit neighboring estates. This way they could avoid paved roads and the danger of the ever-increasing numbers of automobiles.

The Private Lanes Association was formed in 1920 and became the Bedford Riding Lanes Association in the 1950s, which today actively preserves and protects over 100 miles of bridle trails. The Goldens Bridge Hounds was established in 1924 as a hunt club. By 1970, they realized the importance of protecting and maintaining these trails and established a separate group, the North Salem Bridle Trail Association, to care for and promote them. One relatively new group, the Lewisboro Horsemen Association, was formed by residents in Lewisboro in 1990 to provide riding opportunities.

If you hike in Kitchawan Preserve, it is possible you might see an old trail marker for The Dirt Trails Association (DTA). Formed in 1934, they established equestrian trails south of the Croton Reservoir. It no longer exists, but their trails were still visible in the late 1960s. Some of these trails have been incorporated in parks while others had simply been neglected and have disappeared.

bridle trails. These riding trails have become an integral part of Bedford, making it possible for equestrians to ride between residences. Some trails are open to the public and others are for members only. Hikers who join this organization increase their hiking options.

In the 1950's, suburban encroachment and pressure by land developers began to take a heavy toll on these trails, most of which existed as a result of hand-shake agreements made decades before. Construction of the Saw Mill River Parkway sliced right through the trail system and the western section fell into disuse. More recently, BRLA has taken an active role in revitalizing the network. It is encouraging landowners to sell or donate easements to permit riding on private property, pushing to preserve other open spaces, and working to extend trails into parks and other public areas. In addition to the parks listed below, BRLA trails are along dirt roads in Bedford and in Beaver Dam Sanctuary, Merestead, St. Matthews Woodlands, and Ward Pound Ridge Reservation. For more information about these trails, see http://www.bedfordridinglanes.com/

The 0.2 mile of trail in Palmer H. Lewis Wildlife Sanctuary on Route 121 in Cross River connects to BRLA trails in adjacent woodlands. In 1967, Hope Lewis Bedell transferred the property to the National Audubon Society who, in 1999 transferred it to the Bedford Audubon Society [41.231462N 73.619887W].

Guard Hill Preserve

Bedford Village • 1.7 miles, 62 acres

Wetlands seen from the entrance of Guard Hill Preserve might lead you to think you were in for a wet hike, but because of the dense vegetation you cannot reach the standing water that pools in the interior of this preserve. The trail, marked with BRLA signs, skirts the edge of the property. In 2000, Brian and Amy Pennington of Shannon Stables purchased 62 acres to prevent its development. They donated the land to the Westchester Land Trust to permanently protect it.

From Guard Hill Road, the trail skirts a field in Sunnyfield Farm to the right and a large wetland to the left. At 0.4 mile, it leaves the fields and passes side trails looping to the right for 0.3 mile. At 0.5 mile, the main side trail rejoins the main trail. After crossing wetlands on an embankment, the main trail passes a house at 0.8 mile. Turning left at 1.1 miles, it goes along a farm road beside pastures, steeplechase course, riding ring, and barns. The main trail ends at Guard Hill Road at 1.4 miles. A portion through Shannon Stables is open only to BRLA members.

DRIVING: From I-684, take Exit 4 (Route 172) and drive 1.2 miles east. Turn left onto Clark Road and right at Guard Hill Road. It is 0.2 mile from the turn to parking on the south side of the road, next to the entrance sign [41.205733N 73.663662W].

PUBLIC TRANSPORTATION: None available

For contact information, see Appendix, Westchester Land Trust.

John Jay Homestead.

John Jay Homestead

Katonah • 1.0 miles, 63.6 acres

For hikers with a keen interest in American History, a visit to the John Jay Homestead is a real treat. A distinguished public servant for 27 years, Jay served in more key capacities than any other of our founding fathers, including president of the Continental Congress, first chief justice of the U.S. Supreme Court, and the second governor of New York. Jay's unassuming house, built in 1799, is set back from Route 22. Jay retired here in 1801 and five generations of his family lived in the house until 1953. Its rooms are shown as they might have been in the 1820s. The grounds are open to walkers and equestrians year-round. There is a charge to tour the house.

Interpretive signs point out features and show what changes have occurred. The 0.2 mile Beech Allée, with copper and silver beeches, was planted in the second half of the nineteenth century. It leads to Lyons Ridge Road (no parking).

BRLA negotiated with the state to allow horses on the property, an activity not often permitted at an historic site. Equestrians are restricted to the marked bridle paths along the edge of the property. The 0.8-mile BRLA trail at the Homestead connects with BRLA trails across Route 22. A 0.5 mile trail from the back of the property connects to additional BRLA trails at the Harvey School.

DRIVING: From I-684, take Exit 6 (Katonah) and go east on Route 35. Turn right onto Route 22 and head south for 1.5 miles. The entrance is to the left with parking at the end of a long entrance drive [41.250589N 73.659237W].

PUBLIC TRANSPORTATION: None available

For contact information, see Appendix, John Jay Homestead.

Colonial Greenway

Scarsdale, Eastchester, New Rochelle, Mamaroneck • 15.1 miles

Encompassing an area rich in Colonial history, the Colonial Greenway connects seven parks in lower Westchester: Saxon Woods Park, Hutchinson River Pathway, Twin Lakes Park/Nature Study Woods, Weinberg Nature Center, Leatherstocking Trail, Larchmont Reservoir, and Ward Acres Park. The Colonial Greenway is described in detail within the chapter for each of the parks it connects. The road walks between the parks are described here.

The Colonial Greenway is a 12.3-mile outer loop and a 2.8-mile connection across the center. This 'cross piece' makes it possible to have two shorter loops: the 9.4-mile west loop through Twin Lakes/Nature Study Woods and the 8.5-mile east loop through the southern section of Saxon Woods. Parking is limited and in some instances, there are nearby streets with parking for one or two cars. Sometimes it is necessary to park and take another trail to reach the Colonial Greenway.

OUTER LOOP

Beginning in the parking lot in Saxon Woods South, the 12.3-mile outer loop of the Colonial Greenway is described in a counterclockwise direction.

Saxon Woods South to Saxon Woods Golf Course   *Length: 2.3 miles*
The Colonial Greenway is co-aligned with Loop 1. It leaves the park, parallels the Hutchinson River Parkway, and enters the Weinberg Nature Center. Upon reaching Mamaroneck Road, it turns right, follows the sidewalk, crosses over the parkway, turns left to cross Mamaroneck Road and joins the Hutchinson River Pathway. For a full description and a detailed map, see Saxon Woods (in Large Parks).

Saxon Woods (Mamaroneck Road) to Mill Road   *Length: 4.2 miles*
The Colonial Greenway is co-aligned with the Hutchinson River Pathway as it parallels the Hutchinson River Parkway. At 1.2 miles at Pinebrook Boulevard, turn left to follow the section to Ward Acres Park, Larchmont Reservoir, and the Leatherstocking Trail. There is no parking at Pinebrook Boulevard or Mill Street. (For a full description and map, see Hutchinson River Pathway in Linear Corridors.)

OUT FOR A WALK

In 1976, John Varvayanis wanted to go for a hike near his home which had plenty of park and open space nearby, but the parks were not connected. So he obtained permission to walk over the connecting property and then asked again for his hiking club. Realizing that with private and public support, a permanent trail was possible, he worked to create an eight-mile loop, the Westchester Greenway Trail, which opened in 1988. In 2001, spearheaded by the Town of Mamaroneck, the surrounding communities and the county obtained grants to extend this trail. Five years later, the Colonial Greenway Trail became a reality.

Road through Twin Lakes/Nature Study Woods   *Length: 2.6 miles*
From Mill Road (no parking), the Colonial Greenway is co-aligned with the Hutchinson River Pathway for 0.3 mile as they enter Twin Lakes Park. When they split, the Hutchinson River Pathway goes left to parallel the Hutch and the Colonial Greenway turns right toward Reservoir #3. They join at the dam of Reservoir #3 and are co-aligned for the next 1.3 miles. The trails split 100 feet before reaching the entrance to Nature Study Woods on Webster Avenue. (For a full description and map, see Twin Lakes/Nature Study Woods in Afternoon Jaunts.)

Nature Study Woods to Pinebrook Boulevard   *Length: 1.4 miles*
A lengthy road walk connects Nature Study Woods to the Leatherstocking Trail. Along the route, one has the opportunity to look at the architectural variety of private homes and their gardens. From the entrance to Nature Study Woods, cross Webster Avenue to follow Flandreau Avenue. At the intersection with Argyle Avenue, turn left, walk one block to Calton Road, and turn right. Follow Calton Road to the junction with one-way Glenfruin Avenue and turn right, descending behind New Rochelle High School. Turn right onto Braemar Avenue and cross North Avenue to reach Broadview Avenue. Thomas Paine's house is to the left, one block north. Follow Broadview Avenue for 0.7 mile to end at Lyncroft Road. Turn left and walk one block. Just after #316, turn right and walk down the grassy strip along the sewer easement to Hillside Crescent. Follow Hillside Crescent downhill, cross Pinebrook Boulevard, and reach the Leatherstocking Trail. (For a full description and map, see Leatherstocking Trail in Linear Corridors.)

Pinebrook Boulevard to Saxon Woods South   *Length: 3.1 miles*
The 2.6-mile Leatherstocking Trail goes from Pinebrook Boulevard to Old White Plains Road. (For a map and full description, see Leatherstocking Trail in Linear Corridors.) At the end of the Leatherstocking Trail, continue 0.2 mile through the

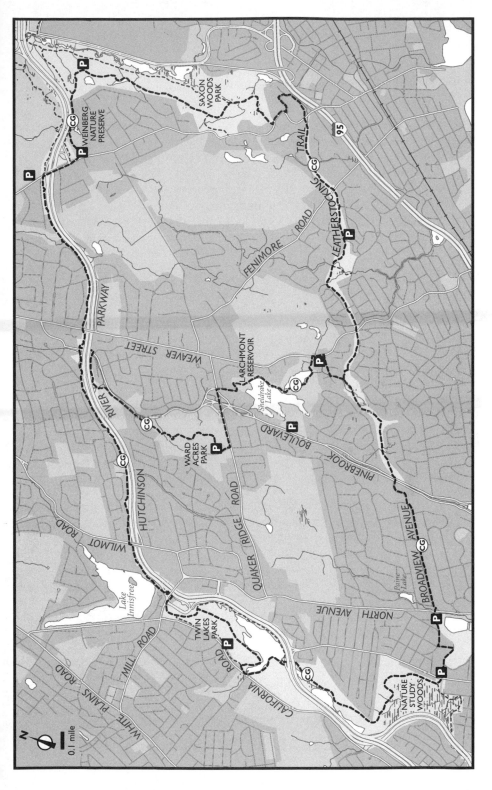

woods to Rock Ridge Road. Turn left to reach Deerfield Road and when it reaches Old White Plains Road, turn right. Old White Plains Road is narrow with a short sight distance. To walk facing traffic, it is necessary to cross the street and then cross it again to order to enter Saxon Woods Park South shortly after passing #1011.

CROSS SECTION

Two shorter loops are possible with the Colonial Greenway because a section of the Greenway connects the Leatherstocking Trail to the Hutchinson River Pathway. This 2.8-mile section goes through Larchmont Reservoir and Ward Acres Park.

Leatherstocking Trail to Larchmont Reservoir   *Length: 0.3 mile*
On the Leatherstocking Trail, at 0.7 mile from Pinebrook Boulevard, a wooden bridge and boardwalk lead to Addie Circle. Turn right onto Bonnie Way. At Weaver Street, turn left to reach the parking lot for the Larchmont Reservoir.

Larchmont Reservoir   *Length: 0.7 mile*
For a full description and map, see Larchmont Reservoir in Pocket Parks.

Larchmont Reservoir to Ward Acres Park   *Length: 0.6 mile*
At the end of Dennis Drive, cross Quaker Ridge Road. Follow it along the sidewalk to the Ward Acres Park entrance on Broadfield Road, across from William Ward Elementary School.

Ward Acres Park   *Length: 0.6 mile*
For a full description and map, see Ward Acres in Afternoon Jaunts.

Ward Acres Park to Hutchinson River Pathway   *Length: 0.9 mile*
From Ward Acres at Pinebrook Boulevard, the Colonial Greenway turns left to

Colonial Greenway, Larchmont Reservoir.

follow Pinebrook Boulevard. At 0.5 mile, just past the driveway at Temple Israel, it enters the woods and heads uphill. The trail reaches a fence which separates pedestrians from traffic on the Hutchinson River Parkway and follows it. At the end of the fence at 0.8 mile, it heads downhill and away from the parkway. At Pinebrook Boulevard, turn left, walk along the north side of the road, and go under the Hutchinson River Parkway. Turn right and enter the woods to join the Outer Loop of the Colonial Greenway along Hutchinson River Pathway.

DRIVING: There are numerous access points for the Colonial Greenway. Parking is located at the parks through which it goes, and occasionally on nearby streets. Specific driving directions and parking availability are listed with each park.

PUBLIC TRANSPORTATION: Access by public transportation is listed in the descriptions of individual parks.

For contact information, see Appendix, Mamaroneck (Town)

East Coast Greenway

Portchester to Pelham Manor

What began as an idea at a regional bicycle conference has evolved into the East Coast Greenway, a trail that spans over 3,000 miles, stretching from the Canadian border at Calais, Maine to Key West, Florida. The trail, which is sometimes referred to as the urban sister of the Appalachian Trail, utilizes sidewalks, old rail lines, greenways (such as the greenway along Manhattan's West Side waterfront), as well as roads. It is open to cyclists, hikers, and walkers. Although the trail route is complete, it is still a work in progress as new off roads pathways are added. Over a quarter of the trail is off roads and along traffic-free paths. Eventually, planners hope that all of the Greenway will have its own space.

In Westchester, the lack of an existing right-of-way has made routing away from roadways difficult. The East Coast Greenway currently uses Bike Route 1, part of the national bicycle route system, which generally parallels Route 1 and the Old Boston Post Road and connects to off street routes in Connecticut and New Jersey. The only piece in the county currently off road is the section near Rye Playland. For more information, see www.greenway.org

Hudson River Valley Greenway Trail

Entire County • 57.3 miles

Crossing through urban, suburban and rural areas, the Hudson River Valley Greenway Trail, known to walkers simply as "The Greenway," is a path as diverse as the valley. Built by local communities, it includes riverside walking trails, connecting trails, countryside corridors, a water trail, a bike route, and a car route. The trail is the result of a legislative initiative began in the 1980's that created

RiverWalk in Tarrytown.

an agency, the Hudson River Valley Greenway, to work to encourage local and county governments to engage in regional planning to preserve scenic, historic and recreation assets throughout the Hudson Valley. For details about completed sections and potential routes, see www.hudsongreenway.state.ny.us and search for Trail Plan.

Westchester County has been coordinating its efforts with the Greenway in creating access along the river in the RiverWalk project. The completed portions of it are described in Along the River in Linear Corridors. The Camp Smith Trail, Cortlandt's Shoreline Trail, George's Island Park, CrOssining Bridge, Old Croton Aqueduct, and Rowley's Bridge are described elsewhere in this book. Not all Greenway designated trails are along the river. Local municipalities as well as nonprofit groups such as Teatown Lake Reservation may submit requests to the Hudson River Valley Greenway to have their trails included as a community trail.

For contact information, see Appendix, Hudson River Valley Greenway

Hudson Trail

Yonkers to Cortlandt

Not to be confused with the Hudson River Valley Greenway Trail, the Hudson Trail is a proposed virtual route from Manhattan to Mount Marcy, located in the Adirondacks. Begun in 2007 as a private project by Bob Jessen, it uses existing trails and roads. In Westchester County, it follows the Old Croton Aqueduct, the Briarcliff Peekskill Trailway, and trails in Blue Mountain Reservation. North of Blue Mountain Reservation, the Hudson Trail follows roads to Putnam County. Track its progress at http://hudsontrail.wordpress.com/.

Lewisboro Horsemen's Association

Lewisboro • 20 miles

Founded in 1990, the Lewisboro Horsemen's Association (LHA) develops and maintains bridle trails as well as hosting social and educational events that bring together local equestrians. LHA maintains approximately 20 miles of trails on public and private property in Lewisboro. Levy, Rose, and Old Field preserves have trails which are part of the LHA network. Other LHA trails connect with bridle trails in Bedford and North Salem. The trails on private property are open only to rider members of LHA; membership tags must be displayed. No dogs are allowed on LHA trails. For more information see http://www.lhatrails.org/

Trails in North Salem

North Salem • 97 miles

Close ties of three groups in North Salem (two equestrian and a land preservation organization) have resulted in about 100 miles of hiking and riding trails. Golden's Bridge Hounds (GBH), the oldest of the three, was founded in 1924. GBH realized a need to maintain trails and in 1970 formed North Salem Bridle Trail Association (NSBTA) as a separate entity. The third group, North Salem Open Land Foundation (NSOLF), was incorporated in 1974 to protect open land through purchase and conservation easements.

Since its inception, NSOLF had protected more than 900 acres through purchase and easements. The portions of the NSBTA trail system on private land are open only to members, but the trails on town property, roads, and land no longer on the tax rolls are open to the public, except where they contain sensitive habitats. The larger NSOLF tracts offer variety of hiking opportunities and include trails in Baxter, Marx, and Hearst-Mead. These properties have posted restrictions as to when dogs must be on leash.

The 0.3 mile trail at Gaymark Preserve near Peach Lake goes through woodland, wetland, swamp, and field. It connects to a 0.8 mile trail open to North Salem Bridle Trail Association members. North Salem Open Land Foundation purchased the property from the Scheuer family in 2005 with funds donated to NSOLF and the support of neighbors [41.361424N 73.562780W].

The open field at tiny Sporn Preserve in Salem Center is where neighbors can take a quick walk. It was donated in 1999 to North Salem Open Land Foundation by Samuel and Ellen Sporn [41.326145N 73.614809W].

For contact information, see Appendix, North Salem Open Land Foundation

Durand Preserve

Salem Center • 0.5 mile, 10 acres

From the right side of the Ruth Keeler Memorial Library in Salem Center head toward the woods. A sign indicates the beginning of a nature trail with numbered posts. After passing through a wetland and crossing a stream on a bridge, the trail reaches the North Loop at a T intersection. Cedar Lane goes across the loop, making a shorter loop hike possible. The trail intersects with three equestrian trails on private property.

DRIVING: From northbound I-684, take Exit 7 (Route 116) and turn right at the end of the exit ramp. Follow Route 116 as it turns left onto Route 22 (north) and then right to leave Route 22. From where Route 116 leaves Route 22, head east 3.4 miles to North Salem Town Hall. Turn left and head toward the library at the rear of the property [41.329802N 73.597828W].

From southbound I-684, take Exit 8 (Hardscrabble Road) and follow Route 22 south. At the intersection with Route 116 where Route 22 goes off to the right, follow Route 116 and the directions above.

PUBLIC TRANSPORTATION: None available

For contact information, see Appendix, North Salem Open Land Foundation.

Hayfield-on-Keeler Preserve

Salem Center • 1.2 miles, 38 acres

Lots of grass grows on the slopes of the hill dominating Hayfield-on-Keeler Preserve. A mowed path goes around that hill along the right hand edge following the equestrian jumps. On the far side at 0.5 mile, a path descends to cross a stream and enter private property, closed to the public. Instead, continue left around the edge of the field and over the hill to parallel Keeler Lane and close the loop at 1.1 miles. A 0.1-mile trail bisects the loop.

DRIVING: From northbound I-684 take Exit 7. Turn right at the end of the exit ramp, then left onto Route 22. Turn right to follow Route 116 (Titicus Road) for 4.6 miles. After Route 121 joins from the right, go 0.7 mile to turn right on to Keeler Lane where parking is along the road. The tract entrance is to the right just beyond the bridge by a stone wall [41.334095N 73.570129W].

From southbound I-684, take Exit 8 and follow Route 22 south to the intersection with Route 116. Follow Route 116 and the directions above.

PUBLIC TRANSPORTATION: None available

For contact information, see Appendix, North Salem Open Land Foundation

Cross-country skiing at Saxon Woods Golf Course.

OTHER PLACES TO WALK

- Provide ideas for quick, easy-to-manage, and nearby, walks
- Help establish a fitness routine
- Increase comfort level of walking outdoors
- Are found throughout the county

Other Places to Walk

Parks and preserves are great for a walk, but there are other places that can be just as rewarding. Walking is an inexpensive means of exercise and it's often just what the doctor ordered. With so many options available, it's a prescription that's easy to fill. Use the following list to help you discover other places to walk close to home.

Cemeteries: Paved roads in large cemeteries meander past rustic resting places. Mt. Hope, Sharon, and Kensico cemeteries are just three of the many large cemeteries in the county. Because of its history and bucolic setting, Sleepy Hollow Cemetery has been written up in Pocket Parks.

Enclosed malls: Think of a mall walk as a welcome haven when the weather is just too miserable to be outside. Some malls have walking clubs that meet before stores open.

College campuses: Colleges in Westchester County range in size and suitability for extended walks. They also vary in how willing they are to allow the public on campus. Manhattanville College is on the grounds of a former estate, Ophir Farm, once the home of Whitelaw Reid, publisher of the *New York Herald Tribune* and ambassador to England. At SUNY Purchase, the road around the academic buildings has shoulders wide enough for walking, running, or cycling for most of its three mile length.

Dirt roads: In the northeastern portion of Westchester County, there are many dirt roads with little traffic. The rustic lanes north and east of Bedford can be shared with slower-moving traffic, equestrians, and leashed dogs. Reservoir Road, near Route 22 and the Cross River Reservoir, is an example.

Golf courses: Although not good places for a walk during golf season, county-owned golf courses are open for cross-country skiing and snowshoeing in winter. Mohansic Golf Course in Yorktown has a section of a former equestrian trail that paralleled the Taconic State Parkway. A portion of this trail passes a barn, now in disrepair, and connects with other unmarked trails on the property. There is a trail system in Saxon Woods, including the Hutchinson River Pathway and the Colonial Greenway. Access to private golf courses is extremely limited.

Long stretches of sidewalk: A sidewalk with few street crossings is neither a bike path nor a walk in town, but it does allow walking with minimal interruptions. Two examples are the path along Route 117 from Katonah to Bedford Hills Memorial Park and the path along Playland Parkway.

Measured loops: Walking on school tracks provides an easy measure of the distance walked. People who are beginning a fitness plan or recovering from an injury find tracks useful because they can easily stop when they become tired. Although not a track, a three quarters-mile path circles Huguenot Lake at New Rochelle High School. The paved path around the reservoir in Ossining's Wishnie Park is a third-of-a-mile.

Preserved open space: New York State, New York City's Department of Environmental Preservation, Westchester County, local land trusts, and non-profits have protected many acres of land. Some parcels are not as yet developed with trails; others are left undisturbed because of the terrain or a species needing protection. A few are 100% wetland. Bushwhacking or foraging your own path through open spaces without trail systems can be hearty exercise and a unique way to observe nature. Trump State Park (Indian Hill Section) is a large undeveloped tract with the potential for trails.

Tiny neighborhood parks: Tucked behind houses or along streams or wetlands, these smallest of parks are open municipal properties, sometimes the result of roads never built. Red Maple Swamp in Scarsdale is between two sections of Valley Road and has a 0.1-mile trail. Carpenter Pond, once part of the Larchmont Reservoir system, is on Daisy Farm Drive, just off Weaver Street in the Heathcote section of Scarsdale.

Town ball fields, tennis courts, schools, and swimming pools: Some of the many small parks in Westchester have ballfields, tennis courts, or swimming pools. Frequently overlooked as places to walk, they often have trails, grassy areas, or paved paths. Stonegate Park in Valhalla and the Town of Cortland Park on Croton Avenue have trails looping through adjacent woodlands. A quarter-mile bike path circles the lake in Pleasantville's Nannahagen Park. Trails adjacent to Increase Miller Elementary School in Goldens Bridge connect to Fox Meadow Town Park.

Utility rights-of-way: Utility companies have purchased easements on private and public land. Because they have edge environments, the areas are great

places to watch wildlife. Access to sewer, gas, phone, and power lines rights-of-way varies. However, along some sections with posted "No Trespassing" signs, the well-worn paths indicate that restrictions are being ignored. Examples include a gas line and an AT&T rights-of-way across the northern part of the county.

Along the gas line.

APPENDIX: CONTACT INFORMATION

Visit www.westchester.nynjtc.org for any recent changes and public transportation-based hikes.

MTA • http://web.mta.info/mnr/html/planning/schedules/

Beeline Bus Schedules • http://transportation.westchestergov.com/timetables-and-maps

Bedford Audubon Society • 914-232-1999; www.bedfordaudubon.org

Bedford Riding Lanes Association • 914-234 2752; www.bedfordridinglanes.com/ Bedford, Town of—Recreation and Parks Dept. • 914-666-7004; www.bedfordny.info/html/recreation.html

Buchanan, Village of—Recreation Dept. • 914-737-1033

Cortlandt, Town of—Recreation Division • 914-734-1050; www.townofcortlandt.com

Croton, Village of—Recreation & Parks • 914 271-3006; www.crotononhudson-ny.gov

Dobbs Ferry, Village of—Dept. of Parks and Recreation • 914-693-5505; www.design-site.net/dobbsferry

Eastchester, Town of—Recreation Dept. • 914-771-3311; www.eastchester.org/departments

East Coast Greenway • 401-789-4625; www.greenway.org; for NY: www.greenway.org/ny.php

Franklin D. Roosevelt State Park (FDR) • 914-245-4434; www.nysparks.com/parks

Greenburgh Nature Center • 914-723-3470; www.greenburghnaturecenter.org

Greenburgh, Town of—Dept. of Parks and Recreation • 914-693-8985; www.greenburghny.com

Greenwich Riding and Trails Association • 203-661-3062; thegrta.org

Harrison, Town of—Recreation Dept. • 914-670-3035; www.town.harrison.ny.us/recreation.aspx

Hastings-on-Hudson, Village of—Parks and Recreation Dept. • 914-478-2380; www.hastingsgov.org/Trailways

Hilltop Hanover Farm and Environmental Center • 914-962-2368; www.hilltophanoverfarm.org

Hudson Highlands State Park • 845-225-7207; www.nysparks.com/parks

Hudson River Valley Greenway • 518-473-3835; www.hudsongreenway.state.ny.us/

Irvington, Village of—Parks and Recreation • 914-591-7736; www.irvingtonny.gov/

John Jay Homestead State Historic Site • 914-232-5651; nysparks.state.ny.us/sites

John Jay Homestead, Friends of the • 914-232-8119; www.johnjayhomestead.org/

Kensico Dam Plaza • 914-328-1542; www.co.westchester.ny.us/parks/ParksLocations02/KensicoDamPlaza.htm

Larchmont, Village of—Recreation Dept • 914-834-6230; www.villageoflarchmont.org

Lewisboro, Town of—Parks and Recreation Dept. • 914-232-6162; www.lewisborogov.com

Lewisboro Horsemen's Association • www.lhatrails.org

Lewisboro Land Trust • www.westchesterlandtrust.org/lewisboro

Lytle Arboretum • Croton Arboretum and Sanctuary, Inc.; www.crotonarboretum.org

Mamaroneck, Town of—Conservation Dept. • 914-381-7845; www.townofmamaroneck.org/conservation_dept

Mamaroneck, Village of—Parks Dept. • 914-777-7754; www.village.mamaroneck.ny.us/

Marsh Memorial Sanctuary • 914-241-2808; www.marshsanctuary.googlepages.com

Mianus River Gorge Preserve, Inc. • 914-234-3455; www.mianus.org

Mt. Kisco, Village of—Recreation Dept. • 914-666-3059; www.mountkisco.org/departments/recreation

Mount Pleasant, Town of—Recreation & Parks Dept. • 914-742-2310; www.mtpleasantny.com

Mount Vernon, City of—Dept. of Recreation • 914-665-2420; cmvny.com

The Nature Conservancy • 914-244 3271; www.nature.org/wherewework/northamerica/states

New Castle, Town of—Recreation Dept. • 914-238-3909; www.town.new-castle.ny.us/parks.html

New York-New Jersey Trail Conference • 201-512-9348; www.nynjtc.org

New Rochelle, City of—Parks and Recreation Dept. • 914 654-2087; www.newrochelleny.com/parks.asp

New York State, Dept. of Environmental Conservation • 845-831-8780 ext 309; www.dec.ny.gov/lands/34976.html

North Salem Open Land Foundation • 914-669-5860; www.nsolf.org/preservesmap.html

North Castle, Town of—Recreation and Parks Dept. • 914-273-3325; www.northcastleny.com/recreation.htm

Old Croton Aqueduct State Historic Park • 914-693 5259; nysparks.state.ny.us/parks

Old Croton Aqueduct, Friends of • 914-693-4117; www.aqueduct.org

Ossining, Village of—Recreation and Parks Dept. • 914-941 3189; www.townofossining.com/depts/parksrec.htm

Peekskill, City of—Parks and Recreation • 914-734-4228; www.ci.peekskill.ny.us

Pelham Manor, Village of • 914-738-8820; www.pelhammanor.org

PepsiCo, World Headquarters • www.en.wikipedia.org/wiki/Donald_M._Kendall_Sculpture_Gardens

Pound Ridge Land Conservancy • 914-372-1290; www.prlc.net

Pound Ridge, Town of—Recreation Dept. • 914-764-3987; www.townofpoundridge.com/parks.cfm

Rockefeller State Park Preserve • 914-631-1470; www.nysparks.state.ny.us/parks

Rockefeller State Park Preserve, Friends of the • 914-762-0209; www.friendsrock.org

Rye Brook, Village of—Recreation Dept. • 914-939-3235; www.ryebrook.org

Rye, Town of • 914-939-3075; www.townofryeny.com

Rye Nature Center • 914-967-5150; www.ryenaturecenter.org

Saint Matthew's Church—Woodlands Commission • 914-234-9636; www.acswebnetworks.com/stmatthewsbedford/

Saw Mill River Audubon Society • 914-666-6503; www.sawmillriveraudubon.org

Sheldrake Environmental Center, Inc. • 914-834-1443; www.sheldrakecenter.org

Sleepy Hollow Cemetery • 914-631-0081; www.sleepyhollowcemetery.org

Sleepy Hollow, Village of—Recreation and Parks Dept; 914-366-5109; www.sleepyhollowny.gov

Somers, Town of—Parks and Recreation Dept. • 914-232-8441; www.somersny.com

Tarrytown, Village of—Recreation Dept. • 914-631-8389; www.tarrytowngov.com

Teatown Lake Reservation • 914-762-2912; www.teatown.org

Weinberg Nature Center · 914-722-1289; www.scarsdale.com/recreation/weinberg.asp

Westchester County Dept. of Parks, Recreation & Conservation · 450 Saw Mill River Rd. Ardsley, NY 10502 914-231-4500; For parks not listed because they don't have an office, see http://parks.westchestergov.com/parks-destinations;

Blue Mountain Reservation · 914-862-5275; http://parks.westchestergov.com/blue-mountain-reservation

Bronx River Parkway Reservation · 914-328-1542; www.co.westchester.ny.us/parks/ParksLocations02/BronxRiver.htm

Cranberry Lake Preserve · 914-428-1005; http://parks.westchestergov.com/cranberry-lake

Croton Gorge Park · 914-827-9568; http://parks.westchestergov.com/croton-gorge-park

Croton Point Park · 914-862-5290; http://parks.westchestergov.com/croton-point-park

George's Island Park · 914-737-7530; http://parks.westchestergov.com/georges-island-park

Glen Island Park · 914-813-6720; http://parks.westchestergov.com/glen-island-park

Lasdon Park, Arboretum & Veterans Memorial · 914-864-7263; http://parks.westchestergov.com/lasdon-park-arboretum-veterans-memorial

Lenoir Preserve · 914-968-5851; http://parks.westchestergov.com/lenoir-preserve

Macy Park · 914- 946-8133; http://parks.westchestergov.com/v-e-macy-park

Marshlands Conservancy · 914-835-4466; http://parks.westchestergov.com/marshlands-conservancy

Merestead · 914-666-4258; http://parks.westchestergov.com/historic-sites/merestead

Mountain Lakes Park · 914-864-7311; http://parks.westchestergov.com/sal-j-prezioso-mountain-lakesMuscoot Farm · 914-864-7282; http://parks.westchestergov.com/muscootfarm

Playland · 914-813-7000 (pre-recorded); www.westchestergov.com/playland/

Read Wildlife Sanctuary · 914-967-8720; http://parks.westchestergov.com/read-wildlifesanctuary

Ridge Road Park · 914-946-8133; http://parks.westchestergov.com/ridge-road-park

Saxon Woods Park · 914-995-4480; http://parks.westchestergov.com/saxon-woods-park

Sprain Ridge Park · 914-231-3450 (summer only); http://parks.westchestergov.com/sprain-ridge-park

Tibbetts Brook Park · 914-231-2865; http://parks.westchestergov.com/tibbetts-brook-parkV.E. Macy Park · 914-946-8133; www.co.westchester.ny.us/parks/ParksLocations02/VEMacy.htm

Twin Lakes/Nature Study Woods · 914-961-3102; http://parks.westchestergov.com/twin-lakes-park

Ward Pound Ridge Reservation · 914-864-7317; www.co.westchester.ny.us/parks/ParksLocations02/WardPoundRidge.htm

Westchester Land Trust · 914-241-6346; www.westchesterlandtrust.org

Westmoreland Sanctuary · 914-666-8448; www.westmorelandsanctuary.org

White Plains, City of—Recreation and Parks Dept. · 914-422-1336; www.ci.white-plains.ny.us

Yonkers, City of—Parks, Recreation, and Conservation Dept. · 914-377-6450; www.cityofyonkers.com

Yorktown, Town of—Parks & Recreation Dept. · 914-245-4650; www.yorktownny.org

APPENDIX: ADDITIONAL RESOURCES

For a more comprehensive list of materials used, see Westchester.nynjtc.org

Printed Matter

Busch, Akiko. *The Incidental Steward: Reflections on Citizen Science.* New Haven, Ct. Yale University Press, 2013.

Cooper, Linda G. *A Walker's Guide to the Bronx River Parkway Reservation.* White Plains, NY: Westchester County Department of Parks, Recreation & Conservation, 2000.

Cooper, Linda G. *A Walker's Guide to the Hutchinson River Parkway Trail.* White Plains, NY: Westchester County Department of Parks, Recreation & Conservation, n.d.

French, Alvah P. *History of Westchester County, New York.* New York: Lewis Historical Publishing Company, 1925.

DeLuca, Dan W. *The Old Leather Man; Historical Accounts of a Connecticut and New York Legend*, Middletown, Ct. Wesleyan University Press, 2008.

Koeppel, Gerard T. *Water for Gotham: a history*, Princeton, N.J, Princeton University Press, 2001

Lederer, Richard M., Jr. *The Place-Names of Westchester County; a Dictionary of Origins and Historical Meanings*, Harrison, N.Y., Harbor Hill Books, 1978.

Pessoni, Philip A. *Historical Notes on the Ward Pound Ridge Reservation.* Boutonville, NY: Landmark Document Services, 1995.

Weigold, Marilyn E. *People and the Parks: A History of Parks and Recreation in Westchester County.* White Plains, NY: Westchester County Department of Parks, Recreation & Conservation, n.d.

Williams, Gray. *Picturing Our Past: National Register Sites in Westchester County.* Elmsford, NY: Westchester County Historical Society, 2003.

Wittner, Phyllis. *A History of Conservation in the Town of Mamaroneck, 1948-2006*, Town of Mamaroneck, 2007

Websites

Civilian Conservation Corps. Civilian Conservation Corps Legacy. <http://www.cccalumni.org/>.

Cooney, Patrick. NY-NJ-CT Botany Online. <http://www.nynjctbotany.org/>.

Subway. New York, Westchester & Boston Railway. <www.nycsubway.org/nyc/nywb/>.

Westchester County, NY. Westchester County Archives. <www.westchestergov.com/wcarchives/>.

INDEX

Page numbers in **bold** refer to the primary park description.

We invite you to join

the organization of hikers, environmentalists, and volunteers whose skilled efforts have produced this edition of *Walkable Westchester.*

The **New York-New Jersey Trail Conference**, founded in 1920, is a federation of member clubs and individuals dedicated to providing recreational hiking opportunities in the New York-New Jersey region, and to representing the interests and concerns of the hiking community. The Trail Conference is a volunteer-directed public service organization committed to:

- Developing, building, and maintaining hiking trails.
- Protecting hiking trail lands through support and advocacy.
- Educating the public in the responsible use of trails and the natural environment.

Join now and as a member:

- You will receive the *Trail Walker*, a quarterly source of news, information, and events concerning area trails and hiking. The *Trail Walker* lists many hikes in the New York-New Jersey metropolitan area, led by some of our more than 100 member hiking clubs.
- You are entitled to purchase our authoritative maps and books at significant discounts. These highly accurate, up-to-date trail maps, printed on durable Tyvek, and our informative guidebooks enable you to hike with assurance throughout the region.
- You are also entitled to discounts of 10% (and sometimes more!) at most local outdoor stores and at many mountain inns and lodges.
- Most importantly, you will become part of a community of volunteer activists with similar passions and ideas.

Your membership helps give us the clout to protect and maintain more trails. As a member of the **New York-New Jersey Trail Conference**, you will be helping to ensure that public access to nature will continue to expand.

New York-New Jersey Trail Conference
156 Ramapo Valley Road ⬩ Mahwah, NJ 07430 ⬩ (201) 512-9348
www.nynjtc.org ⬩ info@nynjtc.org

Other Hiking Books Available From the Trail Conference!

Authoritative Hiking Maps and Books by the Volunteers who Maintain the Trails

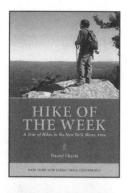

HIKE OF THE WEEK

First Edition (2013), Daniel Chazin

A selection of 52 hikes in the New York metropolitan area—one for each week of the year. The hikes are taken from Dan Chazin's popular Hike of the Week column in The *Record* and are organized by season and level of difficulty. Each hike is accompanied by a map and a sidebar that focuses on some interesting aspect of the hike, such as history, geology, wildlife, etc.

sc. 358 p. 5 3/8 x 8 1/8, B&W photos and maps

HIKING LONG ISLAND

Fourth Edition (2014), Lee McAllister

Whether a resident or visitor, become acquainted with the beauty of Long Island's woods, fields, pine barrens, and beaches. A comprehensive book with information on geology, flora, and fauna. Each hike includes a schematic map and public transportation information when available.

sc. 444 p. 5 3/8 x 8 1/8, photos and maps

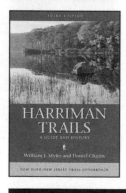

HARRIMAN TRAILS

Third Edition (2010), William J. Myles and Daniel Chazin

Bill Myles' original guidebook to the trails in Harriman/Bear Mountain State Parks has been completely revised by Daniel Chazin. It is much more than a guide. Years of research have produced a fine history as well. Marked and unmarked trails, lakes, roads and mines are all covered in depth. A complete reference work, with many historical photos.

sc. 421 p. 5 3/8 x 8 1/8, B&W photos